FEAR AND HOPE

FEAR AND HOPE

Three Generations of
the Holocaust

◆

Dan Bar-On

Harvard University Press

Cambridge, Massachusetts

London, England

1995

This book is printed on acid-free paper, and its binding
materials have been chosen for strength and durability.

Library of Congress Cataloging-in-Publication Data

Bar-On, Dan, 1938–
[Ben paḥad le-tiḳṿah. English]
Fear and hope : three generations of the Holocaust /
Dan Bar-On.
p.   cm.
Includes bibliographical references and index.
ISBN 0-674-29522-6
1. Holocaust, Jewish (1939–1945)—Personal narratives.
2. Holocaust survivors—Israel—Biography.
3. Children of Holocaust survivors—Israel—Biography.
I. Title.
D804.3.B3525   1995
940.53'18'0922—dc20
[B]   94-42016
CIP

Designed by Gwen Frankfeldt

*To my grandparents and parents,
from whom I have absorbed
so much love and caring*

✦

"There are trees in the orchards that have wonderful foliage and fruit, and suddenly their rootstock is attacked and starts to deteriorate. We then plant a new sapling out of harm's way next to the trunk, and we graft it onto the bark. When this young sapling has taken, its roots replace those that have been damaged, and the tree is saved: Once again it has foliage, a trunk, and roots ... Our family, after the Holocaust, was like a tree that has lost its roots, and now when we sit around the table, Grandma and Grandpa, my parents and us, I feel that we are like the support graft of the family."

Contents

The Interviewees

THE BELINSKYS
Genia
Tzipke
Ganit

THE LERMANS
Ze'ev
Hannah
Yoav

THE ANISEVITCHES
Olga
Dina, Benny
Orit

THE SEGALS
Anya
Tamar and Ya'acov
Dafna and Idit

THE GUETTAS
Laura
Vittorio and Paula
Liat

Author's Note

The names of persons interviewed in this book are pseudonyms, and place-names have been concealed. The interviewees gave their consent to their participation in the study on which this book is based and to its publication under this condition. The study was sponsored by the German-Israeli Foundation.

FEAR AND HOPE

◆ ———————— ◆

Prologue

I grew up with a peculiar combination of fear and hope, an experience shared by many of my generation. It was the legacy we received from our parents—Jewish survivors, escapees, and immigrants from Europe. We had to navigate our way to adulthood between these two poles, trying to overcome the fear while providing hope for our own children. It is this peculiar combination of feelings that this book tries to address. Today I believe it seemed peculiar because we never knew exactly where we were: Were we afraid because something terrible had happened—or might happen? Could we hope for something better? These two feelings have been—and maybe still are—so deeply interwoven in our lives that we can hardly separate them from each other. I suspect that it has to do with the sense of being uprooted that we all grew up with. We did not really "belong" to a new stem, yet the old one had been abruptly cut off. One can fight uprootedness or behave "as if" it does not exist. Or one can accept it and try to live with it. Have we transmitted our feelings of uprootedness to our own children? Have we succeeded in working them through or, at least, in acknowledging them? These questions are the focus of this book.

While growing up I was very lucky to have grandparents as well as an uncle, my mother's brother, and his family. I did not know how lucky I was until many years later, in therapy, when I reflected on my childhood. It suddenly occurred to me that when all the grandparents in my German-speaking neighborhood would meet to play cards together, as they did regularly in a café on Mount Carmel in Haifa, they did not occupy more than two, maybe three small tables. Most of the children in my neighborhood grew up without grandparents. By the time they were six or seven, they had no grandparents—or uncles, aunts, or cousins—anymore. Those who stayed behind in Nazi-occupied Germany were murdered in what came to be known as "the Holocaust." My parents' generation grew up in a world without a Holocaust, but for us there could be no such world. Did having grandparents shield me from fear, from feeling uprooted? Perhaps that is true to some extent, but I really don't know, since I have no other experience to compare it to.

When I was about a year old, World War II broke out. One of my earliest memories is, at about the age of three, being pulled out of my bed in the middle of the night to go down to the little shelter we had dug in our garden. I can still smell my grandmother's gray leather handbag (in which, I was later told, she would take all her jewelry). She must have held it at about the height of my head. For many years afterwards, that gray color evoked for me that specific smell. Other people said that I was very jolly during those Italian air raids on the oil refineries in Haifa bay, that I used to entertain everybody. But I only remember clutching my grandmother's hand fiercely every time I heard a bomb explode in the distance.

Since my father was not around (a physician in the British army, he was stationed in Egypt), I used to spend many hours with my grandfather. I especially remember his eyes, which conveyed warmth and truthfulness. He was bald (I am today) but had a little mustache, and he carried a wonderful old walking stick, which still exists somewhere in the attic. We used to take long walks during which he would tell me all kinds of stories, in German of course. My grandparents did not know Hebrew. They had arrived in Haifa two years prior to my birth, after my mother had returned to Germany to take them out. Had she not done so, they would probably have stayed behind, as many of their generation did, and suffered the same fate. My grandfather was a real German patriot. He had fought in World War I and saw no reason to leave his homeland. So I grew up within a wonderful German culture of language, music, food, clothing, and furniture (which my parents were still allowed to bring with them in 1933). But I also remember hearing Hitler in BBC radio broadcasts, shouting in the language my family was so fond of, and being frozen with fear.

At that age I guess I could not make sense of it all: Was being German good or bad? Hopeful or dreadful? I must have known something, however, because, as they used to tell me years later, in moments of rage (of which I had quite a few) I would yell at my parents and my brother: "You are all Germans, I am the only Jew in the family" (meaning that I was the only one who had been born in Israel). However, at that stage of my life, almost the whole neighborhood was composed of this Jewish-German mixture. At the dinner table at home, after my father returned from the war, we used to talk in three languages: my parents spoke German (or English when they didn't want us to understand), while my brother and I spoke Hebrew.

They also say that I played all by myself for hours in our tiny apartment in a prefabricated copper house imported from Germany. I used to arrange the room for chamber music the way I saw my mother doing in the evening. I must have sensed in her a love for music and an urge to make music, her way of maintaining her sanity in a world that had gone crazy. Some of the people who came to play were British; a British camp bordered our garden. For my brother and me this camp was a constant source of fear, but for my mother it must have provided a sense of security. The family story is that my father convinced my mother to emigrate from Germany to Palestine in 1933 only because "it was, after all, a British dominion." However, in the end, it was the British who drove us out of our home, when, prior to their evacuation, between November 29, 1947, and May 15, 1948, they set up a security zone into which they gathered all their forces.

We were transferred by the British into a large stone house with a marble floor in the German (Templars') colony. At that time this area was inhabited mainly by Arabs, and just before the War of Independence broke out we were the only Jewish family who had a phone in that quite hostile neighborhood. I remember a picture of our living room, my mother serving tea to the British soldiers who maintained order in the main street outside our house with a Bren gun, while in my father's clinic, a Hagana group (a Jewish, and at that time illegal, self-defense force) was holding one of their secret meetings and making phone calls.

I also recall a discussion between my parents: My mother wanted to leave Palestine with the British. She did not trust the Middle East without their presence. My father, being a little more integrated into the emerging society of Israel, wanted to stay. So did we. It is a frightening recollection. Only in retrospect does it become positive, and positive only in the sense that they discussed these issues openly in front of us. It would have been much worse had they tried to hide their feelings, doubts, and contrary opinions from themselves and from us. That is what happened in many families that projected the image of being more "Israeli" at that time. But, because I was a child, this discussion only made me more frightened: Are we going to stay? Are we going to leave? Who *are* we in relation to the more "integrated" settlers who believe wholeheartedly in what is going on here? Shortly after this discussion my brother and I had to be evacuated again, because Arab snipers were shooting at our house. However, this time we were able to come back within a few days.

In 1948, during Passover week, Haifa was liberated. We could feel the cost of this liberation. An Arab woman named Jamilla took care of us and helped my mother with the housekeeping. She would bring us sugar and flour, because at times we could not get our own supplies. She was a warm woman and we all loved her very much. One day, while my brother and I were away, she came to my parents in tears and said that her family was leaving for Lebanon, since "they had lost the war." My father tried to convince her to stay, that he would take care that nothing would happen to them in the newly born Jewish state. But she could not decide on her own, and her husband would not stay. She had six children at that time. They probably ended up in a refugee camp in southern Lebanon. In years to come, when I was assigned to night patrol on the northern border during my military service, I would imagine that some of her children might try to come back as saboteurs . . .

My brother, at sixteen, was too young to fight in the War of Independence. Still, he brought home Israeli stories and songs about the war, went to the scouts' youth movement, and considered going to a kibbutz during his military service. He paved the way for me in these matters, because my mother associated those "militant tendencies" of Israeli culture more with fear than with hope. She calmed down only when he finally went to Cambridge, England, to study mathematics, later to become an economist. I took the Israeli pioneering course more seriously. At the age of sixteen I left home, changed my last name to a Hebrew-sounding one, and joined an agricultural high school. The Kadoori school had the prestige of being the "breeding place" of the Israeli "Palmach"[1] leadership in earlier days. At that point in my life I wanted to get away from the complexity of my family's European heritage, a heritage I still could make no sense of in the Israeli context. I simply wanted to become a "Sabra" (a native-born Israeli). My parents had made it clear that they would not agree to my joining a kibbutz without first learning a profession, so I decided to outsmart them: I became a farmer.

These were wonderful years. I enjoyed the freedom of living on my own within a youth culture composed mostly of boys. We would go on long hikes almost every free weekend and got to know every corner of Galilee by foot. The school also had the tradition of an "honor system": the teachers did not watch us during examinations; if we caught someone trying to cheat, we would run him out of the school ourselves. We assigned work according to a complicated, but very egalitarian system. We dreamt of establishing a new kibbutz in the desert with a nearby agricultural school, which was composed mainly of girls. We ended up joining Kibbutz Revivim, an established kibbutz far down in the desert, which had just succeeded in getting a pipeline bringing fresh water from the Sea of Galilee to the Negev—the dry south. The kibbutz needed professional farmers in order to use this water commercially, and about twelve of us from the school joined it.

I joined right after my military service. We cultivated fruit trees in the desert where they had never grown before: peaches, pears, apricots, grapes, and later, avocados. We tried to develop ways to save water by using a drip system invented and manufactured in a neighboring kibbutz. We devised a way to save manpower in thinning the peaches. We smuggled new varieties of fruit into the country from Florida and California. I was totally absorbed in my activities, totally identified with what I was doing: working hard and hoping for a better, more beautiful future. I completely repressed my family's past and its unresolved dilemmas and fears.

Maybe not completely, because I dragged a cello with me, both to school and to the kibbutz. I tried to keep on learning and making music, a pursuit that, in the pioneering spirit of those days, provoked ridicule, but which was also my only conscious connection to my parents' heritage. I was, however, very distant from my parents and my brother, both physically and mentally. And my fear was gone. At least I did not feel it, and I behaved as if it had vanished.

I married and had two children, a girl and a boy, by the time the Six-

Day War broke out. Then I was recruited into the pathfinding unit of an armored division that fought its way to the Suez Canal. I lost a good friend, who was in a subunit of the same division, with whom I had been managing our fruit tree plantation for the previous two years. The war ended with the euphoria of triumph, but I came back full of fear. It was my first combat experience, and I saw people near me get killed. Life and death were at those moments purely a matter of chance. My own protective shield started to crack, although the legitimate discourse around me did not change. I wanted to study. I considered both biology and psychology and ended up choosing the second, not yet fully understanding why (we can always say something about what we are doing, but that does not mean we know why we are doing it).

My personal, full-scale crisis came a few years later, after the Yom Kippur War broke out. Again I was in a pathfinding unit, this time on the Syrian front, trying to liberate Israeli posts that had been captured by the Syrian army a couple of days earlier. I recall seeing a few young and beautiful soldiers dead in the trenches and getting others out of the bunkers in deep shock. This time it was really rough. I came home after six months of military service a very different person. I could not adjust to regular kibbutz life. I could not talk about my war experiences with anyone. I was elected secretary of the kibbutz and was supposed to help others, but what really kept me going were my children and my master's work in psychology, which I was trying to complete. During those difficult years, fear prevailed.

My family life disintegrated. I joined the army for a year as a field psychologist and began therapy. Toward the end of the year my parents became ill, and my brother and I took care of them. It was the first time I had experienced that turning point in life when your parents cannot look after you anymore and you have to start looking after them. Beginning in 1957, when they started receiving restitution from Germany, my parents used to go to Zermatt, Switzerland, every summer. They did not like to travel in Germany, but the Swiss Alps were a refreshing and relaxing change from the hot summer in Israel. Perhaps it was an enactment of their fantasy of returning to their own "roots." That summer we decided that my older daughter and I would join them, since we felt they would not be able to manage the trip by themselves.

We sailed to Europe on a luxurious cruise ship. My mother was deeply depressed during the whole voyage; however, on the evening of our arrival in Geneva, after my father and daughter had gone to sleep, she asked me to accompany her on a walk along the lake. It was like watching a flower open up before my eyes. The elegant Swiss shops, the old houses illuminated along the lake, the sound of European languages—suddenly my mother was full of life again. Only then did I fully grasp what it had been like for her to live in Israel all those years, waiting eagerly for her next trip to Europe, her home continent.

We spent two weeks together, and it was not easy for me. I suddenly realized that some part of me felt what my mother felt. It came through in particular during our strolls in the woods. I had the strangest feeling of knowing those woods, their smell and composition; although I had never experienced them before, they were not alien to me.

I was still in therapy, still quite fear-ridden, but very slowly, hope came back. I remarried and had a son shortly after my father died of his second heart attack during one of his summer visits to Switzerland. During the previous couple of years my father and I had enjoyed some good conversations in which we broke through the silence that had so often surrounded him. I realized that I had inherited my parents' (my father's unspoken, my mother's manifested) longing for their home culture, from which they had been cut off so abruptly. Through trial and error, I learned that separation is a process that involves a lot of leaving and returning. I developed professional contacts in Europe and began to go there quite regularly myself. In 1985 I launched a research project in Germany: interviewing children of Nazi perpetrators of the Holocaust (Bar-On, 1989).

During one of my research trips, my mother agreed to meet me in Hamburg and show me her "hometown." We spent two days walking along the canals in the neighborhood where more than a hundred members of our family had once lived. She told me endless stories about many of them in the wryly humorous way she had of talking about people. But it was also very painful for her. There was no door she could knock on and say, "Hello, I am back," only memories of old times that had gone forever. In 1992, at the age of 85, my mother died in Haifa. I was with her in the hospital during the last week of her life. She spoke a mixture of English (when she was angry), Hebrew, and German. When I wanted to comfort her, I spoke German with her. After her death, when I locked up her apartment before going to stay with my children in Tel Aviv, I had a last tearful look at the empty rooms. I felt that I was closing the door on an era that would never return.

In the mid-seventies, when I started to work as a therapist in our region's kibbutz clinics, my first client was a thirteen-year-old boy with beautiful dark brown eyes, who sat in his chair and said nothing. I did not know what to do, so I suggested that we take a walk. I had already done this with my own little son: while we walked we would talk, just as, years ago, I used to have conversations with my grandfather. The boy, Nitai, was burdened by his parents' recent divorce. We had a few nice walks and talks, his situation "improved," and I, along with his teachers, felt he needed no further therapy.

A few years later, Alon, his younger brother, was referred to me. He was rebellious at school and at home, and his mother was very anxious about his "situation." After talking with him a couple of times, however, I felt that he was just a typical adolescent. Since his mother, Dvora, was still worried, I proposed that she come for therapy (which I probably should have done before, when the older boy was referred to me). Only then did I learn that she was a child survivor of the Holocaust. As a girl of five she went into hiding with her mother and brother in occupied southern France. Her father "vanished" while still in Paris shortly after the German occupation had begun.

During that time, Dvora tried to clarify, for the first time, exactly when her father had been brought to Auschwitz and gassed. Her father and mother had divorced shortly before the outbreak of the war. Thus, as a child, Dvora "lost" her father twice, first in the divorce and then in the Holocaust. She had tried to commit suicide during her early years in Israel, while living with a group of French child survivors in an Israeli kibbutz, and was hospitalized briefly after her second attempt, but the Holocaust was hardly mentioned in her therapy sessions during her hospitalization. Her mother and brother were still living in Paris, and she went to see them from time to time, but she was not on good terms with either of them, especially her mother.

I asked myself how Dvora had managed over all those years to "normalize" her traumatic experience and navigate her way in a very demanding society (especially in the kibbutz context)—as a youngster, a spouse (for a few years at least), a mother, a very competent chemist in local industry, and a daughter and sister—without ever reflecting on that past and its relevance to her present feelings and actions. I asked her to tell me what she recalled of her experiences while in hiding as a child and later during her early years in the kibbutz. We met weekly for two-and-a-half years. Ours was an unusual kind of dialogue that I had never experienced before. She struggled to find a way to talk about many issues, while I looked for a way to understand what she said within my own frame of reference. I had to rely on her way of making sense and her reactions in order to lead her into making them into explicit discourse.

In one of our early meetings, Dvora told me about a dream she had had: In it, she was a child of four in an embroidered white dress listening to her father play the piano (he did indeed know how to play). Suddenly, German soldiers broke into the room, seized her father, and left her there alone. At the time Dvora connected the dream to her sadness. She missed her father, whom she was very fond of as a child, and hoped he would return one day, a hope she had never abandoned. She was fearful and still suffered from terrible guilt feelings toward her brother and mother (while in hiding, they had attacked her for being a naughty and inconsiderate girl whose careless behavior would expose them to the Germans).

A year later, Dvora had the dream again. This time, however, she saw the same events from her father's perspective—enjoying playing the piano with his young daughter sitting by his side. I noticed a connection between the second version of the dream and her present reality, which was steadily improving. She was less anxious about her sons, who grew up and went their own way. Some time later we decided to end the therapy.

After some months, however, Dvora returned: she had had the dream a third time. This time, she was one of the German soldiers who had come to take her father away. As she saw it, this was the first time she was consciously able to be angry at the father who had "left" her when he had divorced her mother. As she expressed it, she wanted to "kill him in her dream."

Except for this, she felt well and had decided to leave the kibbutz to pursue her own professional career. A few days later, she called me to tell me that she had just recalled her last meeting with her father: he had come to her mother's house, but owing to the tension between them, he had left quickly without really saying good-bye to her. Several months after this, Dvora came by again, trembling and crying: her brother had committed suicide without any warning. To her, he had always seemed such a rational, steady type. His wife and two children were completely at a loss. Dvora herself went through a very difficult time over his death, but she was able to cope with it, she said, owing to the insights she had gained through our meetings.

Every now and then I see Dvora, since we now live in the same town. Her dream has not recurred. When I showed her my written version of her three dreams before its publication in *Legacy of Silence* (1989), she turned to me with a big smile and, in Hebrew still touched with a light French accent, said, "Dan, it was not that way at all."

My experience with Dvora's therapy helped me to begin to understand how difficult it is to find a way between the past and the present, between fear and hope, especially when the past includes painful events or facts that can never be fully verified, yet have altered forever one's basic assumptions about the benevolence of the world and one's value in it (Janoff-Bulman, 1992). How does one raise children all alone while still being driven, day and night, by such traumatic experiences? Dvora had clearly done the best she could, but it was unreasonable to expect that she could manage it all by herself. Once her children had started to have problems of their own, she needed help in differentiating between her problems and those of her children. She needed reassurance that she could create a normal life for herself and her children even though hers had been distorted by the conditions of an extremely difficult, and to some extent "abnormal," life history (Felman and Laub, 1992). I asked myself, "How have other people with similar life histories, who have not had a verification system, managed to get on with their lives (and life stories)?"

Dvora's recurring dream led me to examine the question "What is the truth?" more closely when listening to people's life stories. There is, of course, a "historical" truth (what happened), but there are also several "narrative" truths (how someone tells what happened) (Spence, 1980). The different narrative truths associated with her dream are probably related to the reality of Dvora's life when her dream recurred. When she stopped having the dream, was it because the "right solution"—a specific memory—had surfaced? Friedlander (1980) quotes Marinek, "with acknowledgment, memory comes as well." Will we "know" if there was a "solution"? Finally, there is the posterior evidence when, a few years later,

Dvora laughingly said, "It was not that way at all." What did she mean? Why did she laugh?

The answers to these questions become more complicated when we listen to the stories of Holocaust survivors. On the one hand, we feel we are missing something: indeed, we have not experienced what they have. On the other hand, they also feel that something is missing: it is so difficult to describe what happened to them in everyday language. The very structures of thought and language are so fragile, they can easily break in our attempts to create a bridge between memory and feeling, and the present reality (including the presence of the listener), which are often contradictory in more ways than one. How can they "translate" their horrible experience into ordinary language? What sense can those who have not experienced these things make of their discourse? Which part of this discourse, if any, do they transmit to the following generations? What are they able to work through because of new life experiences?

At the outset of "The Psychosocial Aftereffects of the Holocaust on the Following Generations," a course I teach at Ben-Gurion University, I have my students interview a Holocaust survivor about his or her life. The students then transcribe these interviews and bring them to class. During one term, Ela brought the story of her grandfather, who had become a physician in Poland shortly before World War II broke out. When the Germans marched into his town and rounded up the Jews, he and his wife gave their newborn daughter to a gentile former patient of his and went into hiding with the partisans. He served as a physician with them until the war ended. When they returned, the gentile woman did not want to give back their daughter. They had to go to court in order to get her back. This child was Ela's mother.

In the beginning of the second semester of the course, I ask the students to interview children of Holocaust survivors. Ela decided to interview her mother. Finally, toward the end of the course when students have to carry out an independent research project, she and a fellow student interviewed the whole family: her mother's three siblings, her own brother (aged sixteen), and the eldest child of each of her aunts and uncles. It was an amazing accomplishment on her part, both the interviews and her analysis of the interviews. Ela and her friend showed the ways in which the descendants of her grandfather tell the family history, some stressing the heroic aspects of the past, others the more painful aspects, but each one speaking from his or her own present perspective.

Ela's interviews inspired a larger project: interviewing families of Holocaust survivors and talking with three generations in each family. Several years ago, a group of my students undertook this research, using the framework of a course taught by Gabriele Rosenthal that dealt with biographic and narrative analysis. I had met Gabriele in Germany during my research on children of Holocaust perpetrators. She was one of the few gentiles I met there who understood immediately what I was trying to find out. She had developed a method for analyzing the stories of her subjects, a method I was not familiar with but which immediately "spoke" to me as suitable for the complicated issues the students in my course were attempting to understand. Thus began a collaboration that brought Gabriele to Israel to teach narrative and biographical analysis in the behavioral sciences department at the university, and, during the years 1989 to 1991, and again in 1993, to undertake interviews with German-speaking Holocaust survivors.

This book is the result of the teamwork that grew out of that course. Noga Gil'ad, Julie Chaitin, Bosmat Dvir-Malka, and Einat Weiss participated throughout the entire project. In the interviewing and preliminary analysis, Amaliya Gaon, Dina Vardi, Tova Milo, and Yardena Levi also took part. During the second analysis, Gadi Ben-Ezer and Max Lachman joined us. To all of them I extend my gratitude for their assistance, curiosity, enlightenment, and helpful comments. I also wish to extend my gratitude to Professor Gabriele Rosenthal, who encouraged us to continue and accompanied us on our difficult journey. Miriam Keren is fondly remembered for her willingness to volunteer her time whenever we needed a translation from the German.

Other readers generously shared their comments and thoughts: I especially want to thank Professor Amiya Lieblich of Hebrew University in Jerusalem and Mr. Zvi Dror of the Ghetto Fighters Museum at Lochamei Hagetaot. During the editing stage, Dr. Nitza Yanai, of the behavioral sciences department at Ben-Gurion University, offered comments and suggestions that were irreplaceable. Later, Dr. Joseph Albeck of McLean Hospital, Professor Bennett Simon of Harvard University, and Professor John Forster of Cornell University provided very insightful and important remarks on an earlier version of this manuscript, which greatly aided me in revising it. I also wish to thank the German-Israeli Foundation (GIF), especially its head, Dr. Amnon Barak, for funding the research, thereby enabling us to undertake and process the interviews. I wish to thank Julie Chaitin from Kibbutz Urim for her fine and thoughtful English translation. Finally, I want to thank my youngest son, Haran, and my wife, Tammy, for their patience. So often I could not attend to their stories because I was deeply involved in the stories of other families.

It is impossible to begin this discussion without mentioning the period during which this book was written: the Gulf War. I remember one day when I was trying to concentrate on a particular interview analysis but was unable to free myself of an image of my nine-year-old son from the night before: his frightened eyes behind his gas mask looking first at me and then at his mother as we sat in our sealed room. In those moments I could not help but ask, How many more generations of frightened young eyes will there be before we reach safe shores?

Omer, Israel, May 1991—Cambridge, Massachusetts, June 1992

Introduction

During the 1989–90 academic year, my students and I interviewed three generations in each of twelve families of Holocaust survivors: the survivors themselves, their adult children, and their grandchildren. The decision to go ahead with this research stemmed from the experience of Ela, one of my students, who had undertaken a similar three-generational research project for one of my courses at Ben-Gurion University. We based the decision on a number of factors: the results of a questionnaire distributed in 1988 and 1989 to the grandchildren; the timing of the project—not too early and not too late from the perspective of the survivors themselves; the results of previous studies about the effect of the Holocaust on the children of survivors; and a methodology that emphasized how the storyteller structured the story. We will examine each of these factors in turn.

The Questionnaire Results

We were in the middle of a study of how Israeli and German youth, primarily those of the third generation after the Holocaust, relate that chapter of the past to their perspective on the present. In Israel, we were concerned about Jewish-Israeli identity, attitudes toward Arabs, democratic thinking, and political orientation (Bar-On and Selah, 1991). In Germany, we chose similar local social and political issues. We hypothesized that youngsters held an oversimplified view when relating the past to the present: Israeli youth tended to overextend the relevance ("the past is extremely relevant for our present-day reality"); German youth tended to de-emphasize it ("nothing of the Holocaust is relevant for today's perspective").

This hypothesis was confirmed by the results of the 1988–89 questionnaire (Bar-On et al., 1993). We then looked at both samples to identify those who had succeeded in developing a deeper, more qualitative approach: instead of stating that the past is always or never connected to the present, they asserted that there might be relevance, but it would depend on "when and how and in what ways." For these young people, it is the *mode* of relevance that is central.

We put forward a further hypothesis: that those capable of developing a "partial relevance" mode had worked through the Holocaust psychologically, and come closer to it emotionally, than those who had opted for a more simplified attitude ("everything is relevant" or "nothing is relevant"). The latter group found it emotionally difficult to approach what had happened during the Holocaust and as a consequence of it. Among other things, their simplified attitudes helped them distance themselves from this man-made calamity.

We acknowledged the fact that the young usually tend to see complex subjects as "black or white," since at this stage of their lives it is difficult for them to emotionally process complexity (Erikson, 1968). When it came to the Holocaust, however, we assumed that there was another reason above and beyond the usual "black or white" perspective: the difficulty of the two previous generations in processing their own emotional and moral relationship to the Holocaust. We could hardly find "partial relevance" among the parents and grandparents.

What is this psychological "working through" that we expected in relation to the Holocaust? The concept was developed by Freud (1914) to describe the process between patient and therapist in individual therapy. It was used to explain the laborious psychological process, over and above a one-time "insight," through which the individual confronts repressed childhood experience. In the absence of this process, such repressed content may interfere with an individual's ability to relate feelings, attitudes, and behavior to the present (Novey, 1962). Freud's original concept has been broadened over the years to cope with social trauma and post-traumatic stress disorder (PTSD) (Rothstein, 1986). And the original goal of the process, "letting go" of the influence of repressed content, has been replaced by a more modest one, "living with" the pain of the traumatic event (Lehman et al., 1987).

Clinicians have adopted the concept of "working through" to describe how survivors have coped with the traumas they experienced in the Holocaust. The concept has helped to explain what might seem like extreme behavior as a "normal," delayed reaction to abnormal circumstances and terrible loss (Danieli, 1980). The same concept has also served those who wished to conceptualize the possibility of "living with" feelings of loss and helplessness in one's contemporary life. It has helped us understand how many survivors were able to function for years without exhibiting any pathology, until a time when, for whatever reason, the repressed contents suddenly surfaced (Davidson, 1980).

The concept of working through has been further extended to include the children of Holocaust survivors. Clinicians have assumed that these adult children have had to work through the traumatic content their parents could not discuss openly. Although these children did not experience the horrors directly, they nevertheless absorbed them, especially if their parents did not talk about these matters in an attempt "to protect" them. Paradoxically, the pattern of silence that developed around the survivors "transmitted" something of this content to the children (Krystal, 1968). I have made a similar attempt to describe the process children of Holocaust perpetrators have undergone in struggling with their knowledge of their parents' atrocious actions (Bar-On, 1990).

In approaching the relationship of the grandchildren to the survivors, we need to reexamine the concept of working through, to ask, in their case, a working through of what? Is there some ongoing need to confront repressed experiences that have been passed on from one generation to the next? Even if this is so, for the third generation it could be extremely difficult, especially if they have been silenced by their parents as well. At the same time, a new generation opens up new possibilities for dialogue about issues the survivors have kept to themselves all these years.

We hypothesized that, for the third generation, the working-through process includes five basic stages (McGuire, 1973):

1. Knowledge: an awareness of what happened during the Holocaust, and, if their family was involved, what happened to them during that time.

2. Understanding: the ability to place a knowledge of the facts within

a meaningful human, historical, social, or moral frame of reference.

3. Emotional response: the emotional reaction to this knowledge and understanding; in Israel typically anger (usually toward "the world that stood aside"), fear ("it could happen again"), shame (resulting from "the degradation, the fact that people did such things"), and pride ("for remaining humane," "for fighting back") (Wax and Belah, 1989).

4. Attitude: the attitude toward what happened based on this knowledge, understanding, and emotional response and their implications for the present and the future.

5. Behavior: the effect of knowledge, understanding, emotional response, and attitude on specific behavior patterns in relation to the past, the present, and the future.

In our study we found that a "vicious circle" interfered with the spontaneous working-through process (Bar-On and Selah, 1991). Knowledge, understanding, and emotional response were not correlated to attitude and behavior. At the same time, however, attitudes toward the past were highly correlated to attitudes toward the present. It made no difference whether these attitudes reflected a political orientation on the "left" or the "right." We concluded that attitudes toward the past and the present reinforced each other to form a kind of "vicious circle," a self-reinforcing way of thinking on which knowledge and understanding of, and emotional responses to, the Holocaust, the primary components in the working-through process, have no impact. This "vicious circle" may be the source of that simplification we noted in the third generation—"total relevance"—thereby making "partial relevance" difficult to achieve.

We interpreted our findings as showing that, in Israel, in the late eighties, the Holocaust was being appropriated by a complex and polarized social and political situation (Segev, 1991). While the political right made a claim on the Holocaust through assertions such as "we learned that we must be strong and that no one will help us in our hour of need," the political left, in contrast, stated that "we learned that we must be sensitive to other minority groups." We found that using the Holocaust as a way of finding one's place in the present-day reality of Israel was common among youngsters, whether of Asian or African, or European or American origins. Quite surprisingly, a family's history during the Holocaust had almost no effect on that "vicious circle."

We then moved into a more qualitative stage of the research. We wished to clarify, through interviews, what factors help young adults develop a more refined approach to the Holocaust and to their present lives compared to those who were caught in the "vicious circle." We decided to focus on the family: how did the family influence the young adult's approach to the past and the present? As I have noted, we were already aware of the great influence the polarized political and social reality had on their thinking. We estimated, however, that within the prevailing polarization it would be possible to differentiate between family patterns of confrontation and working through, relating the past to the present in a more refined way. We assumed that the more progress the older generation had made in their working-through process, the less their children's patterns of thinking would be affected by the "vicious circle."

The Timing of the Project

Many researchers have studied the "conspiracy of silence" surrounding the Holocaust, which characterized Israeli society over four decades (Porath, 1986; Segev, 1991). But more than just a "conspiracy of silence" existed. It was accompanied by harsh value judgments, which blamed the survivors, who went, it was said, "like sheep to slaughter." This was the title of an unfortunate pamphlet on the Holocaust published by the Ministry of Education in the early fifties. In the atmosphere that prevailed in Israel during and after the War of Independence, one tended to legitimize only those who had fought in the ghetto uprisings or with the partisans. Only they had measured up to the model of "fighting for one's existence."

Yet, paradoxically, the pattern of value judgment and blame must have served a "need" of many survivors; otherwise, it is difficult to understand why they accepted the verdict of silence. They had their own reasons for repressing what they had gone through: feelings of guilt about family members who had perished, difficulty in dealing with the ever-present images of horror, the pain of separation, and a sense of helplessness in relating all of this to the new, very different Israeli reality. In addition, obsessive talk about the horrors did not take into account the listeners' ability to absorb them, and ultimately had an effect equivalent to silencing.

The survivors wanted to forget and make others forget. They were trying to "save" their children from having to face such difficult memories (Kestenberg, 1972).

We know from other contexts how impossible it is for parents to protect their children from their own oppressive memories. "Untold stories" often pass more powerfully from generation to generation than stories that can be recounted (Grossman, 1986; Bar-On, 1986). In addition, children are sensitive to their parents' need for silencing. A sort of "double wall" forms between the two generations: parents do not tell; children do not ask. Even if one side tries to open a window, they usually confront the other wall. We have found almost no spontaneous incidence in which both parents and children achieved this openness simultaneously, allowing feelings to be mutually shared and accepted (Bar-On and Charny, 1992).

Over the last ten or fifteen years, however, there has been a noticeable change in Israeli society: it has become less judgmental toward Holocaust survivors. While interviewing high school students before their class trip to Auschwitz, for example, we found that they admired those who survived the Holocaust and very definitely did not view those who perished as going "like sheep to slaughter" (Assa and Degani, 1989). At the same time, if for different reasons, many survivors felt a greater need to tell their stories. A few were influenced by the growing willingness of society to reserve judgment and listen. As time passed, the need to talk, to give evidence that would be passed on to future generations, became greater than the need to maintain silence (Felman and Laub, 1992). In addition, the survivors' fears about being unable to build a normal life for their children after what they had been through diminished as their grandchildren, the third generation, grew up. Now the survivors had enough evidence that they, their children, and their children's children were "normal," and this success made it possible for many of them to open their hearts at last and speak (Berlazki, 1991).

In my course at Ben-Gurion University, we spend the entire first semester analyzing the interviews; in effect, they shape the seminar throughout the year. Listening to these interviews has become more difficult from one year to the next as the interviewees speak more openly. Ten or fifteen years ago, we would not have received such varied, detailed testimonies. In fact, one can actually sense that something is changing, not only in the young students who do the interviewing but in the older people who are interviewed. When we began the second year of our research, the research team, composed mainly of graduates of the course, many of whom themselves came from survivors' families, were excited about interviewing family members over three generations. We had the feeling that this was the right time—perhaps the only possible time—for undertaking interviews such as these. Years ago it would have been too early; many of the survivors would have refused. A few years from now it would be too late, since many of the survivors would no longer be alive.

Our German colleagues did not believe themselves capable of interviewing German families on the delicate issue of the Holocaust. They were afraid that the first generation, those who had lived through the period of the Third Reich, would say no to their request for an interview. There is no way of knowing whether their fear was realistic—or whether they were afraid of what they might discover.[1] For whatever reasons, we took two different paths: the German team concentrated on interviewing members of the third generation, and we began interviewing families, talking with all three generations in each.

This is the place to bring up an important question of definition: who, from our standpoint, falls under the category of "Holocaust survivor"? *The Encyclopedia of the Holocaust* gives no definition of this term (Gutman, 1990). From a legal-historical point of view, one may define anyone who lived under Nazi occupation during World War II, and was threatened by the policy of the Final Solution but managed to stay alive, as a Holocaust survivor. However, there are many problems with this definition. It is clear in relation to refugees from the ghetto and from concentration or death camps, but does it also apply to those who escaped to Russia and left their loved ones behind? Does the same definition apply to children as well as adults? Moreover, does this supposedly objective definition reflect their subjective feelings? Many people in the fifties felt stigmatized by being defined as survivors. They tried to minimize this connection or to avoid it altogether. If this is the case, who decides who is a Holocaust survivor?

Two years ago, two of my students interviewed a sample of men and women who had immigrated to Israel from Europe between the years 1935 and 1939 and whose entire families, or most of them, had perished in the Holocaust. From the standpoint of long-range psychological effects, it became evident that they were no different from many other Holocaust survivors. They suffered from the same kind of "survivors' guilt" (Kestenberg, 1972), and kept silent. Their willingness to discuss their feelings, and what had happened to their families, depended mainly on the extent to which they had succeeded in helping those who stayed behind before it was too late. In addition, many of the interviewees felt that their guilt and helplessness were in some way illegitimate because they had not "suffered" like the "real" survivors (Dvir-Malka and Gil'ad, 1989). Their sense of illegitimacy was one result of the official, "objective" definition.

Two other students who interviewed survivors of what was known as the "Kastner train" had the same findings. Some of their interviewees had survived difficult periods in labor camps and faced the very real danger of annihilation before they boarded the train that saved them. They spent months in Bergen-Belsen and suffered illness and starvation. Yet almost all of them still had difficulty relating what they had gone through to the experience of "real" Holocaust survivors. In this instance, their sense of illegitimacy was subjective: they had survived through "improper" means. They felt guilty about the way in which Kastner achieved their freedom (by negotiating with the SS) and about the decisions regarding who would get on that train (Mandela and Frankel, 1990).

What our findings suggest is that survivors see things according to a hidden hierarchy of suffering. A cruel stratification takes place under a magnifying glass: every survivor is seen in relation to what other survivors did or experienced, in a kind of hierarchy outsiders can make no sense of. Internalized definitions of the aggressor may also affect this hierarchy. Mixed families, for example, who survived because of their Christian origins, define themselves as half-Jewish, unwittingly using Nazi terminology. Those with a number on their arm are thought of as "real" survivors. Similarly, among those who were in the ghettos but did not reach the camps, there are some who try to minimize what they experienced: the so-called "Asians," who escaped to Asian Russia, and those who immigrated to Israel before World War II do not consider themselves Holocaust survivors. Clearly, it is very difficult to address extremes of human pain and suffering without attaching to them comparative values and norms: more or less, better or worse.

All of this is complicated enough without getting into a discussion about the subjective "truth" of members of the fighting Jewish organizations and members of the Jewish police, or Judenraat (Zuckerman,

1990), of the "drowned and the saved" (Levi, 1988), or of camp survivors and Jewish *kapos,* who served the Germans in the camps. These are extremely harsh issues, and still very difficult to deal with. In trying to examine them, one cannot escape a feeling of helplessness and emotional stress (Segev, 1991). In contrast to those who tried to develop a scale of suffering according to some private list of criteria, there are others who state with a certain amount of relief: "The only thing possible was escape. The person who did not escape may have a problem with definitions, but not me." The disagreement seems to be between those who relate to the truth of their own subjective feelings and those who try to employ an objective yardstick to measure their suffering.

We understood that nowhere is there a complete overlap between subjective and objective definitions of a family's relationship to the Holocaust. How individuals define that experience depends on their sense of the legitimacy of what they did or experienced as much as the legitimacy given to their feelings by the society around them. Families often struggled with this issue—"who was there and who was not there, where, and when." We do not wish to get involved in these arguments: who are we to sit in judgment? Almost everyone paid a terrible price, some in one way, some in another. We lean toward a subjective definition of a Holocaust survivor, one that includes those who escaped to Russia or came to Israel before the war but left families behind. This period deposited heavy emotional burdens of loss and separation on many who did not have direct experience of its horrors.

In the results of the questionnaire given to the third generation, the grandchildren of survivors, we found an echo of the confusion these difficulties have engendered in people's hearts. Some youngsters defined themselves as having "no family ties to the Holocaust," even though their grandparents clearly were survivors who had immigrated to Israel after the war. It is even highly probable that some family members did indeed go through the Holocaust, yet tried to avoid the label "survivor." Other youngsters, of Asian or African origin, defined themselves as having family ties to the Holocaust on the basis of a single distant relationship. For them it served as a sort of "calling card" for entering Israeli society. One may assume that these differences will only widen in the future, when the survivors have died and different "collective memories" reinterpret their relationship to the Holocaust (Segev, 1991).

It is interesting to note that the distortions we discovered among the German youngsters were not minor ones either. Half of the German sample of 1,100 had no idea whatsoever about their grandparents' involvement during the Third Reich. Among those who did know, approximately a third reported that their grandparents had "opposed the Nazi regime," while only a quarter reported that their grandparents had "actively participated in the Nazi regime." We can only imagine how this distortion will look in the next generation.

The Aftereffects of the Holocaust

We find it necessary to question some of the underlying assumptions of the psychological literature about the effects of the Holocaust on the following generations:

1. How can we separate the aftereffects of the Holocaust from other simultaneous processes (emigration, changing family structures, and individual processes)?

2. Does including the third generation change the role of the second generation as it is portrayed in the literature?

3. Will a different methodology (one that uses biographical and narrative analysis) change the focus from hard normative psychodynamic assertions about identity to the softer theoretical constructs of biography reconstruction? What new information and ideas will emerge from a new methodology?

Most psychological studies have dealt with the long-range effects of the Holocaust on the second generation, the children of survivors. These studies have viewed this generation as being influenced and activated by the events their parents experienced many years before. This conclusion was a breakthrough, since earlier research and therapy had ignored the possibility of such long-range effects altogether (Danieli, 1980). However, the results were not as clear as one would expect. The argument developed mainly along two axes that only partially overlap: that of clinical research and that of "negative" effects versus "positive" ones.

The discussion centering on the first axis grew out of clinical findings that identified long-range effects on the second generation. For example, children of Holocaust survivors had difficulty with individuation (emotional independence from their parents), were less likely to express anger, and had a stronger need for achievement (Kestenberg, 1972; Krystal, 1968). But these findings, which were based primarily on clinical reports, were not confirmed when random sampling was used, including control groups (Reick and Eitinger, 1983). It is also unclear whether the instruments in the controlled studies were sensitive enough to test the effects found in therapy or whether the results found in clinical self-selected samples were valid for the population at large.

The discussion along the second axis focused on clinicians' assertions that the second generation *suffered from the burden* of the Holocaust, which their parents carried and silently transmitted. Other researchers pointed out the *positive achievement-oriented* response, a kind of over-response, due precisely to the fact that these were children of Holocaust survivors, and thus showed a better ability to cope with current problems.

An illustration of the former assertion is found in a study showing that children of Holocaust survivors who suffered from battle shock in the Lebanon War of 1982 did not adjust as well to daily life two or three years later as the control group (Solomon, 1989). Studies illustrating the latter approach show that members of the second generation had more education and achieved greater economic success than peers who were not children of survivors (Reick and Eitinger, 1983). This argument partially overlaps with that of the long-range effects. As a rule, clinicians present data about the negative aftereffects, while researchers who have undertaken controlled studies usually show either a lack of effect or one of relative advantage.

Another line of research, based on more complex assertions, has tried to overcome the contradiction between clinicians and researchers by suggesting *interpersonal differences.* Danieli (1983), for example, categorized the second generation's reactions according to their parents' objective experiences during the Holocaust (camp survivors as opposed to partisans) and their own subjective way of coping (fighting versus resignation). In another study, Vardi (1990) proposed that families of Holocaust survivors "chose" one child to fulfill the role of a "memorial candle," and this child carried the emotional burden the parents did not work through.

According to Vardi, the "memorial candle" child is the one who generally seeks therapy because he or she feels more burdened than the other children.

Clearly, these categorizations and diagnoses served clinicians working with families of Holocaust survivors in the diagnostic process, in choosing the type of therapy, and in evaluating the prognosis. However, these categories do not always help us understand the phenomenon of *intergenerational transmission* in the shadow of the Holocaust. Indeed, most Holocaust survivors and their families did not seek therapy. How, then, did they deal with a similar traumatic burden? If we assume that they succeeded in normalizing these emotional burdens (Rosenthal, 1987), we might ask, When is normalization a proof of competent functioning and when is it a proof of malfunctioning passed on from generation to generation? Did working-through processes develop spontaneously and not in the frame of therapy, and how are they different from or similar to the working-through patterns initiated by therapists?

The primary wish of most survivors was probably to achieve normalization after the Holocaust as quickly as possible. However, one could claim that this wish was simultaneously functional and dysfunctional. It did help the survivors return to "normal" life, avoiding the burdens and frightful memories of the past by performing regular, everyday tasks in the present. But the same normalization could at some point become dysfunctional, since survivors thus avoided a necessary psychological mourning process and thereby became committed to the past (Davidson, 1980). Although accepting that normalization is a "normal" reaction to abnormal and extreme life events, this approach assumes that survivors or their descendants should be able to go beyond normalization to develop a more open strategy for working through the past (Vardi, 1990).

Though quite sophisticated, this still amounts to a normative approach. First, I would ask, How can we actually know in what way survivors developed normalization strategies different (or more extensive) from those of other émigrés? Did immigrants from Asian or African countries not use normalization strategies in overcoming the emotional upheaval of being uprooted? Did people born in Israel not have to develop normalization strategies while fighting in the War of Independence in 1948? What were the particular qualities of the normalization processes of Holocaust survivors and their families?

Second, how do we know if normalization implied hope for a better future or if it was mainly a way to control the fears and memories of the past? Perhaps we can find better answers to these questions through "softer" conceptualizations:[2] by analyzing the narratives of survivors describing their life stories. For example, can we recognize traces of fear and hope in the interviewees' biographical reconstructions? Have their children internalized the parents' normalization strategies? Will they express feelings of dread or relief, fear or hope, or some mixture of both in their narratives? I believe that if we can find answers to some of these questions, we may better understand the link between normalization strategies and the working-through of traumatic events, and their intergenerational aftereffects.

The reason we are leaning toward "softer" concepts is first and foremost because of our inability to isolate processes and study them separately. In fact, every researcher looking at intergenerational transmission has to deal with four distinct processes that have affected their interviewees simultaneously: uprooting owing to emigration, immigration into the new culture of the absorbing country, specific family structures and processes, and personal processes. These processes are interwoven in the burden the survivors carry with them and cannot be separated from it. I will briefly try to show how these processes are interwoven.

First, most Holocaust survivors experienced emigration, which has its own psychological toll: severance from family, tradition, culture, language, and childhood. Rarely does emigration allow a gradual parting—a movement back and forth in the émigré's imagination between the old and the new reality until the final choice matures—which would best suit the dynamics of psychological processes. For example, Aroian (1990) showed that Poles who immigrated to the United States and were struggling with their uprootedness integrated better into their new culture only after they had revisited their homeland. This solution is considered in Israel to be a "luxury," and it is most characteristic of emigration from wealthier countries.

In contrast, most emigration is characterized by a final, one-time severance, which does not allow the objective possibility of returning and reexamining things in their original context in a "backward and forward" process. In such cases, psychologists suggest, difficulties in the working-through process can be observed. Rapid severance makes separation harder. The émigrés become involved in the new reality, but in their repressed or unconscious thoughts they still live in the old, which represents what they have left behind or what they believe they have left behind (Bar-On, 1986). We can differentiate between several types of severance. Thus we can see *compulsive severance* in emigration from Asian or African countries, and identify illustrations of *severance by choice* among the pioneers, who were firm believers in the Zionist ideology. The essence of the concept *aliyah* ("ascent," the word used to refer to immigrating to Israel) reflects the atmosphere that accompanied severance by choice.

For survivors of the Holocaust, however, the process of compulsive severance did not begin with emigration, it ended with it. Most were compelled to sever their ties with their place of origin violently and unexpectedly, while still within their home context. This severance usually caught them in life-threatening danger, unprepared for emigration, and it was, therefore, extremely traumatic. Keilson (1992) refers to the three stages of traumatization experienced by Holocaust orphans: the stage of separation from their family (parents, children, spouses, wider family network); the process of survival during the war; and the stage of returning to find "what no longer existed" at the end of the war. The final stage, he asserted, was the most traumatic, because then many survivors understood the irreversibility of what had happened: everything dear to them was lost forever.

Emigration from Europe became for many survivors not just an act of severance (that occurred anyway) or leave-taking (most people did not have a person or a place to part from), but rather a *corrective act*. It enabled them to make a new start, to erase or forget what had happened. At that point, it was, in fact, an expression of their strength. The survivors did not concern themselves with how and when they would deal with the process of leave-taking; during this period they had to prove to themselves and to others that they were capable of living, and not only according to physical and technical standards. Olga Anisevitch (see Chapter 3) represents this kind of inner command of "rebuilding a life."

Immigration was accompanied by harsh value judgments on the part of the Israeli society that absorbed these survivors (Yablonka, 1990), and this was viewed by them as a threat: it labeled them as incompetent. It was the pinning on of a "blue and white star" in place of the Nazi "yellow star" from which they had just been freed (Segev, 1991). All new immigrants, for better or worse, endured this judgment. It created the possibility of a new taste of freedom, an Israeli taste, one that was different from everything that they had known; it was possible to assimilate and forget one's past identity. But because external judgments were internalized, some survivors came to see themselves as weak, and this only added to the emotional burden they already carried with them and made it even more difficult to work it through.

In the early days of the young state, a complaint about emotional burdens by any segment of the Israeli population was considered inappropriate. During the forties and fifties the model of the "Sabra"—which focused on struggle and action, on contributing to the welfare of society at the expense of individual emotional needs—dominated Israeli culture. Not until the seventies and eighties was there any acknowledgment of complex emotional processes, of the need for self-actualization, or of differences between individuals and generations. By then, a more mature society had emerged, one that had learned to acknowledge the high cost of the previous behavioral and cultural patterns. It became clear that some of the difficulties suffered by Holocaust survivors were also evident in other emigrating segments of Israeli society.

To both of these processes, emigration and the changing values of Israeli society, we must add the interfamilial process. All families have characteristic patterns of confronting external and internal family pressures (Cohler and Grunnebaum, 1981). They express such differences especially when they speak about emigration and changes in social values. According to Bar-Semech (1990), these differences can be charted on two central axes: continuation of the family's original practices, as opposed to inventiveness based on the changing norms of the environment; closeness and intimacy, as opposed to independence and/or loneliness; investment in personal growth, as opposed to investment in group cohesiveness; and symmetry (or competition) between the spouses, as opposed to complementary relations.

In addition, each family has its own "clock," or timetable, of births, weddings, aging, and death, all central life events that bind families together. The family has been defined as a unique system that one can join only through birth and marriage and leave only through death or divorce (Carter and McGoldrick, 1988). The Holocaust "caught" families at various stages in their family timetables, speeding up some and completely disrupting others, usually irreversibly so. It wiped out the possibility of a *full life cycle* of multigenerational families, where daughters learn how to be mothers from their own mothers, where grandchildren hear stories and get a sense of continuity from their grandparents (Cohler and Grunnebaum, 1981). All this happened in addition to the distortion of family timetables caused by emigration, which was already quite painful in itself.

One would expect people to tell their life stories within their family context, unless that context was disrupted by external life events such as the Holocaust. For example, Dvora described how her father "vanished" a short while after the Nazis conquered France. In her family Dvora was "daddy's girl," and his disappearance was extremely difficult for her to bear. For her it was his second disappearance: the first had occurred when he and her mother divorced, and he came to visit only occasionally. For Dvora, the first trauma was her parents' divorce and staying with a mother who projected her anger toward her husband onto her daughter, who loved him so much. One may suggest that the disappearance of Dvora's father during the Holocaust had a degree of finality about it, one that effectively made her parents' divorce irreversible. However, we will never know how each trauma separately affected Dvora, since, for her, they are both interwoven in her memories and her life story. Her recurring dream illustrated how she went on reconstructing her relationship to her father, as her life conditions changed.

To all of these, we must add personal processes. In any given emergency, people will react in different ways. There are those who see the challenge, who discover strength and insight they did not know they had. But there are others who perceive the same challenge as a threat and respond with helplessness and despair. The same person may respond differently to different pressures or to the same pressure at different times. Dvora's brother reacted very differently to his father's disappearance. He was "mommy's boy" in the family, more introverted, and seemingly more "normal," than his "temperamental" sister. One day, however, without any warning, he committed suicide. Can we connect his suicide to the Holocaust? or to the social and familial processes intertwined with it? Perhaps his more introverted personality, which at first helped him normalize his traumatic past, turned on itself owing to unresolved, and now unbearable, conflicts. How can we ever know for sure?

The differences between people and within people add another layer, which intertwines with family patterns, emigration, and societal value judgments. This makes the study of the aftereffects of the Holocaust extremely complicated. Indeed, one can find many human dramas among immigrants from Morocco, Ethiopia, or Argentina. In these families, there are traumas resulting from family separation, the loss of one's birthplace, one's language, and one's culture that have not been processed and are thus transferred from one generation to the next. It is almost impossible to *isolate* the Holocaust as a component in attempting to investigate its multigenerational effect.

One may hypothesize that the Holocaust is the major cause of the similar patterns we can identify among families of émigrés from other countries. However, one may also hypothesize that the Holocaust had a qualitative influence unlike that found in any other combination of processes. It profoundly disrupted the continuity of the family context. Within a "softer" conceptualization, one could hypothesize that *historical events* flooded the frame of the *personal life story* far beyond its regular family-bound context (Rosenthal, 1987). The life story of the Guetta family from Libya (see Chapter 5) will serve as a reference point for testing this hypothesis. It is difficult to find clear answers to these questions, given the multitude of intertwined variables. Most studies have attempted to describe the long-range effects of the Holocaust as a unique phenomenon. This could also have had a political agenda: a need to show the world *what was done to us.* Yet it is important to emphasize that those things considered to be aftereffects of the Holocaust have never appeared independently; they are always compounded by other components.

Adding the Third Generation

This multitude of interwoven processes inspired us to examine such effects on three familial generations (Carter and McGoldrick, 1988; Chang, 1991). In fact, the third generation is the first that is relatively liberated from the actual act of emigration of the first generation and the reaction to it of the second generation. In the case of Holocaust survivors' families, we may find that the need for normalization has been transmitted to the third generation or, conversely, that they have been freed from it thanks to the working-through processes of their parents and grandparents. In addition, the grandchildren may have introduced a new sense of hopefulness into the family by establishing a complete, natural life cycle (Carter and McGoldrick, 1988) and opening communication with grandparents.

Through my students' interviews, for example, we learned of instances in which the grandchildren had prepared a family "roots" project in school and thus heard their grandparents' stories about the Holocaust for the first time. Their parents, the survivors' own children, became acquainted with these stories only when they read their children's school reports. As I mentioned earlier, this may be the result of a number of factors: the change in values that has taken place in Israeli society, the progressive stages of a survivor's particular biological clock, the communication patterns in a specific family, or the presence of a curious, open youngster.[3]

By adding the third generation, we get a different perspective on the role of the second. Now they are not merely passive or active responders to their parents' fate and normalization but mature persons in their own right, parents of their own children. Furthermore, as I have already suggested, they had a complicated task: navigating between their parents and their children. On the one hand, they wanted their children to enjoy their grandparents, a privilege they had missed in their own childhood (Vardi, 1990). On the other, they wanted their children to grow up free of the constraints they had experienced as children. We will see how difficult this task is, one Tzipke Belinsky can reflect on but others cannot (see Chapter 1).

We should, however, remember that by comparing the life stories of three generations, we compare very different life perspectives: the retroactive one of the survivors, who look back wanting to tell a story that reflects the major events in their lives; that of the middle generation, still in their active years, still creating their own life story but also finding themselves at a critical moment (midlife crisis?) as their children grow up and begin to leave home; and that of the third generation, who may not yet have much of a life story to tell. These young people are on the threshold, struggling with basic questions (who am I?), and feeling hopeful (the whole world is open) or afraid (look what others have done with their lives, will I be any different?). These perspectives may be impossible to compare, a priori. What pushed us in this direction was our attempt to reframe our perspective on how descendants of Holocaust survivors are portrayed in the literature by introducing the younger generation.

IDENTITY AND BIOGRAPHY

Earlier, in discussing the psychological literature on the aftereffects of the Holocaust, I mentioned what I believe are the main problems with research in such a multivariate field. I would further argue that this research has shaped an identity for Holocaust survivors and their offspring that many of them have regarded as stigmatizing and tried to get rid of (Fischer-Rosenthal, 1992). By that I do not mean that these studies did not identify important issues; they did. But these issues were *partial truth* presented as *total truth* (Langer, 1991). Even more, quite a few of the people involved felt that the way their identity was framed by the professionals made it more difficult for them to overcome their subjective hardships.

We wanted a methodology based on "softer" assumptions, one that focused on how the storyteller reconstructed his or her biography (Felman and Laub, 1992).[4] This is different from a hermeneutic approach, in which the researcher conducts the reconstruction of the narrative provided by the storyteller (Rosenthal, 1993). The underlying assumption of the present approach suggests that storytellers reconstruct their own life stories, from their own perspective and backward and forward simultaneously (Abelson, 1976). However, we did not assume that this implies a total subjectivization of these experiences independent of their historical context, but rather, that one should try to learn more about the relationship between the biographical reconstruction of a life story and the life history (or life events) in which that story is embedded and from which it is reconstructed (Rosenthal and Bar-On, 1992).

We will see, for example, that the life story of Laura Guetta, who grew up in Libya under Nazi occupation (but with a much less effective extermination policy toward the Jews) centers on events *internal* to the family, although she suffered very painful losses in her family (see Chapter 5), while the other four survivors of the Nazi extermination process we interviewed tell life stories in which *external* events invade the personal, tearing apart the internal family history. We will suggest that one of the effects of the trauma of the Holocaust is this disruption of the natural process of biography reconstruction.

This question became even more central when we tried to assess the intergenerational aftereffects of the Holocaust. It is so difficult for researchers, even when they are trying to be "objective," to put themselves in their interviewees' shoes. At the same time, it is hard for survivors to verbalize what they experienced, especially the feelings that accompanied those experiences. The researchers, through their too rigid conceptual framework, may overlook the fragile language structures survivors have developed to describe those events and their reactions to them. In addition, the researcher may, unwittingly, use a rigid conceptual system as a protection against an interviewee's painful life experiences. This may be especially true of researchers or therapists who find it difficult to become emotionally exposed to their subjects or patients (Danieli, 1980; Langer 1991).

During my interviews with children of Nazis in Germany (Bar-On, 1989), one of my interviewees told me that in therapy, each time she tried to bring up her father's involvement in the Nazi extermination process during the war and her need to clarify and confront this involvement, her therapist would tell her: "This has nothing to do with you, you are running away from dealing with your *real* problems." There are situations in which such a statement could be valid, but in this case, one might suspect that it was the therapist who was trying to avoid these issues and projected this difficulty onto her patient (Schmidt and Heimannsberg, 1994). Danieli (1980) found similar countertransference difficulties among therapists working with Holocaust survivors.

In another study, Rosenthal (1987) describes how her interviewees in Germany, who had participated in both world wars, told their life stories. She then compared how each of them spoke about the two wars—where they spoke at length and where they were brief—and tried to come up with a hypothesis to explain why they told the story the way they did. For confirmation of her hypothesis, she looked in the texts themselves. She was committed to the original text—the way the interviewees themselves had reconstructed their autobiographies—with few preconceptions on her part. In their stories she found an endless process of choice that moved forward and backward. This pattern reflected the tension between *conservation* of the past and *change* in the present and future.

Rosenthal suggested that the reconstruction of their life story by her interviewees was not coincidental and reflected their *normalization strategies*, their ways of facing a threatening past and an uncertain future. These strategies allow people to "smooth corners" in their stories, especially corners they have found difficult to confront in the present (Rosenthal, 1987, 1989; Rosenthal and Bar-On, 1992). Other approaches look for the "historical truth" underlying the subject's distorted report, much as an archaeologist attempts to recreate a version of a pitcher from its broken pieces (Spence, 1980). This approach asserts that a kind of "narrative truth" can be found in every strategy. Here, the question is not which historical truth the story reflects but rather, how the strategy that underlies the story serves the narrator's goals from his or her present perspective.

This method of analysis demands an appropriate interview method. The interviewer must refrain as much as possible from presenting directing questions, since these might shape the structure of the interview, thereby producing the interviewer's, instead of the subject's, structure. In effect, interviewers ask interviewees to tell their life stories as they have experienced them. It is permissible to ask clarifying questions if something is unclear, if there are contradictions in a person's story, or if a noticeable segment of the person's life history has been left out. We often find, however, that the interviewee's original omissions and contradictions were not accidental, so the interviewer must be careful. The interviewee may perceive questions as value judgments. Their purpose should be to clarify whether the contradiction or omission was intentional or a result of the interviewer's misunderstanding.

This method does have its limitations. It is a hermeneutic method that emphasizes the differences between people, an idiosyncratic approach that places subjective experience in the center. Much effort is invested in the analysis of each interview. It is difficult to make generalizations because of the lack of randomized sampling procedures—one cannot prove whether the sample is representative of the wider population. In addition, reliability between analysts may be low; there may be differences in the ways researchers suggest hypotheses and find confirmation of them in the text. Another danger is that one will stray from the text itself: to what extent do researchers "find" in the text ex post facto confirmation of their ideas? (Langer, 1991).

We were conscious of these limitations and knew we were choosing a difficult path—it is relatively easy for researchers to know a priori what categories they are going to use in analyzing the interviews—but we chose it because we wanted to focus on how our interviewees organized their life stories. It suited their perspectives, their need for "normalcy." It also helped us to refrain from being judgmental, a characteristic problem of narrative-analysis in which the reader has the feeling that the investigator "shaped the text" to suit his or her understanding of the interview.

Given these a priori and ex post facto pitfalls, the possible range of the researcher's exploration is quite limited, nor do we claim that we did not have our own views, perspectives, and even ready-made theories about what we would find. That is to say, at the start we had a kind of basic "map," which helped us find our way through a sea of details and undeciphered dependencies. We assumed, for instance, that all interviewees had developed core strategies around which they structured their interviews, that their life stories and life histories corresponded in different ways. However, it was not clear to us beforehand what the quality of each strategy of each interviewee would be; we had our doubts about the usefulness of our "map" and of its "coordinates." We looked for additional "axes" or dimensions, beyond the ones we believed we had already identified.

Once we moved into the domain of biography reconstruction, we wondered how it would affect our questions about the intergenerational aftereffects of the Holocaust. First we would have to try to discover how each interviewee reconstructed his or her biography. Then we could ask questions about how these reconstructions related to each other, to parents and children, and to grandparents and grandchildren. To what extent did they call on the same normalization strategies? What in the life histories of the survivors has affected their life stories (Spence, 1980), and how did this in turn affect the life stories of their offspring? Only then would we be able to go further—to consider what one generation has transmitted to another, what has been worked through, and how we could identify it in the texts of the second and third generations. In many cases, we will be able to suggest only directions for further investigation rather than full-fledged theories.

Issues in Narrative Analysis

The issues involved in discourse or narrative analysis are much more complicated than my brief treatment of them here implies. Let us take for a moment the issue of fear, which I mentioned earlier when I outlined my own life story. How do we know, from analyzing texts, if a person is afraid or not? Wittgenstein (1953) referred to this issue in his *Philosophical Investigations:*

> What does the sentence "I am afraid" mean? We can imagine all sorts of things, for example:

"No, no! I am afraid!"

"I am afraid. I am sorry I have to confess it."

"I am still a bit afraid, but no longer as much as before."

"At bottom I am afraid, though I won't confess it to myself."

"I torment myself with all sorts of fears."

"Now, just when I should be fearless, I am afraid."

To each of these sentences a special tone of voice is appropriate, and a different context. It would be possible to imagine people who . . . used different words *where we used only one.* (p. 88; my emphasis)

I can think of additional expressions of tacit fear: for example, "I am not afraid at all, never." Monk (1990) adds to this passage from Wittgenstein his own point of view: "There is no reason to think that a general theory of fear would be of much help here (still less a general theory of language). Far more to the point would be an *alert and observant sensitivity to people's faces, voices and situations.* This kind of sensitivity can be gained only *by experience*—by attentive looking and listening to the people around us . . . But at a deeper level, some people, and even whole cultures, will always be an enigma to us" (pp. 547–548). Monk identifies two tensions, one between a "theory of fear or language" and "experience and sensitivity," the other between the latter and a "deeper cultural level of enigma and mystery." How do we find our way? Again, Wittgenstein makes a suggestion:

#244. How do words refer to sensations? . . . Don't we talk about sensations every day, and give them names? But how is the connexion and the thing named set up . . . the name "pain" for example . . . A child has hurt himself and he cries; and then adults talk to him and teach him exclamations and, later, sentences . . . the verbal expression of pain replaces crying *and does not describe it.* (p. 89; my emphasis)

Here, almost in a Freudian way, Wittgenstein describes talking of or about pain as a result of a socialization process, a kind of "sublimation" of the child's "cry of pain." However, the words do not "describe it." Unlike Freud, Wittgenstein skeptically elaborates on what one person understands when another says "I am in pain" just as he did with "I am afraid." Still, he did not clarify how we would relate to sensations or feelings that have no criteria (voice, context, history) at all. As Kripke (1982) comments:

any view that supposes that . . . an inner process always has "outward criteria," seems to me probably to be empirically false. It seems to me that we have sensations or sensation *qualia* that we can *perfectly well* identify but that have no "natural" external manifestations; an observer cannot tell in any way whether an individual has them unless that individual avows them . . . It is the *primitive part of our language game of sensations* that, if an individual has satisfied criteria for a mastery of sensation language in general, we then respect his claim to have identified a new type of sensation, even if the sensation is correlated with nothing publicly observable. (p. 103, n. 83)

Although Kripke has addressed our present issue more clearly than Wittgenstein, his remarks bring up several new problems:

1. Can we always identify "perfectly well" sensations of the non-verifiable kind? Does the concept of identification assume determinant relations between feelings and words? Or does the former only have to be "captured" (identified) by the "correct" wording?

2. Do we have no way, as observers, of feeling or even telling of the sensations experienced by another individual unless that individual "avows them" as Kripke claims? Don't we all have innate, non-verbal ways of communicating about feelings, ways that were well refined long before we mastered verbal expression (or "avowal") of our feelings?

3. Why is our avowal of these sensations "a primitive part of the language game" of sensation? Why "only if an individual has satisfied criteria [can we] . . . respect his claim [for] a new type of sensation"? Does Kripke's conditioning not suggest that even he felt uncomfortable with nonverifiable sensations or with our ability, or lack of ability, to communicate them?

In this book I will primarily discuss those feelings for which we have neither a mutually agreed upon nor an external criterion for verification beforehand. The fear or hope survivors felt after undergoing traumatic experiences during the Holocaust is just such an emotion, *nonverifiable and multirepresentational*. We will see that when Ze'ev tells his life story, his fear surfaces only when he refers to his grandson Yoav's approaching military service. Was Ze'ev never afraid before? We could look at examples referring to half a dozen other emotions and ask the same question. This puts an enormous responsibility on the interviewer and the interpreter. Critics can always ask: "How do you actually know? Is it not all in your mind?"

We found it necessary to develop a kind of agreement between the interviewee's verbal expressions, the interviewer's ear, eyes, and heart, and the interpreter's mind (and heart). Clearly, some of what I will discuss here also has relevance for sensations about which we assume we have such mutual or external criteria. However, the absence of such obvious external correlates or agreed-upon criteria creates special problems in "knowing" what we feel and communicating those "feeling-facts" to others.[5]

The Family Interviews

I will now briefly describe how we worked. First, we attempted to locate families that met a number of criteria: The first generation had gone through the Holocaust under the Nazi regime, immigrated to Israel, and lived there today (we tried to find "representatives" of different segments of the Holocaust: those who survived extermination camps and ghettos, who hid, who joined the partisans, who escaped to Russia, and who lived under the fascist Italian regime in northern Africa); three generations in the family were living in Israel during the interviewing phase and consented to the interview (the third generation had to be at least sixteen years old); at least one representative from each generation would be interviewed (Ela interviewed her family on a much wider scale, but we could not follow that pattern because we were afraid it would put too much stress on us and on the families). In one family, however, we did interview both members of the first generation, since they had lived through totally different experiences. In another family, we interviewed two siblings from the second generation; one brother immigrated to Israel before the war and his sister was left behind with her parents and survived the Holocaust in hiding. We encountered a few difficulties. Two families changed their minds about being interviewed after having given their initial consent, and the poor quality of one of the tapes made it impossible to transcribe and process one set of interviews.

The interviews usually took place in the subjects' homes. We began by interviewing the first generation; then the same interviewer, or pair of interviewers, continued, interviewing the remaining family members. The interviews with the survivors were long (two to three hours, on average), and those with the third generation relatively short (one hour, on average). As it turned out, we interviewed more women than men. (Was this because our staff was mostly comprised of women? We have no explanation beyond coincidence.)

We asked our subjects to tell us their life stories and tried not to interrupt them during the first part of the interview except to ask clarifying questions. (The interview texts will show, however, that—unintentionally—this was not always the case.) Afterwards, we asked a few questions of our own, especially if the interviewees had not touched on them, mainly about holidays and family gatherings; who was included in the family; the objects and myths that were transmitted from one generation to the next; family names—who chose them and who the children were named after. We gave a questionnaire to members of the third generation that was identical to the questionnaire we distributed during the first year of the research project. Even though we worked a great deal on using a common interview format, differences between the interviews were inevitable and may be due in part to the interviewers' different interviewing skills.

The interviewers taped the interviews, and then transcribed the tapes, including what they recalled of the interviewees' nonverbal responses. They also added a description of the subject, the interviewing process, and their own feelings during the interview. When they were finished, we began to analyze the interviews together. Moving from the role of interviewer to the role of analyst demanded more than a technical transition, and it was difficult for all of us. We became so involved in the interviews themselves that it was hard for us to maintain the necessary emotional distance needed for the analyses. Because we were under pressure to finish the initial analysis within the time set by the research funding, we decided to meet again during the following year in order to make our analysis more explicit.

For this project the question of methodology is critical—a kind of "to be or not to be." The field of Holocaust studies is already too full of verbosity, of statements loaded with trivialized emotion. So much has already been written about the Holocaust, and all of us are emotionally involved in one way or another. As researchers we had to make choices. Using the method presented here, we wished to inject fresh air into a smoke-filled room—to create fresh possibilities, to reexamine well-established truths.

Conclusion: What This Book Is About and How It Is to Be Read

It is one thing to conduct a successful interview and analysis and another to write a book about the process. Had we troubled readers with the elaborate process of hypothesis generation and testing throughout the text, it would have detracted from our intentions. Instead, we started at the end and worked our way back through the process to consider the main issues that came up repeatedly in our analysis and to follow them through at least parts of the original interview texts. At the same time, we wanted to maintain the original structure of the personal accounts, so they would unfold for the reader as they did for us. Clearly, there is a tension between these two aims. Our text represents a compromise between the major issues as they emerged and the initial unfolding process.

This book consists of five main chapters, one chapter per family. Each chapter was written by the two members of the research team that interviewed that family and analyzed the interview text. Each begins with a short family chronology, which briefly describes the family biography, and an introduction, which includes our initial, tentative questions about the family, based on this biography. We then present full or partial accounts of the interviews,[6] starting with the first generation—the order in which we usually met with family members. At the end of each interview is a short discussion of the interviewee, and at the end of each chapter, a discussion of the family emphasizing the specific issues that emerged in their personal accounts.

Overall, the main issues that concerned us included:

1. *The biographical reconstruction process:* the relationship between the life stories and the life histories of the survivors and those of their offspring. What are the major life events around which the biography is reconstructed? To what extent does the interviewee succeed in maintaining the family context of his life story, in spite of the traumatic external events that threatened to disrupt it? In what

way are these reconstructions different from or similar to *identity conceptualizations* as found in the psychological literature?

2. *Transmission of feelings, or patterns of thought or behavior.* We found, for example, that the strongest form of transmission was the "untold story" obscured in the text by the "told" story. This is a tricky concept, because untold stories are *imagined structures* we impose on the text when we determine what is there and what is missing.

3. *Fear and hope in the more symbolic sense,* fear representing the negative emotions, the shattered assumptions (Janoff-Bulman, 1992) we assume are a negative aftereffect of the Holocaust. (One could just as well suggest anger, hate, helplessness, shame, or guilt, since they all appear in the text or underlie it.) We felt that ongoing fear represented the negative aftereffects of the Holocaust in the broadest sense, while hope represented belief in a better future in spite of all that had happened. Again, this is a tricky concept, since we can talk of hope and not be hopeful, or seem to be pessimistic but also harbor an underlying hopefulness, as we saw in Wittgenstein's formulation (Monk, 1990). If genuinely felt and expressed, however, hope is, in our opinion, an amazing achievement in the shadow of the Holocaust. We will see how difficult it is to maintain a genuine quest for hope in the interviewees' narrations and in their current lives. Although we have tried to attend to Monk's assertion and warning (we have no theory about fear or hope, nor about language), one could ask whether we have imposed a theme on these texts a priori.

   With these two symbolic feelings, fear and hope, we can associate the tension between remembering and forgetting, between preserving the past and moving forward to "rebuild a life." These are the two contradictory exhortations of Holocaust survivors, which their children and grandchildren have had to struggle with. However, remembering the dreadful past does not always imply fear, or "rebuilding life," hope. As we shall see, the relationship between these constructs is much more complicated.

4. *Working through the burden of the past, especially by the second and*

third generations. For its initial formulation, we have assumed that this process takes different forms, and we will try to identify some of these forms by *reframing* previous life stories: for example, when children or grandchildren ask new questions or try to give new answers to old formulations, especially in relation to core events that had a strong impact on the first-generation storyteller. When Ganit or Orit (see Chapters 1 and 3) make assertions or ask questions about their grandmothers in new ways—different from those of their parents—it is a sign that something has been re-framed (and possibly "worked through"). This is different from the transmission of patterns, which we will see more clearly in the case of Dafna and Idit (see Chapter 4).

5. *The second generation as navigators between the first and the third generations.* To what extent did the interviewees of this generation develop their own frame of reference, independent (that is, neither dependent nor counterdependent) of that of their parents, while at the same time trying to help their own children to become independent yet maintain close bonds with their grandparents—a difficult achievement in any family, but especially so in the shadow of the Holocaust.

Following Chapters 1 and 2, on the Belinsky and the Lerman families, we will compare the two members of the first generation: Genia, a survivor of Auschwitz, and Ze'ev, a member of the partisans. We will try to clarify for ourselves which parts of their biographies color their life stories and how these are referred to by their children and grandchildren. Following Chapters 3 and 4, on the Anisevitch and the Segal families, we discuss why Dina and Tamar, the daughters of Olga and Anya, were less successful in navigating between their parents and their children compared to Tzipke and Hannah, the daughters of Genia and Ze'ev. The Guetta family, of Libyan origin (see Chapter 5), clarifies how indirect experience of the Holocaust lessened the "penetration" of external events into the personal life stories of members of different generations. In that family, *intrafamilial* events were central.

We conclude with a discussion in which we will try to evaluate to what extent we have succeeded in developing a new framework for understanding the intergenerational aftereffects of trauma. In addition, we present an appendix discussing the methodological problems that came up during our analysis.

This book will not answer the expectations of those looking for pre-packaged formulas they can use in tomorrow's therapy session or those needing a neatly formulated sequence—what we searched for and what we found. However, for those who are genuinely interested in trying to understand what Holocaust survivors, their children, and their grand-children tell us, what they struggle with, this book is intended as an ori-entation map, still open to their participation in constructing it further yet detailed enough to show where to look and which path to try.

1

THE BELINSKYS

Out of the Camps

with Tova Milo

Genia lost her entire family in the Holocaust. She herself was at Majdanek and Auschwitz. She immigrated to Israel and raised three children; today, she is the grandmother of six. We might assume that Genia left death behind and turned to her new life. It is more difficult to understand how she might contain both death and life within her. What did she teach her children about remembering and forgetting? How did her family absorb the burden and find their own way between life and death? How do they perceive it today, two generations away from those unbearable events? We will look for answers in the interviews with Genia, Tzipke, and Ganit. They represent three different perspectives: the grandmother, a survivor, in the latter part of her life; her daughter, a mother, and, at forty-two, in midlife; and Genia's eldest granddaughter, a young woman at the end of her army service and the beginning of her independent adult life. Each is a person in her own right. Are they all part of a common process?

Genia

"Our hearts were burned in the camps"

Genia opens the door only after she has looked through the peephole. Her face has a fierce look. Inside, the table is already set for two. She wants to begin her story while we are still standing and I am busy looking at the

1922   Genia is born in Warsaw, the third of five children.

1939   The war: A bomb falls on the house on Rosh Hashanah eve. The family moves to the synagogue, and from there they are taken to the ghetto.

1940   On Passover, Genia's mother becomes ill. She has stomach cancer and dies soon afterward.

1942   Genia's brother is killed in a concentration camp. She works in a German factory that manufactures uniforms. Her brother-in-law is taken away to a concentration camp. They hear about Treblinka.

1943   *April 19:* The ghetto uprising. Genia finds a bunker for her father, her two sisters, her nephew, and herself.
        May 2: There is a fire in the ghetto. Genia is caught and sent to Majdanek. Six weeks later she is transferred to Auschwitz, where she remains for twenty-two months.

1945   The Russians liberate them, and they are handed over to the British. Genia arrives in a camp in Lindenberg with a friend. There, she meets and marries Laibel.

1947   Tzipke, a daughter, is born in Leningrad.

1949   The family immigrates to Israel. They settle in Ramat Gan.

1952   Yudke, a son, is born.

1956   Tova, a daughter, is born.

1966   Tzipke marries Yosef.

1967   Ganit, a daughter, is born to Tzipke and Yosef.

1970   Ziv, a son, is born to Tzipke and Yosef.

1978   Nira, a daughter, is born to Tzipke and Yosef.

1981   Yosef's father dies.

1986   Ganit finishes school and enlists in the Israeli army.

1989   Tova Milo interviews Genia, Tzipke, and Ganit. Ziv refuses to be interviewed.

pictures hanging on the walls. "There are always the same pictures, the same furniture," I say to myself as I set up the small tape recorder on the table between us. I am now more prepared to look at her face and hear her story. From what I have heard, I know it will be difficult.

To tell you that I didn't have a chance to know what the word *mother* is? I was seventeen in 'thirty-nine when the war began. The most difficult thing that I went through in my life was on Passover evening. Mother said that she didn't feel well. She was forty-five and a half, almost forty-six. At home we didn't know how old Mother and Father were. *(Genia is trying to remember.)* My mother said that she didn't feel well, she had pains and she said "it hurts me." I had a younger sister, she was fourteen or fifteen, I don't remember. I had a brother who was older than me by a year and a half, and a sister. That is, we were four sisters and a brother. The ghetto wasn't in existence then and my father had a good business. Every day he brought, he brought sacks full of money *(excited)*, as if God had sent him to be medicine for my mother.

After the seder my two older sisters and I went to a professor. He examined my mother and said: "Your mother has cancer of the stomach, without my needing to do any tests or anything" *(agitated)*. What was the reason? She had lost weight, that was the sign—a loss of weight—it came out with blood, so I ask in Polish: "What is cancer?" In Polish, cancer is *rak*. And I ask *(coughs)* him: What is *rak*? We told him that the first bomb on Rosh Hashanah eve in Warsaw fell on our house. We were five children and my sister with her husband, with their one-year-old son, and the first bomb fell on our house. We were left without a house and we went to sleep in the synagogue. Then we lived in the synagogue, all of us: Mother and Father. Later on, at Passover, we saw that Mother wasn't herself, she wasn't herself anymore *(coughs badly)*. We were only Father and five sisters and the child and my brother-in-law. On Friday we were told to leave that place and we really slept in the cold. That was at the end of 'thirty-nine. Afterwards, we moved into the ghetto.

In the ghetto we all lived in one room, without my mother. We were three families, five children and Father in one room, and there was a second family there in one room, I don't remember how many people were there, anyway I remember that there was a kitchen, three families and three rooms. Later on there was a time when we didn't do anything and Father would bring us pieces of bread. He was everything. Mother wasn't alive anymore. Mother had died . . . and that was the way we managed, and Father would worry that we would have pieces of bread and we didn't do anything.

"We didn't do anything." It is as if Genia is saying, "If we had only been able to do something when it was still possible."

My brother-in-law was the first one to be taken away. We remained.

That was in 'forty-two. Meanwhile, there were all kinds of "actions" when the Germans came, I don't have to tell you about that. I went to work, the Germans opened up their factory. I worked in a factory and sewed buttons for the Germans. I needed to finish, for example, twenty uniforms each day. I needed to do this and that, but I have always managed well in life and if I didn't manage, I wouldn't work, and there would have been no Majdanek and no Auschwitz. For example, we needed to make twenty uniforms every day and there was a storage room above. It was a house, an entire house, there were sewing machines and there were people who sewed by hand, and I made the buttonholes. So every morning when I would come, I would go upstairs to the storeroom, and I took the sewn German shirts and I didn't do anything. And when we went home I had twenty pieces ready, like I needed. By doing that, I never worked for them.

One day in 'forty-two we were on the street. There were announcements that by ten o'clock we needed to go where the trains were. They will give us food and we can work and do what they ask. Already then, I said, "I don't go." My father said that he believed the Germans. Why? Because he used to do business with them. He knew the Germans very well, he would go to Katowice. He had connections with the Germans, business, and he said: "It can't be." But we knew that there were crematoriums. We didn't know what they were called, but we knew that they took Jewish people and burned them.

We knew that there was no work, we just knew that they took them and burned them. The fact that one day they took away my friend's brother, they took her brother, they took him away and burned him. That is what we said then in the ghetto. One day, we were in the ghetto, we saw him, and all of the ghetto came to ask him how did you come here? Then he told us that he was on the transport to Treblinka. There were trains and they told the Jews to take off all of their clothes and to walk naked and there they will receive other clothes. And they put all of their clothes on the train and they were like cattle and he had a goy [gentile] there who saved him and put him in among all the clothes. He put him in there and that is how he came back to Warsaw, and he told us what was really going on there. And later on, there was an "action" in which everyone had to be at that place, and then my father knew where he was going, he knew but he did not believe it. Germans—"such a culture and such intelligence and the Germans would not do such a thing." And he didn't believe anyone. That was how the poor man died *(agitated)*.

I wandered around looking for a bunker and I found a bunker and I said that I was coming with my whole family. That is, with my sisters— my brother wasn't alive anymore either. Ten healthy men picked up my brother on the street and they took him somewhere in Warsaw, I don't know where. He was seventeen. They told us later on that they made a mass grave *(sighs)*. I don't know, I wasn't in Poland and I won't go there. I am not interested and I don't want to see the graves. I came back, I don't want to tell you what I saw. I looked for them. I saw someone who had a head, but who had no face. There was a time when there were "actions" all the time and I remained to work in the German ghetto. Sometimes I would get bread and sometimes I would get soup. We managed, we weren't dying of starvation, we weren't living luxuriously, but we had our piece of bread, until the nineteenth of April 1943. I was at 15 Karmilitzka Street and it was an open house, they opened up the gates. It was called "Shops," the name of the factory where we worked for the Germans. There was a small shop, there were all kinds of things, not just clothes, all kinds of shopping. Then they closed the shopping and we went in. They would tell us: "Come, we are sending you to work, you will have it good." And that was the *yekeh* [nickname for Jews from Germany], the one called Schultz. Then I hid. We were a few families and I was alone— I had no one. I had a boyfriend, but it wasn't serious. Who thought then. We had our troubles. They put in the apartment, we were eight or nine people, there was a family with a small child. I was with my girlfriends and there was a window. I didn't live in the Warsaw ghetto, it was like the distance from here to the next theater, across the street. That was also a ghetto, there was Leshnov; Zamenof and I lived in a place where there were a few streets that were a kind of no-man's land. That was the nineteenth of April in the early morning. It was quiet. We went outside and the Jewish police came, Jewish police who said that there was an uprising in the ghetto. And it didn't take an hour or two. We went up to the house and we stood on the street, and we heard thousands of tanks and police and soldiers and planes. You might think that there were a million or half a million Jews in the ghetto.

A few days later, a girl and I went to the ghetto. We walked on the burnt and broken glass. We were so stupid and we did risky things, but we didn't think about where we were going, whom were we going to look for. We arrived there, we didn't see anybody and that was a few days after the uprising. You only saw the houses that had been razed. We returned home. On the first of May in the morning we saw from the porch that the Germans were holding a stick and a rag and were climbing up. In the afternoon we smelled something burning. We moved the cabinet, we climbed up on top, and we saw that everything was burning. They put kerosene on the rag, they put it in the attic, and from the attic it traveled down. That was on the fourth floor and we were on the first.

I took the girl upstairs and together with a few boys we climbed up on the roof. On the other street there was a one-story house. We jumped from the roof of the third floor to the first floor of the next house and we climbed up on the roof there. Hundreds of Germans were yelling that we should give up our weapons and we said that we had no weapons. Meanwhile, some other people came from their houses that had also been burned and they had managed to escape. The Germans took us to the same street. There was a house with a long wall and we [were told] to take off our clothes, put our hands behind our backs, and next to each one of us there was a German with a rifle. They waited and talked: to kill them or to let them live? *(choking)*. The elderly, the young, said, "Shema Yisrael." And then they said the word *anziehen* [get dressed] and that is how we got to the *Umschlag* [the deportation place].

We were there one day and on the second of May they put us onto trains and we went from there to Majdanek. But what there was in Majdanek was not easy. Only a few of us arrived. From Warsaw to Majdanek we held our hands up. It was so crowded and the next day we were completely free with our hands down and three quarters of the other people were dead. And we walked on the dead in the train and we did whatever people need to do, without food and without anything. We stopped somewhere, I don't know where, people were dying, and we asked for a little water, we were dry for five hot days. And the Poles said five hundred zloty. We didn't have five hundred cents. We were that way for eight days. But I want to tell you that all of that was nothing compared to what we went through in Majdanek.

I was in Majdanek for six weeks. I don't know what we lived on. I only know one thing: my father had a friend. His son, I arrived and he knew me. Then he said: "Genushka, when the first transport comes, get out of here." I said: "What are you doing here?" He told me: "I am [working] for the Germans." He brought me a long loaf of bread and a few eggs, and all the girls were jealous of me. I didn't tell anyone and I put it between the clothes. I had my clothes. I put the bread there so I would have it to eat, I didn't give any to anyone else (*makes a movement with her hands as if hiding her chest*).

And then there was the selection. They took five hundred of us young women. We arrived in Auschwitz. I don't remember what the date was, was there a date? Who knew dates? Passover, Succoth, we didn't know anything. Only one thing, how to find a piece or a peel of potato. Once I tried to get some potato peels and I got such a beating, I was unconscious. We were in houses like, did you see those houses? In barracks, they were soldiers' barracks. It was so crowded that when one turned to the right, everybody turned; when one turned left, everybody turned left. There could not be one person turning right and one turning left, the place was so narrow. In winter, it wasn't too bad. We were there for an entire month and we were forbidden to move from there. They guarded us as if we were diamonds. I met someone who worked in "Canada,"[1] who would bring me clothes, some pieces of bread, a little food.

Then a German woman came and took fifteen girls to work, to pick potatoes, for the Germans. Everyone wanted to go. I was lucky that it was an old German woman who had a green number. That is, she was either a prostitute or a thief. And she saw me twice and saw that I was not standing in the front line and that the others wouldn't let me get there. She called me "the gypsy." That was a wonderful place; there were po-tatoes. I worked and I had potatoes and I brought some to the camp. I went to the clinic and I brought them potatoes and they gave me some-thing else. I had enough bread. I always carried my kerchief like the gypsies and I held my bread in it.

God gave me that one day they took me away to work. Winter was coming, it was a long way to walk, and I could tell that it wasn't for me. A goy came, he was either a carpenter or a plumber, God knows, and he said to me in Polish: "Maybe you know who has diamonds or gold to sell? I will bring you cigarettes. I have enough bread." And I went up to the German woman [in charge of us]. I say to her: "Do you have gold and diamonds?" Then she told me that she has gold. And I said that there was a goy who wanted to give, how much should he bring? I said: "To-morrow he will bring it," and the next day I come and tell him that I have twenty gold pieces, what will you give me? "I will give you eight hundred cigarettes, bread every day." And I go to the German woman and I tell her: "He will give you four hundred cigarettes," and then she says: "Won-derful." The next day she gave me her gold and he gave me eight hundred cigarettes, but where will I keep my part? Every day they make a selection in the block. Those who remain in the block are sent to the crematorium. Where to keep it? Then I knew, a woman who watched the barrack, she saved it for me. That woman from the block knew that I had cigarettes, so she called me and said: "Genushka, I want a cigarette" three times a day.

And God gave. Later on I contracted typhus and it was winter. I gave her a cigarette and she sent away her secretary and left me in her room. I didn't get up for roll call, I didn't go out into the cold. And that was the best time for me in Auschwitz. And the place where I worked, there was a girl named Yanka, she was the Germans' informant, a little girl of thir-teen, she would bring all the announcements to the block. She said: "To-morrow there will be a selection, tomorrow to the crematorium." I said: "I have cigarettes." She wanted only fifty. I gave her fifty. We are standing at roll call and suddenly they call out my number and the next day they took us to "Canada." It was such a hard winter, I don't remember having a bra or underwear. Afterwards, when I walked to "Canada," I already had shoes, clothes. From where? From the people who went to the cre-matorium.

"And that was the best time for me in Auschwitz." Only those who were there could talk about the death camp in this way. Genia looks at me, though from a great distance.

We were animals, not people. For twenty-two months we saw how people were burned. They take a wagon with two wheels and they put the Jews on it, and we saw that for twenty-two months. And it worked twenty-four hours a day, and you saw fire come out. Each transport took mothers and children, and people did not know where they were going. They said: "You will meet your children at the place where we left Auschwitz." I saw with my own eyes how they yelled at and beat the children. Twenty-two months it takes me and a day. The screams of the children: "Mama, Papa" *(crying)*. I remember those screams to this day. To this day I can't fall asleep without pills. And the poor second generation, all of our nerves, *they got all of our nerves (breathless).*

And we had an old SS man who once saw that we weren't working; we waited every day for months for the day that they would take us. And he said that he would "take care not to give us too much gas" [speaking in German], and that was our hope, that they would come to take us away and we would get too little gas, and we believed him. Not too far away from the crematorium was a house, but no people. One day I came to work, and there was a lot of blood near the little crematorium. So we asked the SS man what had happened. He said that he had brought men to be burned there and they knew it, and then there was an uprising and they shot them. They knew where they were going. There were mothers who killed their own children because they cried. Our child did not cry. He knew that there was no food and that it was forbidden to ask for food *(sobbing).*

You see, I have no tears—my eyes are dry. I had a woman friend, Peleh. Each piece of bread that we got we measured with a string. You were in trouble if you took a millimeter too much. We didn't have hair but we had nails. Then everything was in the face. Not to believe what I am telling. That's from the movies, it can't be believed. Days without food, full of fear, cold. Days without food. On the eighteenth of January in 'forty-five we left Auschwitz. They took us to all kinds of camps and there were Ukrainians there and it was terrible, it was terrible. We left. On the way we saw Russians that had advanced and yelled at us. We went into a German house. The Russians came in through the windows and made trouble for us. We were young women.

Finally we went to the consulate and said that we want to go to America. Then they took us to another camp, a prison camp. That was after the war. I was there with Peleh and there was one mother from Canada [the real Canada]. She had a daughter our age, they came to Israel, and I was in their house twice in Toronto and they would bring a lot of money for us *(pauses, looks at me).*

I have a son, in Washington. He got his doctorate in 'fifty-seven. He finished the Technion in three years, not four. He got a scholarship. Afterwards he got married and went to Atlanta. Not only did he not pay for his studies—he got money. His wife worked in the Israeli consulate and he worked on his doctorate. Afterwards, they took him into the Air Force.

He was there for seven years and he moved to Washington and there the Air Force gave him a green card. In Washington, he was in NASA. Now he is a scientist, and he makes a good living. Next month he will be here with the children. I haven't seen them for two years.

And the children know what I went through. My daughter Tova was in Los Angeles for seven years. She got married, she didn't have it so good. When her daughter was six, they got a divorce. The things I suffered. "Mother," she came to me, "I got divorced." She is a closed person. I don't ask her. My granddaughter, if I want something from Tova, she goes to her mother and says: "Grandma is asking."

I notice that when Genia has finished her description of Auschwitz, time has lost any sense of sequence: there is almost no "before" and especially no "after." She can read my thoughts.

We escaped from the Russians. There were problems. We moved to the British, that was a prisoner of war camp, a free camp. There were British there. They wanted to send us to Bergen-Belsen, but there was an English captain and he worried about us and thanks to him they sent us to Lindenberg. We were given a home in an old age home for all of the Jews. It was sort of a rendezvous point. We were sixty or seventy Jews, we would eat there, there were single rooms, a bathroom, a kitchen. Peleh and I were in one room and two men lived in the other. They were brothers, Zvi and Laibel. They began visiting us. They would sit in our room and Peleh went crazy: this is the boy for you. And she forced me into it and so I married Laibel *(now Genia is crying)*. But nobody was left for me. They burned seventy-seven people in our family. Peleh loved Zvi. In the end, we married: Laibel and me, Peleh and Zvi. I never heard bad words from him in my life. He was nervous, he was from Lodz. They were in a few camps, but work camps. They made money and with that money we bought a carpentry shop and some fancy machines. There was already a state; meanwhile I lived with my cousin in Tel Aviv. I bought an apartment, we opened up a factory. I didn't think that I would reach sixty-eight, that my husband is ten years older than me. The Germans didn't think that I would reach this age. It can't be, to believe that after all of the things that we went through, that we would live.

The second generation is the most miserable *(Genia has tears in her eyes)*. The broken life in the heart. They were the victims. I didn't have anyone *(crying)*, I was alone, a dog. My husband went to work in the morning, the children annoyed him. I was the one who needed to give the spankings and then they would repent. My children never got a nice word in their lives. Because of that, Tova is in the situation that she is in. I love them and Laibel loves them. The year of their divorce was hard. My daughter never wanted children. She was married and she got confirmation from the doctor that she was pregnant. She didn't want [it] and we were so happy. For me, it was the happiest moment and for her, the worst. When we heard that she was pregnant, my husband and I kissed each other as if we were eighteen. I didn't know that she was unhappy, they were both crazy and they didn't get along.

I bought her an apartment with three-and-a-half rooms. Her daughter says that she has two houses. In my opinion, my daughter has suffered terribly to this day. My granddaughter was three years old and she said, Grandma, Mother did this to Father, Father did this to Mother. Tova was earning three thousand shekels a month; all of that money went for clothes. He wanted her to bring home the money and she spent it all on clothes. Whenever she had money, they fought. That's not life. Sometimes it's better to be alone!

Tova is also a story for me. When I got pregnant [with her] I wanted to have an abortion. On Friday we paid the doctor and after the factory, Laibel said he would take me to the doctor. I told all of my girlfriends that I was going to have an abortion. Friday night, my mother came to me in a dream. She came to me and told me not to, and I decided that I wasn't going to have the abortion. Laibel began crying, I asked to remain pregnant and to give my older sister's name, Gita [in Hebrew, Tova]. My husband did not want it. He said: "I am old and I have no patience." In the end, I maintained the pregnancy and he loves Tova the most, but I pity her.

Our hearts were burned in the camps. I didn't care. We were animals— it mattered more that we were alive—for a piece of bread, and we weren't responsible at all. The girls that were together with me, Mengele came and made a selection and put us in Block 25. The next day a garbage truck came and they knew where we were going, and we saw how they threw them on like the dead. It did not hurt us. Animals are worth more than we were. There were things that people saw, "Oy ve'avoy." The heart was burned. I have often said to myself: "Genia, how can you still see with the same eyes?" But the truth is that I saw it. I went through two years. I became an animal. For a piece of bread, we were willing to hit each other.

Genia offers me more cake and cookies. I accept, even though I have lost my appetite. I wipe away the last few tears that have been running down my face during most of the interview. "It isn't only what she went through, it's also how she talks about it," I say to myself. It is one thing to reach the state of "becoming an animal" in Auschwitz and it is another thing to be aware of it today, to know that it has a continuing effect on her children, and, moreover, to tell a stranger about these feelings. We are quiet for a few moments and I try to compose myself. "Do you have any objects or things that remained from your house?"

I don't have anything, nothing is left from what I went through; I only have my memories. Two days after I was liberated from the camp I didn't remember, I don't remember people. A friend's brother brought me a picture from my home and, to this day, I have no idea where it is. There is no place that I didn't look for it, and I didn't find it; it's as if someone came along and took it. A picture of my mother that I wanted so badly! I have a picture of my older sister, it's a picture of a couple of women and some cousins and two of my younger sisters. I have a dream that is like that picture of my mother.

"How do you celebrate the holidays?"

I keep a kosher house, Passover is Passover, up on top I keep all of the pots, forks, pots. Every day of the year I have [separate] milk and meat [dishes]. When I came from Germany, I didn't know what it was to keep kosher. I was able to eat pork. But I had an old cousin and an uncle and he visited us. He didn't want to eat anything in my house, he was an old man. There was an old man that had a store on the corner. I threw everything away, my dishes, and I bought dishes from him. I told her [my cousin]: "Racheli, come over tomorrow and see what is new. I bought everything new." And I began keeping kosher. When the children wanted to peel an orange they asked me which knife to use.

"In your parents' home did you keep kosher?"

Of course, at home father wore a yarmulke. My father wasn't religious like the Jews before the war, but before the war we didn't know what it was to observe Shabbat. I light candles, my husband goes to the synagogue every year. He likes it. We are traditional Jews, not religious Jews.

"Do your children know Yiddish?"

Only Tzipke. Tova understands and Yudke understands. To this day, I speak Yiddish with Tzipke. Sometimes it annoys me that she speaks only Yiddish with me, but I don't want to tell her. When we came to Israel, Ben-Gurion said that we don't have to speak with the children, that's the way it was. They said absolutely that we shouldn't speak, and during the whole year we never spoke about the Holocaust. My children were the only ones in their class who knew the word *Holocaust.* I have a seven-year-old granddaughter, Talia. When they asked her a week ago in school, "Who has a grandmother that was in the camps?" she immediately raised her hand and said: "My grandma." Another girl raised her hand too. Then her teacher said: "Perhaps you will ask your grandma to tell us something about the camps," and then Talia said: "I don't know if it will work out because my grandma has trouble with her leg. I need to call her." Talia told me: "Grandma, are you willing to come and tell us something about the camps?" I told her that I am having trouble with my leg, but if I am healthy next year, I promise to come and talk. Talia knows, I told her that her grandma was in the camps. All of my grandchildren know.

"They heard it from you, did you tell them?"

When they were little, I told them of course. The first thing that they saw was the [tattooed] number, so they would ask why do you have that? How did they do it, Grandma? I told them that they did it with needles and that it hurt. Why is that? I told them it was because I was Jewish and so that I wouldn't run away from the camp. That's how I explained it. You know, I was in Germany last year. It was the first time since 'forty-nine that I was there. I didn't want to go, I couldn't see them. But when I got to Frankfurt and I left the airport, it tore me apart. Why did I go? Every German that passed me, I said: "He was probably the one who burned my father, he burned my father into his grave." I felt like I was in hell. Maybe I am exaggerating, but I am never going to Germany again.

"Why did you go to Germany?"

They told us, if you go there for the first time and go see a doctor, he writes that you need to take a bath, and then when you are done, he writes you a letter. I went to Ma'aleh Hachmisha [health center] around fourteen times. All of a sudden, they told me that I was healthy and that I wasn't entitled to go to a health spa, and then I wanted to make the trip. It's true that I took six baths and it made me feel very good and it's just like a

Jacuzzi. Why do you need to go there? But I thought that if I sent a letter from the doctor it would help me. But here I just threw away my money. I sent it to Germany after they told me here that I don't need it and that I am already healthy.

"Does this subject come up during holidays or Shabbat?"

No. On Holocaust Day, yes. My husband and I speak about it, I talk about it a lot with Tzipke. She has a [good] memory. Yesterday she reminded me of something, and I said to her: "How do you remember?" But there are things that I do remember. My house. I barely remember my life. But with my children, except for Holocaust Day, the subject doesn't come up. When we were young, we played, we used to have a good time and we used to say: "Do you remember how it was?" [in Yiddish] and to remember Auschwitz. We don't do this anymore, its time has passed. It's been fifty years since the camp.

I went to order a skirt not too long ago. I was looking in the mirror and the woman was measuring the length, and a woman came up to me and said to me: "Genia, don't you remember me, you had a sister Gita and Surele, don't you remember me?" "You haven't seen me for forty years, how do you remember?" Then she said: "Your profile, your shape." My husband is standing there and looking at my face, amazed.

"Did you try looking for your family after the liberation?"

Yes, I knew that my mother had a brother in Argentina. I wrote him a letter through the Joint [Joint Distribution Center] that my mother's last name is Zuckerman, I know that my mother always said that she had a brother in Argentina and that his name was Yosef, but I got a letter saying that it wasn't him. I thought that it was my uncle but he wasn't.

"How do you know that the rest of your family died?"

In 'forty-two they took 30,000 Jews to Bejinksi and I knew that they were there. No one from my family remained alive. I had a cousin here but I didn't know where. After the war, soldiers stayed with me and one of the soldiers was English and he told me they were going to Palestine. I told him: "You know what, I have a cousin that I got a letter from in 'thirty-nine that said that she got married, but I don't know where she lives and whom she married." And I told him that her name was Rachel and she got out of the Holocaust that year and came to Palestine. He placed an ad in the newspaper and her downstairs neighbor called her— she lived in a little barrack—and she told her what was written in the newspaper, and she fainted. They brought her water and she immediately wrote me a letter saying that she is in Tel Aviv, that she got married, and that she has a house. She didn't tell me that she lived in a wooden barrack and that she didn't have children. One day the neighbor got a letter, she got a letter and she took the letter out and said: "Genia, bring me my letter," and I tell her: "Give me yours." We look and see the same address, the same handwriting on her letter. What happened, that her mother and aunt were two sisters and that was my cousin that married him, a second marriage. Then we were a family and still today we get together. The cousin from America and the cousin here did a "roots" project. I don't remember anything, I don't remember anyone, I don't even remember one cousin. I was a child of twenty-two or twenty-three and I don't remember anyone. My pillows were full of tears.

I stop the tape recorder. Genia goes back and tells me more about "Canada," about the diamonds and the transports. Again and again she says: "We were like animals. The children were the victims. I have no heart." There is a moment when I cannot take it anymore. When I say good-bye, she looks at me with the same fierce look with which she has welcomed me. "What a strong woman!" I say to myself as I go into the street.

Genia's speech is abrupt, as if words almost fall apart under the load of suffering and death she has experienced. In extreme conditions, she actively struggled against being swallowed up by the power of death. She fought for survival in every situation she describes: she "managed" in the factory that made uniforms; she found a bunker for her family and herself. In Auschwitz, she traded gold (for the German woman who was in charge of the work) for cigarettes. These cigarettes saved her life when she contracted typhus, and they helped her reach "Canada" (what a privilege in those days!). For Genia, in Auschwitz, hope meant that when they were to be gassed, the person in charge promised "not to give us too much gas" and "we believed him" (we do not know if he meant they would be tortured or have a better chance of being rescued).

She and her husband raised a family and built a new life in Israel, yet all her courageous actions, even her new life, are undermined by her narrative. Nothing can compensate for the losses she has witnessed and suffered, which still have a strong grip on her. For Genia, death began in 1940 when her mother fell ill during Passover. She opened the interview with a surprising statement: "To tell you that I didn't have a chance to know what the word *mother* is." She was already seventeen years old and there is no doubt that by then she had learned the meaning of the word *mother*. We do not know whether she means that she felt helpless and abandoned because of the losses that started with the death of her mother, or whether her mother's illness and death symbolized for her the loss of her feeling of being alive and of family intimacy, which she had experienced before the Nazis came. Perhaps what Genia wanted to say was that her mother's death occurred within the framework of her family life and family story, unlike what followed afterward.

The rest of her family was murdered. They disappeared one after another: she specifically mentions the disappearance of her brother-in-law, her brother, and her father. Twice, her voice has an edge to it when she speaks of her father, who believed in the Germans and their culture, even though the family knew what was happening in Treblinka ("my father knew where he was going, he knew but he did not believe it"). In her narrative other family members, including her nephew, who was still alive during the Warsaw ghetto uprising, simply blend together into an amorphous mass ("they burned seventy-seven people in our family").

The demonic force of death, further accelerated by her many months in the camps, still creates an extreme feeling of loneliness in her life: "I don't have anything, nothing is left from what I went through." She also says: "Nothing is left to remind me . . . a friend's brother brought me a picture from my home and . . . I have no idea where it is." Furthermore, the dead have power to govern life: when her mother appeared in one of her dreams, Genia changed her mind about having an abortion (reflecting her own wish or conflict? We can only guess). For a moment, it seems as if life has won out over death: here, even her husband, who first said: "I am old and I have no patience," in the end "loves Tova the most." However, Genia concluded with a dissonant chord: "but I pity her" (referring to Tova). There is a bond of suffering between Genia and Tova, something Genia feels she cannot control or change.

In this ongoing cycle of suffering, Genia takes responsibility for the miseries of her younger daughter and the distancing of her son. It seems as if these events fit her expectations: they point at the assumption that "nothing good will come out of me after what I have been through" (or what I have done?). Perhaps it is "survivor's guilt," which forbids her, or those she feels responsible for, from having any happiness because of what happened to all the others. We find evidence for this when Tova tells her she is pregnant. There is a moment of happiness: Genia and her husband are happy. Alas, they do not notice that their daughter is miserable ("For me it was the happiest moment and for her, the worst"). That is to say, when I am finally happy, I ignore the fact that my daughter is miserable, and her misery is my misery.

"Mothering" has a special meaning in Genia's private language, reflecting her struggle with life and death. The opening sentence can also be read as if the usual positive meaning we attach to the word *mother* has now become impossible. The memories from Auschwitz, which she was afraid had affected her children, focused on mothers and children on their way to the ovens: "There were mothers who killed their own children because they cried. Our child [Whom did she mean? It is not clear] did not cry." And again: "The screams of the children: 'Mama, Papa' *(crying)*. I remember those screams to this day . . . I can't fall asleep without pills. And the poor second generation . . . *they got all of our nerves.*" She continued: "The broken life in the heart. They were the victims . . . my children never got a nice word in their lives." It is as if she is saying: "How can one live without suffering after witnessing these sights and living these memories over and over again?"

One could say that Genia must be exaggerating the impact these events had on her children. But we believe there is no objective yardstick for such a statement: it is how she felt, how she reconstructed her biography. To cross the sea of death and climb the rocky coast back to life, she had to develop extreme survival strengths. Yet the horrors still penetrated her life story and destroyed all her positive feelings about herself in relation to her family, and her family in relation to herself. The Dutch psychiatrist Jan Bastiaans (1988) formulated it in this way: "They came out of the oven, but the oven continues to burn within them." More than once Genia says, "Our hearts were burned," and she is unable to free herself from this fire. "I have often said to myself: 'Genia, how can you still see with the same eyes?' But the truth is that I saw it . . . I became an animal . . . we were willing to hit each other [for bread]." Her eagle eyes see through the sometimes healing barriers of forgetfulness and repression. Genia is not proud that she has survived, but she is not ashamed either. She accepts it as a sort of fate. If only the oven would stop burning inside her, if only she could stop "seeing it" all the time, if only she could relieve herself of the presumed influence it has had on her children: this is her loneliness, her "vicious circle of suffering," which nothing has succeeded in relieving.

How have Genia's painful memories and her discourse affected her daughter's and her granddaughter's reconstruction of their life stories? Have they succeeded in working through this inheritance? Has Genia's unusual awareness enabled them to choose life over death—which is not a part of their own life history? Perhaps Genia's suffering and loneliness have been passed on unwittingly. Tzipke, the eldest daughter, was born only a few years after her mother's hellish experiences in the camps. It is interesting too that Genia did not mention Tzipke until I asked her if she speaks Yiddish with her children and she told me only with Tzipke. Does it mean that this daughter was outside Genia's "circle of suffering"? How did Tzipke experience her own role as a mother after hearing and seeing Genia's unbearable torment, and what can she tell us about her own childhood? Tzipke is the only child who has chosen to live near her mother. She built a family and her children are now grown up. How does Tzipke find a way to reconcile her mother's experience, her own childhood memories, and her children's future?

Tzipke

"A person needs amazing motivation in order to want to live"

I meet Tzipke at her home in the early morning. She greets me with a smile. She is wearing a loose, brightly colored dress, perhaps in order to minimize the size of her heavy body. She walks around the room freely trying to straighten up the mess. When she is ready for me, I ask her to tell me her life story. She asks me: "What exactly?" and gives me a quick look. "Whatever seems to you significant or important."

Okay, I was born in Germany after the war. We arrived in Israel when I was a little over a year old. We lived in Ramat Gan and I went to elementary school and high school there. I was never an outstanding student *(laughs)*. I was in the scouts, I served in the army, I met my husband when I was sixteen. I was twenty-one when I got married. I have three children. I didn't work for a number of years. I raised the children. When my youngest daughter went to nursery school, I decided to go to work. I now work as a secretary in Kupat Holim [the general health insurance agency] and I try to see that it doesn't adversely affect my home. There is always tension and a lot of running around so that the house will go well. That's it in general.

I wait a moment, looking at her as if asking her to go on. This cannot be her whole story.

Look, I have a brother and a sister. My brother is in the U.S., my sister now lives in Israel after having lived abroad for a long time. My parents are the things that I guard the most and I am the only one who does. My sister does not help me at all; all the responsibility falls on me, all of it *(crying)*, and it's a heavy burden *(continues to cry)*. It's heavy because there is no one to share it with, I do it all by myself. They are very dependent on me now. And now, since I began working in Kupat Holim, I don't have a day that I don't have to run to a doctor or worry about getting them special preference. I do it from love, but it is still a burden. I don't believe that my children were ever as dependent on me as my parents are. They don't take a step without me. What can I tell you, it's suffocating. When my father was in the hospital, I had no one to share it with. My brother is abroad, it is impossible to talk to my sister, so I run around. I worry about the doctors and look for special connections, surgery and so forth.

Tzipke wipes away her tears. I am unsettled by this abrupt shift in mood.

I am now going through the pain of raising parents. I go someplace, I need to call them. I call them at least once a day so that they will hear that everything is all right and that I haven't gotten lost. I think that they demand things from me they would never ask of my sister. When my sister goes away, she never goes out of her way to call. I get into trouble if I don't call two or three times a day. It's not a punishment, that's clear, that's the way it needs to be. If I go somewhere, I am walking around and then all of a sudden I remember, oy! I didn't let them know, they'll look for me and not know where I am. What can I tell you? It is dependency, like the way I worry about my children, perhaps more. My children will verify this *(smiles)*. I don't know if it's because of their past. I don't see such a strong connection between my husband and his parents.

"Where were his parents during the war?"

Here. They immigrated in 'thirty-two. They immigrated with the Beitar movement from Poland.[2] They came as teenagers. The parents immigrated and their family stayed and died in the Holocaust. His mother was sixteen when she left her parents and home. What courage *(makes a sign of admiration)* to come to such a godforsaken country. I sometimes ask my husband: "Did you talk to your mother yesterday? No. What? It's been a week!" Something is not quite right. Now his mother, his father died and his mother now lives with another man, and there is a break between them. I don't get it. I told him many times: "What, you didn't phone her? Is she alive, dead—is she coming?" He says: "If something happens, they would let me know." Such things don't happen with me. For example, yesterday I was at work and I looked at my watch and saw that it was one o'clock in the afternoon and I hadn't called my parents yet! I phoned them immediately. How are you? Everything is all right, okay, I can go home. Last night I was here, downstairs, in a shop, and I saw a nice suit and I thought about my mother. When I go to buy myself some clothes I automatically think about buying her something as well. So I told her that I found something for her, but today when she came to buy the suit, it had already been sold *(in Yiddish Tzipke says: "They stole the bargain")*.

Every now and then I think about leaving Israel, or moving to another city. With the money from this apartment I could buy a much bigger apartment in Herzliya, Ra'ananna, so that each of my children could have their own room. But I wouldn't consider leaving them. I said to my husband: "Are you crazy? I am going to start running between Ra'ananna and Ramat Gan? How can I do that?" I need to be where they are. Not with them, but not far away, so I won't have to travel long distances in order to check what's going on with them. And there is nothing to say about leaving Israel. I wouldn't do such a thing to them. To move away [and leave them] without a protector and savior, it's impossible to do that.

"And what does your husband think about this?"

He takes it fine. He loves them a lot, more than his own parents, I think, because the worry that they worry about me they also give him. If he needs to ask somebody for advice, he talks to my father. He thinks that he is a smart and understanding man. That never bothered us in our lives. The opposite is true; he goes to fix their faucets, to oil things, whatever needs to be done. In that respect there are no problems. He loves them because they love him; they also give him their love.

"But it still bothers you?"

Yes. They need to be involved in everything, in the children's tests, their grades, everything. I never tell them everything in order not to cause them heartache. My son went on a trip with his girlfriend to Tiberias for three days and I told them about it only after he got back. If I had done otherwise, I would have suffered. I think that their worry about me is sometimes greater than my own worry for the children. If the children cause me grief it bothers them more than it does me. I let it go by; they ask questions and go on and on, how did they do and what did they do. They worry about me, so that I will be freed from worrying about my children, so that they will grow up by themselves, succeed in their studies, that everything will be all right.

"What do you remember about your relationship with them when you were a little girl?"

I think that things are better today than they were when I was a little girl. We had a lot of disagreements because I didn't want to study. We would have terrible screaming fights. "Don't go out, what are you wearing and how can you . . ." I do not restrict my children today. There isn't anarchy, but I do not turn their studies into the focal point. When I think about that I try not to make the same mistakes that my parents made with me. My daughter comes back at four o'clock in the morning and I'm happy that she's back. I don't wake up the entire street like my mother, who used to stand on the porch. My mother made such scenes that my husband and I were embarrassed about going outside for a week. If I was to adhere to my mother's way of raising me, I think that I would be in a convent today. She is very conservative. I think that it is just her character, she is like that. When she is watching a movie on television and there is some sexy part [she says] "awful, disgusting, they should be ashamed of themselves" *(laughs)*. If I were to live according to her rules, I would end up in a convent.

Tzipke takes my hand in order to get my full attention.

Look, when I was still living with my parents, there were many nights when I would wake up from their screams, from their dreams. Especially my father, he would scream. That follows me to this day. I will never forget it. He would wake up with such screams and come down and check that we were in our beds. And what can I tell you, our house was not a happy one, like it is in my house, it wasn't such a happy house. You know, I sometimes compare myself to my neighbors who are all Israeli born, with parents who had not been in the Holocaust. I see the differences. But I don't know if it's due to their different personalities or because they lived in a different atmosphere. I don't know, it seems different to me. You know what, there they cannot see each other for four years, they come or they don't come, they phone or they don't phone. It's true that my brother lives far away geographically, but he needs to phone and see that everything is all right. I think that they taught us to stay in touch with each other. Today, my children, one will walk on the left and one on the right and they will barely say hello to one another. No matter how much I try, there is a distance between them. That seems very strange to me. When my brother was in the army, I worried about him so much. It's different with my children. My youngest daughter got mad at Ganit beforehand when she didn't straighten up the room and she yelled out: "Why are you serving [in the army] near here in a noncombat unit? Why didn't they send you to Um el Fachum [a distant Arabic town], so that you wouldn't be home for a week and make a mess of my room?" *(giggles)*. I tell her: "God, you are so funny, this is your sister!" And she answers me: "So what? It's my sister." In my home, we worried about one another, we were always together so that the package wouldn't come apart. Fate wanted my brother to be abroad and about Tova—you know her story. When she was in America, my mother would call her three times a day. She missed her terribly. We, my sister and I, would talk once a week. That also seems strange to me. I tell my children that I don't understand it. It's just like her *(she points to the neighbor's door)*, none of them care about each other. So then I think that it is because their parents weren't there, that they didn't live through such things. The relationships between the children are not strong, I don't know—it's not clear to me.

Tzipke becomes quiet. She has almost managed to clarify for herself the paradox in worrying too much and too little, but from her choice of words, it is clear that she is still thinking it over.

The way in which they *(points in the direction of the children's bedroom)* grew up on stories of Red Riding Hood, Snow White, and children's tales, is the way that I grew up with stories from the Holocaust. It's true. At some point I said I didn't want to hear any more. When I met my husband he would get them to talk about it. Those stories, he had never heard such stories. All of a sudden he came to my house and he heard such interesting stories. On the evening of Holocaust Day, he went to my parents to get them to talk. This year we were here, and friends were visiting, and he wanted to go see my parents and so we went with our friends. We went together to hear a few stories about Auschwitz and Majdanek *(sarcastically)*. He asks them a lot of questions, he milks them: "Tell us what happened then." They always told stories on Holocaust Day. I was always the interesting one in class; I always knew how to tell the most interesting stories. My mother told me, and she was a certified source. They talked about it a lot. They did not believe in not passing on the message and not including the children in their stories. The opposite was true—let the children know and not forget. These stories need to be passed on. My mother also tells my daughters her story. They also learned a lot in school. On Holocaust Day, they brought stories from their grandmother. They were really authentic, they told their stories and included us. It wasn't buried under the rug. These were things that I lived with.

My mother has stories, she must have told you . . . It is very hard to understand how people remained alive and survived. I have a hard time understanding it. They would sometimes say: "Grandma is nervous." Then I would tell them, what do you want from her, after what they went through? This week I took her to a doctor about her leg. I brought her to my boss who is a cardiologist, but also knows about her problems. He examined her and she did not let him touch her leg, it hurt her so much. And he said: "Your mother is spoiled." I laughed: "What my mother has been through—my mother went through Hitler" *(proudly)*. How can she be spoiled? On Sunday, I got her an appointment with a good surgeon.

I think that people who go through things like that and survive are made out of material that does not exist anymore. Sometimes I go on a diet, I am hungry and I always say to my girlfriends: "Tell me, how did people live through that?" I don't eat for two hours and I go crazy, how did people live through concentration camps, not eating and suffering so much? I don't believe that we who are so spoiled could withstand it! The pictures that you see here *(points to the wall)* are my friend's, who has cancer. She has been fighting the disease for seven years. I would sometimes say: "Dear God, where does she get her strength?" Enough, give up, it's over. No, another treatment and another one, and she's been trying them for seven years. That seems to me to be worthwhile, to fight in order to live. A person needs amazing motivation in order to want to live. I don't compare the two, but perhaps it is almost the same thing. I guess that when you are faced with it, you get superhuman powers, I guess!

My mother, when I think about it today, did not manage to get over the trauma of my sister's divorce. She has not yet recovered from that. How she lived through Hitler, believe me, I don't understand to this day. Perhaps it is already enough. How much strength can a person have?

Tzipke pauses, still thoughtful about her last sentences.

"Was food a subject in your family?"

(*Laughs*) See what I look like today. They shoveled food into us! When I look through a photograph album, I am always holding something—a banana, an apple—always! There are no pictures without food. They say that Holocaust survivors pushed food. But all of us were, thank God, overweight, we began our diets early. Perhaps I was like this when I was a baby; otherwise, I wouldn't be as fat as I am. Ganit, when she was born, would not eat and she would also throw up. My mother dragged me quickly to the doctor and told me: "Look at your daughter! She doesn't eat anything." I told her: "Leave her alone, let her be, don't push her, if she throws up she'll throw up." When I threw up, they would feed me again with what I had vomited. But, thank God, today Ganit already needs to diet. My mother checks every day—"Did you have lunch?" If I need to be somewhere, first of all there should be lunch: eat lunch. My children don't worry me. I worry about my husband. He works with a lunch break. He gets home at noon and it is very important for him to have a hot meal. When a man goes out at five in the morning and comes back in the evening, and he has a two-hour break—sometimes I am not at home at noon, I work from twelve—I make sure that one of the children will heat up his food. He won't heat it up by himself. I always laugh and think about the food container that my father would take to work in the afternoon, to the carpentry factory. But my husband doesn't eat outside of the house, he has a problem. He had a gall bladder operation and he is very sensitive to fat. So, I don't leave the house without having food to give Yosef to eat, it doesn't matter what, but it has to be a hot meal.

I wonder whether the food is simply a response to what happened in the camps or whether it replaces something that is more difficult to give here and now? "How did people at home show their emotions?"

(*Pause, thoughtful, silence*) My mother is not the type of woman who gives kisses and hugs. She is very loyal and worries a lot, but not in an emotional way. When my father would come home in the evening, after his day of work, they wouldn't hug each other like I do with my children. My girlfriends ask me sometimes: "You still kiss and hug your son?" I tell them that [I will do so] as long as he will let me, as long as he agrees. Then there was no outward expression of emotions!

We didn't celebrate birthdays either. We would celebrate them in the kindergarten and that was the end of the story. Birthdays passed quietly. I think, when I was fourteen years old, I created a scandal. I told them that I wanted everybody to make me a birthday party—a big celebration. Since then, they've given more concern to birthdays. I bother about reminding them so that they won't forget my birthday. My sister and brother already enjoyed this. My bat-mitzvah was celebrated at Beit Ha-ezrach [The Citizens' House]. They stood me up on a chair like an idiot; I had to thank the guests, I stood there in my dress mumbling. They brought the dress from Canada. Bat-mitzvahs were events celebrated in halls *(angry)*. I celebrated with my children in a different way. When my daughter reached her bat-mitzvah, I said that I would not let her go through the traumatic experience I'd had. When Ziv reached his bar-mitzvah, there was a problem and there were arguments. I said that I was not going to stand in the doorway, shaking hands and taking checks. That disgusts me. I don't like it. Then we really celebrated! I made a lunch after the service in the synagogue. It was a wonderful bar-mitzvah, but it wasn't like they wanted—with a hall and all the ceremony. When it came to my children's bar-mitzvahs, it didn't help them. For Ganit, we ordered a bus and a guide and we took her class for an outing to the Beit Guvrin caves. Even today, no one has forgotten that experience!

Tzipke now sounds more decisive, more sure of herself. She is no longer belittling herself in comparison to her mother. She looks at me hesitantly before going on.

My mother was very nervous and she would hit us for everything, it didn't matter for what. When I raised my hand, I would think perhaps three times. Sometimes I feel that I could tear the chair apart *(agitated)*. But she would hit and scratch. I have a lot of memories of beatings and outbursts. In that respect, she was very emotional, very.

I am struck by this new meaning of "emotional."

I connected it to evil. The evil was hitting *(with emphasis)*. My father never raised his hand at us. I got a slap on my cheek once in my life from my father and I will never forget it. It was on Rosh Hashanah eve; he had come back from the service and I was standing around with my friends. I was wearing black, I was in black, I was standing with my entire class, perhaps, it was when I was in eighth grade. He saw me, came over to me, and gave me a slap: "Do people wear black on Rosh Hashanah?" I will never forget that. That was the only slap I ever got from him. I remember it to this day. But my mother was always very actively involved. I don't remember about my brother and sister, but with me, she was active. I would also do a lot of things just to annoy them. I would deceive them. Whatever was important to them, I would do the opposite.

Today I am sorry that I didn't listen to them. Then we had a lot of conflicts about studying. That was the subject at home. I needed private lessons and she would surprise me and wait for me outside so that we wouldn't waste time, so that I could read another page in the book. Every day she would repeat that Hitler took people's gold and everything else. He didn't take away the studies from those who had learned. Today, I say the same sentence in my house, but I don't pressure my children, not even a quarter of how they pressured me. I see results; my parents didn't get results from me.

I also relate it to her being "Polish." Everybody's children study. How can it be that she has a devil at home who doesn't study? Everybody else's children study. My aunt's children, my cousin, it was only in her house that she suffered from this kind of problem. A child that does not want to study needs to be beaten so that she will study. Her daughter spends time with boys instead of studying—what a terrible thing this is! It was really terrible. She made my life very bitter because of the studies. She would lock me in so that I wouldn't go out if I had a test. The subject of studying was awful.

They also had obsessions about clothes. When I came back from my dates in the evenings, I had to hang up my clothes. They would wake me up in the middle of the night: "Hang up your clothes." Today when I go to work I say to myself: "Wow, if a burglar comes, he will probably think that someone was here before him. What a mess!" I don't drive my children crazy, not over clothes. They can throw them around, they can leave them everywhere—it doesn't bother me at all. I don't attach any importance to it. When it becomes impossible to walk between the piles, then I begin to yell. My little one picked it up from them. She walks around all day picking up and straightening up *(laughs)*. Yesterday she woke me up with a lot of noise. I asked what happened. Do you have to be at school early? No, she has to clean up the kitchen and I didn't let her *(pauses)*.

You see, things should be orderly. One needs to take care of one's clothes—you don't buy new clothes every day. When my mother comes over she feels sick. How many clothes, who needs so many clothes. You know, when I buy something new, I don't let her know about it, I don't tell her about it at all because she will tell me: "How much do you need? How many clothes does a person need?" If she sees me wearing something new, I tell her that it's old. Everything I have is from last year. That bothers her a lot. It doesn't bother my father, but it angers my mother. It seems criminal to her. I waste all my money on clothes and, because of that, I haven't achieved anything and I will have nothing. At home, she never thought that I needed more than two dresses, one in the laundry and one to wear. How many clothes does a person need?

(Sighs) I feel I am making up for the lost years. They didn't make us do with little, but it wasn't given with pleasure. My greed, it turned out to be also true of my sister, seems to be a reparation for the years that we didn't get so many clothes or as much money that we thought we were entitled to get. Again, maybe it's due to their personalities. Even today there are people who feel that spending money on clothes is a waste. They would cut the shoe off from here *(she measures it on her fingertips)* and they would pass the shoe down from one child to another. It was also the atmosphere of the period. They didn't buy a lot of things for themselves either. For instance, I want them to go to Switzerland for a month, sit by a lake, and let them clear their heads. Come back and be new people. They answer me in Yiddish: "You want me to sit by a lake for a month and eat in restaurants endlessly?" *(laughs)*. Sometimes, I am amazed by them.

My father told me that he doesn't want to be a burden for me when he grows old. That is the line that directed them their entire lives. They saved money for their last years. All in all, they were wonderful parents, but they worried too much. We developed better relations after I left home. Only when I was liberated from home did we develop better relationships. I don't know, perhaps the fault lies in me? I don't know why, but it was only after I left home that our relationship changed. That's it, I have nothing more to say.

Tzipke gets up decisively and goes into the kitchen to make coffee and comes back with two cups and a plate of store-bought cookies. I ask her about objects.

I am attached to objects. I got this *(points to a necklace)* from my mother, and I don't take it off. I [also] have something in gold that belonged to my mother. It's a medallion with a picture. I don't wear it, but I don't let my children touch it so that they won't lose it. In all of the photographs of her, she is wearing that medallion. At some point it broke and it needed to be fixed. I told her: "Don't fix it, give it to me so that I will have something of yours." She's had it for a long time. I guess that my father bought it for her after the war. It's not from her childhood *(sighs)*. I wasn't crazy about jewelry at all. As much as I can remember, my mother loved jewelry when she was young. My father would also buy her jewelry. Whenever we had a bar-mitzvah, my father would buy my mother a piece of jewelry. So I said then, I want something too. And he bought me something *(she points to a bracelet on her arm)*. I told my mother: "You see, I learned something from you" *(laughs ironically)*.

"How do you define your family's boundaries?"

How do I define my family? My extended family, including my aunt and my cousins, my Aunt Peleh [my mother's friend from the camps], I can't imagine an event without their being there. It is the only family I have. When I was a girl, I was very jealous of people who had grandparents. We had an upstairs neighbor who was in my class. Her parents were born in Israel. She would go to her grandparents during vacations. I would imagine a make-believe grandmother. I would go visit my Aunt Peleh for three days and tell everybody that I was visiting Grandmother.

I tell my children every now and then: "You don't know what it's like. Enjoy the fact that you have a grandfather and a grandmother." Really, they take it seriously; they go to visit, they pop over. I don't need to pressure them. Ganit goes to see them at least once a week and Ziv goes over every now and then. Nira would go every day if I let her; she would spend a lot of time there. It is very important for them. I drilled it into them that having grandparents is a privilege. Not everyone has it. When

I was a child, I missed it terribly. My entire family was Aunt Peleh and my other aunt, Tamara. Today, I don't have any connection to her whatsoever or to her children. With my other cousins from my father's side, I have a lot of contact. We meet on holidays and celebrations. We call each other every now and then, the contact is kept up. There have been changes over the years. Everyone got married, had children, there are always additions and they always invite us. Birthdays, even when I come without the children, because they are already big.

"How do you celebrate holidays?"

We try to be together during the holidays. I will never go away over the holidays. Every holiday, Rosh Hashanah, Passover, Succoth, Shevuot, outings. Last year my sister said she was going away over the holiday. I won't go away, I won't leave two unfortunate parents alone with only their walls for company. I cannot do such a thing to them. My children already do that to me. I don't care, they know that I won't care. They should go and enjoy themselves. But leave my mother during a holiday? I can't think about that and there is nothing to talk about. A few years ago during Rosh Hashanah, they went to Ma'aleh Hachmisha. They said it was the first and last time they will leave me alone. I wasn't alone. I made my mother make fish for me before she went away. I invited friends over and I celebrated the holiday with them.

We celebrate according to Jewish tradition. I can't invite them over at Passover. My house isn't kosher, we always celebrate at my parents' house. I don't keep pork in my house. Milk and meat I separate—sometimes yes, sometimes no. I have separate refrigerators for milk and meat. My parents eat here often. In winter, I make cholent every Shabbat. Whenever I make cholent, they come. I fill the pot of cholent with sixteen liters! A Shabbat with cholent is a celebration, full of friends and good smells. When people come in they say: "Ah, what a Jewish household." My sister taught me how to make cholent. My brother will arrive at the end of the month. He has already put in his order for cholent; he wants cholent. My husband wants me to open up a stand with cholent so that people can come by with their pots on Friday and buy. I try to make sure that everyone is home for the Shabbat meals. Not on Friday nights. I can't limit the children. Do they need to be punished? At home, I had to come back from the beach and not to enjoy it until the end. I needed to be home at noon.

Therefore, I don't care. If they will be here, they'll be here. If not, not. How long can you hold on to them? Ganit has a boyfriend, Ziv has a girlfriend. I leave them food for whenever they show up.

My parents did not tell us other stories than about the Holocaust. Today they will tell stories about what it was like when "I was a child." When Nira went to ice skating lessons, my mother talked to her for an hour and a half about how she would ice skate as a child. She never told me about that. Today, because of the children, my mother tells us that she came from a very cultured family. Her mother would go to the opera, she was a very beautiful woman and she always dressed well *(sighs)*. But she doesn't remember a lot of her childhood, she only remembers certain things. Today, only my mother tells stories. I only heard from my father for the first time last year about everything that happened, about what he went through during the war. Maybe I was never interested. Only last year I sat with him for two hours, with my husband, of course, and asked: "What exactly happened? When?" He was very open.

I think about how the grandchildren have created new opportunities for Grandmother Genia to touch on her childhood memories.

I brought up the idea of going to Poland with them. It was rejected immediately even before . . . my mother said that she will never set foot on Polish soil. So I said: "I am not interested in going without you." I wanted to see where she lived. I have a grandmother buried in Lodz, my father's mother. He says that he will never find the grave; a jungle has grown over it. They do not want to even bring up the possibility. I am the one who is interested, but not without them. To go for what—to see where they planted trees in Auschwitz? That's of no interest to me *(angry)*.

I want to tell you that I was in Germany. We went to Europe, I told my husband that I didn't want to go to Germany, I wasn't interested. But we traveled from Switzerland to France and we were with our car and we came to Fribourg, on the border, and my husband wanted to go to a casino and . . . we changed our plans. Germany wasn't in our plans. He wanted to go to Baden-Baden to the casino. Okay, I said. One night only, I don't want to be there. We went into the casino and I showed them my passport, which says that I was born in Germany. They began speaking to me in German. At that moment, I felt as if I was being bitten. I felt like a stone, everyone there seemed to be either a Nazi or the son of a Nazi.

We had an incident there, we went into Baden-Baden. We were driving slowly and looking for a hotel. All of a sudden a car stopped next to us and a girl around eighteen years old got out and asked us in English if she could help us. I told her yes, that we were looking for a decent hotel. Then she said: "Follow me." She was with her mother and father. They took us to a hotel. She came over and asked us if we were Israelis and I said yes. She then asked us for our address and she began writing us. She belongs to some sect [Aktion Sühnenzeichen, "The Sign of Atonement"] that wants to bring peace to the world. I told my husband then: "Her father was probably a Nazi and she is trying to atone for his sins." I didn't close my eyes all night long and at six in the morning I woke Yosef up: "Let's get out of here, I can't stay here." We crossed the border and there were soldiers standing there in uniforms. I . . . felt as if I was back in the war years.

Imagine what it does to my parents. My father used to go often to Germany because of the reparations and I told my mother: "Why don't you go also?" She won't leave us alone, she doesn't want to see them and doesn't want to hear them. A few years ago my mother was in Germany, they crossed the border and they left. She will not step on German soil and there is nothing to say about going to Poland, because the Poles were worse than the Nazis. I may go see where I was born, to Lindenberg, if my mother and father will go with me and show me the hospital, where we lived.

My Aunt Peleh wants to go with her daughter and she invited me. But I am interested in my mother showing me where she played, where she went to school. I am not interested in just going for the trip, just to be there. I go crazy from all those people who go. Believe me, it drives me crazy. They eat out for a dollar, "We ate there" (sarcastic). I told them: "Are you normal? You are giving the Poles dollars? They are anti-Semites and you are helping their economy!" I don't understand it.

I wonder how Tzipke feels now, as we approach the end of the interview. "How was this interview for you?"

It was hard for me to be open in the beginning. Even though I am an open person, I don't have psychological barriers. When I feel something, I let it out. It was hard in the beginning and it became easier later on. We are delving into private areas. If you were to talk about it with my sister, you would get a different impression. She is younger than I am. I got married when she was a child of twelve. When I was four years old I was more mature than my daughter at age nineteen. I was more emotionally mature. The mistakes they made on me when I was growing up perhaps had the effect of preventing me from making them on her. *(She thinks for a moment and takes back what she said.)* My mother made a terrible mistake with my sister. She reminded her that she never wanted to have her and that she was on her way to having an abortion. When I hear that, I could kill her.

Genia doesn't relate to me that way. I am big and smart and I handle things in the right way. Tova doesn't. She does silly things and she has to be protected. She gets on their nerves. I try to avoid making the same mistakes with my children. But my mother is the same. She comes over and says more than once: "I don't see you in bed with a book!" I tell her *(laughingly):* "You came at the wrong time, they already finished reading." I also told them once: "Read the telephone book, but read something." Today, it's too late.

(Silence.) She is thinking for a moment, as if deciding whether to tell something else.

You know, I don't have a VCR mostly due to Ziv. As a child he made me very bitter because he didn't want to study. Today, he is finishing the twelfth grade. I feel like I undertook an amazing project. It was my life project that he went to study at the Ort School. It was like a slap for me. My brother even wrote me and phoned me: "Why are you sending him to the Ort School? You're not normal. Statistics show that anyone who studied at a technical school will not go on studying." I said: "So he won't go on, the main thing is that I will know that he is in a scheduled framework and not wandering around the streets." I, it cost me my health. Today he is finishing computer electronics *(proudly)* and he finished his matriculation exams. I can't believe it. My father is really celebrating. But it took its toll on me, it took its toll on me.

He was born with a birthmark. It was terrible. Today there is no sign left. He was a wonderful baby. Ganit would cover the mark with her hand. I told her to take her hand away and not to give him a complex about it. When he was five he went to the grocery store and a woman asked him: "What do you have on your face?" He said: "Have you looked at yourself in the mirror?" A five-year-old boy, he grew up without complexes. Today, the birthmark has faded completely.

When he was seven, before Passover, that is a day that I will never forget. Ziv went to a friend, and I heard screams all of a sudden. I ran outside and Ziv was in a pool of blood. The boy was pouring blood. He fell on a fence and cut himself here *(points to her cheek)*. The insides were showing. I flew to the hospital straight to the emergency room. I was waiting and the blood wouldn't stop coming. I got mad and yelled that I wanted a plastic surgeon to come immediately and take the boy to surgery. And they gave him stitches and today there is no sign. I learned from my mother that when you need a doctor, you go to the best.

They would call me at school every day because he made trouble. When he went to Ort, I really watched over him. I wanted to meet every one of his friends. I got rid of a lot of his friends until he realized that you can't make friends with everyone. Today, when he is finishing high school, he still studies. That is the surprise of my life. He chose it himself. When registration was over, he called me at work to tell me that he registered and arranged everything. Because somebody canceled his registration, all he needed was my signature and confirmation. He arranged everything and that was his beginning, the surprise of my life. I think it's due to his girlfriend's influence, she is a very sweet girl. Her father is an electronics engineer. It must be due to her home's influence.

Tzipke looks at me, proud about what her son—and she—have accomplished.

When my brother was five, we knew that he would be an aeronautics engineer. I would go crazy. After all, in my home we spoke Yiddish. What did they know about aeronautical engineering? They put it into his head, and look, from five years of age! Ziv, I don't know whether it's an intelligent decision, but I don't say anything. You see, that soldier that committed suicide in the army base last week. I said that it was a suicide full of gall! What does that mean, what is so bad? *(angry).* You are not in the Intifada, no one is throwing stones at you. No! You want to be near your mother, what is this all about? If my son was in the same base, I would kiss the mezuzah every day and say: "Thank you, God." The guy committed suicide because they didn't let him serve near his home *(sarcastically).*

I have a neighbor who has a son, he is a real gorilla, and they sent him to a combat unit. He decided that it wasn't for him, so what did he do? He ran away and disappeared. He sat in jail. They let him out and returned him to the same base. It was terrible, he wanted to be a cook and so they punished him. If you don't want to be in the combat unit, you are considered a failure. They didn't send him back to his work and he ran away again. Sometimes the army also makes mistakes. Why did they have to be bothered with him? Perhaps the next time, he will use a gun? He is a boy from a good home, he is a good boy. Where does he get the courage? And his parents are so unhappy, they suffered a lot. I told my husband, that example worries me. Perhaps it will influence my son? I say that we are also to blame. We spoil them and wrap them in cotton. Whoever heard of such things, every day a soldier commits suicide, whoever heard of such a thing? This mess of suicides is really terrible.

I try to understand what Tzipke is talking about: about her son, who has found his own way? About herself, who has also found her own way? And perhaps the images of the birthmark, the pool of blood, and the anger over the soldier who committed suicide reflect her fears: how difficult it is to guard the fragile line of life against the dangers inside and outside the home.

We part with a warm handshake. I am soon swallowed up in the tumult of the street. For a few minutes I try unsuccessfully to find the house I have just come out of, but they all look alike. I wonder what the neighbors know about Tzipke's life, about her mother's? And perhaps there is a story behind each door? Perhaps no one has the time to listen to these other stories. On my way home, I try to figure out how it is to be the daughter of Genia, who is now so dependent, the mother of Ziv, Ganit, and Nira. It seems to me an extremely difficult combination of roles. There is so much to worry about.

Tzipke's narrative is not abrupt like her mother's, but it is loaded with weighty expressions. After a very short, almost neutral opening, Tzipke, crying, talks of the heavy burden she has, worrying about and taking care of her parents: "My parents are the things that I guard the most and I am the only one who does." She has to do it all alone, since her brother is living in the United States and her sister Tova "has her own problems." Her husband's attitude to his mother and her parents is not worrisome: "He loves them because they love him." She worries about them even more than she does her own children. We hear of her current role in her parents' life, another contrast to her rebelliousness during childhood. Can Tzipke find no independent—neither dependent nor counterdependent—place for herself near her parents?

It is interesting to follow how, in successive interviews, new aspects unfold that are central to that particular narrator, but not necessarily so to the former one. Tzipke's narrative is quite a contrast to Genia's, which hardly mentioned her daughter's special role in her current life. Are these, therefore, merely Tzipke's worries or are they her parents' actual needs and demands, which Genia diminished? Perhaps, owing to her own harsh life history, Genia can relate in her biographical reconstruction to those events in the lives of her children that have an obvious external correlate (like her son's distancing and Tova's divorce), but she cannot grasp Tzipke's less obvious, less verifiable sense of burden and loneliness. From Genia's point of view, Tzipke is doing fine, she does not need special concern or attention. However, Tzipke also sometimes gives one the feeling that she "searches" for her parents' dependency: "I wouldn't do such a thing to them. To move away [and leave them] without a protector and savior, it's impossible to do that." But Tzipke tries not to be totally absorbed in her worries. She is struggling now to develop an independent career. But it is not easy, since she also puts her children before her career: There is always tension and a lot of running around so that the house will go well."

Is Tzipke's worrying, as the sole caretaker of her parents, a pattern that has been transmitted to her from her mother? Is it a continuation of Genia's "vicious circle of suffering" and loneliness? Is she or Tova Genia's "memorial candle" (Vardi, 1990)? The struggle for independence from her mother is difficult, because Tzipke adores her mother, how "she lived through Hitler." (How? "I don't understand it to this day.") Tzipke was well informed during her childhood about what her mother went through, but she finds it difficult to imagine what these events were actually like. She tries to make real for herself the difficulties Genia had to deal with through her own dieting or her friend's struggle with cancer. But even when she describes her mother's lack of emotion ("my mother is not the type of woman who gives kisses and hugs"), Tzipke is unable to be angry and say that she missed it. In contrast to her parents' lack of emotion, she tells how she hugs her children. She does not compare "my parents as opposed to me and my husband," but rather, "my parents as opposed to me and my children." Are they compensation for what she did not have in her own childhood?

Only later in the interview does Tzipke tell how she suffered from Genia's harsh mothering. These are the concrete experiences Genia referred to when she said she "took it all out" on her children. Tzipke mentions the numerous beatings she got from her mother (she "was always very actively involved"), who woke her up in the middle of the night to hang up her clothes. Tzipke says, almost sarcastically, "In that respect, she was very emotional, very." She relates these beatings to evil: "The evil was hitting." By doing this, Tzipke is perhaps trying to distinguish between her "mother" and the "evil" that permeated her mother's life during the Holocaust. In reaction to this evil, Tzipke rebelled. At that stage, it gave her life meaning: "Whatever was important to them, I would do the opposite." Yet even this Tzipke describes, in retrospect, as "what I did to them," not as a reaction to what they did to her. However, she concludes, quite openly, that it was not a happy house, thereby pointing out the suffering that permeated her own life story. The only slap she remembers is one she got from her father for wearing black on Rosh Hashanah. It is very symbolic: the struggle between black and white, evil and love.

Her struggle over her complex relationship with her parents is expressed in her attempt to compare herself to her neighbors. Tzipke begins with a description of her parents' nightmares and fears. She would wake up at night to her father's screams, and it "follows me to this day." She continues: "Our house was not a happy one." In her Israeli-born neighbor's house, "I see the differences," but she is unable to describe that happiness because it would sound as if she were criticizing her parents. She concludes: "It seems different to me . . . [it is all right if] they cannot see each other for four years." That is, at our house we had nightmares and life was not joyous, but we *cared* for each other. Tzipke admits that this caring has no limits. She raises the possibility that her parents' overdone worrying drove her brother and sister to the United States. Still, she cannot make up her mind, moving between "when my brother was in the army, I worried about him so much" (having a positive meaning) and "it's different with my children" (also having a positive meaning). Her smile tells us that, although she complains about their seeming lack of care for each other, she feels that they are behaving more *naturally*. They have a legitimate right *not to care*, more than she did at their age. Still, as her words show, Tzipke is wrestling with the distinction between how much care is too little and how much is too much.

In light of her childhood, how does Tzipke view her own motherhood? She has tried to "learn from the mistakes they [her parents] made" and given her children more freedom in terms of their studies, their reading, when and what they eat, and how they keep their clothes, just as she allows them to choose how to celebrate their bar-mitzvahs and spend their Friday nights. But her way is not simply to respond by acting counter to her parents. She also exhibits insight, even a process of trial-and-error learning from her own experience; for example, on Shabbat she prepares cholent and wants to have everyone "together," and her guests say: "Ah, what a Jewish household." However, Tzipke is also aware that her children want their privacy and she therefore looks for the right balance that will let them go out on Friday night and be together with the family on Saturday afternoon. This is her inventiveness, which she did not learn from her parents—or from overreacting to them. Perhaps her husband has been helpful in encouraging her in this kind of path-finding.

In this respect, Tzipke has made the longest journey with her second child, Ziv. In the beginning, her fears and her reactions "spoiled him." But when there was a danger that he would not be able to continue in school, she recognized her overreaction and, against her brother's advice, saw it as her "project" to help him get into Ort School, "to liberate" him from his less desirable friends and help him finish school. Tzipke had to find a way to avoid overreacting to her own childhood and repeating her parents' kind of discipline. She received a "bonus" when Ziv decided to continue his studies after finishing high school. In her eyes, her "life project" had succeeded.

Against this background of hopefulness, Tzipke's anger about the Israeli soldier who committed suicide ("a suicide full of gall") expresses her fears, but probably also her insight: "I say that we are also to blame. We spoil them and wrap them in cotton." She is able not only to respond to her parents' "mistakes," but to set limits for her son. Tzipke comments that she has learned how to respond decisively but in a way that is not aggressive. This is her achievement. She is able to work through her mother's heritage, navigating carefully between her own experience with her parents and finding a new way to help her son.

Ganit

"It happened and it is impossible to go back and fix it"

I feel uncomfortable returning to Tzipke and Yosef's house in order to interview their daughter, so I invite Ganit to my house. She willingly agrees and I am full of curiosity: Who is Ganit like? Her mother? Her grandmother? I am not thinking about her appearance. After all, Tzipke has already told me that like her, Ganit needs to diet. I think about the different possibilities that face Ganit. Is she completely wrapped up in the Israeli reality of the late eighties, ignoring the burdens of the past? Does she revolt against her parents as her mother did? Perhaps she has something new to offer us?

My name is Ganit, I am nineteen and a half. I am a soldier, I serve in the adjutancy unit in Ramat Gan. I am the office clerk. It's very uninteresting work. I don't have a lot of hobbies; I read a little. I am now studying English so that I can take a matriculation exam. I am the oldest child of three in my family. That's all.

The interesting subjects in my life were the death of my grandfather, my father's father, and the transition to high school, to the ninth grade. It was a very big crisis for me. I went into high school with a few children from my old school but I was put into a different class. It was very hard for me to get acclimated, to get to know people, to get over the first stages. I left the "incubator" of elementary school for high school. In elementary school everyone was an individual. In high school, I became a number without a name. It was a sort of crisis. Mostly because I was alone, I was completely alone.

When I took my matriculation examinations and when I did basic training in the army, these were pressured times for me. Especially when they pressured me to become an officer. They thought that I had leadership ability. And then, when I went home for the weekend, I heard that my father needed to have surgery and, at the same time, I broke up with my boyfriend. Except for that, it was a good period *(smiles)*. That was the nicest period of my army service. I don't enjoy it now at all. At first I served in a place where I was a clerk in a more interesting office. But I had an officer I couldn't stand. He was disgusting, selfish, a real bastard. He had a different absurd idea every day. I didn't have the patience to put up with his ridiculous ideas. I have enough problems of my own, I don't need to suffer because of his problems also. I changed jobs by pulling some strings. It's the same story everywhere. It's an easy job; the hours are good. I don't work in the evenings or special shifts or do kitchen work. I don't work late hours. It's comfortable for me, I can study. When I finish the college entrance exams I want to study psychology here. I may begin to work a bit *(awaits my reaction)*.

The truth is that I thought my army service would be different. I wanted to be a welfare officer. I went to pre-army courses and they told me that I was suited for work in electronics, but I had no interest whatsoever in that. Since I wasn't accepted into the program, I said that I wouldn't make a fuss. Whatever they give me, I'd take. When I got to basic training, I had an interview with an officer in charge of women, the officer who chose soldiers for the different army branches. I talked to her and they told me that they took a small number of girls and so I got into the navy with the use of some "pull." I am a little bit sorry, but . . . it's not too bad. I like helping people a lot. It really hurts me that I wasn't accepted into the welfare program. Maybe I will become a psychologist *(giggles)*.

I remember almost nothing from my childhood. Only pictures, I remember things through pictures. I remember that I cried and that I didn't want my mother to go, that's the only thing that I remember. All in all, I didn't have problems. I was like every child: small fights, nonsense, nothing drastic *(silence)*.

I have a sister, Nira. She is a wonderful child. I am a very sociable person and it's hard for me to see that she doesn't have girlfriends. I think that it's because of the framework that she's in. In her school people aren't friendly. I am used to parties, movies. I took a lot of classes—folk dancing, drama, ceramics, enamel work, basketball. I was always active and I had friends over all the time. For her, the subject of friends is a hard one and that makes me unhappy. She is a charming child. She helps. One day she got up at six in the morning. She was depressed because she needed to clean up the kitchen *(laughs)*. She's got a good soul. She gives with her whole heart.

But that subject really bothers me, it hurts me. Maybe things will change in high school. Her entire class doesn't participate in the youth movement either. I was in the scouts, but I left the counselor training program because of school pressure. I am only four years older than her but right now the difference between us is great. I don't remember her growing up. I remember visiting school. I guess that I have a selective memory. I remember what is comfortable for me to remember.

The relationship with my brother is all right, but it's not so deep. They thought that we would be very close but there is something that divides us. We grew up together, we went to summer camp together, I was dependent on him *(smiles)*. It's not so much that way today. He has his life with his girlfriend, I have mine with my boyfriend. Everyone has their own world. We sometimes sit and exchange experiences. Where were you? Where did you go? I helped him out a bit with his school work. But we don't have an intimate relationship where we spill out our souls to each other. I do that with a good girlfriend of mine. I always had a lot of girlfriends. When I joined the army I cut down a lot. My boyfriend in the army is two years older than me. I met him when he was in twelfth grade. We have known each other since the ninth grade. I went out with other boys during that time. I didn't know if that was my future. We are now back together again after we broke up. I didn't believe that I would go back with him. There was a little bit of pressure, but I don't know. When I broke up with him, I became impatient and apathetic about everything that went on around me. I am impatient with him and I don't see such a great future for our relationship. Meanwhile, that's the situation *(silence)*. Do you have any questions?

"How do you define your family?"

My close family, mother, father, my brother, my sister, my grandfather and grandmother on my mother's side, my grandfather on my father's side who died. And my aunt from my mother's side, but the relationship with her is not so close either. The relationship with my father's sister isn't so close either. The close family is mother, father, my brother and sister, my grandparents on my mother's side. That's it. We usually see each other on family occasions—holidays, weddings, circumcision rites. We also meet on Saturdays and on birthdays, but mostly on holidays, Passover and Rosh Hashanah. Events that are bigger, big occasions. We celebrate the holidays with a very small circle [of people]. Since my grandfather died, we meet a lot less. Grandmother went crazy a bit and so we go more often to visit her. For instance, on Passover, she invites people over less. It used to be on every occasion, every Shabbat, at least once every other week. Today it's a lot less.

On Saturdays we travel and we eat on Yom Kippur. Everyone does what he feels like doing. I need to fast, I fast because of my diet *(giggles)*. For the lie here and the lie there *(embarrassed),* in order to repent, to atone for it. I have fasted every year since age twelve. We are Jews and we have to keep up the tradition, on Passover as well.

When I become a mother and have a family, perhaps I will celebrate these holidays. I won't necessarily go to services. Up until a few years ago

I went to services on Yom Kippur and on Passover. I would go with my father. I felt like I was a Jew. I don't eat pork. I learned that at home, mostly from my mother's side, from my grandmother. My grandfather is traditional and he goes to services almost every Shabbat even though they drive on Saturdays. They keep kosher, there are dishes for milk and meat and they sometimes have special dishes. At home we do less, we don't have separate dishes for milk and meat. I never learned to keep kosher in my house *(silence)*.

"Did you ever make a family tree?"

No, Nira did, I didn't have a project like that. She interviewed the grandparents as well. It bothered me a lot that I didn't have that project. But all of that has no connection to the way that I was brought up and to who I am. I have my family, my parents, my society, my environment. The past does not have a deep influence on me.

"When did the subject of the Holocaust come up in your life for the first time?"

From Grandma or from Mother? They talked about it when I was little. I don't remember how much it affected me until I heard about it in school and when I went to Yad Vashem [the Israeli Holocaust Memorial Museum]. Up until then I didn't really understand. When I grew up I understood more *(silence)*. My mother talks about it sometimes. For her, Holocaust Day isn't like it is for Grandma, but you still feel it. It is close to us, yet far from us. The day itself is shocking, the atmosphere of that day. It hurts me to see how my grandmother looks on that day or how she talks about those she lost. I think that it mostly affected the cohesiveness of our family.

The stories of my grandmother from the Holocaust, tales, not stories. What she was like, her family, Grandfather's stories. The whole subject of death camps. She doesn't talk about things that happened before the war. She told me that she was a beautiful young woman. That left the biggest impression on me. That is the topic, the most shocking experience, the trauma that she won't stop speaking about. Grandpa talks about it a lot less. He is a pretty closed person, he barely talks. I sometimes get tired of hearing about it *(sighs)*. It happened and it is impossible to go back and fix it. It's far away from us. It's far away from me. I don't feel like I can help to make up for what Grandma lost. Even though she talks about it,

I am sure that she wants others to talk to her about it. There is no reason to go backward, to bring it up all the time. We need to be reminded so that we won't forget, but beyond that, nothing will help *(sighs)*.

The framework of Holocaust Day is heavy. It helped my grandfather and grandmother get over it. I feel that I belong to that framework, to Holocaust Day. It touches me. It takes me back to thinking that I could have had a much bigger family. Can you imagine how the human mind could do such things? It is really shocking. I am part of these things, we are united because of them. Otherwise, it would be each person, each person for himself. The whole subject touches me mostly because my family went through it. It's like on Independence Day, Memorial Day, the soldiers. Every soldier and all of that terrible loss.

I feel that it has been pretty much erased for most of my girlfriends, for most of the youth, for society. This year, on Holocaust Day, I wanted to see the television programs because it is close to me. My girlfriends spend that day as if it were a regular day. If things were open in the evening, they would go out. I respect that day, I respect the losses. I wouldn't go out. When I was in school and we talked about it, a lecturer would come, or someone to tell a story, I felt it. I was closer to it. I feel more removed in the army. It is a date and it goes by.

I am sure that when I am a mother I will talk about it. I will tell my children about its meaning. I will try to remember it and pass on the message. I hear, I listen. People around me don't pay attention to it so much. They go bowling on the same day. People don't pay attention to the day anymore, including people who are older than I am. We lost a lot of people in wars and people don't relate to that so much either. For people who are close to it, they have memorial services, they remember the wars and the void that fell on them. It only touches those who are really close to it.

I talk about it more with my grandmother. She begins talking. It isn't discussed during the whole year, only around Holocaust Day and on the day itself. We are a very warm family, we are very close to my grandmother and grandfather, mostly on my mother's side. It's very important. She lost her entire family and I think that family is the part that you can't choose in your life, but it is a very important part. As long as it exists, you need to keep it together. The family is very small; I feel bad that it's so small. I hope that I will have a bigger family. When we get older and now as well. I see how we celebrate holidays, we sit together, small gathering. My mother's brother is in America, my mother's sister is divorced and she only has her daughter, and then there are us and Grandma and Grandpa. I don't have aunts and uncles and cousins who are closer to my age. On holidays we get through the day. On Passover, we read the Haggadah and eat and there is nothing beyond that. We don't have happy holidays, we don't sing and tell stories. It would be very nice if we did, if we sang. When there are opportunities for celebrating and being happy, it's nice to celebrate with more people *(uncomfortable)*.

I hope that I will have a bigger family. Even though I say that I will have a family that fits the number of rooms I have *(laughs)*. I suffer from it. I share a room with Nira. I don't really suffer, but I don't have privacy. I don't think that it will leave its mark in the future, but it might add something, it's missing. Everyone needs their privacy.

Ganit uses words in a different way than either her mother or her grandmother. In comparison to Ganit's brevity, Tzipke's animation and Genia's grim facial expressions are overwhelming. Ganit is a minimalist, as if she is talking about herself from a certain distance, which conveys a sense of an underlying burden, although Ganit refers to it only indirectly. She describes her present life in tones of gray. After all, her own life is not special: "like every child: small fights, nonsense, nothing drastic." Ganit talks about herself, about her brother and sister, her grandmother and grandfather, but she barely speaks about her mother and father. Tzipke appears in only one faint early memory: "I remember that I cried and that I didn't want my mother to go." However, she is completely missing from Ganit's narrative of the present, almost as she was missing from Genia's narrative. Why do both her mother and her daughter exclude Tzipke from their life stories?

Ganit's minimalist speech and gray description of her present reality may be a reaction to her mother's overwrought descriptions and her grandmother's horror stories. In the army, she does not make "a fuss" about the job she is given when she is not accepted into the program she wanted; "pull" did not help because "it was the same story everywhere." She went back to her old boyfriend eventually, after they had broken up, because she was "impatient and apathetic about everything." But, she does not see a "great future" for the relationship. Ganit speaks little about her past: "I remember almost nothing from my childhood." If she has memories, they are negative ones: the death of her grandfather (her father's father) and the crisis of moving into ninth grade: "I became a number without a name" (a dreadful association with Genia's "number"?).

Ganit speaks openly, and in a way that reminds us of Genia, about the lack of control she feels she has over the past and the present, although without the uniqueness of her grandmother's story. Ganit adds irony where Genia's story has more substance. For example, when she talks about Yom Kippur she says: "I fast because of my diet *(giggles)*. For the lie here and the lie there . . . in order to repent, to atone for it." Her unhappiness is expressed mostly in her description of the holidays: "We sit together, small gathering . . . we get through the day. On Passover, we read the Haggadah and eat . . . We don't have happy holidays, we don't sing and tell stories . . . it's nice to celebrate with more people." We hear the echo of family losses in the distant past that are still causing unhappiness today, especially on holidays.

Ganit talks more emotionally and more favorably about her grandmother, adding some color to her that we have not heard about before: "She was a beautiful young woman. That left the biggest impression on me." And around Holocaust Day, "It hurts me to see how my grandmother looks . . . how she talks about those she lost." Ganit adds: "It's far away from us . . . I don't feel like I can help to make up for what Grandma lost." Ganit has found a way to be empathic to her grandmother but not overwhelmed by her, unlike her mother, at least with respect to Genia's past. Ganit also sees wider consequences: It hurts her that people "remember the wars and the void that fell on them. It only touches those who are really close to it." She feels a closeness to this suffering, even though she too "sometimes gets tired of hearing about it." She concludes angrily: "Can you imagine how the human mind could do such things?"

One might assume that Ganit's realistic, somewhat dull outlook on life would color her sense of the future, yet her comments about the future are actually full of optimism and hope. She wants to study psychology because she "likes helping people." When she has a family of her own, she will celebrate the holidays because she identifies with the Jewish tradition, even if she doesn't go to services. She hopes that "I will have a bigger family," and she reflects: "Even though I say that I will have a family that fits the number of rooms I have *(laughs)*," mentioning the dilemma that arises from having a family and maintaining privacy (which right now is very important to her).

In relation to memories of the Holocaust, Ganit notes: "I am sure that when I am a mother I will talk about it. I will tell my children." It seems that she believes in the possibility of interweaving hope with remembering to make her own way forward while being aware of the difficult legacy of the past. Though she is at an early stage in her life, she may be a step further than her mother in working through the past: looking hopefully toward a different future.

The Aftereffects of the Holocaust

Genia, Tzipke, and Ganit—three women a generation apart—struggle with memories of the Holocaust. It is possible to label them with psychodynamic labels: "depressed personality," "individuation difficulty," "memorial candle." Tzipke could be identified as "typical" of the second generation (just as Genia is a "typical" survivor), living near her parents, guarding them, still lacking "boundaries" between dependence and counterdependence; Genia revives her dreadful memories, setting in motion a vicious circle of suffering for herself and her children. One could even argue that she is a borderline case, not really within the normal range of behavior and narrative. While such claims characterize something in her discourse, they overlook other aspects.

In the "strong" tradition, Tova could be seen as Genia's "memorial candle." Yet it could also be Yudke, or even Tzipke: in a way, each of them is a different kind of "memorial candle." Yudke, who is successful professionally, lives at both a physical and an emotional remove from his parents. From Genia's perspective, Tova is part of the "circle of suffering" that also includes her. These are all partially true statements, yet they lack something. What is it exactly?

What these labels overlook is Genia's opening statement: "To tell you that I didn't have a chance to know what the word *mother* is." This statement, almost an exclamation, is not based on historical truth. It is strongly personal and subjective: Genia's life story begins with death and her never-ending confrontation with it continues. Against the background of her experiences in the camps, no normative solution—how one should think or behave—is relevant. Strong conceptual systems that are based on normative expectations, whether they are psychoanalytic or not, fall short of understanding Genia's subjective narrative truth (Spence, 1980). It is as if within such a life history, anomaly becomes normal and the normal anomalous: Genia manages to maintain a deep sense of caring despite the terrible things she has endured.

Genia cared for her family while it was still possible; she cared for her own life when nothing else was possible. Though she claims otherwise, Genia remembers a great deal, including "unheroic memories" (Langer, 1991): how she would scratch her girlfriend, for example, because a piece of bread had not been cut precisely. She fears that her children were her victims and sees their difficulties (such as Tova's divorce) as examples of "her [own] burned heart"—a heart that could not hold what it had experienced, could not mourn for her sisters, her brother, her mother and father, or for all the children whose screams she still hears today. The vicious circle of her suffering is this fear: remembering the dead and fearing what she has handed down to her children. Genia tells us how terribly difficult it is to maintain hope with such a life history.

There is no truly objective measure of Genia's normalcy. One could argue, however, that an objective measure could be developed for the second and third generations: after all, they did not experience the horrors directly. Perhaps we can define what for them is "normal" or "correct" behavior? We can assert, for example, that Tzipke's adolescent rebellion, in reaction to her abusive mother and her passive father, was functional at the time in developing her independence, but it did not help her separate from them in a "healthy" manner. A symbiotic relationship still exists between them. Tzipke has raised her children in reaction to her own harsh childhood memories: her parents' nightmares, her mother's beatings, and so forth, a reaction that lacks the "expected" liberation and individuation which should happen between generations at an earlier stage.

The psychological literature dealing with the second generation of the Holocaust is full of such "strong" assertions, which are all based on the assumption that we know the "correct way" to grow up in such a family. The research team has reservations about this assumption and the literature upon which it is based. In our opinion, it is better to be modest, to state "softly" that we do not know how we ourselves would withstand such pressure—like Genia? like Tzipke and Ganit? We want to learn from them how to deal with the unforgettable reality of death, the grim memories of animal-like behavior, and the ongoing awareness of such issues as they are transmitted or worked through from one generation to the next.

We learn from Tzipke that she is trying to construct her own career as she did her motherhood, in a way that is different from that of her mother (for whom even the simple name "mother" was destroyed by the war). It is difficult, because, while Tzipke criticizes and negates her mother, she also admires her. As a daughter, she suffers from an "abusive" mother, but she also knows enough to account for it as the "evil" her mother internalized. One may assert that Tzipke has slowly learned, by trial and error, how to develop a strategy for relating to her parents and her children. She has found a way to give her children a taste of the childhood she missed, including having grandparents.

How does she do it? She lets her children have a degree of freedom she did not have because her parents were fearful, harsh, and self-absorbed. She understands that her children should read because they choose to do so, not because their grandmother wants them to. She tries to imbue barmitzvah celebrations with a different significance, one that is relevant to her children's interests. She attempts to create a feeling of "togetherness" and a "Jewish home" by making cholent on Saturdays. When her son "makes her life miserable" because of his school problems (just as she made her parents' lives miserable), "her life project" is to get him to continue with his schooling at the Ort technical school, and it is her victory that he finishes high school with a "desire to go on." At this stage Tzipke is ready to reflect on the past. She tries to convince her parents to go with her to Poland, where they grew up. They refuse, but she still hopes that someday they will change their minds.

Clearly, Tzipke has suffered some failures. She makes a statement and contradicts herself. She goes forward (with her children's independence) and backward (with her parents' dependence). Perhaps this is a testimony to how difficult this navigation between generations is for her: it is a mission that she carries on all alone. She does not see herself as very strong (in her dieting, for example) and those around her do not give her a lot of support in her struggles. From her remarks in the interview, it seems that her husband—who is in awe of her parents and their stories, which he never heard from his own family—does not recognize her needs. Her sister is wrapped up in her own problems and her brother lives far away. She does not seem to have a *"validating other"* to offer support. She gets it only through her own experience, along with the positive feedback she receives from her maturing children.

Ganit is not yet ready to give her mother such support, to step into her mother's shoes. She is busy building her own identity, and her life story has not yet taken its final shape. It seems to her that her story pales compared to that of her grandmother. There is no "drama" in it. The gray tones of her present-day army life bear testimony to that burden. When Ganit relates to the past, she speaks lovingly of her grandmother and feels her pain, but she is also able to state that she can distance herself from it and that she is unable to make up for what Genia has lost. This is how she can handle it at less than twenty years of age. She is actually able to draw a thin line that differentiates the two of them, although perhaps not yet one between her mother and herself. This demarcation does not find expression in her present life but rather in her thoughts and hopes for the future.

Ganit could also be defined as a victim of her legacy: she is "depressive," "lacking in self-confidence," "low in self-esteem," and has an "undeveloped sense of feminine identity." To a certain extent, all of these are true. However, once again, we would ask: What is the objective yardstick for Ganit's way of coping? Should we measure "what is the expected response of a woman her age"? Or should we use Ganit's perception of her world— one constructed at a distance of fifty years from the "animal behavior" and death of Auschwitz and meshed together with the day-to-day results of her interaction with her grandmother, mother, and aunt. Ganit is not yet a mother, so the problems so characteristic of motherhood in her family are as yet too distant from her. However, she prepares herself for this role through her imagination and her hopefulness.

In the Belinsky family there is still more fear (anger, pain, helplessness) than hope (assertiveness, strength), and the present entails more past than future, more transmission than working through. We could conclude our analysis in this way, but we would rather avoid making such generalizations. In the following chapters we will get to know other patterns and different strategies. We assume, however, that each of these strategies serves a similar function: to struggle with the legacy of the past. The three

Belinsky women are evidence that this is not a simple task and that it cannot be achieved completely after one or even two generations.

The unique path of each one of these women is worthy of respect. We wish to understand their special language, which we have not yet mastered, and to apprehend in their fragile words the light and shadow of human reflection.

2

THE LERMANS

Among the Partisans

with Bosmat Dvir-Malka

Ze'ev was born in a village in Belorussia in 1922, the same year Genia was born in Warsaw. Like her, he had a large, traditional family that was almost extinguished in the Holocaust. Both of them lost nearly everyone and everything that had been dear to them before the war. Both survived due to their resourcefulness. However, Ze'ev's story is different from that of Genia, at least during the war: he escaped, joined the partisans, and fought with them until they were liberated by the Russians. If Genia represents camp survivors, Ze'ev represents resistance-fighters. We have seen that Genia needs to confront the memories of hunger, sickness, and helplessness connected with Majdanek and Auschwitz. Does Ze'ev have more positive memories because he enjoyed relative freedom of action? What part of his life history dictates or colors the construction of his life story, the loss (the similarity) or the war experience (the difference)? Which of these similarities or differences has been passed on to the following generations? Perhaps there are other aspects of his life story that are not reflected in the similarities and differences mentioned here? In search of answers to these questions, we turn to our interviews with Ze'ev, Hannah, and Yoav.

Ze'ev

"It's good being alive"

I meet Ze'ev in his apartment in Rommema on Mount Carmel. The apartment is simply furnished in an almost Spartan fashion. From the patio, there

1922	Ze'ev is born in a small town between Minsk and Vilna, the fifth in a family of three sisters and three brothers. The family is religious but not orthodox.
1939	The Russians invade the town after the Ribbentrop-Molotov nonaggression pact. The family remains together under harsh conditions.
1941	The Germans take the town. "Actions" begin, and Ze'ev's mother and sisters are killed. His father and older brother are sent to work camps. Ze'ev escapes to Vilna and from there to the forest, where he joins the non-Jewish partisans.
1942	In the woods he meets and aids a Jewish family.
1945	He returns to his village and retaliates against the gentiles. He marries Rachel, a daughter of the family he met in the woods.
1947	Hannah, a daughter, is born.
1949	Ze'ev and his wife and daughter immigrate to Israel. They stop first at the "Immigration Gate" in Haifa and from there move to Kiriyat Eliezer, Haifa.
1950	Dina, a daughter, is born.
1956	The family moves to Rommema on Mount Carmel in Haifa.
1969	Hannah marries Moshe, a Sabra, and they move to Upper Nazareth.
1971	Yoav, a son, is born to Hannah and Moshe. Dina marries.
1973	Shani, a daughter, is born to Hannah and Moshe.
1983	Raziya, a daughter, is born to Hannah and Moshe. The family moves to Tivon, a suburb of Haifa.
1989	Yoav is preparing to go into the army. Bosmat Dvir-Malka interviews Ze'ev, Hannah, and Yoav.

is a beautiful view of Haifa bay. Ze'ev points proudly toward the port and says in a voice with a clear Russian accent: "I arrived here exactly forty years ago. I remember it as if it were yesterday." We settle down in the living room. I set up the tape recorder and look at him attentively.

What do I remember from my childhood? I was born in 1922. Are you already taping? *(laughs).* I was born in a small place in Belorussia. It's near Minsk, midway on the road that leads to Russia. Yes. And I grew up there in a family of six children, father, mother, grandfather and grandmother, cousins, and a big family in a big house. In the middle there was—how can I explain it?—it was like a hall. But this hall was bigger, let's say, than this entire house *(Ze'ev gestures with his hands)*. We lived on one side— father, mother, and the children—and on the other side lived my grand- mother, my father's mother, and her sister with their big family as well.

It's a small place, let's say, with about 150 to 200 Jewish families. I am not talking about the gentiles, just about the Jews. I finished elementary school. I would go to the rabbi, the learned man, you know, in a type of *cheder* [religious school]. We learned the *chumash,* Bible, a little Hebrew, and a little Yiddish. Yes, my house wasn't orthodox, it bordered on being traditional. Shabbat is Shabbat, on Friday you go to the synagogue. There was a synagogue. And to services during the week, once yes and once no. We had kosher dishes, you know, divided in that way. How can I say it? We weren't very rich, but we weren't poor. There was bread, potatoes, there was what to eat, the basics, what I am telling you. The rest—we didn't have luxury items. And we grew up. It was a small house: this child *(points at himself)* grew up on the sofa with very wide wooden boards without a foam rubber mattress and without all the extras. And we all grew up, each one of us, nice, straight, and healthy.

And the war came. The war came, and so this small house was taken apart, the house that I loved that was not luxurious but that was loved so much. That is everything that was dear to me. Everything was made by hand, with love. In my mother's house, we would make bread. Every Sunday morning we would make bread. And what I remember, each loaf of bread was like half a table. Six loaves of bread for six days and on Sunday we would make more bread for another week. And that's the way it always was until . . . the Russians came. The Russians came on the eve of Rosh Hashanah, 1939. Can it be? When did the war start? The Russians came and . . . with that my studies came to an end. There were those that tried to continue but it was very hard. It wasn't organized like in regular life.

"Everything was made by hand, with love": the warm memory of his childhood house. Ze'ev is well prepared to tell this story. He builds it slowly and gradually. Yet I am tense. His intonation reminds me of my own family from the same generation.

And we began working at home, helping out the family. And I did all kinds of jobs, whatever there was. This child worked and he didn't get tired of it. The main thing was that the house would have what it needed.

Since my childhood I had, how do you say it, what is it called in simple Hebrew? I already had it in my head—I need to do things, to hold things together, to do maintenance work. And I did everything, I would go, we had a factory in the town where they would cut timber. And they needed to put together crates for apples. In the winter there was a forest where they would cut wood in order to prepare it for cooking in the summer. Whatever there wasn't, we made. The main thing was to have enough to live on. And the Russians came from 'thirty-nine till 'forty-one. And in 'forty-one, the Germans arrived. The Germans, aahh . . . *(as if shouting and sighing simultaneously),* they came and they started killing the Jews, each time a little bit more. And later on whole families, until they killed all of the . . . they killed the entire town. Not one Jew was left. Whoever ran away, ran away. Whoever didn't escape was killed. In a mass grave: the grave has remained to this day a mass grave, there in the town. If you would take me there today, I would be able to find the exact place. It is something that you can't forget until you die *(there is a fierce look in his eyes).* I ran away from there and I wandered around to all kinds of places, hungry, troubled, without shoes. You know, when you are separated from your home, the mother and three sisters were murdered and the father and the three sons were still alive. After the war was over, my father and my eldest brother died. My younger brother and I remained alive. I live in Israel and my younger brother lives in Canada, in Montreal. That's the background of the family. That's Chapter One.

"That's Chapter One." I shudder: How is it possible to summarize what was left of an entire family in three words!

The second chapter: I wandered around until I arrived at the Vilna ghetto. In the Vilna ghetto I worked in all kinds of places. God knows how I got out of there alive. There is a place called Ponar and it is well known: everywhere they dug ditches. Each ditch was, let's say, fifteen meters by fifteen meters in order to kill Jews. And they would bring Jews there. That's where I worked. I worked on the railroad tracks in the winter. In short, I worked there for a few months and one day I left Vilna ghetto and I never went back. I got to the forest and I was accepted into the partisans. The first day that I was with the gentiles, the partisans, and until [the end] of the war I was a partisan.

"That's where I worked": the Nazis made it possible to term clearing the tracks for the murder of your people "work."

The war ended, there were episodes, you need a book. No, you need to sit with me day and night. It's not a short story, I am telling you everything briefly. The war ended, I met a girl whose family I knew from the forest. How did I meet the family in the woods? I once went to do some mission with the goyim [gentile partisans]. And I see fire at a distance. Far away in the forest. I go, I see sitting there, how can I say it, perhaps eight to ten people, with women and small children among them. One of the girls lives in Rishon le Ziyyon now. What can I tell you, I see that they are making soup. And the soup was as black as the oil in a car that has already run. Why? There was a hole in the bucket and it was stuffed up with a rag and so when it was on the fire the fire would burn it, it would burn the rag, and the water would run out and so they would add more water. I went there and I saw them, that picture, it was very frightening. I couldn't help them in the forest, but I promised them. I said: "I am going out on a mission. I will be gone for two weeks perhaps, perhaps three. It depends on how successful we are getting there. But I promise that I will come back and I will bring you a bucket." And to bring a bucket was like a house today. Understand, with that bucket you washed, you needed to make soup and with that bucket you needed . . . and it's a family.

Yes, I promised it and I did it and the goyim laughed at me. "What a Jew. Why are you dragging that bucket?" Go tell them that I promised to bring one. My commander, I requested that we would go back the same way that we came. And I gave them the bucket. So one of them, she also died in Israel, she said to me: "We have cousins, pretty girls. If we stay alive, come to us and I will introduce you to a girl, to my cousin." And fate, fate is that after the war was over the army took me to Minsk, and there I heard that it is possible to go to Israel through Poland. On the way I said that I would go into that town that they came from. Perhaps I will find [them].

I went there and I found all of them that had gone back to their town. So she told me, "Come, I will introduce you to my cousin." And I entered the house and I found a girl and three sisters. The youngest one was ten and my wife was the fourth, the eldest. And I met her and I married her. So I took a wife and her three sisters were immediately ready to come *(laughs)*. Yes, and not too much later we went to Germany and from Germany to Israel. And three sisters live here, they are all married, they live not too far apart, in the northern part of the country.

I am completely wrapped up in the story. "With that bucket . . . and it's a family." When Ze'ev talks, I find myself reading some new Bible in which only the nice stories are narrated and the rest is described briefly.

I raised a family. I have two daughters, two successful daughters, and I have no complaints about them. And I have a grandson and four grand-daughters. One has a grandson and two girls and the other has two girls. My grandson went into the army two weeks ago. He went into a very elite unit *(proudly)*. He is very talented and yesterday was his first day in uniform. When he came to see me, there was great happiness. We made a meal and he went back today.

I came to Israel. I came with money and I lost all of the money here, to my last penny. It didn't work, it's not that I didn't want, I wasn't lazy. I decided to go to America, my wife has a big family in Texas, a very rich family. And they sent us papers to go there. In the end I changed my mind, I said: "I came here, I want to be here." And just as things were going downhill, the wheel turned around. And I worked in all kinds of jobs, whatever there was. I brought a big welding shop from Germany. We were four partners. And I worked in construction with steel. I did it all and in the end I threw it away and I bought a laundry. Forty girls worked there, in the bay, near Kfar Ata. I was successful there, and that's the way I live. Now we live here in Rommema. This is our third apartment.

How can I say it—it's not luxury, but it's good to say: "It's good being alive." How do you say it? "Happy with what one has." If you say: "The shirt that you are wearing is the best one," that is, you have it good. I have a good wife, I have good daughters. They both finished the university. I enjoyed teaching them. A great family and that's the way we live. That is, I have no complaints against anyone. And how to say it . . . it's like I didn't like Israel when I arrived. When I arrived here, I didn't love Israel. I didn't adjust, everything was for me, it was something else completely. Now everything is turned upside down. Let's say, when I am riding down the street and I see someone damaging a tree. I will stop and say to him: "Sir, why are you doing that? Why are you damaging it?" That is, over the years the whole thing turned around. That's it. I don't get involved in politics. And it doesn't matter who's in charge or who isn't in charge. There are problems, it hurts when they do the wrong thing. There is blackmail, thieves, there are such things. But I saw that it is everything and it won't help you. Whoever is strong controls. That's the situation, there is nothing to be done. What else do you want to know?

"Whoever is strong controls." Ze'ev has a philosophy of life that was formed during the war. It doesn't seem to mesh with caring that a tree is being damaged. I try to bring him back to his childhood.

What happened at home? To begin with, we had a piece of land and outside of that we lived [far away] from a big place. We lived a hundred kilometers from Vilna. It's not like today, you get in your car and you go to Tel Aviv very quickly. An hour there and an hour back. It wasn't like that then. Then there was a horse and wagon and to go to Vilna and to bring back merchandise for the stores would take a week. And there we had fall and winter. It was a difficult winter, forty degrees below zero and the bathroom was outside. And all kinds of jobs, how can I say it? It was a hard life. It's not like today. The roads here are wonderful [in comparison] to what was there.

Anyway there were a lot of young people who came out of Jewish families and came to Israel. They are here today, today they are already old. When they came to Israel, I was a boy of six. So today they are already eighty. You have to understand, they live in Nahalal, in Haifa, all over. But they all know me and I know all of them. I was in my place, I knew, I was very mischievous. I never rested. If a gentile boy would hit me, I didn't let it go by. I needed to give it back to him so that he would know that he couldn't get away with that with me. And that's the way I got to the partisans. And I went back to my place, where I was born, and I burned the place *(tense)*. And I settled the account with the goyim that killed the Jews. I settled the account completely. That is, I have experiences, I am not, I am not sorry for what I did to them, I did them justice!

Ze'ev's look hardens when he remembers his revenge. The pain shows in the way he holds his mouth, but his description is brief.

And that's that. Now my cousin wants to go to the town where we were born. He is from Bat-Yam and he was there. He made a movie. He took a video camera and he made a movie that you can open the television and you can see a movie. I promise you that when the movie will be ready, I'll give it to you, so you can see. He was in the town where we were born. He told us that the only thing left was the well in the middle of the village. The well, where we would get water from. From that well . . . *(chokes)*. I have another cousin, his brother. I met them in the forest and they were little children. And it was exactly then that the Germans arrived. Not one German, they took thousands of soldiers from the front, and they searched through the forest in order to catch the Jews. And the boys needed to move from place to place and I met them. I was already in the partisans and I saw that child. They couldn't walk another kilometer. I walked with them all day, let's say like from here to Tivon. They walked a hundred meters and sat down. They had no strength *(very excited)*.

I put that boy into a sack on my back. That child, I said: "Stop crying! If you cry, I am going to put you down. I will leave you here." Then he stopped crying. He was four or five. He had the brains to stop crying. I brought him to another place. No, no, I didn't leave him. My aunt and uncle had already died, but all of the children were alive. The one who lives here in Israel is the one I carried on my back. The rest are in America. That is, the family remained a family. What can I tell you? To this day, when I want to visit him, I don't have to phone, there is no need for that. I go and see him. There are no barriers between us. That is to say, the family is very close and that's the way we remained, what can I tell you?

"There are no barriers between us." The family here knows no borders— does that compensate for what has been lost? The richness of what Ze'ev has said makes it difficult to identify what he does not feel inclined to tell. For example, in remembering the town well or the boy he carried on his back, he finds it difficult to express the feelings that accompany these places and moments.

I am very close, for example, to my brother who lives in Canada. He can pick up the phone, talk to me for an hour, an entire hour. In the forest he would go and look for bread. He stayed alive in the forest. At night, he would go to the gentiles and ask for bread to bring to his family, to his aunt who saved him. During the war he was little. He is nine years younger than me. He went to Canada, he got married, and he is doing well. He is doing better than I am, but I don't envy him *(laughs)*. He was here in the summer. He didn't say that he was coming, he just showed up with his wife. He was here for a week and he went back. He came to talk to the family *(looks at me and smiles)*.

"What else do you remember from the beginning of the war?"

The Russians arrived and the place stayed the same. The worst was when the Germans arrived. The Germans arrived, then the gentiles, the neighbors, were worse than the Germans. They always hated the Jews but they were quiet about it. It was quiet as long as the Russians were around, but when the regime gave them freedom, the Jews were sacrificed.

"What do you remember from when the Germans arrived? What did you know?"

We didn't know what they would do. But, I don't want to go into great detail. We wrote a book, I wrote part of it. I don't want to talk about that a lot, but the moment that I got a rifle, whatever I could do, I did. I did [what I could], and my children know now that my cousin was there and he made a movie, so they asked if I am still alive . . . they remember me well. I burned all of their houses. No, not the Jews' houses . . . the Jews were no longer alive. I didn't want the goyim to use our houses. There were a few of us who remained alive and we did enough. Enough, enough.

We are back in the half sentences of Ze'ev's act of revenge. It is difficult for him to talk about the story with his cousin in the forest and about what the Germans did. Perhaps he still feels helpless and does not wish to relive those atrocities. It appears as if his caution is deliberate (Is he afraid of the law? his children's judgment?), in contrast to the unconscious repression of his feelings of helplessness prior to joining the partisans. "How did the Jewish partisans get along with the non-Jewish partisans?"

There were no problems. Look, during the two years that I was in the forest with the partisans, I was always in action. I was always leaving the camp. Once with ten people, once with eight. There, you needed to go out at night and to sleep during the day. I was in the unit that laid bombs. I would walk on the train tracks at night and lay bombs. Later on, I was moved to the convoy. We got close to the town that I was born in and I knew the places. I was in the convoy for a while, but I was always in action. That is to say, I didn't have time to think. Time went by quickly. And that was a time . . . then nothing was of value. We were alive then . . . nobody knew what tomorrow would bring.

And I can tell you, I lived in the forest with those partisans. I lived through it by drinking, I was always half drunk. No, not enough to make me lose my head. That is, let's say that when I needed to go lay bombs on the railroad tracks, it wasn't because I was Jewish. There were six of us. Each time another one would go. There was somebody who would carry the bombs and someone who would carry the explosives. The explosives without the bombs wouldn't work. Then, I couldn't go if I didn't have a little to drink. I had a bottle made from tin here on the side, like I had two grenades. That's the way I held it. I drank a little and things went well. When a person is alone and he knows that he has no family

... then I didn't know that my father and my older brother were still alive. I escaped by myself to the Vilna ghetto. We didn't see each other. We met when the war ended.

"When did you find out what happened to them?"

When they came, when the Jews started coming in 'forty-five. They brought my little brother to me when they went to Poland. Then I sent my younger brother to Canada. My mother once said, we were sitting at home, that she had sisters in Canada and when he gets older we should send him to Canada. I remembered that. There was the Joint [Distribution Committee]. We wrote and got replies and he went there. He was eleven and they took him into their family as if he were their son. And he grew up and he studied and later on he got married. They opened up a factory for children's clothes and they did very nicely.

From Ze'ev's words, one can hardly learn anything about the mood of his meeting with his little brother: was it only happiness? I sense more, since only the two of them remained alive out of the whole family. Is that the reason Ze'ev sent his brother to Canada? What actually happened to his father and his older brother? How did they die? Ze'ev is a lot less clear about these parts of his story.

"How did you find out about your mother?"

I knew that immediately when I ran away. I knew that they killed my mother and sisters when the tumult began. I escaped. They caught [them] and immediately brought them to one place, let's say it was like a movie theater, and they burned them alive. They brought them there and they killed the rest. They took my father and my older brother to work, to a different place, and that child, my younger brother, my younger brother was taken out of the movie house by my aunt, who was a good seamstress, by the aunt whose son I carried in the forest. Then the Germans took her out, they knew that she could be useful and they took the entire family. They knew that she had six children. However, one of the six was missing, he had run away and was hiding somewhere. So, she grabbed my brother's hand and she took him out of there and that is the way he remained alive.

Ze'ev, perspiring heavily, moves uncomfortably in his chair. I imagine him running away while all of this was happening. Feelings of fear and anger still well up inside him.

These are all things that are not written down, and that are impossible to believe. Impossible to evaluate. What can I tell you? There was a time when people took reparations from the Germans. I didn't. I said that I wouldn't sign. What I went through, I paid my dues to them. I don't want their reparations. I don't want the good or the bad. I will manage. If I am young, I can manage. It is good to work and to have a country and things will be all right.

Ze'ev looks tired and I suggest that we take a short break. He agrees willingly.

I don't sleep so well now. The boy, Yoav, my grandson, went to the army. What can you do, things aren't quiet and I don't sleep. Yesterday he was here and he didn't feel so well. I told him to ask for a day off and stay home. Really, he had a fever. He said no, not in our [his] place, where they are a cohesive group. "If I don't go back, others will suffer." He went back this morning.

"Did you tell him your stories?"

He knows, he knows. The children know, my daughter knows, the daughter passes it on to the grandchildren. They both speak Yiddish. They learned it at home. And they pass it on to their children. The children, the grandchildren, don't speak Yiddish any more, but there are expressions. Let's say, "Volfi, kum tzim tish." Do you know what that is? "Grandpa, come to the table." They learned it then, they learned something. And they know where I was born. I went to visit and I took both girls. It was fun with the girls. The whole trip took two weeks. We just talked about keeping the family together. They know everything.

"It was fun with the girls." We take a break on the patio and I gaze out at the wonderful Haifa landscape. It is so pastoral, especially in comparison to what Ze'ev has just been telling me. When we go back in, I ask: "When did you start talking about the war? Did they ask or did you start telling?"

They are very thirsty to know everything. But the things, what I think about the Holocaust, I didn't tell them. I didn't want to. They said that the Germans came and killed the Jews. But the roots, the troubles they went through, and what they did with the little children, they don't need to know the details. I didn't want to tell them everything. And they are so pedantic, they write down everything. And my girls already managed by themselves. There was a different regime there [during my childhood] for children. That is, children wouldn't go out and wouldn't take things without permission. I think that they are very talented. They are on the right road, all of the family *(looks at me, proudly)*.

When I began my immigration to Israel and I came here, it was 'forty-nine. We came on the ship *Negba* and we arrived in Haifa. We stayed in immigrants' dwellings, Shaar Ha'aliya [The Immigration Gate]. We were there for a month and a half. The mayor gave us a piece of land and we bought barracks from Germany. We were four partners. We brought the barracks to the country and we set them up in the town. I didn't do so well with that, I already told you that. And thank heavens that I never gave up, I looked for something else. Then I found the right thing and I went into the laundry [business]. The laundry worked for a hospital and from there things went well. I managed. My wife brought up the two girls. Why? I'll tell you. When I left in the morning they were sleeping and when I returned in the evening they were sleeping. And it wasn't like that for one day, it was like that for a number of years. To say "Enough, I won't do any more," I didn't do that. I always went on *(sighs, somewhat sadly)*.

Ze'ev reveals some of his difficulties: He does not wish to and is not able to tell his children about the "roots" of what had happened during the war. In Israel, he was busy trying to make ends meet and didn't have time to help raise his daughters. Does "root" refer to the pain over what he lost—about which he is unable to speak and which he tries to forget through hard work? He says: "And my girls already managed by themselves" with more than a hint of fresh pain: I am alone; are they alone too?

We are close to one another, the family, I have no complaints. Now I, I will pick up the phone and tell both of the girls: I want you to come over now. They won't ask why, they will both be here fifteen minutes later. On Pesach, during the holidays, we don't leave the house. There is food, there are festivities, everybody sits together, it is everything. If you let yourself be a part of it, it's festive *(coughs)*. Rachel's cousin is going to come from Russia. We are waiting, he should be arriving soon, in November. She is already excited. We are looking for a house. He is coming with his family. We wrote them. They are from Minsk. First they need to learn Hebrew, right?

Both of my girls grew up with a silver spoon in their mouths. I didn't have a car. It was my dream, but for my girls I paid five Israeli pounds an hour so they could learn English. They speak English, America is nothing. I gave everything to them. There are families, you know, that leave home. Here, they didn't leave home. They got married and had children.

"They didn't leave home. They got married and had children." This is his unique way of saying that he feels his girls are still living "at home," and he does not wish to—or is unable to—let them go.

I have a childhood friend that lives in Canada and his grandson came. He is in Israel now and he speaks Hebrew. I took him for a little bit to the place where my grandson is doing his preparatory army course. There are tents there near Jerusalem in some remote place. Yoav said: "Let's go home, it's hot here." I told him: "It's hot for you now. You are going to have to live for three years in this heat." I educated him a bit *(laughs).*

"I educated him a bit." Ze'ev talks about Yoav as if he is his youngest son. I think: he was a partisan, but he didn't have a son whose army experience could be a "corrective experience" for himself.

I gave you a small picture of our family, how can I explain it, there are no demands—things are good for us the way they are. That is, it is impossible to do what you cannot do. Here, it is a hard country and the weather is not good, with people from all over the world who are nervous. And it hurts me that our youth run away from here. The best run away from here. They have no foundations here. He finishes the army, he can't go and live with his parents. They all want to leave because to buy a house here is very difficult. It is a lot of money and all of this [political] regime isn't good. These children, they are our wealth. We need to keep them here. Are we missing land? The Jewish National Fund has as much land as you need. But they want money for it. For what? Is it theirs? Give it to these children. Give it to them! They finished the army. If they go to school here, they won't run away. But, in Europe we would say, "A bird in the hand is worth two in the bush."

Ze'ev sounds more frightened than he did at the beginning of the interview. Is he afraid that Yoav will want to leave Israel when he finishes his army service? Is he afraid of being alone again? After all, what young people want to do with their lives is no longer under his control. Ze'ev walks me to the door as if it is also difficult for him to part from me. I am not in a hurry and we talk for a while as we stand there. I decide to walk down Mount Carmel on foot. It has been years since I have done so. On the way, moments from the conversation with Ze'ev come back to me: his boyhood house with the large hall in the town; the bread they would bake that was as big as half a table; the story about the bucket in the forest that led him to his wife, Rachel.

I now notice for the first time that Ze'ev has barely mentioned his wife in relation to later events (he has said only: "I have a good wife" and "My wife brought up the two girls"). The discrepancy between description and narration is clear in Ze'ev's case: the former is concise and stands in for the emotions he has trouble feeling and expressing. The latter expresses the grim historical truth with which he has had to live in peace. However, there are questions in connection with this truth that remain unresolved: Is being "alone" the moral of his heroism? Is being "together" strength (as in his idyllic childhood) or is it weakness (when he needs to run away)? This is the fact of life underlying his difficult transition from the high alert of an emergency situation to the day-to-day routines of a strange country, a country that treasured heroism but had no place for him because he was busy making a living, raising his daughters, and dealing with his memories.

For a moment, I have a picture in mind of Ze'ev hugging his entire family and refusing to let any of them go. And then I think of the fear in his eyes when he talked about Yoav and the young people who leave Israel, and of his difficulty in saying good-bye to me at the end of the interview. In contrast to my usual habit, I phone him that evening and I tell him I greatly enjoyed meeting him. He is happy and says again, almost as he did during the interview: "It was a very short story. I told you everything briefly." "But you said a lot in a few words," I reply warmly.

I try to imagine my conversation with Hannah, his daughter, whom I am scheduled to meet the next day at her home in Tivon. Does she know how to tell wonderful stories like her father? Does she feel that because of the stories of his heroism, she has no story of her own to tell? Will she react to his "untold stories"? Perhaps she is also a partner to her father's criticism about what is going on around him in Israel: "Here, it is a hard country and the weather is not good, with people from all over the world who are nervous." Or has she built her identity around "Israeliness"? Does she, like her father, feel that family is a protection against the fears of the past? Or does she see it as a burden and prefer that "each one should be for himself"? I go to Tivon the next afternoon with these questions in my mind.

Hannah

"I really don't know where or how to start . . . Perhaps it is my life story?"

Hannah, a woman in her forties, has deep blue eyes. The interview takes place in her garden, to which she directs me and from which she disappears for over half an hour, with no explanation. During the entire interview, except for a handful of times, her eyes are tearful and her voice quivers with emotion. I think she is afraid, although whether of me or of herself I don't know. She expresses a great deal of suspicion toward me. I ask her to tell me her life story and she looks at me in surprise.

I am not, I really don't know where or how to start. You know, when I talked to Father I thought that what you are interested in . . . [she means, it seems, the connection of her family to the Holocaust], but I didn't think you were interested in me.

"What is important to me is your life story and the way you decide to tell it to me. I am not looking for anything in particular."

What department are you from?

"Behavioral Sciences, Ben-Gurion University . . ."

What in the behavioral sciences? Is it psychology or sociology, this research project?

"The project is in psychology," I say quietly, asking myself: Will she trust me?

Yes? *(silence, for five seconds)*. It's very hard for me. Are you taping already? Look, last year I was on sabbatical and the courses I chose were really different and unconnected. I didn't focus on one thing; rather really . . . every day I did something else, and there was no connection between the things. One day I learned photography and one day I learned merchandising; each day was dedicated to a different subject. I didn't see how the things were connected. Later on, when I thought about these things, I thought that . . . perhaps I don't progress really in one area and take it to the end, but do all kinds of things superficially. Why am I telling you this? Perhaps it is my life story? *(laughs)*. I go along like that, instead of going into depth in one area, I go in all kinds of directions *(silence)*. I don't know, when you say life story, what things interest you? *(she gives me a straight look for the first time)*.

"Why am I telling you this? Perhaps it is my life story?" *I feel the demand (it is unclear whose) for some focus (which she feels does not exist) and her dissatisfaction about what is happening. Perhaps Hannah has never told her life story as one sequence?*

"Everything is interesting to me. Perhaps you will pick a starting point and simply start talking from there."

I don't know what to concentrate on *(silence for ten seconds)*. I don't have a dramatic story to talk about or events that are extraordinary. Don't you have any question that you can ask me to help direct me?

"I don't have a dramatic story to talk about." Hannah looks at me and I understand that my conversation with Ze'ev is now an obstacle between us. Hannah has no stories about a bucket in the forest, about blowing up trains, about burning houses. Does this mean, therefore, that everything she has done (which, in her opinion, is neither focused nor goes together) is worthless in her eyes? Hannah already interests me, but I do not wish to "rescue" her from her uneasiness. I give her a little rope: "No, there is nothing specific I am looking for. For the most part, people your age do not have dramatic stories to tell, so anything that you tell me will be both relevant and interesting." *Hannah looks at me a bit disappointed, searching for a way out.*

I don't know. The interview will be very boring, I can't focus on anything specific *(laughs, silence)*.

"I am sure it will be interesting. I have already done a number of these interviews and you can believe me that I always find them interesting, even though no one has changed the world or anything like that" (we both laugh). A few seconds later the telephone rings and Hannah goes to answer it. She returns with a more determined look in her eye.

We will begin with what I do today. I work. This year I was on sabbatical. Now I work in an *ulpan* [Hebrew school for new immigrants], and outside of work, any subject connected to literature is of interest to me. I follow it, I read and participate in literature classes and in literary groups, groups where you read [and I am also] a group leader. The people in the groups come from different backgrounds and interests. The members' level of knowledge is also different, there are many different levels *(hesitates)*. Perhaps it is important for me to have friends, but there are many times when it is not important. I often feel that I don't really try. I get tired of it sometimes and I feel that I need to be alone *(cries)*. But when I am alone, I have the feeling that something is missing after all. That is to say, my life story is different *(mumbles something quietly to herself)*. My family is important to me. I am lucky that I have such a good husband, that I have succeeded from the point of view of family. That is, the children, the relations between us. I think our relations are good *(looks at me)*, a boring story, what can I tell you? *(laughs)*.

It turns out that Hannah does have a life story, but she judges herself harshly as, for example, in her statement "I don't really try." All in all, she sounds positive. Unlike her father, she begins with the present. She works, she is interested in literature, she has a successful family. She has friends who are interested in many different things and wonders how much time she should spend with them, how much time she should give herself. Yet she concludes with the statement: "[It is] a boring story, what can I tell you?" Hannah laughs when she senses my response. Then she falls back into her silence, but this time, she goes on without my prodding. Still, in the beginning it is difficult for me to follow what she is talking about.

It must be very important for me, and I've thought about it a lot. To participate and to listen and to be near, to pay attention. I am also lucky, but it is not only luck, I know. I have also invested a lot of thought and attention. For example, my work in the *ulpan* is very interesting for me because of working with people. It may be because there are different people from all over the world, of all different ages and from all different kinds of interest areas, and I need to hear them all the time. On the other hand, I also get tired of it and I feel that it is hard for me when I feel that I do my job like a robot. If there is a group that I become especially close to, I ask and give and listen and then all of a sudden I feel that I am unable to look at more people *(laughs lightly)*. That's the way it is—the thing and its opposite *(silence)*.

I like Hannah very much. When she talks of herself she is charming, probing deeply into her feelings. The word different *seems to reappear every few sentences, why, I don't yet know. Hannah is trying to explain to herself and to me how she is drawn to working with people until she becomes tired of it. Why does she invest so much in others? I look for a way to elicit her chronological life story. It seems that it is not so important to her.*

"Were you born in Israel?"

No, no, I was born in Germany *(silence)*. About Israel, I really feel that I love this country and I feel as if I am part of it . . . I really feel as if it is my place, like . . . flowers and plants. I belong here, and I really care and I see that things bother me, they really bother me, but I don't see that I do a lot [for it]. Perhaps it will come, and I will feel that I really want to do more than what I . . . I meet a lot of people from outside of the country at work and they speak about all kinds of things. Even when they are right, when they criticize something about Israel, it really annoys me. I don't respond, but I still feel that I care *(silence)*. Who are the other families that you interviewed?

A pattern has already emerged: when Hannah has difficulty saying something about herself, she turns to me with a question. It is interesting how similar Hannah and Ze'ev are in expressing their connection to Israel. They feel that there is something in them that cares, and that annoys them. I ask myself: If the new immigrants' criticisms bother Hannah, is it because she herself identifies with them? I tell her I have met with many different kinds of people.

I know that when my parents arrived in Israel they went to Shaar Ha'aliya, and then they moved to Kiryat Eliezer and later on to Rommema on Mount Carmel. After we had lived for a few years in Rommema, I got married and we moved to upper Nazareth and we lived there for a number of years. Later on we came back, closer to Haifa, and moved to Tivon. My early childhood was in Kiryat Eliezer. I wandered around a lot then *(long silence)*. My first memories are really from Kiryat Eliezer. My parents came there from Germany and there they built, they brought a kind of hut. That is, they brought from Germany a kind of a wooden house. And they brought a factory and I wandered around a lot. I remember that I was the only child, I think. The others hadn't yet . . . everyone there were young couples. And I was the first child and . . . *(tears)*. They spoke Yiddish and I went from house to house and they gave me food. And I know, we went barefoot then, and I think that it was taken for granted that that's the way new immigrants were. Then, I didn't see new immigrants as being something exceptional. It is only now when I see new immigrants, people who come from Russia, and I talk to them and I hear them speaking Yiddish with their children, and then I remember. All of a sudden, these memories arise, memories of my childhood.

My mother had some family here that were long-time residents in Israel. They came, I think, during the second wave of immigration, in the twenties, and they adopted us. They came to receive us and they invited us to Petach Tikva, and I remember that, as a child, I loved visiting there. Now I think it was because their house was much better equipped and furnished. It had more room and swings in the garden and a library and all kinds of things. I remember, when I came, they gave me all kinds of books and stamps and I remember that she was a very beautiful woman. She was older, with silver hair, and I talked to her about Grandmother and Grandfather. She told me that she was willing to be my grandmother if I wanted *(smiles through her tears).* I was very happy with this adoption, and I remember it today when I meet Russian immigrants in their *ulpan* classes. I feel as if there is a sort of meeting. I am becoming sentimental.

Hannah is very emotional and I suddenly have this image, a scene from the movie Avia's Summer. *It now becomes clear that her story also has a past, but it is a painful one, even though she states: "I was very happy with this adoption."*

I have a boy in class who is seventeen, and he talked about how he made his plans to immigrate to Israel. He talked about all kinds of Yiddish songs that he knew in Russia. Then I remember that these were also the songs that I had heard at home *(crying).* My parents, when I think about it today, were really very young after everything they went through. They would talk about it. It's not like, you know, I have heard about families who don't talk about it. They really talked, and when they would meet friends, they would then bring up all kinds of stories. Maybe it was because my father was a partisan. And they would really talk about all kinds of things, they would tell about real stories of heroism. I remember that it was an event for me. As a child, I would sit and listen and they would talk about how a specific case had occurred, how they did those things. My mother's story, she spoke about it a lot. It's interesting. Today, when I try talking to her about it, she is not as willing to talk. Then it was in the family. They talked, they told stories, quite a lot.

"It's strange that your mother talked a lot about it then and that today she isn't willing to talk."

I don't know if it is that she is not really willing to talk. She says that she is not willing to talk, but she does talk about it within the context of story-telling. If we try to ask her formally, then she will say that she is not interested. But I want you to know that she talked a lot at home, and I thought that it was that way in all the homes. I thought that in all the homes, people talked.

Songs in Yiddish and stories of heroism, as well as her mother's stories and silences: the songs belong to her childhood experiences, but Hannah needs to meet a new seventeen-year-old immigrant to remember them, and she tells me about it with tears in her eyes. The stories of heroism belong to her parents; she listened to them as a child, but she doesn't describe what she felt. Perhaps her mother's recent silence is an expression of desperation—that people won't understand her—a desperation that Hannah also feels? Before I can ask another question, Hannah continues.

In connection with my childhood, in Kiryat Eliezer, I was accepted socially. I had girlfriends, and I was in the middle of everything. And then, when we moved to Rommema, I had it a little harder in a social sense, that is, to enter into another social class. I think that the families were of a higher economic class. It was no longer a neighborhood of new immigrants like it was in Kiryat Eliezer, and it was hard for me, the difference. I don't know if I all of a sudden felt more introverted and shyer *(silence)*. This week I read an article by Amos Oz, and he referred to this matter in one sentence and said that in those days, they made all kinds of mistakes. He said that, when the immigrants came and we related to them as if they were people who needed to contribute to the new state, I had the feeling all of a sudden that he was talking about me. I felt insulted *(silence)*.

To call it a crisis? I don't know whether to call it a crisis, but it was a very short period in my life. I think that it went on for two years. Later on, I adjusted to the group, I was in the middle of things and I had friends. I was in the scouts and the whole story. But sometimes I think that when I would meet girlfriends from "old timers' " houses I would still feel . . . feel that my parents didn't know Hebrew well and all that *(she looks at me shyly)*. What else? My life is a pretty routine one. I was in the army, I got married after the army and I began studying.

It is hard for Hannah to say that she is still angry that she was considered to be inferior because she was the daughter of Holocaust survivors who did not speak Hebrew well, was not so well established economically, and was less involved in what was going on. Perhaps it was a crisis for her because, among other things, she heard stories of heroism at home and knew that she was entitled to more, not less. Perhaps that explains her feeling that she does not know how to connect outside and inside.

"You spoke earlier about a feeling of alienation. Is it something that you felt about yourself or about your entire family?"

I think it was everything all together *(silence, tears)*. It was more my feeling, an inner one, and I didn't talk about it. That is, I was never really completely alone. I always had a friend to be with. My father is a more sociable type and likes activity and noise. He relates more to people, he asks and talks. That is his basic personality. But he was simply very busy. He worked very hard and was almost never home. My mother didn't. She worked very hard, but she was at home.

My mother's story, she remained when the Germans arrived in her town. Then, actually, after a period of time she stayed with her sisters, three sisters, and she was the one who actually worried about them, and she stayed there with them during the entire war. When my father married her, he always says that he immediately had three more daughters and afterwards four wives, and that he married them all. In the beginning, they would all come and visit us, but over time . . . that is, to this day I feel that it is very important for my mother, the business about families, everything should be arranged, how the table looks, with all of the dishes and everything else *(cries)*.

But what I remember was that it was very difficult. Because she worked so hard, and no one ever helped her, and she always felt as if she was the victim until it would sometimes take the fun out of it. I think that during the last few years it has become easier. She lets others help her a bit . . . she is a character. I think that she is a classic "Yiddishe mame" in the sense that "I do and I do more and I work and I am falling apart and I . . . " *(silence, tears)*.

Hannah is trying to reflect on her own memories ("It was very difficult") and her mother's (which she may only partly know). Her father is a social type, but he was never home. Her mother had a hard life: during the war she took care of her sisters. Hannah says about her mother that "she always felt as if she was the victim until it would sometimes take the fun out of it."

"Was there any change in the relationship between you and your parents from the time you were a child until now? Was there a change in the atmosphere in the house?" Hannah thinks about it for a while.

No, I don't think so, I don't think that things have changed. I think that it is because of their background, events they experienced, and because I am a girl and not a boy. Their concept of a girl is "be a good girl, be pretty and shut up" *(giggles)*. It is something like that. Perhaps there were times when we had a few conflicts over it but . . . it seems that now, things have calmed down a bit. Perhaps it is because they are getting older. My father had a heart attack and he stopped working. Perhaps it is due to my growing up and my willingness to be more accepting. That is, they are the way that they are, and if they have their special things, it's all right, that's the way they are.

There were times when they would comment about the way I do things, things that they didn't like or that they didn't really agree with. I would get angry, I would try to explain, or I would get into an argument with them. Now I don't . . . but there weren't any dramatic conflicts *(laughs and becomes silent again)*. All kinds of things about approaches to things and views about what needs to be and how things should be, even about the way I relate to my children. Then I listen and I say: "All right" or I smile or I say: "That's it, that's the way it is." That is, I don't argue with them.

"Be a good girl, be pretty and shut up." Hannah feels that she was less valuable in her father's eyes because she was not a son. It now becomes clear whose criticism she has internalized: who complained to her that she was not "focused" enough or "devoted" enough to people and things. Perhaps it is why her story begins in the present; it is only lately that she has begun to work through his criticism, to find work and to lead literary discussion groups. However, she has also come to accept that "they are the way that they are, and if they have their special things, it's all right, that's the way they are."

"Do you remember when you left home?"

No. Sometimes, when I look back, I am really amazed how it was that I never . . . I was never alone and I never needed to make my own decisions and I was always protected *(laughs)*. I don't know whether that is being lucky or not. Really, I sometimes think that it is perhaps lacking in me, perhaps it is even a flaw. I was never, I never faced hard situations when I was by myself and I needed to solve a problem. I can even say that life spoiled me . . . perhaps I lost out on something, in the sense that if I needed to deal with something by myself I would learn something from it.

I remember Ze'ev's comment that, in his mind, "they never left home, they got married and had children." Hannah herself says: "Life spoiled me." Indeed, compared to what her father and mother went through, she was "always protected." She still speaks of herself in the way her parents have defined her. Why have they defined her in that way? Perhaps it is a cover for something they are unable to confront—something that Hannah symbolizes?

"Your name, your sister's name. Do they have any special significance?"

Yes. I am named after my mother's mother and my sister is named after my father's mother, who perished . . . *(silence)*.

"Do you like your name?"

It is possible that I would have preferred a more Israeli-type name, something less ghettolike. But it's not really a problem.

"And your children's names?"

Yes, the same thing. It is really out of respect to my parents. Yoav is named after my father's father. Then his name was Yovush. When Yoav was born, perhaps it really fit him, it's part of being in a family. It was on Shabbat, a Shabbat in February. It was such a beautiful day, a sunny day, and in the nursery in the hospital there were, I think, fifteen people from the family who were waiting for him to be born. My parents, my mother's sister, and my husband's parents, and my uncle's brother. Who wasn't there? It was really something. I don't even remember that I said that I was going to the hospital. Everyone gathered and waited. The first birth in the family after many years . . . and it was a boy *(laughs and cries alternately)*. I am now so worried about him, I am afraid. He is going into the army and it is a difficult unit *(silence)*.

"And the girls' names?"

My eldest daughter is called Shani [Scarlet]. And when she was born, we were looking for a name, and my father came to the hospital and said that he wanted me to call her Yifat [the Yiddish equivalent]. I understood immediately, because he had a sister whose name was Shayna. You know that Shayna means "pretty" in Yiddish. Then he said Yifat or Yafit or something like that. I told him: "Daddy, really, and what will happen if she is ugly?" Then he said: "What are you talking about? I saw her and she is really beautiful!" And then I had a great idea all of a sudden— Shayna is very much like Shani. Yes, then he was very happy, and that makes me feel good because he really liked that name and he is always proud of it. I also think she is pretty. She even tells her girlfriends and they call her affectionately Shayna or Shayndele. That is, I see that it doesn't bother her, rather the opposite. She tells the story. And Raziya [the younger daughter], we called her that just because we thought it was a nice name. All of the grandmothers' names had already been given out because there were a lot of births in the family.

"The stories that your parents told you about the war, about the Holocaust, do you remember listening to them because you wanted to, or was it burdensome?"

No, it was not burdensome. They weren't aimed at us directly either. They would just sit and talk, like you do, when they would meet friends; people that were with them, or when the family would come over. They have a lot of relatives in America. When they would come visit they would always prepare a meal and after the meal they would sit around and my father would tell stories. My father was also thought of as a hero in my family *(silence)*.

"Did you have nightmares because of their stories?"

No, almost never. I am an optimist, I try to see the good side, the nice things inside and outside the house. I am sometimes angry at myself for not being sensitive enough to the pain of others, to what happens to them and to their problems. When I hear about people's problems, I think that perhaps I don't listen enough, I am too detached, I am not . . . *(silence)*.

We part with a warm handshake. Something has happened between us during the hours we have sat together in her garden. Something in Hannah has touched me, and perhaps something in me has touched her as well. Even though we are very different, we also have something in common. On my way to the bus, I realize that the interview ended with the same words with which it began: "I am not . . ." But now Hannah adds the explanation: "I am sometimes angry at myself for not being sensitive enough to the pain of others" and "I am an optimist, I try to see the good side, the nice things inside and outside the house." She seems to move between these two extremes, which perhaps accounts for her frequent use of the word different. *On one side is her "sociable" father, who loves life, and on the other, her more introverted mother, who sees herself as "the victim." And perhaps Hannah moves between them—between being "together" and being "alone." Perhaps her parents' legacy is her feeling that she has no life story of her own, that her parents define her. At the same time, she is trying to construct her life in an optimistic light, one that tries to get closer to people (friends, new immigrants), to participate in literary groups, to be part of and enjoy her family.*

Hannah had no ready-made story to tell, but I feel that she has said a lot, both in words and in the silences between them. After I leave I suddenly realize that Hannah did not talk about herself as a mother. She speaks briefly of her worries about her son, who is going into the army, gives a short description of his birth, and adds a few words about the children's names, but she contributed these details only in response to my questions.[1] I wonder why her mothering is not part of her life story. Is it somehow related to the fact that it has only begun to take shape? Will it include mothering experiences at some later point? She stands in dramatic contrast to Tzipke, who told me at length how different a mother she is to her children than her mother was to her. Hannah does not speak about it at all, although she described the difficulties of her childhood well, and with tearful emotion. Perhaps it is connected to her assessment that "I am not sensitive enough to the pain of others, to what happens to others and to their problems." Does she consider her children to be among these "others"?

I begin thinking ahead to the interview with Hannah's son, Yoav: Will he see himself as a continuation of the stories of heroism and strength associated with his grandfather? Or has he developed the same kind of harsh self-criticism as his mother, to the point of feeling he does not have a life story? Is he a lone wolf or a social animal? Will I find in his story some clues to why Hannah's mothering is not part of her life story? I call Yoav during the weekend and set up an appointment.

Yoav

"Life isn't the time that you are alive but what you do with it"

I return to Tivon a few weeks later to meet Yoav, eighteen. He is between a shower and a friend's party. His room is a mess—typical for a boy his age— with giant posters and a model F-16 airplane that looks as though it is going to land on us at any moment. He is tall, with a full head of hair, warm eyes, and a mischievous look. "Can I offer you something to drink?" He echoes his mother's tone of voice, but he is also trying to create an easygoing atmosphere for the beginning of the interview. After all, there is usually a moment of uneasiness during a first meeting. He seems less uneasy than his mother did.

"I am interested in hearing your life story. Tell me about yourself, about your life." Yoav becomes serious all of a sudden and tries to focus his gaze on a specific point in space.

I am trying to check whether there are really things that influenced my life, special things that happened to me, that helped me to get to where I am today. Shall we begin from the start? I was born into a family, I think, that was pretty normal. The relationships, I won't define them as being ideal, as much as I know and as much as they showed me, and I don't think that they have a lot to hide from me. That is, a family in which all of the ends are closely connected. We give each other compliments. I think that it was expressed to a great extent in my childhood. That is, I was quite spoiled, I got what I wanted more or less, sometimes a little less, sometimes a little more, but I was never denied anything. In the beginning, we lived in Rommema, later on in upper Nazareth. I don't think that there is anything outstanding. I had a completely normal childhood, and as a child what I liked to do a lot was to concentrate on specific hobbies and to know them. That is to say, to become an expert in certain things, if you can call it that. I had an aquarium at a very young age and I knew about all kinds of fish, even about fish I didn't have. I read at a relatively early age and what I read weren't books from school, things that I needed to read. I read about fish in the "professional" literature: names of fish. I mostly recognized them by their pictures and things like that. And before I became interested in fish, I was interested in cars. I think that these were my obsessions: that isn't exactly a life story . . . that is, I am talking about things that interested me.

I nod my head in confirmation that what he is telling me is fine with me and recall Hannah's inability to "focus."

I would identify cars by their wheels. I was a boy that loved keeping myself busy. Perhaps I was hyperactive in a way? Within the limitations of family behavior, I would find myself all kinds of things to keep busy with. I even got carried away sometimes, in the sense of typical interests for a child that age. Perhaps it was to direct my hyperactivity in a more positive direction *(smiles to himself)*. I also hit other children a bit in the kindergarten *(laughs)*. Later on, in the first and second grade, I got into sports, all that energy. Then, I would wander around the neighborhood, play soccer, basketball, whatever came into my hand, and that was what I mostly did. Today I have less time for it. There are things that from a logical viewpoint are higher on my list of priorities: I prefer them to sports. But the moment that I begin playing, I am unable to stop. That is still true today. I would also go out with my friends, with the same friends, because then everybody played soccer. It is as if I dragged my friends into my excitement. I think that I was always involved with people who played a lot of sports. I was obsessive about sports; I would play the entire day.

"Hyperactive," "obsessive": I ask myself where Yoav gets this psychodynamic terminology? I follow the flow of his narrative.

Afterwards, around the sixth grade, I became interested in computers. I put a lot in that, I loved it a lot. That is, I didn't go and study it. I loved to take computer programs, to take them apart and understand them by myself. That gave me a lot of satisfaction, to be able to understand them by myself. I think I also understood them more. I also liked to play a bit, but I liked to make up programs by myself the best. Also here, when I would sit there I couldn't stop, day and night. I didn't have patience for school. I would wait to go home and continue the program.

In addition, I continued with sports. I reached the age when I could get into a competitive group. I began playing tennis—I actually began that in third grade. I was quite serious about it. I was in one of the teams five times a week, three hours each day, and I reached a competitive level. I won a few small awards, and it gave me reinforcement to continue. And when we moved to Tivon, I became more interested in handball, because I thought that I was better at that. I put a lot into tennis, but I wasn't as good at it. I was in the Hapoel All Stars in handball a year after I began playing. I thought that my chances were better there. I also liked it more. I think now, looking back, that the moment that it was a little more difficult for me to get to practice and I saw that I wasn't so good, I stopped playing tennis and became interested in handball. Then, I practiced with two teams, because it wasn't enough for me to practice only with my age group. I played handball every day and . . . I barely saw my girlfriend. When I had a girlfriend or something, they would complain that I didn't have time for them. What interested me was that I was incapable of stopping. I couldn't think—I need to go to my girlfriend, so I won't stay after practice to throw the ball a bit or I won't go to the soccer game. And . . . that's it.

Yoav smiles a wonderful smile and looks at me as if to get confirmation, especially from me, since I am a girl. I smile back, as if being his girlfriend for a moment, and also think to myself that Yoav demands of himself a serious attitude toward everything he does.

I had a crisis from the social standpoint. You must have interviewed my grandfather: he also had crises. However, my crisis was having to move from upper Nazareth to Tivon. In Nazareth, from the social standpoint, it's a kind of incubator where you know everyone. Especially in the seventh grade, there is a class that is actually made up of all the children your age in town. It was a kind of united class, where everyone simply knows everyone else from a very young age and we were all closely connected. In terms of time and closeness, they were like my brothers, because I lived three houses away from them. There isn't too much going on there—we were always together in a group. It was very hard for me to leave them. And what made it more difficult was that here things were so different in all those ways. It seems really unimportant when I look back on it from where I am today.

"For example?"

For example, which clothes you wore there, it was different . . . I never wore, I didn't wear jeans until I came to Tivon. Today it seems strange and weird not to wear jeans. Till today, perhaps, I am still a bit different, I don't look for elegant clothes or for what is in fashion. I simply look for what looks nice to me and is natural, but I am incapable of wearing worn sweat suits. When I came to Tivon, everything that seemed natural to me before changed. Perhaps I am simply different because I underwent so-cialization within a small group. But when I arrived in the seventh grade, all these small details of clothing, and even the way we entertained our-selves and the relationships between the sexes [were important]. I had girlfriends in Nazareth that were . . . there was less going out and having a relationship. I had a lot of friends who were girls and I would go visit them in the afternoons. Just like that, I would go over and go in, it was nice like that. In Tivon, it was very binding, it was special. Perhaps it's not like that now, but in the ages of seventh and eighth grades, it was very committing. They made quite a big deal out of it. In Nazareth, everything is much freer at those ages. Now, when I talk about it, it seems like nothing, but then it was a crisis for me. Those two things together, mostly the difference, but also the separation from my friends in Nazareth. Then, it was quite hard for me.

I think that slowly, slowly in the eighth grade, I got used to things and I fit in. I didn't have a real problem finding new friends; it was more of a problem breaking off from the old ones in Nazareth. In the beginning, I would go to Nazareth on Fridays and every chance I had, I would talk to them on the phone. It is difficult for me to analyze it exactly according to time, but in the end I think that I fit in here quite nicely. I didn't try to push myself into the group or anything like that, I just found my friends and I think that what characterizes me, perhaps, is that I know how to find my friends wherever I am. It's true, I am capable, if I feel something bad toward someone, I tell them directly. It's also a way to get into trouble. If you look at what is written about me at school, I think that I was one of the more conspicuous ones in the history of the school, because I always needed to say something. That is, I couldn't keep quiet about things that I didn't think were right. I was thought of as being mischievous, yes, but on the other hand, I was never rude to a teacher and I never picked up a chair, even though I wanted to. In the army, I understand that I will need to keep that under control, but in school I simply thought that I could talk. Because of that, I think that the people I didn't get along with—I had no problem breaking off the relationship in a way that I think was relatively respectable. I am very happy over the friends I found here, and I still keep in contact with my good friends from Nazareth, and in that way I enjoy both worlds. And all in all, it was a very positive move from my point of view.

I listen intently to Yoav and wonder how many eighteen-year-old boys are so outspoken about themselves. The crisis caused by the move in seventh grade, the way Yoav describes it, including the jeans and the girlfriends and boyfriends—how he saw it then and how he sees it today, and how I see it.

Here there are more possibilities, because at a certain stage, in the eighth and ninth grade, people feel strangled in Nazareth. In the tenth grade I went into high school. In terms of studies—I continued with the handball with great intensity—from the study aspect it was simply a waste of three years. I didn't do anything in school. Every now and then I would become motivated over some test because of my parents, but on the whole, I didn't study for tests. I didn't go to classes I didn't think were important, like Arabic, which I quit in the middle of the year. I would go and play handball.

"Were you pressured at home to study?"

No, that is, my report card wasn't bad, because there were a lot of kids like me and the pace was very slow and there wasn't any problem making up missed work. So, I didn't have a terrible report card and my parents didn't think that I was mixed up in a bad crowd or anything like that. They just didn't bother me. Every now and then they threw out something and I related to what they said. They more or less directed me, they didn't allow me to really mess up in school. I was a pretty good student. Perhaps I could have gotten better grades, but it wasn't that important. In addition, in handball I was on the All Stars at one stage. It was one of the high spots for me. Now, it doesn't seem important any more, but then it interested me a lot, the fact that I was in the Hapoel All Stars. That is the name of the National Youth Handball All Stars Team. At one point, I was taken out. There was supposed to be a trip abroad at the end of the year and the All Stars coach didn't let me go. He had very different theories than my coach here. And I admired my coach here and I admired the other one less.

It seems that, for the first time, Yoav is searching for words.

I liked it a lot. I thought it was an honor, and I wanted to be there, but I guess that I wasn't good enough, and I thought up all sorts of excuses. It heightened my motivation to play, to train. All in all, handball became the most important thing and I played it all day long. For me, it was the most important thing because we got into the national play-offs and then . . . that was also a high spot, I think, in comparison to what you will find in this family. In short, these are the sort of things that I was busy with in my childhood, all of these things connected to sports.

"A high spot . . . in comparison to what you will find in this family." I wonder whom Yoav is competing with, his grandfather? his father? Yoav moves uneasily in his chair. He is looking for a way to get over his embarrassment and change the subject.

Girls, I always had girlfriends, but there was never anything serious. Every now and then I had girlfriends and every now and then something short term would develop with someone, but it was never really serious. Perhaps it was because I didn't want to be obligated. I was once in love with a girl who was also in love with me. That was also one of my high spots, because I was in love with her for a long time. At some point, she asked me to go out with her. I got very excited and I made a lot of blunders on the date. To this day that girl has a lot of very funny stories about that date. In the end, after two or three dates, she made it clear to me that it had no future *(looks at me with an embarrassed look)*.

Now I have a girlfriend whom I have loved very much for a year and a half, and I think that she has given me relative peace. She is influential in my life. She calmed me down a lot in terms of my hyperactivity. It is as if, when you are nervous or something like that, instead of going to play handball or getting irritated, you sit quietly and talk to someone. You know that if you get annoyed at her, she will get annoyed at you and it won't be good. Somehow or other I learned to control myself. Perhaps it is also a matter of maturity, perhaps it is both of them. And . . . that's it.

Yoav returns to his stream-of-consciousness speech and the warm look comes back to his eyes.

In terms of school, the important decision I made at the end of the tenth grade was to go into the sciences. It is hard for me to remember why I decided to do that, but I think it is because I thought it would be easy for me. They gave us psychometric tests and they directed me to that program based on the results, to the science program. But I don't think that it is representative. If I was to think of it ahead of time, I would have gotten much higher grades if I had studied literature. I would also have had an easier time if I had studied biology. I thought that perhaps I have a mathematical head. I am not sure about that to this day. I was with the kids in the science program, and it is hard for me to compare myself to them, because I didn't work as hard. But my grades were pretty good in the end. I came with a great deal of enthusiasm to the science program and slowly my enthusiasm dampened and disappeared.

"My enthusiasm dampened and disappeared." Now I begin to think how often that refrain appears in Yoav's story.

When the matriculation exams came, and it was clear that they would come, they came when a lot of damage had already been done, and it was hard to correct it. In any case, it was hard to correct it in the twelfth grade. I actually tried hard, that is to say, I studied a lot harder, in a way that I thought I wasn't capable of, and I tried to make up for all of the gaps left from the eleventh grade *(sighs)*. When I summarize my twelve years of study, I think that the school in Nazareth gave me a lot from the educational point of view. There were teachers there who were important. They shaped my character in terms of the atmosphere that they created and all kinds of values that they gave me. Later on, from the eighth to the tenth grade, actually through the eleventh grade, I didn't do anything. It was a waste of four years. The state of Israel spent money on me and it was simply a waste. I think that the twelfth grade was a year of maturity. First of all, I needed to see how I stood up to the pressure. How I manage with the schedule and all kinds of things like that. I think I got better. I am sure that if I was to do my matriculation exams of twelfth grade now, I would get better grades just from the lessons I have learned.

In addition, in the middle of the twelfth grade, the army began inviting me. I think that it is an important thing in life. Should I tell you how things went? I was accepted into a certain unit and I really didn't know what I wanted to do. At a certain point, the idea came up that I would go into a pre-army academic program. But I rejected that idea because I knew I couldn't decide what I wanted to study. Perhaps there was also an unconscious reason, that I didn't have the desire to work for good grades. When I needed to make the decision, it was in the eleventh grade, I was in the middle of my bad grades. I thought, what kind of change do I need to make now? Perhaps I decided not to go into the program out of laziness, perhaps due to my lack of belief in myself.

I don't have any idea what I want to be today either. I got all kinds of invitations that I passed up. The air force and the radio station passed me up. Later on, I got invited to the reconnaissance unit, to what is called an orientation course. During the orientation, they filter out people mostly based on your physical ability to stand up to pressure. They try a little bit to tear you to pieces and to see how you stand up to it. If you are really in good physical shape and you have a little bit of ability to withstand pain, you pass. So I passed the orientation. Looking back, after I went through the orientation it seemed as if it was easy. There were some pretty hard parts, but I never thought for one second that I would quit. I knew that I would finish. It's like a handball game where you need to run a little and you know that you won't stop running all of a sudden.

Later on, they sort you into three reconnaissance groups. The first one is thought of as being the best, and the other two are made up of those who passed, but for some reason or another aren't suitable for the first. That is, there are those who were accepted straight away. Most were cut out and didn't finish out the day. That is to say, approximately half didn't finish out the day, and many got an invitation to the two other groups. The rest went to a psychologist. The psychologist was supposed to cut those who were a little sick, those who weren't suitable. Now, I had an "anti" approach to the first group. They seemed to me to be fanatics. It's nonsense, I simply didn't try to find out anything and like an idiot, I went and told the psychologist that I was against it. They gave me a question-naire and told me to list what I thought my good and bad points were. I thought I was pretty disorganized. I don't know whether it's easy to know but I don't always think about things and I don't always manage with time. And organization as well, that is to say, to organize things . . . I don't know how to explain it to you. For example, even to draw a picture. You see that there is no order in my head.

I wrote all of that and he understood it. If I had wanted to go [into the best group] then I would have written down other characteristics that would have helped me get in. I would make up something, the way a lot of people make up characteristics. He asked me about these things: "What does it mean that you are disorganized?" I told him that I don't manage well with time. After all I didn't want to lose out on everything, I wanted to get into the third group. It was a unit I had heard a lot about. I was also a bit unwilling to take responsibility. I thought that I was in good shape and that it wouldn't be hard for me there. So I told him that I would overcome those faults with willpower if he would send me to the specific unit I wanted to get into. So he took me out of the first, but he didn't throw me out altogether. He gave me the two others as options. I was sure that I would get what I wanted, every third word I mentioned that unit. After a while, I got invited to the orientation for the second unit. I was depressed for two days and then I decided that I would try and see what it was like, and I went to that orientation.

I enjoy the combination of naiveté (the presentation of his faults to the psychologist), his desire to get exactly what he wanted, alongside his acceptance of the decision when he did not get it. Yoav smiles at me in return, as if he perceives my thoughts.

During the orientation, in the beginning, I felt great. I don't like giving up on challenges, that is to say, I can't stop something [I've started]. Even a game. For example, I can play tennis with someone who will tear me to pieces. And let's say I know that later on, that person will go and tell others that he destroyed me and everything else. I can't stop and say that I don't feel well. I have to finish the game. So I said I have to finish the orientation and see what it's like.

In the beginning I felt really good and I enjoyed everything. At a certain point they tried to tear us apart, that is, to push us to the limit of our physical abilities and see how we cope. On the first day, those who weren't in good shape fell and I felt good about it. Later on, it began to be hard for me. The hardest point was when I became dehydrated. It was a little bit disappointing because I thought that it was near the end. After the first two days, each time that I had it hard I looked back at what I had done up till then, that I am in good shape, and I am going to finish the orientation. I thought that if I don't fail in the middle, when about two thirds quit, then I would pass.

Then I got dehydrated. I had a few tears in my eyes and I said that it was a shame about all that effort. They gave me an infusion and I tried to get back in. It was hard for me to return, and I think that they saw the tears. Those leaders there were really something special! I have all kinds of reasons for joining that unit, but if I try to be honest with myself, one of the reasons for being one of them is because they simply personified perfection. In the path-finding as well, you couldn't see a meter in front of your face and they ran. You run behind them. But the thing that amazed me the most, it is simply something internal, that they took such good care of us. On one hand, they brought us to the limits of our ability and on the other, you felt taken care of, you felt that they were paying attention to you. At a certain point I didn't know that I had become dehydrated, because I had never become dehydrated before. You always feel shitty, excuse the word. You don't know—whether you are acting spoiled or whether you are really sick—that something isn't right.

They also looked for leadership, and the leader gave me some things to do. He gives someone responsibility over some activity, and in the beginning I was pretty good at it. Later on, he gave me an activity and I didn't really hear what he said, and I didn't really see him when he talked to me. He saw that I wasn't . . . that I was confused. So he sat me down on the side. I didn't know what was happening with me at that moment. I don't really remember, I don't remember a lot of it. He sat me down in the shade for about twenty minutes. I had a pulse of 110, they got worried and they took me to the clinic right away. I got the infusion there and that's it.

I tried to go back afterwards. I didn't think about whether I was going to finish or not. I said that I had to try to go on. I still didn't feel well, and I didn't know what to tell them once again, because I didn't know if that's the way you feel after you have been dehydrated. They asked me if I wanted to continue and I yelled yes, but I really wanted to yell no. At a certain point I demanded to see a doctor, because I felt that if I would take three more steps, I would die. I am not saying that in order to make an impression, I just felt like I had never felt before.

Let's say, I would also fall in handball and it hurt me. Here, it wasn't pain, it was a kind of . . . no strength, no mental strength either. I simply could not think, I felt nothing. I felt that something wasn't right because it wasn't unimportant. I guess that I had a high fever, so they brought me back and in the end they admired it, because I passed.

I got a bit carried away in the description of the orientation, because it was terrible, it was terrible. There is a lot more, I really cut out some parts of the story. They also asked us not to talk about it. I got carried away a bit anyway.

"I got a bit carried away," Yoav apologizes. Then he looks at me proudly.

Now I look at everything differently. Let's say, when I got back from the orientation, it was a turning point. I felt really good about myself. It is impossible to describe, it is simply a kind of exaltation. It is not haughtiness over others, I didn't feel that I was better than them. But I felt as if I didn't care about the others; do I care about what they'll say? A lot of things seemed to be so unimportant. Perhaps I am exaggerating, maybe the orientation wasn't so hard. But it seemed to me as if it was an effort and that I am capable of doing so much. You can ask my parents about me at that time. For example, I would get up in the morning and I wouldn't go back to sleep. I would wash the car, work in the garden, things like that.

"You can ask my parents." He is such an innocent, even now when he is about to enlist.

On the one hand I want to enlist already and it's not because I love it. It is just worthwhile to begin already, because I am unable to really enjoy anything else. I was on a wonderful vacation at the Achziv Beach on the Mediterranean. It was a feeling of complete vacation, of independence. But it wasn't quite right. It is as if there is something that is coloring all of my pleasures and something that is coloring my disappointments. Because I know that everything is really nothing in comparison to what I am going to go through, from the point of view of difficulty as well as from the point of view of the things that I am going to get out of the military experience.

The course is very difficult, but I am going because I know that I will get things, that they invest a lot in each soldier there. And I am going to work on my character in a way that other people won't have a chance. To acquire all kinds of traits, perhaps skills that are a bit military in nature. These are things that others won't know how to do, that I simply wouldn't get the chance to do if I was to go and be a lawyer or something like that. Parachuting and things like that.

What do you live for all in all? I look at life differently than other people, not only in relation to the army. In general, I don't think that I make a big deal out of life. Let's say, I don't want to die or anything like that, I love life a lot. But, in my opinion, life isn't the time that you are alive but what you do with it. Because you can live for thirty years and be a nobody. It is not that I am belittling it, but every person has his own emotional experiences, his ups and downs. You can even be a respected lawyer who has this case and that case. It's a kind of perspective.

"Life isn't the time that you are alive but what you do with it." What a statement! I am stunned at his sudden maturity. I am listening to Yoav and recall his grandfather, Ze'ev. Didn't I hear a similar approach to life from him? Yet Yoav allows himself to talk about the things that weren't so successful, and about his weaknesses and his own feelings in relation to these things.

I am going to retract, I just wanted to say: it makes me tense, I am afraid, I am afraid of the difficulty. I am not so energetic, that is to say, I was better than average in sports due to my natural abilities. For example, during a game or a training session when it was very hard for me, there were always people who broke before me, and because of them we needed to stop the practice. It was also hard for me, but I never reached my limits. That is the reason why in general, there aren't any athletes in units like those, because they're not used to such effort. It is actually those who weren't such good athletes that tried harder, that are more emotionally used to trying hard. I am really afraid of the effort, I am not afraid of the other things. I have a friend who is enlisting on the day that I enlist. It seems that he is going to go into the parachuters. He was also in the orientation. He is a very good person and he broke at some point. He is still sorry about it. He says that simply at one point he got up and said that he couldn't go on. I also had moments like those. There was a very thin line between the part where you decide to stop or go on. Almost by chance, I passed that thin line and he didn't. He went back home, but he thinks a lot about the army.

One night we talked until the morning about the army because I found someone who understood me. Put simply, he was nervous like I was. For as much as people are close to me, I find out that they don't understand. I tell them, for example, that I am afraid of the unit . . . that is, that I am nervous about it. "You have nothing to be afraid of, you will get through it, you will be accepted, you will finish the course." Things like that. They don't understand that that is not the problem.

(Yoav turns to me) Do you understand what I am talking about? I am afraid that once again I will reach a point that is beyond my capabilities. It is just a horrendous feeling. It's a feeling that you can't take another step and you do it anyway. I don't know how to explain it. It is just the first time that I felt it [was] when I was in the orientation. Perhaps people who have been through more things will make sense of what I am saying. I always think about it . . . I get up in the morning and go brush my teeth, so go faster! It's like a test, and you have no strength, and I want to go slowly, then go faster. It's like you are always being tested. I give myself small tests of willpower. It is all the time, it doesn't leave me, it doesn't allow me to really enjoy my freedom. I can't call it freedom, it's more of a short break. I am talking too much because these are the feelings that I have difficulty expressing in words or in numbers. I was a pretty mischievous child and I was curious and I did [things], all kinds of small stories but, as of yet, no big events have happened to me.

"As of yet, no big events have happened to me"—I wonder what Yoav expects from himself? Does he compare himself to his grandfather and what he went through in the partisans? Up to now, he has not talked about it openly. I try to ask him about his relationship to his grandparents.

Which grandparents do you mean? I never tried to analyze it, but I can't take them separately, it's just that the Holocaust must appear. Because my grandmother and my grandfather on my mother's side, it's as if they need to help us. It's as if they are obligated to us, they need to come and take care of us, Grandma needs to come and clean and she needs to come and cook, she needs to send us food. The other grandma doesn't need to. We visit them [his father's parents] every now and then on holidays. We eat at their house every now and then on Shabbat. I like

Grandma's cooking very much. It is very subtle, it's on a high level. I love them very much, they are nice, gentle people. But they are not as warm as my mother's parents. They do a lot for us. I call that grandma after tests. That is to say, I need to call. I enjoy it as well, I know that it makes them feel very good when I phone. I also call her when I am on a trip so that she won't worry. When I went to Germany, of course I called Grandma and Grandpa. It helped them a lot.

"Did they mind that you went?"

I don't think they minded. They got used to the idea. They simply separate it. It's not that they forgot. They remember every now and then and then they talk about it. They talk about it with a lot of excitement and they really live it. But they separate going to Germany today and doing shopping there and things like that. They don't try to even the score and . . .

Yoav talks about "it," but he hardly brings up the word Holocaust. *I ask him if he has a problem with "it," and Yoav becomes serious all of a sudden.*

I had a problem and I still have a problem with it. I went to Germany with a handball team to a training camp. We were in northern Germany and we were hosted by German families in their homes. So my family was very nice and they had an old grandfather who was very nice. But you always think, nice, what was he doing forty years ago? That is, you need to give everybody a chance. When I met those people, that family, I liked them a lot. Yes, and I felt admiration for their hospitality. They were very good hosts. But I think that even in connection with them there was a sort of feeling that they needed to atone for something. It sounds like something big, but they went out of their way with their hospitality. The way that they took us in seemed like they were trying to be overly nice.

Of course, the subject of the Holocaust didn't come up. There may have been moments, but I really don't remember details. It was when I was in the eighth grade and I only remember that I recoiled from the Germans. Let's say that I don't like them. Perhaps it is unconscious. I see those Germans, I don't say "Nazis," "disgusting people," or "murderers," but I am afraid of them. Somehow, it is connected to my unconscious [thought] of what once happened. I won't feel that way about other Europeans, do you understand? It must be something unconscious that causes someone to feel that you don't like him, that you have something against him. I have something against the Germans. I won't boycott them and I may buy their products. But I feel that I recoil from them. I am just not crazy about them.

I ask myself if I am permitted to tell him that I am not crazy about the Germans either but decide to refrain. I suggest that we go back to his grandparents.

I am already getting into the psychology of other people. Grandma has to do things for her whole family. That is more important than anything else. Do you understand? I also think that the family is important, but she gets carried away sometimes. For example, my cousin and me, I was very busy with my matriculation exams and I wasn't in contact with her. I didn't talk to her on the phone. When I see her, I feel open and I think that we get along quite well with one another. And Grandma, it is very important for her . . . "Did you talk to Na'ama today?" My cousin's name is Na'ama. "And please call Na'ama, she loves you so much, and it's so important to me for the two of you to talk to one another." And that is one of her principles. Grandma is a calm person, but this is something that can drive her crazy. And when you think about the big things that didn't drive her crazy, and this little thing [and], I didn't answer her with disrespect. I said: "Okay, Grandma, I have a test. We'll see about it later on." I didn't really promise and that made her furious. She is not obsessive, she is indirectly obsessive.

I laugh out loud and Yoav joins in. He has just invented a new psychological concept pertaining to Holocaust survivors without really meaning to: "indirectly obsessive."

She won't tell you "Do this or that," but she is capable [of making you], since you love her and you don't want her to get angry, of getting you to do them. And that gives me an unpleasant feeling, because I don't keep in contact with my cousin only in order to fulfill my obligations to my grandmother. She thinks that it is terrible, that family is just above and beyond, it is very important for her and it agitates her a lot.

So that's it . . . I got carried away again *(laughter).* I just never had the chance to talk about my family in this way, to analyze them.

During the last few years, my mother's sister has started coming to the seders: they have it one year with us and one year with their other side. They are very happy and it is very nice having the seder with them. It also widens the seder. It's nice when there are more people, good food, a nice atmosphere, yes. It's not that I look forward to it, but it's nice going to the seder. Every now and then, my father's brother also comes. They usually go to the other side of their family. I love my father's brother very much. I like it very much when they celebrate the seder with us. There is more atmosphere, a lot of humor, and then Grandpa tries to read seriously, and that is very funny, because he does it humorously. He goes into a trance all of a sudden and begins to read seriously. And he skips words and . . . we don't laugh at him, but he's the type that is sometimes serious and sometimes not.

Yoav is beaming and I try to imagine Ze'ev reading "humorously."

Mother always tries to get us to sing. She loves that a lot. Everyone tries to get the others to do what they want, Father with his jokes, and my sister and I sit there and enjoy everything going on. I think that we get along very well. I don't want it to change. I love my sisters. I also love my parents, but it's just a relationship. My sisters and I have gone through so many things together, the little experiences, the stories and games of children. Raziya, my younger sister, there is an age difference between us, but even with that, it makes me feel very good to be with her. She makes me feel grown-up. And Shani, my middle sister, is my friend. She tells me things, we think alike, we think the same things are funny. It's enough for the two of us to look at one another at one of those meals and to laugh and understand one another. I know that she is also good at keeping secrets. Not that I have a lot of family secrets, but if I need her to do something for me, she will do anything for me. She has no problem covering up for me. I don't use it a lot, but I know that I always have someone on whom I can depend. Friends come and go, but the family remains. Even though some of my friends are just like family. My relationship with my sister is a little more [serious].

This time, it is difficult for me to say good-bye. I stay a while longer and Yoav shows me his awards from his handball and tennis games. When we part, I get a warm handshake from him, and he thanks me for the interesting conversation. "It's me who needs to thank you," I answer him with a smile. I leave the house and step into the clear summer air. The sky is full of stars. I can still hear him saying clearly: "Friends come and go, but the family remains." On my way to the bus, I try to remember the questions I had at the beginning of the conversation.

Yoav has really surprised me. His telling of his life story flows so well compared to that of his mother. There is something so free, open, optimistic, and naive about him, which I was not prepared for after my interviews with Ze'ev and Hannah. Even if someone wished to connect his desire to prove himself "in real tests" to his grandfather's partisan past, one could assert that every Israeli-born child has this wish; it is not necessarily related to the Holocaust. On the other hand, Yoav has a love of life. This is what makes him so appealing and why he seems to embody Ze'ev's lessons.

I return to Hannah's mothering. I feel the need to go back to her and tell her: "It is not possible that a son like Yoav came from a background that was lacking a 'mother figure.' After all, it is you who provided the conditions that allowed him to be so free, so sensitive. Why can't you take the credit for what you did?" I try to imagine the two of them sitting in the garden, or in his room, and I realize that Yoav talks very little about his parents, except for his statement that his is a "normal family." I conclude that perhaps some things are so clear, there is no reason to bring them up when one is telling one's life story.

THE LIFE STORY VERSUS THE LIFE HISTORY

We began with a question: "What influences one's life story?" Is there a clear association between the life history and the life story, or are they independent of each other? Is the biography one constructs embedded in the events one has experienced, or is there some other motivating force? In Ze'ev's and Genia's case, we have already noted that they are the same age and from similar family and Jewish backgrounds, even though they were born in different parts of eastern Europe. Both lost most of their family in the Holocaust and survived due to their own ingenuity. In both cases, the traumatic event erupts and floods their life story. However, while Genia spent most of the war in Majdanek and Auschwitz, including the horrific section called "Canada," Ze'ev escaped from Vilna to the forest and fought with the partisans. Both got married immediately after the war and immigrated to Israel in the late forties with a daughter, who was born in Germany. Both raised families in Israel. One can assert that both families are socially and economically stable. In fact, Genia and Ze'ev can look back with pride on what they have achieved, all rebuilt within two generations.

Up to this point, the life histories of Genia and Ze'ev are similar. How have these histories colored their life stories and those of their children?

It becomes clear here that Genia and Ze'ev are telling two very different life stories. Even though Genia was extremely resourceful in very difficult situations, she is preoccupied with the harshness of events: the brutality of the camps, the screams of the children before they went into the gas chambers. Her awareness tortures her, and she feels guilty and responsible because her children have paid the price. In contrast, Ze'ev focuses on the things he did here and there, which include fighting with the partisans, revenging himself on the citizens of the town where he was born after the war, and struggling to make a living in Israel. He is proud of the possibilities he has created for his daughters and his grandchildren. Through them, he feels the sense of belonging he has succeeded in building for himself in Israel. Images of death color Genia's prewar memories. Her life story actually begins with her mother's death from cancer when she was seventeen years old. In comparison, Ze'ev has pleasant, almost idyllic memories of prewar family life and his extended family, until the war came and swept it all away.

It is possible to assert that Ze'ev's wartime history as an active fighter has given the biography he constructs an optimistic resilience. For Genia, in contrast, life in the camps—the helplessness and the suffering that characterized her time there—has colored her story, and caused her to see things from a basically negative point of view. For both, a significant segment of their life history, in their case, what happened to them during the Holocaust, dictates and colors their life stories. Still, this assertion is incomplete: we sense in Ze'ev's concluding words an undertow of fear related to Yoav's military service, which suggests that his activist approach to life perhaps suppresses other, more difficult issues that are only coming up now.

Even if this assertion were true, we could ask whether it is also validated in the life stories of the younger generations. For example, do Tzipke and her daughter Ganit tend to tell their life stories in the negative manner reminiscent of Genia? And do Hannah and her son, Yoav, have the opposite tendency due to Ze'ev's more positive way of looking at the world? It is, of course, impossible to expect a totally consistent continuation: among other things, each generation's life story is also affected by those of other family members (Genia's husband, Ze'ev's wife, Hannah's and Tzipke's husbands), who each have an independent impact on the life stories of the younger generations. However, if we include other factors, the matter becomes more complicated.

If we compare Tzipke's and Hannah's life stories, we discover that they have a lot in common, starting with the difficulties of making a living and adjusting to the Israeli context as children of refugees in the Israel of the fifties. They both married young and focused on raising their children, and they began their professional careers only after the children had grown up. Beyond these similarities, we found that it was more difficult for Hannah to tell (and probably also to reconstruct) her own biography. Next to her father's heroic past, her life experiences appear bland. In addition, she was the daughter of a father who wanted a son and expected her to "be pretty and shut up." Tzipke's confrontation with an abusive mother, who woke her up in the middle of the night to hang up her clothes and pressured her about her studies and eating habits, caused her to rebel, to enter into an open struggle with her parents and, as a result, to construct a life story of her own earlier than Hannah was compelled to do.

One could suggest that the cycle would reverse itself in the next generation: Tzipke succeeded in freeing herself of the burden of her mother's terrifying memories, while Hannah did not manage to escape the dominance of her father's heroic tales from the war. However, there is no such simple, "dialectic" explanation. Perhaps it was the failure of her teenage son's rebellion that has allowed Tzipke over the last few years to work through what she once fought against. Tzipke first reacted to her negative childhood experiences in the way that she has raised her children. She has also tried to make her own way by directing her son's studies, by celebrating her children's bar-mitzvahs in her own way, and by trying to find a way to balance her children's right to privacy and the family's gathering together on Shabbat. The only ones she is still overly protective toward are her aging parents: there, the old dependence-counterdependence pendulum has prevailed, fueling new expressions of the previous patterns.

Hannah does not speak about being a mother at all in talking about her life, which comes as a surprise in view of Yoav's lively story. It seems as if Hannah has begun to reconstruct a positive life story only from what she has recently initiated: working with literary groups and teaching new immigrants. In so doing, she has learned to live and think as someone independent of her father's history. It is, however, a fragile process; she still doubts her ability to succeed. Her interview begins and ends with the words "I am not . . ." She still responds to her painful past experiences with tears. She may also be less verbal than Tzipke. It is clear, after listening to Yoav, that she has navigated quite successfully between her father and her son, but she does not give herself credit for it.

Above and beyond the similarity of their life histories, actions, and reactions, the second generation also share what we might call a cyclic counterreaction to the histories and stories of their parents, the first generation. This reaction is intertwined with their own attempts to develop an independent approach, combining their early reactions and the beginnings of introspection to construct a separate life story. For both Tzipke and Hannah, this independence has developed at a relatively late stage.

What happens in the third generation? As a rule, the grandchildren have not yet developed an orderly life story; it is still in its beginning stages. Here, as in Genia's and Ze'ev's case, part of the difficulty in finding commonalities arises from the fact that we are comparing the life stories of a man and a woman. We all know how different the expectations of society are toward men and women, especially during the period of army service in Israel. It is precisely against this background that Yoav's life story, which is full of incident and experience, flows: it is a combination of a hopeful and youthful naiveté and subtle and complex analysis uncharacteristic of a boy his age.

Both Ganit and Yoav are trying to find their way in the contemporary Israeli context, overcoming the uprootedness of their grandparents without dissociating themselves from that heritage. Ganit does not tell her story chronologically: for her, the past is almost nonexistent. Instead, she examines her present reality in an open, but detached manner and hopes only for a better future. In this she is relating emotionally to her grandmother Genia's life story, and she brings in nice details of her grandmother's youth (her beauty, her mother's love of opera) that were hardly mentioned by her mother and grandmother. Yoav's love of life, his competitiveness, his search for the meaning of life, and his sociability are characteristic also of his grandfather. It is possible to see Yoav's emphasis on action, his search for "high spots," and the tests of strength and ability he puts himself through as a continuation of—or even a competition with—Ze'ev. Is it also the antithesis of his mother's self-doubt or her proclaimed optimism or both? It is interesting that Ganit and Yoav hardly mention their parents with any frequency in their narratives. As we have noted, at this stage in their lives they cannot yet incorporate the complexity of their parents' viewpoint. Ganit identifies emotionally with parts of her grandmother's story; she also possesses some of the shrewd, almost painful awareness that characterizes Genia.

The connection between the life stories of the first and third generations should not be viewed as circular, but rather as spiral. Ganit reacts to Genia's recollections of helplessness by stating that the past "cannot be fixed." Yoav does not try to repeat his grandfather's heroic or vengeful actions. Both live in a new Israeli reality, where the younger generation creates continuity by searching for significance in their own lives while simultaneously relating to what happened two generations previously. In this context, working through means going on reconstructing one's own biography in the present context by examining (rather than denying) the experiences and reactions of former generations.

Ganit and Yoav have not initiated their open search for meaning and significance out of nowhere: Tzipke and Hannah must have helped them find their way, probably with the help of their spouses. Tzipke has developed an active, thoughtful strategy, navigating her way between Genia and Ganit, two generations that are so different in relating life story to life history. It seems that Hannah has moved between Ze'ev and Yoav more intuitively, but she cannot reflect on it within the frame of her life story and will not take credit for doing so. Yet if either had done so in an unintelligent and insensitive way, it might have alienated the younger generation from their "irrelevant" grandparents. Tzipke and Hannah have acted out of their own conscious or unconscious wish to provide their children with loving grandparents. With the Holocaust in the family's background, they have tried to prevent family tragedies reminiscent of Eskimo myths, in which the fate of the elders is to "go and die in the snow" all alone.

The psychological literature about the children of Holocaust survivors is full of descriptions of this generation as carriers of the pain and suffering that is still so alive in their parents. Yet Tzipke and Hannah show that this is only partially true. From their self-structured stories we learn that they not only reacted to the first generation's emotional burden, they also successfully activated a strategy between the generations. Each woman developed her own way, but for both of them it was important that their children would be close to their grandparents without having to take on the emotional burden they carried during their own childhood. Ganit's and Yoav's stories make it clear that their mothers succeeded to no small degree.

As we have seen, there is no simple relationship between the life story and the life history. While the life history frames the experience recounted in the narrative, the relationship between them may take many different routes through the generations. We can identify a pattern of action and reaction, but we also find that new approaches to issues have been identified and worked through. Love for children and for aging parents, although complicating things, has also motivated and enabled this resilience and inventiveness. It may separate life story from life history, but it brings them back together in new ways over time.

3

THE ANISEVITCHES

Out of the Warsaw Ghetto

with Noga Gil'ad

O f the first generation, Olga is the youngest person we interviewed. She is from a "mixed" family and survived thanks to her mother, who sent the child to her gentile father on the Aryan side of Warsaw when she lost hope in the ghetto. Olga, remaining loyal to her Jewishness, joined a kibbutz in Poland at the end of the war and eventually immigrated to Israel. She and her husband, a work camp survivor, settled as pioneers in a *moshav* (cooperative settlement) in the southern part of the country, where Olga is still living. Her husband died of cancer eight years ago.

Olga

"To rebuild life"

We meet Olga at the entrance to her house in a moshav *near a large army camp in southern Israel. She is a small woman, and her face and hands are lined with wrinkles. She invites us into the house, modest, yet well cared for. It is densely furnished in the well-known "Israeli–Eastern European" style, which seems to spell out to you as you enter: "Material goods are not the main thing." On the telephone Olga answered our request positively: "Yes, my daughter Dina has already informed me—you are the researchers from the university." Now she is more emotional: "I know that after such a conversation, I don't sleep so well at night." However, when she turns toward us after serving the coffee, her warm, wise eyes seem to say: "We've been*

ANISEVITCH FAMILY CHRONOLOGY

1930	Olga is born in Warsaw.
1933	Yadek, her brother, is born.
1934	Her parents divorce. Her (gentile) father leaves with Yadek.
1935	Her mother remarries.
1936	Her grandmother visits Israel.
1939	Her mother gives birth to a daughter.
1940	Her stepfather, an officer in the Polish army, escapes to Russia.
1942	Her grandmother commits suicide in the ghetto.
1943	Olga is smuggled out to her father in the Aryan section of Warsaw.
1945	Olga runs away from her stepfamily to a village, where she stays until liberated by the Russians.
1945–48	Olga joins a kibbutz in Kalisz and eventually immigrates to Israel.
1949	Olga works at a police station in Haifa, where she meets Baruch. They marry.
1950	Olga and Baruch move to a *moshav* (cooperative settlement) in the south.
1951	Dina, a daughter, is born.
1954	Dvora, a daughter, is born.
1957	Benny, a son, is born.
1960	Baruch contracts tuberculosis and gives up farming.
1968	Dina studies at the teacher's training college.
1970	Dina marries Yehoshua; they move to Yeruham.
1974	Orit, a daughter, is born to Dina and Yehoshua.
1977	Gideon, a son, is born to Dina and Yehoshua.
1982	Yadek, Olga's brother, immigrates to Israel. Baruch dies of lung cancer. Amnon, a son, is born to Dina and Yehoshua.
1986	Dina, Yehoshua, and family move to Lehavim, on the outskirts of Beer-Sheva.
1988	Olga visits Poland with her friend Shimon and her granddaughter Orit.
1989	*Spring:* Noga Gil'ad and Dan Bar-On interview Olga and Benny, Dina, and Orit.

through so much, we'll survive this too." This look gives Noga and me the
courage to begin the interview. [Dan Bar-On asks the questions throughout.]

So, I was born in 1930 in Warsaw, Poland. My family was mixed and
I had a very happy childhood.

What do you mean, a "mixed" family?

Ah, my mother was from a religious Jewish family, really religious, not
just traditional, and my father was a gentile, a Pole. When I remember
the—my parents were already separated. They divorced when I was three.
Actually I really remember my home with my second father, whom my
mother married when I was five. He was Jewish—both of them were
assimilated. At home I wasn't exposed to Jewish tradition, Jewish language, Shabbat. And I must repeat that I had a very happy childhood. My
mother was a high school teacher and my second father was a sports
trainer, a sports teacher; I don't remember exactly anymore. He also ran
two lending libraries, that is, he was also in business. My parents were
well off financially, and we would spend our summer vacations in the
country. In short, a wonderful childhood—until the war came and everything, everything changed.

At first they put us into a ghetto and then my grandmother came to
live with us. My [step]father escaped to Russia because he was an officer
in the Polish army *(breathes heavily)*. Things slowly became worse and
worse—there was hunger and poverty—till my mother saw that the situation was getting very difficult, and she decided that whoever could be
saved should be saved, and then in, I don't remember exactly, but I think
it was in 'forty-three, it was very close to the ghetto uprising. When that
started I was already on the outside. She simply contacted my father and
sent me to him. It cost her a lot of money to pay the man who smuggled
me out to my father.

At my father's place they didn't really accept me. He had remarried and
had two daughters, besides my brother, who had lived with him since the
divorce. I was placed with some family of my father's because his wife
wasn't really so interested in having me stay with them. I was fourteen
years old already and some of my habits were unacceptable to them. It
bothered her that I addressed my father "per tu"; they were accustomed
to using the third person, very formal. I was much freer in my behavior,
a lot less polite. They placed me with some cousin, and in order to camouflage my dark skin, I was put into a school run by Carmelite nuns. That

turned out to be a very nice experience for me and somehow I remained with this family for a while. Every so often I was moved, I was always sent to somebody else, and that was bad for my studies as well. Slowly, I came to be a maid for these families. Later we went through the Polish Warsaw rebellion, led by Promokovsky. We were sent from the city to a kind of transit camp. My father managed to escape from there. Then I ran away from my father's house because the oppression of his Polish wife was very unpleasant. I ran away and came to a village. In the village I told them that I was willing to do any kind of work for shelter and food. And that is what I really did. That was my first profession—I was a pig herder *(laughs)*—and then the Russians liberated us.

I went back to the city and I didn't find anybody. I didn't find the house—only the walls and the cellar remained . . . somehow I met a former neighbor and she told me to go to a kibbutz. She directed me to a Jewish house, and they told me to go to the orphans' house because, according to my age [fifteen], I belonged there. But I had become so grown-up that I didn't stay there for long. They sent me to the kibbutz and . . . with the kibbutz, through the illegal immigration, stage by stage, we came to Israel. In Israel, we had dreamt about life in an agricultural settlement. We then left the city, came to this village, and built a family here. You know my oldest daughter, Dina. So that's it, in short. Now, if you want me to elaborate on anything, please let me know.

Olga has tried to tell her whole story in one breath. We give her a moment to collect herself. "You've told us everything according to the way it happened until you came to the part about the walls and cellar, and then you were very brief. Perhaps you wish to tell us more about that period?"

Look, Warsaw especially was in ruins, almost completely. What had been left by the Germans after the ghetto was leveled by them during the Polish rebellion. Just to tell about the time I returned to Warsaw and how I survived there would take three hours. I don't know if that is relevant. It depends on what you are interested in.

"Maybe you could tell us a little bit about how it was, how you managed to survive." Olga begins a detailed historical description of how the Russians advanced to the banks of the Vistula but let the Poles rebel against the Germans and let the Germans level the city. I have the feeling that, besides wanting to give the historical background, she is trying to gain time before she begins to talk about much more difficult issues.

I remember that when I used to go out and bring some dry bread from home, everybody in the cellar said, "Quick—run quickly, run," because, in fact, bombs were falling all the time. Later, when the Germans had conquered the city, they deported everybody to transit camps. Whoever was able to manage somehow left the camp. Whoever wasn't went to Germany to work. Warsaw was actually empty when the Russians conquered it, there were no people there. Warsaw was liberated in January 1945. It was bitterly cold and snowy. It was interesting to see how the people wandered back to the city from the country and how they were searching for what was left of their homes, of their families. The Poles also suffered then. Suddenly, they too lost each other. The Germans did not treat them gently. But of course, they weren't as cruel to them as they were to the Jews.

So, when I was liberated, I was in a village. I was in the midst of a very important job. I was sitting in a bomb crater holding two pigs. The farmer's wife was afraid that the Russians might take the pigs away, or perhaps she was afraid of the fleeing Germans. And so her son sat in one crater with two pigs and I in another *(laughing)*. And when the Russians arrived, they told us to come out. So somehow we got home with the pigs. And then they told us that Warsaw had already been liberated. I went there on foot. It was forty kilometers away and the roads to Warsaw were filled with people! Throngs of people, all of them carrying whatever they could, walking to Warsaw.

Warsaw was empty—no electricity, no water, no houses, nothing. And one had to live somehow. For one whole week I sat in the cellar of what had been our house ... besides the mice, there was no one else there. Here and there, I found some dry food to eat. I remember some very dirty sugar cubes.

"You mean your mother's house?"

Yes, of course. I had no further connection with my father, nothing. He also used to be very afraid to go into the street with me. He'd say to me: "If they catch us together, don't you dare say that I am your father." I was dark skinned and I looked Jewish. [He said] I had a "Jewish way" of walking. It seems that he was also afraid that perhaps I knew Yiddish. And I was only a little girl, no? He really was afraid then. I was more courageous than he was. I used to walk around freely in Warsaw. I bought myself a necklace with a cross and, all in all, I managed quite well. I didn't have a lot of problems besides the deep longing for my mother and my little sister, who were still in the ghetto.

There is a quiver in Olga's voice. What a terrible situation: on the one hand, her fear of and estrangement from her father; on the other, her longing for her mother and sister.

So now, how was it after the war, when I came back? After I had sat in the cellar for a week and walked around all day long, I used to roam the streets of the city and, only at night, I slept in the cellar. I was really without any food and I felt that I must, I must get something to eat. Something warm, but—there wasn't anything anywhere. Everything was in ruins. So I was walking along and I passed a woman sitting in a place that had once been a store: only the walls and the ceiling were left. She was sitting there and she had a few cushions and she lit a fire. So, I went in and asked her if I could warm up a bit. She looked up and saw that I was almost frozen and looked pretty unfortunate, so she even gave me some warm water to drink. She heated up the snow, and in that way, she called it tea. She asked me what I was doing, and I told her that I just had to eat something, that I was terribly hungry, and that I didn't know what to do, how to go about it. Then she said: "I have some flour, I'll make some noodles right away." She took some snow, mixed it with the flour, how she did it I don't know, but it turned out wonderful, yes? Then she made me a "work offer": "You'll go out every day and look for things and whatever you find, you'll bring to me. If you find coal, you'll bring coal. You find a cushion, bring me the cushion. And I will worry about giving you a place to sleep and I'll also give you food." I was used to being in situations like this before and so I was quite satisfied with this arrangement. For a month, I think, I brought her all kinds of things. There is even a special word for this in Polish. So we had quite a number of cushions and blankets that I had found—and I was able to sleep, it was warm, in all of this, and that's how we lived.

Olga has a very simple way of finishing up her description of difficult situations: "That's how we lived." When she referred to her father, she said: "All in all, I managed quite well." Yet now, when she speaks to the woman, for the only time, perhaps, during the entire interview, she says, "I didn't know what to do." In my mind, I see her searching for a "mother" to whom she can say what she really feels.

During my wanderings, I met this former acquaintance, and she told me: "You must get out of Warsaw because there is nothing to do in Warsaw." The trains were running for free because the Russians were sending back soldiers and equipment from Germany. People would just go to the train stations and get on the freight trains. One just had to make sure they were going in the right direction. A train would stop, people would get off, or change trains *(laughs)*. And I remember that this woman had told me, "You have to get to Kraków" and gave me an address there. So I arrived in Kraków. It took me several days. I didn't have a train schedule or anything. We just used to ask the conductors and the staff, and hundreds of people traveled that way. Actually, it was nice. We traveled with all kinds of freight and we used to sing; everybody was happy that the war was over. The whole thing was nice—in my eyes anyway.

I got to Kraków where they suggested that I join an orphans' home, but as there weren't any children my age, they decided I should join a kibbutz in Kalisz. There, there was a kibbutz—there were seventeen very young girls there. I got to Kalisz and I really liked it. There were lots of girls and there were two counselors and I was very satisfied. The conditions weren't so good, because, what was it? We did have an apartment on Palmatshe Street, I don't remember, and we slept in bunk beds. There wasn't a lot of equipment and the clothes were from UNRRA [United Nations Relief and Rehabilitation Administration]. There were also American army uniforms. But we had clothes. The situation was much better than before. They also taught us some Hebrew. Later, I had to have some medical treatment for my ear. They sent me to an ear specialist in Katowice. While in Katowice, a pogrom broke out in Kalisz. My best friend, we shared a bunk bed—she slept on the bottom and I slept on the top— she was killed in the pogrom. That affected me very deeply and I didn't want to return to Kalisz. So I stayed on at the kibbutz in Katowice, and they hosted me while I was having my ear treated.

Olga pauses for a moment.

That's it. I came to Israel with this kibbutz, with the illegal immigration. At a certain point we joined the army. Because, in the illegal immigration it was like this: you traveled a bit and then you settled in a camp and, again, you traveled a bit and then you stayed in an agricultural training farm. In the end, the whole process from Poland to Israel took us three years. First we went from Poland to Prague. From there we went to a camp in Germany. From there, we went to the agricultural training camp near Dachau. From there we moved again to Italy, passing through the Tyrolean Alps, which were beautiful in wintertime. In Italy we lived in a refugee camp and there they told us, that's actually where I heard, that the state of Israel had been established. On the loudspeaker they were asking the young people to volunteer to help, because the situation in Israel was very bad.

Most of the people volunteered, especially the unmarried. They sent us to an old castle where they had a rifle from Napoleon's time *(laughs)*. So at least we learned how to open, to close, and to load the rifle. We had a few jujitsu lessons, climbed ropes and drilled. Three weeks, then they swore us in, the oath of the IDF [Israeli Defense Force]. Then, by airplane, we arrived at a small airport near Haifa. My group was mobilized right away, but because of my ear trouble, again I was left behind. That seems to be my luck. My ear always at some stage bothered me, but it also saved my life. Because most of my friends were killed in the battle of Latrun *(deep silence)*.

What a harsh combination of circumstances: the pogrom in Kalisz and the War of Independence in Latrun, and all of that after what Olga had gone through in Warsaw.

For two months they examined my ear and so I was all that time in Haifa, at the old campus of the Technion, where there was an immigration point. Later they began giving us the deserted Arab apartments, and I got a room in the valley, Wadi Nissnas. This was an apartment shared by three families. Each one had a room, and the bathroom and kitchen were communal, and that's all.

Olga offers us something to drink. She is in need of a break, and so are we. I remember Wadi Nissnas from my childhood in Haifa: I would pass by there on my way to school. To begin with, I was afraid of Arab violence, and later I was wary of the strangeness of the refugees from Europe. When we return to the interview, I ask Olga if she ever found out what had happened to the members of her family who stayed behind in the ghetto.

Of course I inquired about them all the time. Even when I was inside the ghetto I used to get out because I spoke Polish well and, I guess, I was a child who knew how to manage. So my mother used to send me out to bring all kinds of things. I was very thin and easily managed to slide under the wall to where there was a sidewalk. The Germans always left a place like that open. So I slipped outside quite easily and went to the market to buy all kinds of things. Among other things, I would, ah, also go to the pharmacy and ask for sleeping pills. My mother used to save up these pills and she would say that if . . . the situation ever got very bad she would end her life with these pills *(silence)*.

Ah, the situation in the ghetto was very bad. My grandmother committed suicide in the ghetto. And she did this because she wasn't working. In the ghetto, whoever was able to work had the right to live and even that was limited. My mother was an educated woman, she spoke Russian and German, and she had a job as an interpreter in the Shulz factory. I know that this was a factory where they sewed uniforms for the Germans. *(I think of Genia, who worked in the same factory.)* My sister and I—I had a little sister from my mother's second marriage—had an *Ausweis* [permit] to stay inside the ghetto. But my grandmother didn't have a permit of this sort. At that time, the Germans used to perform "actions" of this kind: suddenly, they would appear in front of the house and announce with loudspeakers that everybody should come down and then some of the people—those who didn't have an *Ausweis*—would be loaded on trucks and sent away.

For my grandmother we had hiding places where we managed to hide her each time. Once here, once in the shower, behind the boiler, all kinds of places. And—until one day Grandmother had enough. She said it: "Enough!" She had been a midwife, she was already retired. She suffered from diabetes and heart trouble and she used to give herself injections. Then she injected herself with morphine and told us that she wanted to sleep and that no one should wake her up. She explained to me that she was going to sleep until death *(pause)*. I was very close to my grandmother because my mother was always working. After she got divorced she had to earn a living. My grandmother was retired already when I was five and a half and we used to spend a lot of time together *(pause)*. Then—she really did sleep for three days, and in the evenings my mother used to have discussions with all kinds of people, including our family doctor, whether to wake her or not *(silence)*.

I remember this so clearly, as if it happened yesterday. I remember the doctor saying: "We could give her an atropine injection" *(Olga is upset)*. How do I remember the names of these medicines! No, I don't really know, I was then twelve years old, maybe twelve and a half. In the end they decided to let her sleep. I was very interested in this process. All the time I would go and look at her, I would touch her, I would feel her pulse, I saw her turn yellow and yellower and yellower until my mother pronounced her dead. They came and took her away. My mother wanted to go with them to the cemetery. They didn't allow it. The way they took away my grandmother was really shocking *(silence)*. They took her out of our apartment, and on the street there was this wagon with two wheels and a man pulling it from the front—whichever way he wanted—and there were some corpses lying on it already. They then took off what she was wearing and threw it on the sidewalk. They simply threw her on the wagon—hands and feet, in such a humiliating way, and they shouted very rudely at my mother to get back into the house. They didn't let her walk with them even a little bit. That's how we parted from Grandmother.

Olga's voice cracks and her eyes fill with tears. All three of us are upset.

So, I knew that my mother, if things got very bad, she would take the pills and I believed this might be true also for my little sister, who was three years old when I left. For many years I was pretty sure that they had taken the pills. There was a jar so full of them . . . later I tried to find out. There were actually two alternatives—Treblinka or Majdanek. For a long time I thought I would meet them *(long pause)*, for many years *(five-second pause)*. Even when I was already in Israel, I dreamt *(five-second pause)*, but that's it *(silence)*.

"And about your father, did you find out anything?"

My father, I speak of the one who acted as my father, my stepfather, not my real father, whom I didn't love and didn't consider to be my father. He ran away to Russia in 'thirty-nine when Poland surrendered. And in 'forty-two he suddenly reappeared. *(Olga's eyes light up.)* Even the way he returned was very original. He always had a sense of humor. Someone rang the doorbell. There, we didn't open the door like we do here, there was a chain and we would open it a little bit. So somebody rang the doorbell and I ran to open it, I opened the chain and in ran a chicken! *(laughs)*. Already then it was hard, it was hard to get food. I unhooked the chain and stepped out and there he was standing on the steps. Everybody was very happy.

He came and tried to persuade my mother that all of us should move to Russia. He came with some peasant who had a wagon, he was loading up and my father had reserved places for us. My mother had just one night to pack what was essential, because you couldn't take a lot, and to get the family ready and off we would go. Getting the family ready meant everybody. But then my grandmother said she wasn't going because she didn't have the strength. She said she was not well and she would stay in the ghetto. She had two brothers and two sisters in Warsaw. My mother seemed to feel that it was her duty to stay with her mother and so she refused to leave *(long pause)*. She convinced him that he should go because already then they were rounding up men for all kinds of work. And then, really after a whole night of talking, he left *(silence; breathes heavily)*.

I never saw him again. He was in Israel—that I know from my uncle. He left Russia with Andreas's army. They came through Israel and fought in Italy and he was not on the list of casualties. I found that out through the Red Cross, I inquired about him. I guess that he built himself a new life and is not interested in renewing his connection with me. I heard that he had been seen in London. Someone from my family said that I shouldn't make any more inquiries because he built a new life for himself. So I stopped asking *(fifteen seconds of silence)*.

I remember having heard that many Jews had deserted from Andreas's army while it was in Palestine. I ask Olga: "And did he never look for you or your family?"

I don't think so. The person who told me about him is from that part of the family that lived in Israel. They came from Poland in 1933. Several of my cousins came here then, including a close uncle, my mother's brother. My grandmother even came to visit him in 1936; she stayed here for about half a year. She was the kind of person who believed in keeping up family ties. So that person told me not to inquire any more because he wasn't interested. She probably met him in London and told him that there were survivors from the ghetto, because that was rather rare. It was only when I wrote to the Bureau of Missing Relatives from Italy that my uncle found out I had survived. But he didn't succeed in communicating with me until I was almost in Israel, because the letters he wrote me—I had already moved to another place. I received the first letter my uncle had written to me in Italy six months after he sent it.

It is clear that Olga does not want to talk further about her fathers, either the one who remained in Poland or the one who lives in London. I suggest that she tell a bit about her family here in Israel.

In Israel I married a Holocaust survivor. I met him at the police department in Haifa. We both worked there and I married him and we established a family. We had two girls and a boy. He too was alone, one could say, alone—alone. His closest family here were some cousins. And they had been a very large family. Whereas my mother only had one brother, his father and mother had many brothers and sisters. I can't even remember all the names. So he really had a lot of cousins. He was born in Silesia and there more people survived. He spent all the war in camps, that is from 'forty-one until 'forty-five, in concentration camps. They took him there when he was fifteen; they simply caught him in the street. When he was liberated he was almost twenty. When he was liberated, he weighed thirty-five kilos [under eighty pounds]. He was taken to an American army hospital.

He didn't remember how many months he was there. From that period he remembered only that he fought with the doctors who didn't want to let him eat when he wanted to eat. When he got out of the hospital, they told him that his health was impaired. He really was not healthy; he had contracted pneumonia in the concentration camp and he had water in his lungs. And with all these problems he kept on working, without clothes and without food. Later, there was dysentery at the time when he was roaming from one camp to another, and this also affected him. Due to that, he lost a lot of weight. But he was a very brave man, and very, very good-hearted. A personality, one can say, a special personality. Always thinking of others, always satisfied. I was capable of saying: "Oy, how we are living here in this village. We haven't got a decent bed or even water and electricity!" He would reply: "What do you mean, after all, we do have a bed and a mattress! Do you know how many years I had to sleep on a wooden board?" In that way, he always made a joke out of things (laughing).

We had already decided to go to an agricultural settlement after we got married in Haifa. Actually, we had a nice little home there. We had a small room on the roof—we lived together with the pigeons—there was a big dovecote. We had a tiny room, no toilet or anything, but it was very close to the police station where I was working, and we were able to use the bathroom in the police station, even the shower (laughs). We wanted to find a place to settle in, an agricultural settlement, and so we came here. In those days, there was a policy that people should live with their own ethnic group. Here was a settlement of Polish people who had come in the fifties and so we were sent to join them. They didn't check to see if we were suited in age, culture, or mentality—nothing! Just Poles with Poles. So they made this kind of a mess, and it was very hard in the beginning, because the people who were already here were much older than we were and they had different ideas, and we really felt out of place. And for the young people who were here, we were old. My husband, unfortunately, died eight years ago, he died from cancer of the lungs, and I have built myself a new life.

Olga offers us another cup of coffee. At the same time, Shimon enters the room and she introduces him: "This is my new boyfriend," and we understand that this is what she meant by her last remark. I marvel at her will to live—how many times has she already said to herself: "I will build myself a new life!" When Olga sits down again, I ask her how much of all this she has told her children.

My children know everything. Whenever they asked, I told them. What they didn't ask, I didn't tell *(laughs)*. Yes, they asked, indeed.

"When? At what stage?"

It's hard for me to remember. But they asked. First they asked: "Why don't you have parents? Why don't we have grandparents?" That's where it began. "Everybody has grandmothers and grandfathers, only we don't." And so we had to explain to them why they had no grandparents. I think this started when they were quite young.

At this moment Olga's son, Benny, enters the room with his own little boy. She introduces him and explains to us that he lives across the street. He sits down and she turns to him right away as if he had been with us all the time.

How old were you when you started to ask questions?

Benny: I don't remember how old I was, I think it was from the time I could think straight. When Yadek arrived the circle was closed.

Olga, momentarily embarrassed, hastens to fill in what she has left out of her story.

Ah, yes. At a certain stage my brother came to Israel. In 'eighty-two he tried to adjust to life here but he didn't succeed. He had lived all his life in Poland. He grew up in a Polish family and married a Polish woman. He was educated and he didn't succeed in managing here. He very much wanted to be near us, but he didn't find work.

I am rather surprised that Olga tells us about her brother only after her son mentions him as "closing a circle" (what circle?) and I ask her: "What was it like for you to meet him after all these years?"

That was a great event. I dreamt, I always dreamt that I would meet him some day. But my dreams were not that he would come here. Because, in my opinion, he took a step that was bound to fail. I had been ready for immigration after all I had gone through in the war. Besides, I identified myself as a Jew, and it seems that he did not. Or, maybe he did at a later stage in his life. He is three years younger than I am, but when he came to Israel he was already fifty-one. He was an electrical engineer, he had a master's degree, and his expertise was suited for work in the electric company; only they could have hired him or in the Ministry of Defense. The Ministry of Defense was not interested in employing anybody from the Eastern bloc and the electric company was not interested in a man fifty-one years old who didn't speak Hebrew and could not be put in charge of projects.

Is there a touch of sadness in Olga's voice or has her tone become apologetic? I ask her: "Had you been in contact all those years?"

Ah, no. We had some contact by way of poste restante. My brother was living with my father, who was not interested in having him correspond with me. When I left for Israel I took leave of him. I was fifteen and he was twelve. He begged me: "Take me with you," but I did not agree to take him along: the group I was with was unsuitable for him; and he had a problem with his lungs, he was ill . . . there was a spot on one of his lungs. I knew that as long as he stayed there, they would take care of him. If I was to take him through all of the hardships that were in store for illegal immigrants, it would be harmful to his health. He was rather hurt at my refusal: "What do you mean, my only sister doesn't want to take me?" And he, with the imagination of a twelve-year-old, probably thought, God knows, to what paradise I was going *(sighs)*.

Then there was a period, ah, when it wasn't so good to be in contact with Jews in Poland. I tried to contact him. I wrote to the poste restante section of the city where he lived and asked for his address. Then I was invited to come to the Polish embassy in Tel Aviv, where they interrogated me: Why, all of a sudden, was I looking for an address in that city? They explained that I could only do this at the embassy and that I couldn't write straight there. And then I understood that I could actually cause him harm. They really interrogated me, what kind of contact and what kind of . . . as if they had caught a spy *(laughs)*. Finally, from here he went to Germany and he managed very well there.

Benny: That really was very strange! To suddenly come and see a man who looks like your mother. I wasn't able to get close to him. That is, I didn't feel the blood connection. And also, suddenly, you have a grandfather!

Olga laughs and adds: Ah, right, yes.

Benny: It was really strange! You grow up with no family, a mother and a father and that's all. There are distant relatives, cousins, but they're not exactly . . . I thought this was a very interesting experience. But communicating? First of all, there was no language, the mentality was different . . . It was strange, quite strange, to see a brother and a sister, you could easily see where there was a similarity, but that's it. The distance was great and it stopped here. But for me it was very moving to see that my mother had relatives. I mean to say, I was happy for my mother, not for myself. It didn't mean much to me. As far as I was concerned, I had already adjusted—that's it.

Olga interrupts: On the other hand, the girls were really glad. Especially Dina, because he lived near Beer-Sheva. She helped him a lot. They were in contact often. She also understands more Polish because my husband and I spoke Polish to each other in the beginning. It was only when the other children were born that we decided to speak Hebrew to each other.

I turn to the son: "You said your grandfather also came?"

Benny: No, that was a result of Yadek's coming, that is, he spoke about him, he brought pictures of Grandfather.

Olga interrupts again: My father was still alive when my brother immigrated. When he left Poland, my brother told my father that he was going to Israel to attend the wedding of his grandson. My father has only one grandson. Besides him *(pointing at Benny)*, he has only granddaughters. And my father didn't react one way or the other; he wasn't interested. He had never really been interested in me. I had always been the black sheep of the family. And when Yadek came, one of the sisters wrote that Father was very sick. She wrote to my brother and not to me! And later on, he died. And so the children suddenly discovered that they had a grandfather someplace. A grandfather that—what could I have told the children about him before? *(angry)*. That they have a grandfather who didn't want me. What for? If he wasn't a father to me, how could he be a grandfather to the children? The man who had been a father to me had disappeared.

"So when the children asked, what did you tell them? When they asked: 'Why don't we have grandparents?'"

I told them that their grandparents had been killed in the war. I also couldn't tell small children that they were from a mixed family. I don't know how that would have affected them. There were a few families in this village where the husband was Jewish and the wife Polish or Russian, and I would hear the words "gentile," "goy," or "shiksa"—insulting Yiddish words. There, the Poles used to call me a "smelly Jew," so I needed that here? What for? My decision about which group I belong to I made at some point. And that's it. Whatever I left behind didn't exist anymore!

Benny: For us, that's how it was—nonexistent.

Olga continues: Yes, simply, nothing. For me, as well—I remember when suddenly there was contact between my brother and the sisters, that is, my stepsisters, who I—when I lived with my father—how they were treated and what treatment I got. Not that I had anything against these little girls, they were younger than I was, but I didn't feel that they were my sisters at all. They were the "ladies" and I was the maid! *(angry).* There was no fair treatment! And, suddenly, a letter came from one of the sisters and this one *(pointing to Benny)* says: "I have an aunt, too?"

Olga is laughing, but Benny is serious. A frank discussion is developing between them.

Benny: Every time someone dies, someone new is born. It's terrible, it's unconnected, out of the blue . . . The truth is that I don't even remember that this was a problem for me. Perhaps I suppressed it? We always knew more about Father's family than about yours. When people would talk to me about family it was usually about Father's family, and this is how the circle closed for me. It's true, you transmitted a lot of anger about your father. We remember this from the time we were children. You didn't make a big fuss about it, but it was enough to see the expression on your face in order to understand that whatever was over there was no good. *(Olga laughs bitterly.)* So there were questions, and here and there we got an answer. But we understood that it was unpleasant and, therefore, it was better not to ask any more. At least that's how I felt. That is, I didn't insist. I felt it was an open wound.

I turn to Benny: "On the other hand, when you asked your mother, would she reply?"

Benny: We were given answers about that period. Sometimes these answers were evasive, but they were answers. I don't remember all of them. Though I do know that some of the answers were very powerful and some of them were quite weak—I just don't remember all of them. It turns out that I myself have problems with this. You see, I suffer, I think, from all kinds of anxieties, some of them connected to that war. Not relating to the awful stories, but to the symptoms borne by my parents. I have anxieties, questions. That is, when my father died, this came up. Personally, I think I have fears about being left behind, about running away, I am fearful of illness and death. It's very complicated, but it's connected; here and there you can find the connection. If one sits down and thinks about it hard, one can find the connection.

Olga again interrupts him: My husband was a sick man. When I met him he was always coughing. At first we talked about bronchitis; later on, it was already asthma. In the sixties, he became ill with tuberculosis of the lung, with a serious hole in his lung that kept him in the hospital for a whole year. He ended his life with cancer in the other lung, the healthy one. This situation affected our home, even though we didn't make too much fuss about it, but I think the children especially suffered from this situation, because he was sick. He was not spoiled, he didn't ask for special consideration, he simply tried to deal with it, to be active. We built up a good farm, we had many cows—up until the time he contracted tuberculosis and then we had to get rid of the barn. We also had a large chicken coop, the remnants of which can still be seen here, and later he looked for work. It was very difficult for him to find suitable work. But when he found a job as a civilian worker for the army, he functioned just like anyone else. He would get up in the morning, go to work, come home and fulfill all his tasks. If I was to give him a grade, I would say that as a father, he rated an A, yes. That's why I don't think the situation was so bad. But, the problem was always there. We too, always—I personally learned to go on, not to dwell on things. He had a marvelous sense of humor—it was easy to live with him and he really loved life. He loved to sing and dance and travel and see things, to have a drink now and then. He loved life. At least, that's how I see Father. *(She turns to Benny.)* How did you see him and his bad health?

Benny: That's just the problem. It all came out after he died. Because he handled himself—his last illness, in fact, all of his illnesses—so well;

he bore things so bravely. I was unable to understand just how well he dealt with his problems. I was sure that he purposely ignored his illness, it didn't make any impression on him at all! A glass of brandy and everything would be fine. This wasn't exactly the case, I'm just giving you the general picture. I'm not painting it exactly as it was. But inside me, there was a conflict, because as a child, I would lie in my bed and hear him cough and cough really hard. And, as a child, I would make a wager with myself: Is he going to choke or not? Hospitals, inhalations, medicines, whatnot.

Olga adds: Yes, he would have asthma attacks.

Olga sighs and I let my thoughts dwell on the almost mystical connection between the spot on her brother's lung and the hole in her husband's lung.

Benny: Very bad attacks! Anybody who knows anything about asthma knows exactly what I am talking about. And that's what I grew up with. You grow up with—you have a very strong mother and she does many things that are difficult because there are things that your father is forbidden to do. There were lots of times when we would work together, father and I, and if it was real hard work, he would really try and he would work very hard, push and pull and lift, and when it was over, he would spit in all directions. We would sit on the tractor together and work— the smoke would really get to him. He would get annoyed, cough, and yell at me. You live in the shadow, every time it appears in a different place. At some point, I got used to it. It's like, you know, the story about the wolf: the third time, you don't get excited anymore—he'd cough, he'd almost choke, but he lived. It's not serious, he didn't like making a fuss about it. But then, when he died, the hero actually succumbed! That was a shock. How for twenty-five years and then, suddenly—it just can't be. That's it. There's a big conflict inside. Today I'm not certain of anything. I mean, we're not really as big and strong as we think we appear. The first shock occurred and it really frightened me!

Olga is finding it difficult to listen to her son. She looks for a way to change the subject.

There was another thing we tried very hard to implant in our children. We said it all the time—the only thing we can give you is a profession. You must learn a profession, whatever you want, in order to be independent and to earn a living; and don't depend on agriculture *(laughs).*

Benny: You actually did this very gently. I must admit that you let us know this, you told us things, you did it as gently as you could. But today, I find myself thinking like you, talking like you. I catch myself—wait one minute! This isn't me! And I start all over again. *(Olga laughs uncomfortably.)* I'm always getting pulled along. I don't even know that it's happening, I'm not aware that I'm being pulled, but I find myself eating compulsively, thinking compulsively, working compulsively, saving money compulsively, simply—and when I realize what I'm doing, I feel bad. I really do.

Besides being anxious about being deserted, I'm also fearful of death, of illness, of starvation. It isn't a rational fear—it has no foundation *(he hugs his son who is standing next to him listening)*. Then I find myself being afraid for these kids. I mean, if I don't do this, who will? Anxieties—I'm full of anxiety! *(breathes heavily for a moment, upset)*—I think I was expected to do more at home and that expectation grew and grew. For instance, Shabbat, for me Shabbat comes and I don't feel well. I feel pressured, tense. In my heart I hear, "Do something." There was a time after Father died, walking around here I would hear his voice: "This has to be repaired, this ought to be done, that has to be done." There is always something to do, problems with the car, problems with the lawn mower.

I feel as if we have accidentally stumbled into a very important conversation between mother and son.

Olga continues: I also remember, when you were a child we got a Polish record. I bought it in Tel Aviv, a beautiful record. Among other things, there was a song on it: "To my little son, even when you grow up, remember then my hands . . ." and I liked to listen to this song a lot and I would say: "I'll always protect you" *(laughs, embarrassed)*. I had fears too, maybe I wouldn't be able to protect you. Not only financially, I was afraid about my lack of education. My parents were educated people and I was not! And I was afraid that I would have no authority over my children! Nothing could hide it, right? So, I had fears. Of course, I tried to do my best. Parents always try to do the best they know; the fact that they make mistakes can't really be helped.

Benny (softly): Listen, just as I often find myself restless, unrelaxed, and I take it out on my children . . . You say that you made mistakes, I've heard my sister say that you made mistakes with her—I don't think so. I don't think you made mistakes with us. I think you did your best with us. That's the way I always felt, the honesty, your straightforwardness. For example, in the army. One of the letters you wrote me was very moving. In basic training you sent me a letter. I had written that it was very hard for me. I don't remember exactly what, but I was complaining, complaining to my mother. And you wrote me an ordinary letter, but there was one sentence that said: "Listen, my son—we couldn't tell you that the world is—how do you say it, 'cruel,' 'hard,' 'shitty'?" I don't remember exactly what you wrote. "We didn't want to tell you this beforehand, but we knew you would find out in time, so we kept it from you. So now you see that this is the real world, this is reality." That's a nice thing to do, isn't it? You did a very good thing there. It made all the bad times worthwhile. With that letter, you made up, in a way, for the mistakes. I think that you were mistaken in not doing so earlier; but here, as far as I was concerned, you consoled me. You have no idea what that letter did for me. After that I simply straightened out!

Olga, with characteristic honesty: Actually, I don't remember that letter . . .

Benny (turning to me as if noticing me for the first time): I was in a special unit in the army. They pulled you apart; that was the system, to tear you into pieces and then put you back together. It was rough on me—I still have a problem when I go to the army. Today, when I am called to reserve duty and I face the Intifada, there are questions on my mind: On which side am I? On the side of the Jews or on the side of the cross holders? I act, I am often forced to act in a way that I consider to be inhumane. I would often find myself confronting Arab "masked activists," and we had the right to shoot. And from my side, I hear "Shoot, go ahead and fire, come on, shoot!" I am glad that I follow reason, but I really found myself caught between two pictures, as it were, that appear and disappear.

Olga, half listening, continues: I made a promise when I was very hungry, in Warsaw, that if I ever had a home, no one would ever leave it hungry. I always kept this promise. I would go out into the yard with food and coffee. There were years when a Bedouin boy used to come around and he was like one of us. The children saw that they are people just like us. It's possible, therefore, that the army, in order to ensure that this child will learn to protect himself, needs to tell him that other one is not exactly like him.

Benny: I have a slightly different idea. I really feel like a conqueror, a conqueror with a capital C. It's simply disgraceful to behave like that. I walk around with a gun and I say: "Move over—to the right, to the left," and I can decide whether or not someone is going to die. What am I, God? But, in the Second World War, people in my position were God. There is some kind of connection here, and I feel I carry two pictures in my head, one of the Second World War and one of the wars here. These pictures collide all the time, they come and they go. It's very hard for me.

Olga protests: I don't see it that way at all.

We are all weary. Before parting, we touch on an additional topic: How are holidays celebrated in the family?

Benny: What I remember are the religious holidays. Father was in his element then. Absolutely—he came from a religious family, as you know. At any rate, he and God got along very well on Yom Kippur. I think those were the only religious holidays, besides Succoth and—Passover, how did I forget? But, if you ask about Purim, during that holiday I was all right, I must admit, putting on costumes, having fun. In short, apart from the religious aspect, there was a problem here. As the youngest in the family, I felt that something was missing, especially on Shabbat.

Olga answers: I was an atheist. And when I was an adolescent, I encountered Christianity and I rejected it. However, I didn't feel comfortable with traditional Judaism either. The noise from the synagogue used to bother me. In the house opposite us here, there used to be a temporary synagogue for the *moshav*. And it bothered me, the noise of the praying. I never really understood why one should always praise a God who cannot be seen. He never did anything good! And that's why there was a big problem in our family about religious tradition.

The interview ends—never to be completed. We say our good-byes warmly. Perhaps Olga and her son will continue on without us. I feel exhausted as I try to concentrate on driving home in the dark. Noga and I are silent most of the way. I am still under the impact of Olga's openness—and her son's.

I try to reconstruct for myself how many times Olga has had to start over; how many times fate ran her life. First, there was her parents' divorce, then the war, the ghetto, moving to her father's house outside the ghetto, going to the Carmelite school, the Polish uprising, on to the farm, then the return to Warsaw where she met that woman in the storefront. She started a new life, joining a kibbutz, but then had a friend murdered in a postwar pogrom. She joined another group, which came to Israel. Her friends got killed in the battle of Latrun. She joined the police department, married, and went to live on a *moshav*, ran the family farm, and had difficulty making friends there. Her husband became ill and had a hard time providing for his family. Then he died, and she built a new relationship with Shimon.

Noga points out the restrained tone with which Olga has told her story. This is the tone, seemingly detached, used by many Holocaust survivors in trying to describe, in ordinary language, what happened to them. Once or twice, Olga's voice breaks, especially as she describes her grandmother's suicide and the cruel way in which the body was removed. That is probably where her pain penetrates the rational surface she has cultivated over the years.

Later, when we are transcribing the interview, we notice "holes" in Olga's story: the loss of her mother and sister; the disappearance of her stepfather, whom she loved so much; the pain she must feel knowing that he is not interested in renewing contact (and she does not try to do so); the pain of her father's rejection; his treating her as the "black sheep." Even if this could be attributed to the "circumstances of that time," Olga feels that she was more courageous than her father. However, she remains so angry that she does not tell her children about him until many years later, when her brother appears: "What could I have told [them] about him before?" She knows what a real father is like—even if it is not her biological one—but she accepts his denial of her existence.

And then the dreadful events connected with Olga's mother and grandmother. Of all the people Olga has lost, it is her grandmother who elicits her warmest response and identification. She exhibits no anger toward her grandmother, even in the story about the lost opportunity to escape and describes the incident quite clearly while simply sketching in the others. We come to realize that she has mixed feelings about it through hints in the text, but we must make sense of them by ourselves.

Olga tries to reconstruct a coherent biography from several of the possible "identities" she inhabits ("Jewish," "gentile," and "Israeli") and some almost unbridgeable stages in her life. Her mother was Jewish, her father gentile, a combination to which the Nazi era gave a demonic dimension, and she lived with each of them during some determining life experience. Perhaps, therefore, unlike many other survivors, who concentrate on one or two phases of their life history (before, during, or after the Holocaust), Olga tells about all of them: her short prewar life, her life in the Jewish ghetto and in the Aryan section of Warsaw during the war, and the long, complicated postwar period in Europe and later in Israel. Again and again she has confronted agony, despair, and death. How has she overcome them and managed to retain any hope for a new future? How has she bridged the potentially painful contradictions of these "identities" and life phases?

Olga hints at some of this while preferring to remain silent about the more painful aspects of her life history. From the very beginning of the interview, we have noted the contrast between what she chooses to reveal and what she hides, between the "told" and the "untold." She speaks briefly of painful and uncontrollable events, but when these dreadful events threaten to destroy her family and herself, it is the continuity of the family framework that provides a hidden coherence.

Olga begins: "My family was mixed and I had a very happy childhood." In the following sentences, however, it becomes clear that her childhood happiness has nothing to do with having come from a mixed family; rather, she was happy in her mother's home after her mother divorced her first husband and married a second, Jewish one. Moreover, as it turns out, although she mentions her mixed family background at the beginning of the interview, she kept it hidden from her family for many years. Olga did not tell her family about her gentile father until her brother came to Israel eight years ago (and she did not tell us about his coming until her son joined our conversation). Perhaps what she meant was that her childhood happiness began in her mother's home and ended when "the war came and everything, everything changed." Unlike Genia, Olga evokes that early happiness.

In contrast, when she mentions her father's home, in which she found refuge from the death-ridden Jewish ghetto, it is with anger and pain, which seem to be linked to what is revealed and what is hidden: she was saved, but her mother and sister were not. Her father's (and thus, her own) Polish background came to the rescue at a time when Jewish identity meant death. The way her father treated her, however, is still reason for her manifest anger. It was arranged that she stay with her father's family (not of her own will and certainly not on her own initiative), but she could not adjust. Her description of this period becomes more negative and more intense with each sentence: At first it was only her habits that were "unacceptable" to her father and his wife. Then she was placed in a Carmelite school to "camouflage my dark skin." As she continued to be moved from one family to another, her studies were interrupted to such a degree that she gradually turned into a "maid" for the families she lived with. When Olga was no longer able to tolerate the "oppression of [her father's] Polish wife," she ran away and carried on until the end of the war on her own.

Olga's ongoing identity problem as a child of a mixed family comes up several times during the interview. The gentiles (the Poles) called her a "smelly Jew" (it is unclear at what stage in her life this occurred), while the Jews in her *moshav* called people like her "shiksa." On the one hand, Polish is her mother tongue; on the other, these are the people who participated in the extermination of her people in the pogrom in Kalisz. As Olga explains, her son does not know Polish because she and her husband had decided to speak Hebrew after their older daughter was born. But later, she mentions a Polish record she bought in Tel Aviv that included a beautiful lullaby; listening to it, she swore to herself that she would always protect her little son. It is this record that calms her fears. In the interview she is able to talk about these fears and emotions only after her son has told about his own in the Israeli context.

In describing the meeting with her brother, Olga emphasizes that she chose a Jewish identity for herself at an early age— "whatever I left behind didn't exist anymore"; this in contrast to her brother, whose choice of Judaism came "too late" (only in the early eighties when he was already in his fifties). Yet the question of Olga's identity seems much more complicated. First, one may assume that the choice occurred before she was really able to make choices for herself. At the time of her parents' divorce, it was "decided" that she would remain with her mother while her baby brother would go with his father—an unusual decision for a Jewish family. This sealed her fate as a Jew at a time when history had decreed that the Jews should be annihilated. These choices meant many additional hardships, although she always seemed to stumble across trustworthy people, who helped her in her unusual and lonely journey.

When Olga discusses her atheism, she says she "encountered" Christianity and "rejected it." She does not say whether she ever weighed any other possibility. One can only conjecture why for her, the Jewish religion was "uncomfortable"; she says it was the "noise of the praying" from the synagogue opposite her house in the *moshav*. Perhaps by returning to the trivial, Olga is trying to create some kind of balance, as if she is saying, "I did not like any religion." And she adds: "I never really understood why one should always praise a God who . . . never did anything good" (as if saying: "I rejected both Christianity and Judaism, because the Almighty did not save my mother and sister").

Olga's life story centers on her Jewish and Israeli identity. Although her father's gentile background saved her life, it did not provide any further positive meaning. Could Olga have survived without her father's help? Probably not, although she stresses the fact that she had "managed quite well." Yet the anger and humiliation she felt then live on. They are an integral part of her life history reconstruction. She tries to reduce the impact of her hidden pain through irony ("a nice experience"; "my first profession—I was a pig herder"). At the same time, she only hints at the real and continuing hardships: her deep longing (concern and, possibly, guilt) for her mother and sister, the difficulty of having a complex identity, and her lack of an adequate education.

Olga tells us that she returned to Warsaw because "I had no further connection with my father." Later she tells us that her brother, who had lived with her father all those years, was disappointed when she refused to take him with her to Israel. This shows that her brother identified with her and wanted to come along, even though Olga felt rejected in her father's home. It also shows that she maintained some kind of connection with her father after the war. Yet Olga does not mention her brother at all when she describes those three years at her father's house and states only that there was "no connection" after the war.

In a sense, her Jewish stepfather becomes a symbol of this combination of hopefulness and disappointment. Olga describes his return to the ghetto with the joyfulness of a small girl welcoming a rescuing angel. Unfortunately, her mother decides not to go. Olga does not comment further, although this decision had such a dreadful outcome. She expresses no remorse or anger. Still, although her stepfather survived the war and was living in London, she did not try to contact him, mentioning only that from a relative she had heard "he was not interested" in such a meeting. We do not know the details, and none of the other family members even mentions his existence. We can only surmise that such an encounter would have been too painful.

Olga returned to the ruins of her mother's house after Warsaw was liberated to find "only the walls and the cellar." In describing her meeting with the woman who made tea for her, Olga again reveals the emotional cost of losing her mother. To this stranger she admits that she does not know what to do, the only time during the whole interview that she has expressed a sense of helplessness. In the next sentence she immediately downplays this harsh confrontation with postwar reality by stating simply: "That's how we lived."

The intertwined experiences of trust, hope, and disappointment continue after the war: her Jewish acquaintance, the kibbutz and the pogrom in Kalisz, the death of her friends during the War of Independence, the illness and death of her husband. Yet Olga goes on, as if none of these events can break her spirit. First, she is "led" back to her Jewishness. A former Jewish acquaintance, whom Olga meets in the ruins of Warsaw, advises her to go to Kraków to a Jewish children's home. From this point on, however, it is Olga who takes the initiative: to join the kibbutz, to immigrate to Israel, to live as an Israeli, a pioneer, a farmer. It is not a coincidence that Olga tells her story in an eloquent Hebrew much better than that of either Genia or Ze'ev. And her choice of verbs is not coincidental either; she is creating a new reality. One can sense Olga's confusion about her past identities when, during the interview, she turns to us directly: "Now, if you want me to elaborate on anything, please let me know ... I don't know if that is relevant. It depends on what you are interested in." Relevant to whom? The question put to us is also meaningful for her. How can aspects of the past not be relevant from the present Jewish or pioneering Israeli point of view?

In any event, she has tried to make a clear separation between what happened "there" and what she has created "here," a separation that is difficult to explain to her own children. When she mentions what she has told her children ("Whenever they asked, I told them. What they didn't ask, I didn't tell"), she knows quite well that questions cannot be asked about what she has chosen to hide. Her son, referring to this, says: "We understood that it was unpleasant and, therefore, it was better not to ask any more."

With the help of her son, Olga also touches on the painful topic of her education. She comes from an educated family, but she was unable to obtain a proper education because of the war. Again, she puts the responsibility, though indirectly, on her father. Because of him, she had to move from one place to another, which interfered with her studies, and thus she became a "maid for these families." This lack of education would later cause Olga to doubt her authority as a parent, and she urges her children to get an education and, in that way, to guarantee their future: "You must learn a profession, whatever you want, in order to be independent and to earn a living." Perhaps here Olga reveals further doubts about her identity: on the one hand, education was the only legitimate component of the family before the Holocaust and remained so afterwards; it is also a sign of continuity. On the other, education did not save any of the Jews, just as the Jewish religion did not help its believers.

It is precisely Olga's attempt to create for herself—and for us—a picture of normalcy from the extraordinary events in her life that makes the "untold story" so powerful. This story is connected to the relative advantage that her mixed background provided for her in the terrible constellation of the Holocaust—a relative advantage compared to Genia and Ze'ev, and even to her mother and her sister, who could not be saved. It is interesting to note that Olga never mentions the Nazis by name in the course of the interview; only once does she touch on German deeds, and that is in connection with the Poles: "The Poles also suffered then. Suddenly they too lost each other," although "they weren't as cruel to them as they were to the Jews."

Olga finds it difficult to reveal the "untold story" to her children, but her brother's arrival in Israel in the eighties forced her to talk. Even then, she revealed only the existence of the "mixed family" and did not talk about her own identity conflict, perhaps because she was unable to define it for herself. The conflict surfaces again in the apologetic way she describes her brother's failed attempt to settle in Israel: she feels sad that he could not adjust, yet she states: "His attempt was doomed to failure," additional proof of her conviction that hers was the only possible way to be Jewish and overcome the past.

One may also suppose that her father's death at the time of her brother's visit to Israel did not soften her relationship to him but, rather, emphasized her alienation from him. Had there ever been any hope of clarifying the anger between them, his death made it impossible. It is her son who is sensitive to the influence of the "untold story" of one generation on the next. When Benny speaks about his difficulties with the Intifada, he has a hard time defining "whose side" he is on, that of the Israelis or that of the "cross holders." He is referring to the Palestinians, who feel that they are an oppressed people, but in the context of the interview, the cross has another meaning.

It is not by coincidence that Olga reacts immediately, and in her reply there seems to be a contradiction: on the one hand, she has taught her children that an Arab is also a human being; on the other, in the army, "in order to ensure that this child will learn to protect himself," he must be told that the "other one is not exactly like him." It is as if she wants to tell her son, "Know who you are, just as I had to decide who I am."

In the spontaneous conversation that develops between mother and son, we witness the deep feeling Benny has for her. When Olga confesses to mistakes she may have made in his upbringing, he reacts very gently, remembering with gratitude a letter she wrote him when he was in basic training.

Olga has obvious difficulty in expressing her emotions. When her son voices his fears about his father's health or about the compulsiveness he feels he has absorbed from his parents, Olga is unable to deal with his outbursts. She tries again and again, with her light-hearted comments, to lessen the level of emotion. Only once, when she talks about the lullaby on the Polish record, does she give in to her feelings, and then they mesh with those of her son. It is interesting to note that only her son has made his home near his mother; his two sisters have chosen to live farther away. Is he his mother's "memorial candle" (Vardi, 1990), representing the two fathers who failed her and the husband who died?

Dina

Between redemption and survival

Dina, a woman of about forty, receives us at her home in Lehavim, a new settlement near Beer-Sheva, one of those new places where there are only a few signs of greenery and one can easily get lost because the street names are so similar: they are all named after plants and flowers—Narcissus, Anemone, Cyclamen, and others—that do not grow here in the desert. We wander around until we arrive at the right house. Dina opens the door and her blue eyes immediately remind me of her mother's reference to her own "Jewish appearance." Inside, the house is large but sparsely furnished, in contrast to her mother's small and densely furnished house. Noga sits down with Dina while I interview her daughter Orit in another room. When Noga asks Dina to tell her life story, Dina begins immediately.

I was born in the *moshav*, the one you visited when you met with my mother. Today it is green and nice, but once it was the edge of the desert! It's in the northern Negev and was known as a "drought border area,"[1] if that means anything to you. My parents came down to settle this place; they were pioneers—pioneers of the fifties—and the pioneers of those days were not like the pioneers of the eighties.

So, I was born there. Many Poles and Romanians lived in the *moshav*. What was it like? In the first grade there were five pupils. The teacher knew only Hebrew, one boy knew only Polish and another one only Romanian, and someone else only Yiddish—I was the only Hebrew speaker! So, for a while, I used to translate between the children and the teacher. Well, the *moshav* was rather backward, people sitting on their suitcases, but with the years there was progress. Later, I went to a regional junior high school with children from other settlements. That was a big school. Later on in the high school, that was also a big school. Then I came to Beer-Sheva, which then seemed to me to be a big city . . . the village girl came to the big city.

So, I finished the teachers' seminary and started teaching in Yerucham.[2] That is, we got married and then I taught elementary school for nine years. After that I had a year's sabbatical and studied at the university, and I felt as if a whole new world was opening up for me . . . and when the year ended it was very hard for me to return to the elementary school. It suddenly appeared to be such a small and limited world. Then I was offered a teaching position in the junior high school. I took the job and enjoyed the work very much. I taught mainly mathematics. We moved to Omer and lived there, and then we came here. Today I am assistant principal, and there's a lot of work to do.

Like her mother, Dina tries to tell her whole life story in one breath. She rests for a moment before going into detail.

I have three children—Orit, sixteen; Gideon, thirteen; and Amnon, eight. We actually moved to Yerucham temporarily. "You don't raise children in Yerucham," we thought to ourselves. In fact, we felt very good there. But that idea remained so strong in the back of our minds that when the opportunity came along to move here, we didn't think about it twice. Orit missed a bit of the feeling of being involved in building a new settlement because she continued for a while at her old school after we moved here. That was a very special period. That was something wonderful, really and truly. We saw houses being built, we examined the flowers that grow in the desert. Lehavim is situated between the mountains and the edge of the flat desert; there are special plants here. It was so nice to see all this through the eyes of the children—you see a bird, a flower, the leaf of a plant, looking under stones. It was wonderful. It was like the *moshav* where I grew up. There were lots of flowers there too, all kinds and colors, and shrubs; there were so many. Here, I found the same things but in miniature. I don't know what this did for the children, but for me it was marvelous.

I remember the first day the inspector came and looked at the shelter [the temporary school] and the sand all around, and he mumbled to himself: "These people are crazy, they are not normal." But when he entered the shelter he was amazed: everything was there, the floor, an acoustic ceiling, everything new and nice—just like any other school! That was something new, something different, something really exceptional!

Dina speaks so enthusiastically, she gets carried away. Noga tries to bring her back to her childhood:

I was born in 'fifty-one, that was during the time of the infiltrators from the Gaza strip.[3] There were other settlements, but not as dense as they are today. Then it was an isolated area. Today it's altogether different, but then, so they tell me, there was a feeling of isolation, so that saboteurs came in and could do anything. That is, it wasn't only a feeling. The fact was, that was the reality. I even remember there was a time when the saboteurs came and stole the mule, and that was terrible, because, you have to understand, there weren't any tractors or other agricultural machines like there are today. A mule and a wagon were essential, even when you had to take women to the hospital to give birth; that's how they took my mother when she had my sister. I also remember that they stole cows, and in those days everyone got a cow from the Jewish Agency[4] and that's all they had, that was all!

They lived in such poverty that it's difficult for us to imagine today. Today when we say, "There's nothing to eat," we mean that we haven't done our shopping, and in half an hour it can all be done and we can have a whole meal ready. But, I remember, that is, I don't really remember but from the stories my mother told us, that we ate beets and bread. And when they made meatballs they put in a lot of bread, so there should be a lot of food. And today? Today, I don't even put in bread crumbs, hardly any at all *(excited)*. The story is that there was also a lot of, there was a lot of fear. They would come in, there were murders, the papers reported on couples that were killed, they used explosives and blew up houses. That was a very difficult time.

"And what do you remember from that time?"

I remember a lot of nice things! Really! As a child I was so afraid, I probably picked up those fears, I didn't like darkness and I'm not the bravest person in the world, even today. But, I remember a lot of nice things too.

Between the fear and the "nice things," Dina tells about four childhood memories connected to wagon rides. In the first one, she describes gathering bales of hay in the fields and adds: That is a later memory, because by then we already had a tractor. My father was driving and he went up a hill with the wagon and then that huge pile of bales, with all the children, fell on the ground with all the bales of hay and it was a real party!

The second is about another tractor ride, this time, to the beach: It was a wonderful day, and on the way back, when we got to the *moshav*, we discovered that a little boy was missing. A boy is missing! It was terrible. He was the son of a friend of my parents and that was all she had. She didn't have a husband, only this boy. So, naturally, we returned quickly, no, not us, my father with one or two other men, they went back quickly to the beach and they found him sleeping. He didn't even remember falling asleep; he fell off the wagon into the soft, warm sand that felt really nice. Everything was all right; they picked him up, he didn't know—to this day he doesn't know that his mother almost had a heart attack when her son suddenly disappeared.

In the third story, she describes how her father became the milk delivery man for the moshav *because of his poor health.* One day my mother came home—where's my father? There is the horse and the wagon but no driver! He simply fell asleep on the wagon, but the horse knew the way and went home by itself. When it got home and stopped, he woke up— no problem.

She also told us a fourth story: Aside from that, there was a hill, it was really something. Today there is an orchard there, but then it was a hill where there had once been a British army camp. And for us children it was really something special, full of mystery and surprises. First of all, there was a big hole in the ground, I don't know what it was used for, but there was a deep hole, a very deep hole. It had a wide diameter. They filled it in at some point, but we kids went—you know, you probably know that game—you try to frighten and catch the others, and I pretend that I'm going to throw you in ... but the fascination of that hill—you could find all kinds of things left there by the army.

Don't forget—I told you that we were rather poor, actually quite poor. And we found all kinds of odds and ends like a fork, a pocket knife, and it was magical. But even more wonderful were the flowers on that hill. Every and all kinds! Purple, pink, and green—all the colors! There were gladiolus, anemones, I remember, cyclamens, no, not cyclamens—tulips! There were a lot, there were many asters—in many, many colors—really wonderful! I remember that we just simply loved to walk there. I remember how I used to feel there and that came back to me when we came here.

The childhood mixture of magical and frightening experiences is still coming through in Dina's words.

We would swipe a few watermelons. I remember once my cousin from Tel Aviv came to visit. He always wore new clothing. We lived in the country. We didn't see anything, know anything. He came with pants— what were they called, those trousers with a low waist? One day he came with his friend—that was also characteristic of my parents; our little house (approximately sixty square meters), and everybody who came to visit— friends, cousins, everyone—knew that the house was open. That was very characteristic of my mother and father, very characteristic! They never said "No!"—something that I experienced after I left home. Reactions like, "We can't because we didn't prepare enough food," or "I can't give everyone the same food." At the beginning, I just did not understand; then I was insulted, until I realized that there are people that do not behave like my parents did. And so, during vacations, they came to visit and really enjoyed going to the field, picking tomatoes. I can still feel that on my hand, that powder against insects and that green stuff that comes off the tomatoes, it has a special smell, a smell that I like from a distance.

Dina's words are a little difficult to follow; she is telling a story within a story.

So, we went together to that hill, in the evening, we made a bonfire, we went and stole some watermelons. And later, when we finished eating—we didn't have any dishes, we ate with our hands—I was so crazy about my cousin's bald head that I simply put half a watermelon on his head. That was very funny. He put half a watermelon on my head, and that was not at all funny, because he was bald, but I had hair, and at that time there wasn't any water. At nine at night there wasn't any more water. That meant that my hair remained sticky until the next morning.

Dina, as if waking from her memories, says: I don't know if this interests you at all! My parents had friends in Tel Aviv, that is, friends who had come from Poland from the same—places, and they came to visit us in the *moshav.* Here things get mixed up for me. On the one hand, my mother would tell me, actually she didn't really tell me, but she gave me the latent message that they were genteel and nicely dressed and that she was always working hard. They had books and music, and we didn't: "There aren't enough books in this house, and my children don't go to concerts." It's really interesting to see what she thinks about this today, but up to a few years ago when we would talk about it, she always thought that we were lacking things compared to the children of their friends from Tel Aviv. And, with the passing of the years, we don't have less! None of us has less than those children had. In other words, the fact that she said there were no books and no music, it may be that in the beginning we were backward in a certain way, maybe even a lot, but we have caught up—all of us! None of us has remained a dumb country hick in any way, shape, or form.

I remember when they received reparations and built their house. In the beginning, my father didn't want to accept reparations, and right away my mother agreed with him. She said—I remember because I wasn't so young any more—she said: "After they ruined, killed, and finished off my entire family, I don't want anything from them." But, in the end she took [it]. She built our house and bought a record player, and when it came there were lots of parties. There was joy in our house. That's something that has remained with us to this day: when there is a birthday, everybody comes—everybody.

It is a bit difficult to follow Dina's train of thought: she moves from her mother's fears about her children, which, according to Dina, did not come to pass, to Olga's refusal to take reparations, to the record player bought with the reparation money and the happiness in their household that has carried over until today.

But, there was always a discrepancy between how my mother understood her situation and how others saw it. For example, there was once a friend, a truck driver, and when he came he was very hungry and the only thing my mother had in the house was radishes, bread, and butter. She felt terrible that she didn't have anything else to feed him. But, years after, he would remind her: "What a wonderful meal you gave me. It's been a long time since I ate such a wonderful meal like those radishes with bread and butter." He had simply been very hungry and the meal tasted delicious. But there were other things too. She worked very hard in the fields—she's not big but she was very strong and muscular—and her friends used to come from Tel Aviv "all dressed up," delicate ladies with high heels, and she always felt the difference, that she didn't have anything to offer.

"Did they talk about what they had gone through?"

In the Holocaust? Hmm, they didn't talk about it when they were young. I don't think they told us anything, nothing. I remember that when I was older, they spoke of starting a new phase. The past was terrible. There—that is, there aren't any uncles, no family—but they were not going to be seen as being miserable or unfortunate, no! Over time, when television became a part of our lives, they slowly told us things, but never very serious, difficult stories. That came only when we were older, much older, eighteen or so. Maybe by then enough time had passed, or maybe because we started to ask direct questions. I really don't remember any of their stories, stories that had an effect on me. And even when she told the really hard stories, the ones my mother told me—my father never did tell us stories, that was after I had started to work. Earlier, I had heard, read, understood, but all that happened to others, that didn't happen to them. That was how I related to it.

"I really don't remember any of their stories, stories that had an effect on me." I ask myself how parents manage to tell stories in this way.

I always knew that I didn't have grandmothers and grandfathers. That was never a surprise to me. I grew up with it—I knew that my grandparents died in the Holocaust and I haven't got any—we have no family on my mother's side. None, because all of them were killed, massacred in the Holocaust. But these were sort of external words—it wasn't traumatic for me and I didn't see my mother suffering from that. It seems that day-to-day life was stronger. You see, my children are growing up today with grandmothers and grandfathers! A whole celebration with all the things that go along with it—the little games they play and the wonderful love given to them by their grandmother and grandfather. I didn't have that at all! That's how I grew up, it seemed all right to me, I didn't think I was missing anything, that's it!

Dina is upset, even a little angry: At a later stage, when I understood and asked, "Olga . . ." I call my mother Olga, but that doesn't, it doesn't mean, it's because they had a friend who, when they came to settle in the *moshav*, the one whose son fell asleep and fell off the wagon, they said to her: "You take care of the children and we'll work for the police." And it worked for a while. And her son, he's older than I am by three years, he called his mother "Mother" and my mother "Olga," and that's how I got used to calling her Olga. Today, if I called her "Mother," she wouldn't turn around. Olga is Olga—that is my mother. That doesn't mean that we're alienated from one another, that's her name.

I hear her explanation and wonder why, at least until now, Dina has referred to Olga as "my mother."

So, when Olga told me, she told me the terrible things she went through, it became very meaningful when she found her brother. Did she tell you about that? *(she is testing me and understands from my reaction that Olga has told us about Yadek).* So that suddenly I had a grandfather! That was the funniest thing. But then she told me, it was hard for her, she told me in detail, and I, you see, nothing came as a surprise for me, nothing. But this time, things finally got connected. Because before it had been, we had our lives here, their lives and what was happening with them here, all of that was strong enough, so full of stimuli and experiences that I didn't busy myself with their past.

Now it came like a blow. When the letter came from Yadek, I don't know what she felt, but we felt it. The few days after she got the letter, actually it was a whole period *(excited)*. It was even more significant, because my father had just died. And that was a hard time for us, a very hard time and then, suddenly, a letter came from Yadek, saying something like: "If you are still alive, still at the same address, and—all that, how are you?" They started to correspond and then he came here and that's it. On my father's side there are a few relatives, but on her side, none. And all of a sudden, I had an uncle! That was great! And he came from Poland, from a country behind the Iron Curtain.

So when he arrived—she told us many stories. Then she told us, and that left a strong impression on me, first of all, she told us how her grand-mother committed suicide because she didn't want to fall into the hands of the Germans. She didn't want to and she knew that they were going to die. And so she preferred to take her own life, she injected herself with kerosene, and she [Olga] told us that she and her mother and another sister were still in the ghetto. She talked about the sister and hardly men-tioned her brother, and only now do I realize why. The explanation was that her mother and father were divorced, and he, the son, stayed with him and the two girls with her, and the mother went with the two girls to the ghetto. And there, she says, I don't know how and when, they killed them; she didn't go into the details.

Now that Yadek had arrived, she began to tell us stories about how she had survived. I think that story was very significant for me, because—because if I see in our literature, in the policy of the Ministry of Education, of Yad Vashem, of everybody, and of myself in the classroom, how I used to teach the Holocaust as resurrection. Yes, there isn't, it isn't Holocaust in the sense of "Oy, gevalt, they killed . . . we're so helpless and miserable." No. It is from Holocaust to redemption! Look at what they did to us and where we are today. We go on and no one will ever do that to us again. And the stories about how she survived, I think they also helped me change my view.

Dina is very upset, but she does not go into detail about how her mother's stories changed her previously normative perception of the Holocaust.

She told how she tried to live in the ghetto, everything was in ruins, bombed and burned, and there wasn't anything to eat or drink, and she walked around the city . . . and then she told me the story about her father—that story really shocked me! But that wasn't because of the Ho-locaust, but because of the type of person he was! He—no, he wasn't German *(with certainty)*, Aryan *(less certain)*, I don't know, at any rate, he wasn't Jewish. She was wandering around and the police caught her wandering in the streets and brought her to the police station. And then they asked her, "Who are you?" And she said she was Olga Orlovska. "Who is that?" She said her father was von Orlovski, the doctor. So they called him in and he came and said: "Yes, this is my daughter." And when they left the police station, he said to her: "Get out of here, so that I won't have to see you again!" Now that's a story that she told me, and to this day I feel a pang inside: How can a father say such a thing? And then she joined the kibbutz and immigrated to Israel. I'm sure that it really wasn't all that simple, but that story made a strong impression on me.

I understand the connection between Olga's story and her father's cowardice.

Now, when her brother came—that was a wonderful experience! First of all, you could see the similarities between them! They hadn't seen each other for forty years, but you could tell that they were brother and sister, even without knowing, you could see it by looking at them! In their faces and in their movements, in the way they spoke, what they emphasized— it was amazing to see, really amazing! Over the years, I had forgotten my Polish because I hadn't used it. But, it's really funny, it came back to me. That is, when I hear Polish spoken around me, I need a few hours and then I understand it once again! To listen, to speak a little, it's hard for me to make the "zych-zych" sound. I understand better than I am able to speak. And he also understood some English, so we managed—he picked up some Hebrew—we developed a very nice relationship. We found out that my grandfather was still alive, even Yadek told us what a disgusting character he was, even he told us how awful he was.

Olga also told us that her mother had been well educated, as had her father, and her grandmother had been a doctor. It was important to her! This is something she [told us]—not so openly at first; then with some regret, in parentheses, that she didn't get an education. She didn't study! I mean, at the beginning, she worked in the *moshav*, she helped my father. He had been in a concentration camp, he contracted tuberculosis and wasn't treated, and then it turned into bronchitis, and then into asthma, and in the end, he had cancer in the lungs and he died of that. Then, he had many difficult periods, dust and sand, he wasn't built for hard work, working the land. And at a certain stage, the whole farm landed on her shoulders! She did all the work, it was hard! Now, she is an intelligent woman. The fact that she didn't learn, that she wasn't able to get a formal education, still bothers her today. She will be retiring soon and she is already planning her studies. She'll study till she drops; she feels deprived in that area and she will always try to overcome it.

Don't misunderstand me. They really appreciate her at work. That's something she is afraid of, by the way, she does a lot in order not to be alone, and she succeeds in it. Except now, she talks about being tired and it makes me—it frightens me a lot. She has enough health reasons to be tired, and that frightens me—the idea that something could happen to her frightens me. I will be terribly sad, in the real sense of the word.

"And your father, what do you know about him?"

(Chokes): He didn't tell us much. He was a happy man—it's very hard for me to talk about him in the past tense—but that's how he was, a happy man and people really loved him. A month after he died, we sat and talked about what had happened to him, what he had gone through. And then his friends told about what they had been through in the concentration camp, how he and all of them adjusted at that time. Those weren't stories about something heroic that someone had done. What he had done, others had done as well. For instance, how they created confusion in one corner of the camp so that in another corner people could escape, those kinds of things. No, there weren't any horror stories. They talked and they never hid things. I don't remember ever hearing: "No! No, we're not going to tell you. That's not right." I remember that they said clearly: "It was terribly sad, it was awful." But both of them were very young, my mother was eighteen when she came to Israel and father was five years older, and they came here and basically settled down. Here they lived in the present, that was what was strong, that's what they passed on to me.

It was important for my father to go to the synagogue on Yom Kippur. That is something I am sorry about. Because, for my father it was important. His family was very traditional, but he was already less so. There was a time when he only went to the synagogue for the holidays at the beginning of the year. Later on, he became the "gentile of the *moshav*"— he would go with the wagon to fetch the rabbi because all the others were religious. Holidays were important to him. I vaguely remember him saying to my mother: "Once again, my clothes won't be ready for the holidays" or "We still haven't finished preparing the house and getting the food ready and the holidays are already here."

Maybe I'm mixing up things here, I don't know exactly. But after a short time, we all, that is, my parents, didn't bother any more. No candles, no nothing. We only celebrated the rituals of the holidays. For instance, we always lighted the candles on Hanukkah. Now I remember that my father told us that his father would light a candle, bless it, tell them stories from his childhood. But in our house we used to gather together on Rosh Hashanah, always together, and we always had a festive meal and there was a lot of joy. On Hanukkah there were doughnuts, and pancakes for Purim, and we always danced and laughed.

But from the point of view of tradition, religion, nothing. I even re-member hearing, not in a rough way, but clearly: "If you want, go ahead, if you want to honor tradition, if you want to believe, if you want to keep the *mitzvoth*—go ahead, please, we won't interfere." I remember that this was said in association with my mother, not my father. How could such a thing happen, one cannot talk about the Holocaust and God in the same breath. It doesn't go together. And so—there are people, some of the people are evil, there are different cultures, and that has been so always. That is what happened here, and it's a shame that it happened. Today I hear this from Olga in a much more refined way. She discusses the meaning of history, but she holds no religious beliefs.

Dina conveys the different religious nuances that characterized her parents. I ask what her solution was.

When my children were born, I guess all mothers go through this in one way or another, I thought, Shall we light candles on Shabbat? Yet somehow, I never managed to finish work on time on Fridays. I always had to clean on Shabbat—when do I have time to clean in the middle of the week? Really, I never had time. Not that the house was so neglected, but the laundry piled up, and when there is a whole day free, I should sit idly? *(laughing)*. No! I read and write, I hang up the wash, clean, cook, whatever has to be done. There were times that I wanted, I thought that it is something that is possible for a person to do, a person can make him- or herself become used to doing certain things.

"And what did you want it to be like? Did you have a picture in your mind?"

Like the pictures in the books! The pictures that are in children's books, the mother with the scarf around her head, raising her hands to bless the candles. No, I never succeeded. It didn't come from me, it didn't, it wasn't a part of me. It was a nice sort of picture, a picture where the children are sitting around the table, they are sitting there so nicely and disciplined, and the father blesses ... Somehow, it never worked out like that. The children never sat around the table so nicely and quietly, and I never managed to make a Shabbat meal. I don't know why, it didn't work. I was sorry about that when they were young. Today it's not an issue. I have other things. After all, it doesn't have to be so—it's a religion without religion.

Dina's voice seems to have a note of disappointment and apology.

As for tradition, something was created here. Really. When there is a family gathering, there is never a birthday that goes unnoticed. For us a birthday is a birthday. We invite people or we make an announcement and people come to the party. They bring presents and the whole thing has its own dynamics. There must be a present no matter what, that was an underlying message. I remember that we as children prepared, our parents had a wedding anniversary, and we wanted to, but we didn't have pocket money or anything. What to do? I remember that I read in a children's magazine, I was pretty young, perhaps ten or eleven. I read how to make a stork out of a pine cone. I didn't remember the exact directions, but I had the idea. So, when they went to visit somebody, I said to my sister: "Now, we're going to make them a present." It didn't come out right, what a disappointment that was for me! Of course, when they returned and saw us looking so unhappy they asked what was wrong. "We wanted to make you a present and it didn't work out." Their reaction was "Never mind, it was a lovely idea." That's it, that's what is left, nothing else.

"And what are relations like between you and your brother and sister?"

Today, we get along very nicely. There was a time, how can I say it, we always got along fine. We were never angry with one another, we didn't hold grudges or anything, no, there wasn't anything like that. But today we are closer than ever. We're sorry that we live an hour's drive away from one another. I have a sister who lives in a *moshav* in the far south. We really love to be together; we enjoy each other's company very much; we love each other very much; we support each other a lot—emotionally, no, not economically, because we are not in a position to do so *(laughing)*. I am the oldest one and they depended on me. I am responsible. For many years Olga worked until five o'clock, and that meant that I had to do the shopping, take care of the children. My brother is six years younger than me.

"Are there any objects or traditions that have been passed on?"

You know, that's interesting. There was a time, perhaps it's still around, I remember when Olga saved some red kerchief that was pretty shabby. I mean, it wasn't embroidered with any special pattern, just a plain red scarf. I remember that she guarded it and told us that Father used it in the concentration camp. That's it, there were no other objects. I think that they completely shut out the past. They bought some pictures over the years, not too many. My mother found her cousin at some point, he was old, he also immigrated to Israel. Meanwhile, he died. He was really the only one. He had a few photographs and a few letters that she wrote. She doesn't show too much, she never did show much. You could say that she reveals a little and conceals a lot. Why do I say this? Because— my nephew had his bar-mitzvah not too long ago and he worked on his "roots" project. All of a sudden, I hear *(excited)* my mother saying: "Look at this, look at this! This is a letter that I wrote to my Uncle Haim when I was around eight years old." "But Mother, you never told me about this." "Enough, in that closet, there are lots of things. There's a photo of my mother and some others."

Dan and Orit enter the room, and Dina, somewhat uncomfortable, turns to them: How much talking did you do? She *(pointing to Noga)* is asking me about my childhood memories, I could talk nonstop until the day after tomorrow. *(Turns back to Noga)* I left home at sixteen. I was born at the end of October so I was always a year ahead. Pedagogic preparatory courses already existed, and that was very important to Olga, to send me to study because "it's very important to study." So I left home. Now, you have to consider that I left at an age when there are usually battles, explosions. I wasn't home so I didn't have the problems of adolescence *(laughing to herself)*. Until the age of sixteen, I was the older one, and later on, I was out of the house. Now, my sister was home and she was the real "sandwich" child. Just a few years ago, she told me: "You were always the one they depended on. When you are with Olga, no one else exists. The two of you sit there opposite one another and I feel completely left out." We solved this problem quite well, but it had bothered her for many years. She tried everything, tried us all out, when she went through adolescence.

She made so much trouble for her teachers that Olga took her to be examined. Was she able to learn anything? Then they told her: "You have a gifted daughter." But that is probably characteristic of a hundred million other families, right?

Dina looks tired. Perhaps the larger group makes it difficult for her to continue. We are offered some more refreshments, in keeping with the family tradition. On our way back to Beer-Sheva, Dina's closing remarks echo in my ears: "But that is probably characteristic of a hundred million other families, right?"

When Dina, like Tzipke and Hannah, narrates her life story, she reduces its importance in comparison to those of her parents: "My parents came down to settle this place; they were pioneers—pioneers of the fifties—and the pioneers of those days were not like the pioneers of the eighties." Just as Olga downplayed the impact of the events she had experienced during the war, Dina trivializes her own activities in relation to her parents' deeds, emphasizing the continuity of what her parents have achieved during their life in Israel. She reminds us of Olga when she says: "I don't really know if this really interests you at all." It seems as if Dina is also asking herself: Can my story really be of interest to anybody? And again in her concluding sentence, "that is probably characteristic of a hundred million other families, right?"

Dina's life history relates her own pioneering activities. As a teacher, she helped establish a school in Lehavim, a new urban settlement in the desert. This motif reminds her of her childhood. She recalls from the stories of her parents how they had joined the *moshav* at "the edge of the desert," where she was born. In the tiny first-grade classroom, Dina was already given an important task: since she was the only one who understood the teacher's Hebrew, as well as the Polish and Romanian spoken by the other pupils, she translated for them. Was this what led her in later years to go into teaching? When she became involved in building a school from the ground up at Lehavim, she remembers the pioneering spirit of her childhood.

"Pioneering" is repeatedly referred to during the interview. Words like "create" and "strong" appear over and over in different contexts as expressions of action, hopefulness, and novelty. Mixed with this kind of discourse are expressions of transience, danger, and fear. In the *moshav*, "people [were] sitting on their suitcases," and there was poverty and back-wardness. Near her parents' house, saboteurs stalked, stealing cows and killing people. When she is asked about her own memories, Dina replies: "As a child I was so afraid, I probably picked up those fears, I didn't like darkness . . ." Perhaps these fears were related to more than the *moshav's* reality? Dina does not consider such a possibility.

While relating her early memories, Dina's constant expressions of laughter and pleasure mix with those of fear: for example, the loaded hay wagon overturned and all the children fell off along with the bales. It must have been rather frightening, but Dina describes it as "a real party." She also tells about the neighbor's son, who fell asleep and slipped off the wagon into the sand on the way back from the beach, as if it were a funny incident, although the boy's mother "almost had a heart attack when her son suddenly disappeared." The British army camp with the huge hole in the ground is a source of mystery and fear, but the surrounding area was full of flowers of all colors, like a Nature Preservation Society's poster.

Through her lively description of events, Dina's biography reconstruc-tion assumes a particular shape: the pioneering identity of the Israeli child-woman that helped Dina ignore her parents' past. It was not that she did not know. She says, for example, "I didn't have grandmothers and grand-fathers. That was never a surprise to me. I grew up with it." Only when her mother's brother appears (when Dina is already a mother herself) does something new occur: "This time, things finally got connected . . . before . . . we had our lives here . . . all of that was strong enough, so full of stimuli and experiences that I didn't busy myself with their past." Had Yadek not appeared, perhaps Dina would still be absorbed in that ongoing present.

But Olga's ambivalence reappears in Dina's story. Settling in the *moshav* was not a simple issue for her parents: on the one hand, there is the legend of pioneering, accompanied by hospitality and the adventures of farming and nature. Dina very much identified with this part of her parents' story as "something that has tremendous strength." On the other hand, her father suffered from severe physical problems ("he wasn't built for hard work") and her mother felt inferior to their city friends for not having concerts or enough books. Dina's voice assumes a sarcastic tone when she speaks about the "delicate women with high heels" who had no idea what physical work and life close to nature was like. There is also a note of envy of their cultural superiority. The story was Dina's; were the feelings Dina's or her mother's?

What did these expressions of ambivalence, of fear and hope, mean for Dina? During most of the interview, she tries to mitigate their significance. She insists that neither she nor her siblings felt any less fortunate than the city children who used to come to visit them: "None of us has remained a dumb country hick in any way, shape, or form." The push to learn, to obtain an education and a profession, had its origin in Olga's sense of educational deficit. Only recently has Dina come to enjoy studying at the university "for its own sake," which was not true of her early training for the teaching profession. And she admits that it was difficult for her to return to the narrow framework of teaching elementary school after "a whole new world [opened] up for me."

Insight requires tranquillity and free time. Dina had neither, because she was in constant motion. One example is her failed attempt to keep the Shabbat. Identifying with her father, whose own attempts were unsuccessful, Dina tried to practice the Shabbat in her own home. She had an idealized image of blessing the candles, the children sitting quietly around the table in a festive atmosphere. However, she was unsuccessful in accomplishing this ideal. Was it because her children did not go along with it? Or was it that Dina seemed too busy with housework? "When do I have time to clean in the middle of the week?" Partly admitting failure, partly on the defensive, Dina says: "It's a religion without religion." Dina avoids the opportunity to reflect on it. Following her mother's path, she casts doubt on religious ceremonies as well as on the existence of God after the Holocaust.

Dina's compromises are the secular family celebrations, such as birthdays, which are of central importance to the family. These are celebrated with religious zeal—a response to the void left by the Holocaust. They represent family continuity, which was also very important to Olga. The phonograph, bought with Olga's reparation money, became the symbol of "joy and dancing." Again and again, Dina, like her mother, *creates reality rather than experiences it.* It is as if she is still participating in a latent controversy about the success of the family's life in Israel. Whereas her younger brother expresses his current anxieties openly, struggling with his parents' reflection in himself, Dina gives no sign of similar feelings or thoughts.

This becomes obvious when Dina refers to the Holocaust. To begin with, there is a difference in her mind between "resurrection and survival." She grew up on the idea "from Holocaust to redemption," seeing the Holocaust as another form of Israeli heroism. This was the way she was brought up and this is how she introduced it into her teaching, in accord with the Israeli norm that characterized the fifties and sixties (Segev, 1991). At home, the hard times in the *moshav* were widely discussed, but not horror stories from the Holocaust. When, a month after her father's death, his friends came and spoke of their experiences in the concentration camp, Dina adds that they weren't stories "about something heroic," only the regular things that had happened. Though she knew that she had no grandfathers and grandmothers because they were killed in the Holocaust, "these were . . . external words—it wasn't traumatic for me . . . it seemed all right to me, I didn't think I was missing anything."

It was thus surprising to hear Dina's response to the question about objects in her parents' home. She recalled a red kerchief that her mother had kept, the only reminder of her father's time in the concentration camps. Perhaps this was an indication that she associated the Holocaust emotionally with her father rather than her mother. Dina reports that her father was not talkative, and it is difficult for her to talk about her father "in the past tense."

When, as a result of her brother's arrival, Olga started to speak of her father's home, Dina was surprised. She found that she still had a grandfather (Olga's father) in Poland. However, she talks about it in her typical way, mixing contradictory emotions: "Suddenly I had a grandfather! That was the funniest thing!" and we feel her anger and embarrassment. At this point in the interview, Dina stops referring to her mother as "my mother" and calls her "Olga." She tries to explain why she calls her mother Olga (it "doesn't mean that we're alienated from one another"). However, it does not seem coincidental that she starts to relate to her mother this way at this exact point in the interview.

Here, we find the first indication of a boundary between mother and daughter that has not been obvious before. The use of her mother's first name could be seen as a sign of intimacy (Dina had called her Olga during her childhood). On the other hand, it may be a sign of necessary anger at a mother who tried to conceal her past, and perhaps also, anger at the lack of boundaries, which Dina has not succeeded in establishing. Olga concealed her gentile background (and that part of her past) from Dina, who was the eldest child and felt very close to her mother (her sister says: "When you are with Olga, no one else exists"). As this aspect of her mother's past is uncovered, her belief that she is very close to her mother and that the past "was finished with" is shown to be untrue.

Only now does Olga tell her daughter how she survived in the ghetto and after the war. Dina adds: "The stories about how she survived, I think they also helped me change my view." She does not explain how they did so, but we may surmise that, for Dina, the Holocaust does not mean simply redemption, it also means pride in the mere act of survival. In the Israeli context, this constitutes crossing a very fine, yet clear-cut line that divides those who associate themselves with "here" and those who associate themselves with "there." Dina states that "nothing came as a surprise for me, nothing . . . this time, things finally got connected," and we assume that the missing link has been the effect of the past on the present and a new understanding of the meaning of human suffering and survival.

At the very time this happened, several other important events also occurred: Dina went to study at the university "for its own sake." At the same time, she and her sister settled the problems that had caused tension between them ("she was the real 'sandwich' child"). As the older, responsible sister, she acknowledges her envy of her younger sibling, who could afford to "make trouble" for her teachers, while being recognized as the gifted one. Dina, living up to her parents' expectations, saw herself as an "average child," and later refers to her own daughter, Orit, in a similar way.

Still, Dina also continues to admire her mother and identify with her. Her grandfather, condemned by Olga, is now also rejected by Dina. For a moment he turns into "a German" in her imagination when she tells about the incident at the police station, which Olga has only hinted at: "If they catch us together, don't you dare say that I am your father." But where Olga reports on her father's fear, Dina emphasizes his rejection: "Get out of here, so that I won't have to see you again!" and adds: "to this day I feel a pang inside: How can a father say such a thing?"

Was Dina aware that Olga's stepfather was not interested in renewing contact with her? Evidently Olga wanted to spare her these complex and embarrassing details, and Dina is still willing to "cooperate." Indeed, Dina asserts that her mother "reveals a little and conceals a lot." She assumes that there may be other facets to her mother's story she does not yet know about. However, Dina does not ask, and Olga prefers to give letters and pictures from the past to her grandson, who is doing a school project about his family, rather than show them to Dina.

There is only one clue to the way Dina imagined the past, during her childhood, beyond her expressed fears and feelings of danger and temporality: "the fascination of that hill"—the mystery of the British army camp to which she felt herself drawn in her childhood. They played "I'm going to throw you in" near the frightening hole in the ground. They found artifacts left by the army; objects like a fork and a pocket knife, and "we were rather poor, actually quite poor." In contrast, there were beautiful flowers of all colors on the hill. We asked ourselves if this place entailed an unconscious representation of the past for Dina. Was it something like "father's concentration camp" or "mother's ghetto" or "a cemetery for lovers who were not buried"? A place where children could play dangerous games, like the "games" their parents had "played" under the Nazis. However, unlike Momie's games with the Nazi beast in his parents' cellar in the novel *See under: "Love"* (Grossman, 1986), Dina played games unconsciously, if at all.

At first it seemed that Dina had reconstructed a conflict-free biography based on her mother's manifest attitude: "to rebuild life." We asked ourselves if Dina could simply ignore her mother's hidden and conflicting identities by stressing the continuity of her own life with that of her parents? However, Dina's own conscious and unconscious sense of fear and temporality suggests that she has not addressed the unresolved issues of the past but, rather, has silenced and repressed them. In this respect, we learn that she has come a long way when she describes the process in her own mind: no longer only redemption and heroism, but now also legitimization and respect for her mother's act of survival. Also, she has incorporated being Polish into her own identity through her relationship with her uncle, Yadek. Can we claim that these are signs of Dina's own "working through" process? We cannot be sure: the change in her consciousness may also be accounted for by the self-confidence she has acquired through her studies and her position as school vice principal, or by the changes that have occurred in Israeli society as a whole. Nevertheless, Dina is still in an early phase of this process. Her unspoken question still is: How are my fears and hopes linked to what my parents experienced during the Holocaust?

We now wonder what Orit, Dina's daughter and Olga's granddaughter, has absorbed from the stories of her mother and her grandmother? Orit is under no obligation to concern herself with the complicated issues of the past. As a second-generation Israeli, she lives at a distance of fifty years from the events that shaped her grandmother's life and, to a certain degree, her mother's. She was born into a different family framework, one that included grandmothers and grandfathers, and she is growing up in the complicated reality of a contemporary society shaped by tensions between Arabs and Jews, between various ethnic groups, and between the religious and the secular, as well as a stressful economic situation, in which the past is no longer represented except through the stories and sayings of the elderly. She is sixteen and probably busy discovering her own identity.

Orit

From survival and restoration to choosing the future

Orit is a tall, plump girl with long, wavy red hair. Her brown eyes, inquisitive and warm, examine me as she comes forward when her mother calls her to shake hands. We all sit down for a while in the living room to have soft drinks and fruit. Orit is sitting with her bare feet folded under her on the sofa. While we engage in small talk, she remains quiet. After a few minutes, I suggest that we find ourselves a place to talk and she points to her room. "There's a problem with chairs," she says with a smile, "I'll sit on the bed and you can have the chair by the desk." The room is simply furnished, the style typical of a dormitory at the regional high school. As I prepare the tape recorder, I ask Orit to close the door, since we can hear the conversation from the living room, and she agrees. I begin with my usual opening question: "Please tell me the story of your life, whatever you think is important." Orit is a bit embarrassed and smiles shyly.

Where should I start? That I was born in Yerucham. And that I lived there for eight years. It was very nice there; I was part of a small, rather close-knit group. I had friends and it was nice there. I lived there until the age of eight. Then we moved to Omer. That is, our goal was to come here, to Lehavim, but because the house wasn't finished and we hadn't sold the one in Yerucham, we moved to Omer, to my grandparents' house, who were in France at the time.

"Grandparents from which side?"

From my father's side. I lived there and went to school there. It wasn't really so good for me, this move, because I really had it good in Yerucham. I was in the second group that studied in the local school. I had to get used to new friends *(laughing)*. I don't really have such a magnificent history like some other people, I'm just an ordinary girl . . . we came here two years later and I've been here for six years already.

Orit hesitates—should she add something? I ask myself: Why is her description so brief, even in comparison to Yoav's story? "Perhaps you could describe some early memories from your childhood?"

(Thinks for a moment, eyes down) When I play with the kids from the neighborhood, we go to the shopping center near our house and we annoy the shopkeepers, we steal some chewing gum.

"Who is 'we'?"

My girlfriends and me, mainly two. Neighborhood friends of mine. Not exactly neighbors: one was a neighbor and the other lived a little farther away, but we would meet and play together in the playground and go from there to the shopping center *(smiling)*. I used to hide. First, I would say hello to the store owner and then I would go and hide. I didn't steal things *(laughter)*. That was when I was in kindergarten, I think, or maybe first grade. Afterwards, I also remember . . . I liked dogs and cats a lot. So one day, we played in the shopping center, my brother and I, on boxes that were there. Gideon was about one year old and he played with me there. Along came somebody from the municipality and asked, "Where does the Shamir family live?" I answered him right away: "We're the Shamir family." Then he asked: "Do you have a dog?" and we said yes. Then he asked: "Where are your parents?" and I showed him our house and then I heard him tell my mother that our dog had died *(quietly)*. They found him dead, and by the collar, they knew it was our dog. He was sick, he had been poisoned or something like that, and they found him dead. That was very sad for me (*her eyes are looking at me seriously, for the first time*).

"*Do you remember what your mother or father said? Did you cry?*"

No, I didn't cry, but I was sad (*five-second pause*). But I don't think you came here to listen to my childhood memories. I thought you were going to ask different questions (*laughter*) . . . You are interested, after all, in my grandmother's stories and memories about the Holocaust.

I am surprised by Orit's directness. I am still thinking about her childhood experiences, how they are both similar to and different from those of her mother. I wait for a minute. "If that's important to you, go ahead. What is your connection to her stories and memories? What do you know and feel about what your grandmother experienced? When and what has she told you?"

I sort of had to squeeze it out of her. I was in Poland with her last year for three weeks. We were in Warsaw and we visited the places where she used to live. She invited me. It was a sort of a "small revenge" (*she says this with emphasis and a smile*) against Gideon. He was supposed to go abroad this year and my grandmother said: "The first one to go is the oldest." One day when she said that she and her friend, Shimon, were going to Poland, I said jokingly: "Me too." Then she said: "All right, you too." My mother wanted to go also, but that didn't work out moneywise. So, during the three weeks of the trip, I tried to hear from her, to get a little more information, since we were, after all, visiting places where she had lived. And one day, when I tried to ask her in an indirect way, she said: "It's hard for me to talk about that, but if you ask me direct questions, I will give you direct answers." Then we were in Warsaw, and I could see it all coming back to her, because she used to live there and it was in the air somehow. Then she told me about her father and her grandmother.

This has been a long stretch of talking for Orit, and she stops to catch her breath for a moment. I am utterly amazed that I have heard nothing about this visit from Olga or Dina.

She told me how her grandmother used to take her for walks in the forest, some forest near Warsaw, and how she used to walk to a certain tree and play there. There was also a lake near the forest, and they also used to walk there together. She loved her grandmother very much, and I could really imagine to myself how they were together, walking and playing games . . . (*she pauses*).

She told me that she didn't see her father very often because he was a gentile. And when her mother didn't want her to get hurt, when things got bad in the ghetto, she sent her to her father *(quietly, almost whispering)*. She didn't have it so good there. That is, since he was her father, it was clear that she would love him, but she didn't feel good there. She was there for three years. He kept her there and then he sent her to some old aunt. It was very vivid for me, I could feel it in the air, what it was like . . .

There is a knock at the door; Gideon (her brother) comes in. "I just wanted to show you my new haircut. Do you have a minute?"

Not now, later. *Gideon leaves. I am sorry this interruption has occurred at just this point. It will be difficult to restore the atmosphere of our earlier conversation.*

"Let's return to Warsaw. You're walking around with your grandmother. How was that for you?"

It was exciting, I could imagine to myself how she had walked in these same places with her grandmother *(silence)*.

"And did you get emotional about it together? Did you or she cry?"

I don't know. Grandmother doesn't really show her feelings. It's difficult to be emotional with her. Of course, when we stood near her house, or approximately where she once lived—the Poles, after all, did not restore Warsaw the way it once was, before the war—then you could feel her excitement: "Here I am, back home." But aside from that, it was very hard to know how she felt exactly. She told me about what had happened then. I don't know exactly if that was the same grandmother, that is, the mother of the mother or of the father, but when they were in the ghetto and they started to take people out on trains, she didn't want to, she didn't have the strength any more, so she wanted to, she was a doctor and she injected herself with a tranquilizer, that is, she committed suicide *(Orit is thinking to herself and pauses for a few seconds)*.

(Softly) "Did she tell you anything else?"

No *(silence)*.

"When you came back from Warsaw, did you tell your friends, your mother and father?"

Yes, I more or less told them what happened *(she is uninterested now, quiet again)*.

"Does your mother know your grandmother's stories?"

(Laugh) I suppose so, she's nosy like me *(laugh)*.

"Up to now you've told me about yourself and about your trip to Poland with your grandmother. But you have barely said anything about your parents. What memories do you have of them?"

(Surprised) Memories? I don't really know. We used to like to walk, to go for hikes, all the time. For part of Shabbat mornings, we liked to get away from the routine, work and school, and go hiking. That was mostly in Yerucham, but also in Omer. We would go especially when the anemones were in bloom, there was a field there, a field full of anemones. But in Lehavim, because of their jobs, we couldn't go on with this. Mother's job in school [as vice principal] and my father's too—he's in charge of safety in the Potash Works. He checks when there are problems with the safety helmets, or if there is a chlorine leak and people are injured, he has to figure out what happened.

"From what background and ethnic group is your father?"

Father is half and half. He's half Algerian and half Polish. My Polish grandmother from my father's side talks only about her coming to Israel. She has told almost nothing about her family there *(laughing)*. I did not get the story about her family from her. I got that from a relative of hers. I don't know exactly how they are related, but she told me that they lived in a small village not far from Warsaw. They were also a very big family and all of them were wiped out in the camps, burnt in the ovens. She remained behind with a brother and a sister. I don't know where. That is, maybe I knew, but I can't remember. And she came to this country just when the state was being established; she came on a famous boat, the name escapes me, ah, it was called *Exodus 1948,* if I'm not mistaken. My grandmother doesn't have so many memories because she was a very small child during the Holocaust and because they also emigrated to France at a certain stage. They didn't exactly stay in Poland. That's why she doesn't remember events in Poland like she remembers coming to Israel.

"Do you feel that this background influenced your mother or your father?"

(Thinking) I think . . . neither of them . . . because both of my grandmothers, if you ask them directly, will answer: "What was, was—let's forget it. What will be is what's important." And that's why my parents aren't so interested and don't go into it so much, like telling stories about the past or something like that. They talk about the future—what we'll do tomorrow. What happened then is not so important.

"What would you like to happen tomorrow? What are your plans for the future?"

I have big dreams . . . there are all kinds of directions I want to go in. I also know that wherever I end up, that's where I'll stay and . . . I will use whatever I can!

"But what do you wish for?"

To be an economist . . . or to go into the army, the intelligence. From this family, I already have experience in spying (laughing) and, anyway, I want to do something for this country, not just live my life here. That's why I am taking advanced classes in Arabic, so that I'll be accepted there when the time comes (silence).

"Are the names in your family connected to the past?"

Yes, Amnon, my little brother [age 8]. His middle name is Piecke after my grandfather, who died a few months before he was born. And my mother is also called Gita, after her two grandmothers. My name and Gideon's are not connected to the past. Actually, my mother and father didn't want to give us names from the past because our motto is "Don't think about what was in the past." They only wanted to commemorate grandfather, like they say (silence).

"Are there any objects that pass from generation to generation in the family?"

(Laughing) Our chairs. They used to belong to grandmother's brother, Yadek. He showed up one day and lived for a while in an immigration center. Later on he moved to Germany. He didn't manage to live here and he left his chairs with us. I loved him from first sight. I also sort of pitied him. For instance, in the beginning, when he went to the supermarket with my mother and saw all the things on the shelves, he would ask her: "Can I buy everything?" He wasn't used to there being so many things to buy. We mostly talked in body language, because I didn't know Polish and he didn't know Hebrew. Mother taught me a few sentences in Polish, she taught me to say just a few words. My mother knows a lot of languages, a little bit from every language . . . I felt that there was a resemblance between him and grandmother, both of them are quiet and cultured . . . (laughing) in their way of speaking. There is no cursing. At the most, they may say "the devil . . ." My grandmother, especially, speaks quietly, but it sinks in at just the right spot!

"Holidays—how do you celebrate them?"

Not very religiously. At Passover, we don't read the entire Haggadah, we read whatever we want. But the whole family gets together. That includes Grandmother and Grandfather (from my mother's side, although sometimes also from my father's side), and my uncle who lives near them (the son who continues working the parents' farm) and his family. Most of our family live in the central part of the country, except my mother's sister, who lives near Eilat. There is also an aunt that my grandmother adopted or lived with, her son grew up with her children, and anybody who has joined the family over the years *(smiling)*. And then there's Grandmother's borscht and the "aroma." For my grandmother, "aroma" is something burnt; every time she burns the food, and that happens quite often because she is doing ten other things at the same time, she says: "This food doesn't taste burnt, that is the special aroma of this food." In the beginning, my father wasn't used to this: "Why do you like to eat burnt food?" But slowly he got used to it *(she is thoughtful for a moment, smiling to herself)*.

We don't tell stories like "There used to be . . . ." Pictures, yes. Once I was cleaning Grandmother's closet and I discovered pictures of Grandmother when she was little with her mother and pictures of uncles and aunts. But I didn't tell her that I had looked through her things, so I don't really know who was who. Our motto is that one has to live one's life, to use every moment in the best way possible. In the last two years, my visit to Poland changed my way of thinking. One has to live. One should plan what one wants to do, and if something else happens, it's all right. This is what I think I'll also tell my children. I won't tell too many "granny stories." I won't talk too much about what used to be. What good does it do?

Orit ends with this proclamation, which is perhaps closer to what she has heard from her mother and grandmother. We conclude the interview and Orit fills in a copy of our questionnaire. We enter the living room, where Dina and Noga are still talking. Dina is surprised at the length of our interview: "I didn't think that you would be able to get Orit to talk for such a long time. She isn't one of the big talkers in the family." I try not to interfere with the conclusion of her interview. Later, we are offered more soft drinks and fruit. We take our leave and step out into the evening breeze. The first evening shadows of the summer sun race across the hills of Lahav.

As I go over Orit's questionnaire on our way home, I find that in the part on feelings about the Holocaust, she has rated "pride" the highest (3) ("after all, we succeeded in coming to Israel"). She has rated "anger" equally high ("the stupidity of the people who let this happen"). She has rated "shame" medium (2) ("we didn't manage to get to them before six million died") and gives the same rating to "paralysis" (adding in her own handwriting: "It happened to them, will it not happen to us?").

After a brief attempt to follow directions and tell her life story, Orit turns to her interviewer almost as her mother and grandmother did: "But I don't think you came here to listen to my childhood memories." Orit has her own a priori ideas about the interview. She does not think Dan is interested in her in her own right, but rather as the granddaughter of Olga. After two short tales of her childhood in Yerucham (shoplifting from the stores and the death of her beloved dog), Orit comments, "I don't really have such a magnificent history like some other people." This was not surprising in an interview with a sixteen-year-old, especially since she was referred to by her mother as "not being the type who talks much." However, Orit's next phrase "I'm just an ordinary girl," reminds us of Dina's and Olga's self-representations.

For us, the interview holds a surprise: neither Olga nor Dina has mentioned anything about Olga and Orit's trip to Warsaw the previous year. For Orit, this was a key experience: "My visit to Poland changed my way of thinking." Unfortunately, Orit does not clarify in what way. She traveled with her grandmother to her home ground and tries, indirectly, to ask her about the Holocaust, but Olga answers very much in the spirit of what she has said to her own children, "It is hard for me to talk about that," but that she is ready to answer any questions she might have. Orit asked and Olga told her why her mother sent her to live with her father as "things got bad in the ghetto," about the problems she had with him, and about her grandmother's suicide.

Orit acknowledges the feelings between Olga and her father: "Since he was her father, it was clear that she would love him, but she didn't feel good there." Is this the naiveté of a sixteen-year-old who could not imagine not loving one's father? Or is it perhaps her insight into the complexity of the relationship between Olga and her father? At any rate, it is very different from Dina's (and Olga's) formulations. Dina did not consider the possibility that Olga loved her father—a futile love that got little response. Dina only spoke of her mother being rejected by him.

Further on in the interview, Orit displays an unusual talent for identifying people's feelings. Her definitions are clear and concise, without going into motives. When she refers to Olga at the time of their Warsaw visit, she says: "Grandmother doesn't really show her feelings. It's difficult to be emotional with her." She describes Dina as "nosy like me" and her uncle Yadek as like her grandmother: "both of them are quiet and cultured . . . no cursing." Again, reflecting on Olga, "my grandmother speaks quietly, but it sinks in at just the right spot." She explains the lack of effect the past has had upon her parents: both grandmothers have made it clear that the important thing is the present and the future. In all these references, Orit expresses neither judgment nor anger nor fear. Her reflections reveal a lot more than the "black and white" thinking we might expect of a girl her age.

It was Orit who asked to accompany her grandmother to Warsaw in the first place. Even if her initial motive was the jealousy she felt about her brother's planned trip to the United States, Orit exhibits a much more serious approach later on. Her curiosity about her family's past is striking. She knows how to listen to her grandmother "between the lines": "you could feel her excitement: 'Here I am, back home,' " and accepts her grandmother's difficulty in showing her emotions as part of telling her story. Yet her curiosity was not satisfied by hearing her grandmother's personal story in Warsaw. When Orit later states that she wants to serve in the intelligence section of the army in order "to do something for this country," she adds with a smile and a bit of irony: "From this family, I already have experience in spying." Unlike her grandmother, there was no need for her to study in order to "make up for a lack that was created during that time" nor, like her mother, did she have to prove that she had not missed anything by being raised in a backward village.

All of this reflects Orit's own patterns of thought rather than a continuation of her mother's or grandmother's. She became an investigator of the past. Even when she verbally accepted the family's norm—"the main thing is the future, it's not so important to scrape around in the past"— she tried to find out and to understand those things not discussed in the family that relate to the past, to begin to make sense of its hidden complexity. In a few simple statements about Olga, Orit shows that she has captured something neither her grandmother herself nor Dina could clarify through their life stories.

Our question remains: Why didn't Olga or Dina tell us about the trip to Warsaw? After all, it was a central event in Orit's life that "changed her way of thinking." Did Dina and Olga not notice it? In the interviews with both Dina and Olga, moreover, there is no mention of Orit's unique interest and sensitivity, which comes through so clearly in the interview. Both relate to her in a general way. "Orit is an ordinary child," Dina says when describing her daughter's intellectual abilities.

One might suggest that the nonmention of the trip was a by-product of a biased interview. Orit was aware of the subject of our research: You didn't come to "listen to my childhood memories . . . you are interested . . . in my grandmother's stories and memories about the Holocaust." Dina also knew about our research subject, and possibly her mother did too. Perhaps they assumed that we were not particularly interested in their relationships with their children and grandchildren. However, elsewhere in her interview Dina gives a detailed description of the move to Lehavim, of her first teaching experiences, including the period in which she taught her own son, Gideon. It must be asked: Why was Orit left out of her mother's narrative (just as Genia omitted Tzipke from hers)? Why did this omission also include her daughter's and her mother's trip to Warsaw?

It is more difficult to believe that this trip was unimportant to Olga. One can sense through Orit's descriptions how the visit aroused Olga's feelings and memories. After all, it was Olga who initiated the return to her hometown. Yet Olga makes no mention of the trip whatsoever. We know, however, that Olga tells only what she is being asked about according both to her and to her granddaughter's account. If it had not been for her son Benny's interruption of our interview, we might not have learned about her brother Yadek's trip to Israel and what it opened up in her family.

We may assume, then, that it was not a random omission but rather an intentional one. Why did Dina bypass the trip to Warsaw? According to Orit, Olga wanted Dina to come, but it was not financially possible. Was that the only reason? Orit identified with the issues of Olga's father and her feelings in Warsaw in a manner different from that of her mother.

She related to Olga's feelings, not simply by listening to them through Olga's words. Perhaps Dina did not tell us about the trip to Warsaw because she did not share her daughter's insights.

It is more difficult to explain why Olga "forgot" to tell us about the trip. After all, she encouraged Orit's interest in the past by sharing her stories and feelings with her. She had reason to be proud of herself: why did she not show us this pride? It must have been a difficult experience for her to feel at home "there" after she had worked so hard at rebuilding her life "here." Perhaps the trip to Warsaw meant so much to Olga, she could not handle it and at the same time talk about the past. This gap between her stories and her deeds is very characteristic of her.

Olga could not say about her father what Orit stated so simply: "Since he was her father, it was clear that she would love him, but she didn't feel good there." Yadek's visit to Israel opened up new opportunities for clarifying this relationship. Olga shared her mixed background and feelings with her family and the hardships she faced in order to survive both physically and emotionally. Yet, if her brother's visits opened up an opportunity for her to work through her anger toward her father, it was gone when her father died during Yadek's stay in Israel. Thus, another dimension was added to her irreversibly bottled up emotions. Perhaps her father's death sealed Olga's relationship to the past—a seal the trip to Warsaw reopened—but not her version of that past.

Working through the Past:
From Physical Safety to Psychological Security

Olga survived a range of devastating experiences, each of which was accompanied by an identity conflict (Jewish, Christian, Polish, religious-nonreligious, educated-noneducated). In Israel she became a farmer-pioneer, cutting herself off from the other aspects of her identity, and thus not really having a chance to work them through. Dina, with her own childhood memories of danger and uncertainty, continued her mother's strategy, thereby defending herself from her mother's unresolved conflicts. Orit, however, who had a different childhood with more freedom of choice, was able to construct her own relationship to the present and to the past. Unlike her mother, she did not have to make the transition from redemption to survival; and because she was not obliged to identify with

Olga, she had no immediate need to distance herself from her grand-mother.

Olga and Dina have probably contributed in no small measure to Orit's relative freedom. Olga has invested all her energy into rebuilding her life under harsh physical and emotional conditions. Together with her husband, she established the foundation for the *physical security* of her newly established family, since the former one was destroyed in the Holocaust. For Olga, this physical security symbolized the *continuity and coherence* of her life story, despite its hardships and losses. Dina, still aware of a sense of physical insecurity in her own childhood, went on to establish herself in the same physical sense: starting a family, pursuing a professional career, helping to build a school in a new community. Yet Dina unwittingly absorbed the unresolved conflicts of Olga's past. She had the difficult task of fulfilling her mother's manifest expectations ("the future is the main thing"), without much opportunity to delve into untold stories or elicit Olga's complex feelings about her past. Furthermore, Dina had to handle a more complex social environment, in which new values—of pleasure and self-realization—had emerged that were different from the pioneering culture of her parents.

Orit was probably less exposed to the relative physical insecurity, the shift in values, and the direct aftereffects of the past. For her, there are new options for looking into the unresolved, psychological aspects of her grandmother's life, and she has taken advantage of them. By asking questions and looking for answers, Orit has been able to understand the relationship between Olga and her father, Olga's feelings at being home in Warsaw, and Yadek's appearance, as natural life events. This may have helped her develop a new psychological feeling of security, beyond the physical one her parents and grandparents worked for. But she is still very young, and it is too early to say anything conclusive about her strategy. We can only identify the first signs of a new direction.

4

THE SEGALS

Out of Russian Asia

with Bosmat Dvir-Malka

Anya, the oldest of our interviewees, escaped in the footsteps of her husband from land conquered by the Germans to Russian-held territory after the outbreak of the war. She was a Communist. She was saved from the fate of the Jews who stayed behind in the countries that underwent German occupation. Like Genia, Ze'ev, and Olga, Anya lost most of her family in the Holocaust. In addition, during the war years in Russia, Anya lost both the baby to whom she had given birth and her husband, who never returned from his service in the Red Army. Anya and her second husband, Shmuel, are defined as "Asians" according to the common historical definitions of the Holocaust, because they both spent the war years in Asia and returned only after the war's end.

Up to this point, we have met survivors' families in which there are several children. Tamar is Anya's only child. On the one hand, she carries the story of both of her parents on her shoulders, but on the other, she received all of their attention during the first difficult years in Israel. How will this influence Tamar's life story? those of her daughters? (Because of space considerations, we present Anya's complete story and only excerpts from the interviews with Tamar, and Dafna and Idit.)

Anya

"Things that no longer exist one need not talk about"

Bosmat interviewed Anya in Tel Aviv on the day after Holocaust Day: In the entrance to the small apartment, I meet a woman with short, white hair,

SEGAL FAMILY CHRONOLOGY

1905	Shmuel is born. He is a bright student. During the war, he escapes to Russia. Most of his family die in the Holocaust.
1907	Yitzhak is born. A tailor, he survives the war by hiding. His father and brother are killed.
1915	Anya is born. She escapes to Russia in 1939, where she loses her husband and baby.
1917	Esther is born. During the war, she escapes to Russia with her sister. Most of her family die in the Holocaust.
1947	Anya and Shmuel both arrive in Cyprus but do not know one another.
1948	Anya and Shmuel both immigrate to Israel. Family members introduce them.
1949	Anya and Shmuel marry. Esther and Yitzhak immigrate to Israel. They were married in Poland and their eldest son was born there.
1950	Ya'acov, a son, their second child, is born to Esther and Yitzhak.
1951	Tamar, a daughter, is born to Anya and Shmuel. She is their only child.
1950s–1960s	Tamar and Ya'acov grow up in the same neighborhood in Tel Aviv. They become friends in eleventh grade. Ya'acov is released from the army for health reasons and studies engineering at the Technion. Tamar studies psychology before her army service.
1970	Tamar and Ya'acov marry and settle near their parents.
1971	Dafna, a daughter, is born to Tamar and Ya'acov.
1972	Idit, a daughter, is born to Tamar and Ya'acov.
1973	Shmuel, Tamar's father, dies. Tamar and Ya'acov move to Arad.
1978	Tamar and Ya'acov move to Dimona because of Ya'acov's work.
1980	Mor, a daughter, is born to Tamar and Ya'acov.
1984	Tamar and Ya'acov build a house and move to Beer-Sheva.
1989	Bosmat Dvir-Malka and Dan Bar-On interview Anya, Tamar and Ya'acov, Dafna and Idit.

wearing a very simple dress. She invites me in and immediately offers me a cup of tea, a suggestion it is impossible to refuse. When she finally sits down in front of me, she seems to be tense, as if prepared for battle. She reminds me of my own grandmother! I feel from her opening sentences that in order to achieve a sense of detachment, perhaps the interview should be done by a non-Israeli. *There is no way to convey the heavy Polish accent that accompanies her broken Hebrew.*

Look, I was born in a small village called K. There is a book, I will bring it to you in a moment to look at, from the year 1915. What was in my childhood I can only tell you—I was five. My books came, my father was a learned man and he began teaching us. I am just like Tamar, an eternal student. I am always reading, it is my hobby. So that's the way we were brought up. So after the war [World War I], I was seven and I went into the second grade, because then we began learning to write at age seven. But what happened, my brother was ten years older than me so they didn't take him [into school]. There was a teacher in the school, there were ten years between us, I sat at the corner of the table, I learned what they studied and I knew everything. I was only seven years old, I went through to the seventh grade and I finished school. I finished, I didn't have what to do. There were, I had girlfriends, they all went into sewing. I wasn't good at that. From childhood I have been different. For two years I did different things, then a friend of my brother's opened up a printing shop and I went to work there for years and years. I also worked in embroidery, I finished school for embroidery. I also worked in the printing shop where it was better. These ten fingers saved me from death—not neighbors and not friends. Not my husband, no one. It is only because I know how to embroider and to knit and to sew. I am not a great seamstress—what you see on me is what I sewed by myself. But my hands, every machine that they showed me in Russia I learned how to use. I was a *musselman* of thirty-four kilos [seventy-five pounds] and I knew how to make parachutes, other creatures didn't know, I knew. That was the only thing that saved me.

Anya speaks with great power in a continuous flow. I quickly get used to her language errors and am already caught up in her story, which moves rapidly from her childhood to making parachutes in Russia. I note for myself that when I am transcribing, I will need to put in periods, because Anya overlaps all her sentences.

I was very thin, I was the smallest one at home. Observant Jews, with not too much income. We had what was needed, we weren't beggars, but we weren't rich. Father always sat with his books, Mother made the living. Later on, Father left all of that. He was a *buchhalder*, do you know what that is? *(regards me with a look of wonder).* Don't you know what a *buchhalder* is? It is, how can I tell you, my husband was also a *buchhalder* with books. One moment, how do you say it in Hebrew? He worked with accounts, an accountant. So later on, he saw that it was hard, the work, so he went back to the books, it was his life.

That's the way it was and then I was finished. I was, I am not embarrassed to say it, I am proud to say that I was a Communist. Why did I get to that? I didn't have a way to live. I wanted to study. The village didn't enchant me any longer, I wanted to leave. I loved the village, but I wanted books, I wanted to be a person. So I took a lot of courses, I finished more than high school, but I didn't do it systematically. So until the war broke out I worked in Warsaw and I went back home in the summer. I traveled every year, so I worked in the printing shop. Even abroad you need to travel to work. I went back in the summer. I think, I didn't tell my parents, I had a boyfriend, I knew that I wanted to get married, but my parents didn't want him, he wasn't orthodox. So I didn't have a choice. In secret, I packed a big suitcase in order to run away. I didn't manage to run away, the war broke out.

I sit mesmerized, listening to Anya. Her language is full of heart. "She is not only 'there,' " I say to myself, "she is also 'here.' " It is her way of looking at me, how she turns to me every now and then when she is speaking.

The war broke out, no boyfriend, nothing. He came, I couldn't go with him. My mother was ill, I didn't know what she had. We thought that after the holidays we would go to Warsaw and see what she has. Oh, here [in Israel] I understood that she had the beginning of cancer in her eye. I understood it here, but then, who understood? Besides, I was twenty-three and from a small village. What does a young girl from a small village know, I ask, books and books, but those are books, they are not life! *(gets excited)*. We didn't manage to get there. My brother had a wife and two daughters. My sister had two children and a husband. I was the youngest, I didn't leave. I was there with the Germans, that is, when the Germans came. What do you want me to tell you? If there are animals in the world, if there is evil, within eight days, a war of only eight days and all of a sudden one morning, Sodom. So the escapees came, all of the young people were on the roads, and I went back that same night, on the seventh of September, 1939, I went home. I had a dress, not this *(pointing to what she is wearing)*, I had enough dresses. A black dress, I don't know why we wore it. Today we do not understand what we did [then]. And I stood there, I had hair down to here *(she points to her waist)*. I will show you pictures later on.

Anya turns to me: "Drink already," she tells me. I can see how excited she is.

And all of a sudden the bombs began. The same size, I saw them, but on every Jewish house. So I threw something out of the house. Grass, fire, everything was like Hell. I can't understand how there can be a place like that. To this day I don't understand. I ran to my sister, we grabbed her children, the synagogue wasn't too far away. The synagogue was five or six hundred. We, the Communists, said that in time we would make it into a museum. There were three synagogues. I have pictures and I will show them to you. It was [made of] wood, it is impossible to describe what it was like, what was there. The wood was burning, someone came in and expelled us. We saw dead here and there. We ran over to the cemetery, not the Jewish one, to the Christian cemetery. Almost half, or a lot of the Jews of the village were there. We sat there, my father and myself, my sister with her children and my brother-in-law, when all of a sudden someone said: "Father, look, your son isn't here!" Where was the son with his family? To get up? If I was to rise, they would kill all of us with bombs. But I didn't get up, I crawled on all fours and I found my brother, far, far away. And I asked him: "Where are Rachel and the children?" He said that they went to the village in the morning. So I went back, I found my aunt, a sick woman, who had a bag with food. I said: "Give me your bag. And come, follow me." I said to my father: "Look, I brought you someone else from your family." He said: "Good." So we sat there until the evening. If there is a fire, if they burn the forest, this isn't a fire. Because then it is with black and red flames and there everything was red. The fire burned endlessly. We started leaving and we waited. A goy came from the village, we had more money. We had money from merchandise in the shelters. Because we knew that there would be a war. We had a store of leather for shoes. *(She tries to describe the kind of shoes she is talking about.)* It's like, you know, not inside, only on the top. It was owned collectively by us and by my brother and brother-in-law. I had money in my belt, we paid him fifteen zloty, which was a lot of money. The family could live for two weeks on that. I gave him, we went in, my aunt, my mother with the children and my father, and who else? Only the children went by foot, four children, my aunt, my sister, and my other aunt and my mother rode on the Polish wagon, which was full. We traveled, it was dark, but we saw everything around us. Light, fire, we sat there. Father said, when the bombs began, instead of taking a cup or something like that, he went in, he grabbed his *tallith* and his *tefillin* and he closed the door. The keys remained in his hand and that is the way we escaped. But it hurts, the smallest child was a year and a half old. He asked for water, he was frightened. Father went back to the town and he told us that when he went back, he saw burnt soldiers, too many to count, burnt Poles and Jews from the town.

Anya relives the first memories of the war once again. She is excited and remembers everything in great detail. It is not always easy to follow her train of thought. She is having a discussion: who rode on the wagon and who walked, how they had money, and why they didn't have a cup when the baby asked for water.

And then we drove to the town. We arrived in the village in the evening. We entered . . . how do you say it in Hebrew? "A journey?" A goy came out and said: "Come in!" We paid. It didn't work without money. That was on Friday night. It was September, exactly on a Friday. Fish, Mother wanted to make fish. The fish remained on the table, it wasn't important. Life was important. And, Friday night, we were all tired. The children slept on the straw. And I sat in front of Father and said: "What will our end be?" Father said: "Don't worry, we know the Germans, everything will be fine. Who knows what will be?" Okay, in the morning we left. We didn't have anything to eat. I went into the goy's house and said to her: "Will you sell me some potatoes and some bread?" She sold me bread, challah. But we needed to eat. I said: "I want potatoes." She said: "Get out." I picked up potatoes from the ground and I brought them over to her. There were a lot of potatoes. She gave me a bowl and I left. They were very big *(shows with her hands the size of a melon).*

I brought the potatoes and I cooked them. My mother [said]: "Father, will you eat them?" But there wasn't a choice, he was hungry, he was a man. We passed the day that way, Saturday, Sunday, the ninth of September, with the goyim. On the first Friday morning, I went to the house, she said they were selling hot bread. Another goy understood that he could make some money. And he began selling bread, I was standing in line. He said: "Oh, I know you, you are . . . from there." I said yes. I got two [loaves of] bread that were this big. Not like the bread here. I went out with them and I took milk from the goy and that was our lunch on that Sunday morning.

Father said; "Don't worry, we know the Germans, everything will be fine."
I shudder. I am slowly beginning to understand that Anya has a diary in her
head in which all of the hours of the days she was still with her family are
listed.

Later on, it was in the morning, my father said: "Let's go see what is
left." We went back to the village, it was twelve to fifteen kilometers. I
had shoes from Warsaw with high heels. I threw them away, what choice
did I have? We met, Polish soldiers came and they said: "*Nu,* how is the
war?" Later on we understood that they were Jews, they were on our side.
We went to the village, we saw it from a distance. In the beginning, we
didn't see anything, everything was very crowded with small and big
houses. The Jews lived there like they do here, they put one place next to
another. My brother stood where our house had been and he was looking
through the pieces of wood. We found a pot. We found something, we
were happy. My brother had no shoes. I said to my father: "Give him
some money so that he can buy shoes." We couldn't get it. They had
robbed us. Who? It's not important, they robbed everything.

I did not ask who had done the stealing. Anya was answering her own
questions for herself.

But at that moment my aunt, her husband was from another town, said
to me: "Come to my house." I didn't have children, I was free. We went
to see, she left her husband, her children, and her sister and everything.
We went to [her] town. It was the first time in my life, I have forgotten
a lot, but [not] what I saw there. A few Germans had come, holding a Jew
with a white beard. He was a handsome man. His son-in-law was holding
him on one side and his son on the other and the Germans were surrounding them. All of the townspeople, Jews and Christians, came running to see. I had not yet seen a man like that. He was upright, not bent
over, he was straight! And he looked the Germans in the eye! I began
asking why they took him. They told me that he butchered animals according to the Jewish law. He was a butcher, so they caught him and they
brought him in order to kill him. I didn't see the execution, but his face
... and the way he was! I have forgotten a great deal, but [not] what I
saw.

My aunt caught me, she was ten years older than me, and she said:
"Come on!" We walked to her house. The rain began, we walked, we were
drenched to our bones. All of a sudden, [Germans] came from a distance.

I was wearing a skirt from a Christian friend, I had been with the goyim. I will show you the pictures later on. And one of her blouses and a scarf tied here. I must have been twenty-three, but I had a more mature-looking face. They [the Germans] stood there and said: "Come here." I didn't have a choice. We went in, they had a truck. And they asked: "Do you know Yiddish?" *(she shakes her head no)*. "German?" *(again the same)*. I know it, I studied it. I am going to my aunt's house by foot *(she points to her foot)*. Are you married? Yes. Where is your husband? In the army. Do you have children? Yes, four. How old are you? I am thirty-five. They looked at me, they didn't understand, they didn't even understand that I was really that young. Where are they, what happened? So I said: "Look, everything is burned." Where did you live? Here. I didn't really live there. Then the old man took out a package of cookies and a piece of sugar. "This is for your children." My aunt looked, she was gripped with fear, if they kill me, who will be left? Afterwards the German asked: "Where do you want to be dropped off?" On the way there was a sculpture of one of the Christian patron saints. So I said: "I want to get out here because I live here now." They dropped us off and we walked. We went in to where my parents were. I don't know what I looked like, but my mother and father stood there and did not move. I said: "Don't be afraid." The children grabbed the cookies as if it was a dream *(sighs)*.

We went home and we heard that they had opened up our shelters. I went with my brother and father at night. I knew who had done it. We got close and then the bombs started. How can I say it? I stood first in line, I fell down, I let them run ahead. But they didn't beat my uncle, he didn't agree, he told them to leave me alone. He grabbed my hand. Where had my brother-in-law and my brother run to? I didn't know. I found them later on. So my uncle took me by the hand and I ran. There was a shelter, I wanted to go into it with my uncle, my instincts told me to do so. He grabbed my hand and said: "Sit down, come here." And we stood there, the Germans came with their guns. And whoever was inside, was killed. What could we do? I waited in some place on the street until morning. I ran to the house and I found my brother. He was as white as snow. And my hair, I don't know how my braids opened up, he took, he combed my hair. We were happy, we hugged one another and left.

I like the way Anya relates this picture of herself and her brother. It is a moment of warmth and intimacy amid the cruelty of war.

Afterwards, I went from village to village to bring food. Father couldn't walk, neither could my brother-in-law. I walked from village to village. I walked and I brought news about people, and my mother understood that it would be my end. And she [said]: "Start running away, run away! There is nothing for you to do here. I know that I am sick, but I have a son, I have a daughter, I won't remain alone." I didn't take anything with me except my high-heeled shoes. I was an idiot, I could have taken more things. Yes, and I went to a girlfriend, she was like a sister, and I said: "Come with me." She didn't want to. She died, she died like all of them *(cries)*. I told her: "Look, I know that you don't like to work, I will work for you, you can stay at home." Nothing helped. She was a person. She said no, so no *(angry)*.

I walked, we reached the Russian border, me and another nine boys and girls. We couldn't cross the Boek [river]. It's not so wide, but you need to cross it. So, in the middle of the night we went to one of the goyim and he said: "I smuggle people, I will smuggle you across, I know the hours." We waited there for a few days and he brought us to the other side, me and my friends from Warsaw. To this day, I am in contact with a few of them. We went at night, we waited for the guards where the Russians were. They caught us, we went in and said: "Look, we are young, we are Communists." It doesn't matter whether we were or not. It is only important that they brought us. They sent us to Kovno. Not Kovno, I'll say Kovno, it wasn't Kovno. From there, oy *(sighs)*, we looked for a way to live. We were there and we decided to set up a commune. They sent us to some place where whores lived, rich people, goyim who were smugglers. We set up a commune there. There were thirty-five of us. In the same hometown of [Chaim] Weizman, a very, very small town. But there were Jews there. In the beginning of January 1940, they began arranging shipments to Russia. We were the first; we registered, they took our papers, our documents, whatever they could, even our identity papers. We traveled in January, February, on the eighth of March we reached the forest. They told us that we were going to a factory in the forest. They brought us to the forest, a gigantic forest. They only exist in Russia. They put us into huts, big houses. We were given apartments, we worked there. There was a Jewish artist among us from Warsaw. In Warsaw, there had been a small theater from France, she had been an artist there, she was Jewish. The snow was taller than me, but I was tall. We needed to cut the timber and she sang to us. There was no choice, we walked to the center, like they say here, to ask: Look, I had studied, I worked in the printing shop. Here, the second one was a psychologist and she was a laboratory assistant. We could be of use. How were we being of use with this [the trees]? So he said that they needed the wood to fight the Germans. We didn't have a choice so we decided to plan an escape.

I began to be afraid. It was forbidden that someone would say anything because the Russians could take us away also. Everybody escaped, three stayed behind, me and two sisters and another [girl]. I asked them: "Why do you want to stay with me?" I said: "Look, I need to remain, I wrote home, I want to know what is happening with my parents. Who throws away parents? So if you want [to leave], go ahead, I can stay by myself." "No" [they said], "we will wait for you." One day I began embroidering. The Russians like embroidery very much, their *rubeshkot*, I know that. And I always got, I worked for them, I brought home bread, I brought home what I could. So we began managing, we will wait for the holiday, October, and then we will escape. All of a sudden the girlfriends came, here is a letter from my mother. I got a letter—my mother wrote: "We are still living in the town of K. We took your clothing [I left a package, a suitcase with clothes] from your friends, we sold it. And I am living with my aunt, with your aunt and we are writing you. Don't worry. Do you have bread? How are you?" It doesn't matter *(excited)*, I said: "[Now] I can leave." I wrote them, I couldn't write that I was living in the forest. [I wrote] that I had already begun studying in the university and that things were good. Take care of the children. And we began to move east.

I try to make sense of the time frame here and to be with Anya in the Russian forest. She waits for a sign of life from home and tries to convince them that she is studying at the university. "Take care of the children," she says, and heads east, away from them. I ask myself, where did she get the strength? Where was her husband? Was she already a mother? Anya does not mention any of this.

We got vodka, everyone got a bottle of vodka. It was a treasure. We began walking. We went to someone and we gave it to him. We only opened up one bottle, I gave him a drink and I said (this wasn't the truth) that we were freed from our work in the forest and that we want to get to the city of Karpovitz. If you help us, we will pay. We had all kinds of products, because they gave us a lot for the holidays *(makes a sign with her hands up to her neck).* He took a drink and said: "Good, the [body of] water that they call the Lishsenka is bigger than . . . our river here." It was already the month of October, it was winter there. He said: "I will get you to the other side where there is a road. You can go that way." We began traveling, here it was closed, here it was impossible. He said that he would be killed and he left us. We began walking, I had suitcases, my girlfriends had bags on their backs. We walked that way, until we reached a place where we could ride. We went in, I said to the guard: "Look, we have already been freed from work." It wasn't the truth, but we had no choice. We needed to reach Karpovitz. He said: "Look, there are no more ships. There is only one ship for the army, if they will take you with them. But first, come in here, there is a house, and have something to eat." We went in, there was a goy who had nothing, I gave her some beans or something like that, and she made us lunch. A small boat came, it wasn't a boat, I don't know how to describe it. I said: "We have vodka." He said: "First, we'll have a drink." We had a drink and we told him that we were liberated from our work duties, that we want to go to Karpovitz, a very old city, a big one.

"It wasn't the truth, but we had no choice." Anya is still uncomfortable with the thought that in order to survive, she had to lie.

We walked and walked and all of a sudden, we saw a hotel. We went in, they didn't want to let us stay. Again, more vodka, it was only vodka that saved us. We went into the room, we bathed and rested. Suddenly, in the middle of the night, there were knocks on the door. Girls, come with us. Oh, we understood that we had fallen into a whorehouse. We started to leave, the woman said: "I didn't know who or what you were." We decided to leave in the middle of the night. We had addresses. I had the address of my boyfriend and his sisters. So in that way, we knew where to go. We rested a bit, in the morning of the second day, what should we do? So we walked, they said that they needed workers on the trains. We went to work painting, we worked, we were as white as snow. That was in the year of 1941, we didn't even see the color of milk, and here each one of us got their own bottle of milk. We didn't drink it all because we needed to bring some home [*for the baby? I ask myself*]. At night they accepted us for work and we began to make living arrangements. The girlfriend that I was talking about didn't live far away and she decided to go somewhere else, and I wanted to stay because I decided to work in the printing shop and with my embroidery. I thought that I would stay. They came and caught us and took us to prison. Why? What? We knew then that a law had been passed that whoever left work without permission could get between four months and ten years of a prison sentence. We knew about that. They took us to prison. I went to see the officer. I said: "Look, comrade" (it was forbidden for my girlfriend to speak), I said, "What am I, a thief?" But he was quiet. I said: "Yesterday I finished for you"—I already knew—"I finished a *rubashka* for you. Are you going to send me to prison now?" But it didn't help. We yelled! It was impossible to stand. They took us to a special house, how do you call it? To solitary confinement, me and my girlfriend and the other one. When we finally left, we looked funny, nobody had faces like ours. We didn't see, we didn't have a mirror to see what we looked like. But we laughed a lot. We were there for less than four months. We were lucky, no questions, nothing. Among them, there was a Jew from Moscow. He told us: "If you get out of here, go to Karpovitz to the police station and there you can get your identity papers, the papers that you need." He told us this and ran away, they wouldn't see. We understood that he saved us.

This is an endless story of suffering, initiative, and luck. How would I have withstood it? And, had I been her daughter, how would I have managed to listen to Anya's story day after day?

We left the prison, I said: "I have had enough of Russia, I am going to Ukraine." A friend and I, we then got our identity papers, went to the train. We sat down, we were hungry, what is hunger, it is . . . it doesn't matter, she said: "You know what, Anya, in Russian I have a different name, you know—I am going to look for food." She wasn't like me, I am quiet, I don't trust people, so I don't see what they say. I, my daughter is a psychologist, I am a psychologist, too *(smiling)*. I met two Russian soldiers who wanted me to go somewhere with them and they would bring bread. I gave her, we had three or four hundred rubles. It was a lot of money. I gave it to her and she went with them. One hour, two hours, three, it was already evening, and she didn't come back. I began to worry. It's not that I was worried about the money. All of sudden she came back crying, and I said: "Fania, what happened?" They lied, they took the money and ran. I stood there and I said: "Good, you came back, quiet." I took the little money left and went to the window where they sold tickets and I got two tickets. But not to where we wanted. Only to Moscow, there we needed to switch [trains]. We went into the compartment, we felt good. To begin with, you could buy something. We went and bought, we ate, we reached Moscow.

We were in Moscow for two days, not that we wanted to be there. There was no other way. We needed to exchange our tickets, and there you don't go and change your tickets. In every city, I don't know whether we saw two taxis. Empty—the streets were clean and nice, it was like a dream. The metro—a dream. Moscow was a very nice city then. I don't know what it is like today. They exchanged our tickets. We got [tickets] to a small town not far from Kraków. We began making living arrangements, I went into a printing shop, they said no, because I didn't know Ukrainian. So I went to an embroidery shop. They accepted me. So I began working. My friend went and got work in some kiosk, and all of a sudden, on Sunday, the twenty-second of June, war [came], [it was] a few weeks until the evacuation began. Do you know what an evacuation is? They also took us. We went as far as Tashkent, no, Sarytau. In Sarytau, there was a printer. I went in, and all of a sudden we saw, there was someone there from Poland, how to explain it, the one who made the arrangements for the Poles. Good, I got into line, I opened up the door, a man was sitting there *(takes a deep breath)*, oy, oy, you are so and so's sister! I was in your house, how did you get here? I couldn't talk about it. I told him in Russian that I was Biazanca, I am this, and so on and so on. He wrote down two thousand, no, two hundred rubles and a package of food. I hadn't dreamed of that. I said: "Fania, you don't need to go." [But] she also went and got.

Every few sentences, Anya says: "It does not matter, it is not important," with a wave of her hand, as if this movement cuts off the necessity of going into detail for those who were and were not there. Still, it gives the feeling that there is a third, hidden person in the room, with whom she is having an ongoing argument.

She and I were the same. We went and sold things, we bought shoes and decided to go to Tashkent. We reached Tashkent, almighty God. I never saw—there were Jews from everywhere who had run away from every place. I had an apartment, it wasn't an apartment any longer. I didn't have what to eat. I didn't always find work. I didn't have any strength left until I went to the Defense Ministry (I had a note from a friend who was a soldier), and I got a job in a factory. I began working, I made matches out of pieces of wood. They put it in the sulfur. You needed to light it, it was lit on each box, that's Russia. But I paid for that and I got malaria. Then I began losing my strength, but I knew that I needed to hold on to my [work] place in order to be registered.

From there I went into the hospital, I weighed thirty-four kilos [seventy-five pounds]. There was no food to eat in Russia. I don't know what it is like now, then there was no food. You live here, you grow stones, you eat stones. Where you grow bread, you eat bread. But to exchange stones and bread doesn't exist there. Aside from that, there was a war and there they say that a thief sits on a thief with a whip in his hand. And there, one night in the hospital, the commissar came. Do you know what a commissar is? [He said]: "I heard the doctor told you to cut your hair." I haven't had long hair since then. "And I also heard that you won't live till tomorrow." I opened up my eyes and I said: "Look," I know his name to this day, he was a Jew, but a professor, "I will still come back, I will go home and I will see my parents, nothing else."

"I will go home and I will see my parents, nothing else." I echo her statement. After all, it is most likely that her parents were no longer alive. However, that thought kept her alive at thirty-four kilos, when her son had probably been dead for a while (although Anya has not yet mentioned him at all).

He said: "God help you." That night, I got out of bed. Somewhere I saw a nurse who was embroidering and I waited for her to leave. Then, she left, I took the blouse and I began to embroider. She came in, started to look [for the blouse]. Where did it disappear? All of a sudden, she found me. She asked: "Why did you do that?" I told her that I was an expert in work of this sort. And then she said: "Do you know how to do things like this?" I said yes. "That's it," she said, "finish the blouse for me." So I finished it, I got shirts from the doctors, directors, soldiers, generals. I worked only for bread, for food, not for money. They only gave me money to buy thread from Vilna. They didn't have it in the stores, you needed to go to the black market to buy it, and that is what I did. I met people. They took me into their home, it was a good place to live and sleep.

And then, all of a sudden, on one Sunday when I already had, I had a dress and shoes that were rags but they weren't torn. I was already registered to travel home. Then they registered the Poles who wanted to travel to Poland. Behind me there was a tall, well-dressed man. I turned around,

I said: "Look, fella, I am not interested." He said: "I am not looking. I know you but I don't know from where." He began talking, he asked where I was from. I didn't look at him, I was afraid that he would take my bread. He said: "I am from Yosful." It's not far from us, it's on the Vistula. That is the largest river in Poland. Yosful, I had family there. Then I said that I was from K. I am from there. Who is your wife? Miriam. I grabbed his hand: "Where is Miriam?" This Miriam, her mother and my aunt were sisters, and they were living in America. Then he said: "Oy, you are Anya. What you look like! You were beautiful." I didn't answer and he said: "Look, I know that you come from an orthodox family, that your family *(she looks at me—are you tired of hearing about this? Is it hard for you? Are you cold? I will give you...)* is the biggest family in K. Sign this for me. I am going home, I am going to sell your land, because I know that no houses are left, and I will save the money for you." I looked at him: "Who are you to sell our land? Where is everybody, where is everything?" He didn't say anything. He started to walk away. Afterwards he came back and I said: "Look, where is Miriam?" He told me that she was in her ninth month and that she had a boy who was four years old. And Germans had come into the town, they announced that they would leave the women, and at night, the Germans came with their little vans, that's called *gashgupka* in Russian, and they put the women in there and they died. I looked at him and said: "Look, Abraham, if you had the strength to leave Miriam when she was pregnant, then you are not my partner. I have no need for you." I never saw him again.

"Where is everybody, where is everything?" This is the way Anya first hears about the annihilation. She is angry at Abraham that he left his wife and child. Perhaps she is also angry at herself for having left her parents, her brothers, and the cousin who had been like a daughter, behind. Anya continues to describe in great detail the rest of her stay in Tashkent. She talks about another man she met, something else she did. I begin paying close attention again when she begins telling about how, in 1945, she started to receive letters from abroad.

I had letters from all over the world, wherever I had friends. Here are two letters that I got from America. Two letters from two uncles. One uncle wrote that he choked when he read, he got a letter that I wrote from the forest, to my grandmother. It was at my uncle's house in Haifa, they took the letter from there. And in the second one they wrote: "Go to your uncle in Haifa," his name was written there, "we will meet there." I understood it. I answered them that if I need to go to my uncle, I need to go home to Poland. That is, it is impossible to go from here [Tashkent] to my uncle. Okay, they wrote: "When you get to Poland, there will be money there for you." It was true, good. Two weeks went by. Somebody came from the Jewish Agency: "Anya, you have uncles in America. Your Uncle Aaron sent you one hundred dollars. Please take it, go buy yourself something." I said: "Look, sir, one hundred rubles is a whole loaf of bread, that is what bread costs, and I won't take the one hundred dollars. Give it to me in Warsaw or in Lublin." I didn't know where I was going. "Oy, you are so smart, don't you want any help? I will send people from the Joint [Distribution Committee]." "Excuse me, sir, don't send anyone. I won't take anything. I am going away and I don't know where I will be." He came back again. I sent him away and I didn't take anything. I went home, I went there. I entered Poland. I went to the town, I understood from . . . what I saw in the town *(very excited)*, the land, again those goyim. At the end I will show you all the pictures. I didn't find, not my brother, no friend, no cousin, nothing. A piece of land. I went, meanwhile I sold our piece of land. So I bought myself a watch. Tamar broke it with her little hands. That was my entire inheritance.

I wrote to America. My uncles wrote that someone would wait for me in America. I came to France and we arrived in . . . what is it called? It's close to the sea because we traveled by boat. And I got from my uncles, they wanted to give me money. I knew that I shouldn't take it. There was five dollars in every letter that I got in Poland, I had enough. I didn't take anything. In France, I went to Paris, and immediately [they said], you are coming with us to America. I said: "Not now and not later." When I was in the town, I met a gentile I knew from before and he said: "Look, this is your father's will, and he said that he has a brother in Tel Aviv." He didn't say Tel Aviv, he said: "In Palestine you have an uncle, if you remain alive when you go there." So I said to him: "Look, sir, I won't go with you to America, I will go to Tel Aviv, to Israel. I have the certificate from the ship *Theodore Herzl*." What a trip! In the middle a war broke out with the English. We had a lot [of people], we went on Passover.

Her description of the war ended, Anya is tired and becomes quiet for a moment. I decide to ask a question.

"How old were you?"

I was twenty-eight, or more.

"Were you single?"

I had a husband but I don't want to talk about it. He died, he is no longer alive. Things that no longer exist one need not talk about. We reached Haifa port, we had two casualties on our boat. Somebody said to me: "Get off" [in Haifa]. I was sick the entire trip. I didn't want to get off. We went to Cyprus. And I went through the delousing and what is it called? [*I: the camp*] The camp. I was in the camp until the state of Israel was established. And I came by ship to Haifa. A young man came and said that people were waiting for me. I knew [it was] the uncle that I was in contact with. I didn't need anyone. So, there her son was walking and he yelled: "Grandpa, Grandpa! The ship has arrived." I was embarrassed, the whole street came out to see me, I was dirty from the ship. They began [crying]. I said: "Aunt and uncle, I want you to stop crying. I will sit with you." I wanted to open up and say, it hurts me! They didn't want to listen to me. I didn't tell them anything. To this day, it sits here *(points to her throat)*. Why didn't they want to hear about what hurt me? Why didn't they want to understand that I left a sick mother, a religious father, a gentle brother. They didn't want to hear about it. I didn't talk about it, I kept it [locked up] in my heart. Then, I met my husband and we went to live in Tel Aviv.

"They didn't want to listen to me . . . to this day, it sits here." Anya waited for support for such a long time, but there was no one who gave it to her in Haifa. Has anyone ever succeeded?

We lived in Haifa, he was a soldier. He got sick in the army. Heart problems. Here he is *(points to a picture on the wall)*, and he was sick for seventeen years. I lost, Tamar isn't the first, I lost a son with him, and after Tamar, I lost another two children. The doctors said, either him or children. But I had the strength to hold on. I told him that I wanted someone who would remain [after us]. He had the ordination to be a rabbi, I didn't want to be a rabbi's wife. I had been a Communist before. I didn't agree, my heart didn't agree. I held him this way at night (cradled in her bosom) until we moved away from there. My friend came from America. She came in: "Are you living here? Aren't you ashamed?" I told her: "How can I live any other way? I don't have any money." And so one day we were sitting together and someone came and said here is two thousand dollars, buy yourself an apartment. My husband wasn't a good soul, he was evil. Why? He thought I wanted to leave him. He was sick; a man who is sick isn't good, but I don't want to go into private matters.

We bought the apartment. We started cleaning it, Tamar was two and a half or a little younger. I was even pregnant and I got rid of the child. I say, that's it, we are done, we are finished with children. That's the way we began in 1955, we didn't have anything. Another uncle came and bought us a refrigerator, bought us a gas stove. And later on another uncle bought me a washing machine and this too [book shelves].

My uncle was here when my husband had his first [heart] attack. They loved me, I was, I couldn't understand that they would arrange everything for me. It doesn't matter, we are talking about dead matters. Tamar is lacking nothing, whatever there was, I gave her. I don't live for myself, I had a war with my family, with Tamar also. Why are you teaching her, why? Look, leave that to me, I didn't achieve anything, Tamar will achieve [things]. Both families fought with me. Then Tamar grew up, she said herself that she grew up with a sick father. Whatever I could, I didn't have a dress, I didn't have a life, I only wanted to have a book. And he died, he got his last heart attack *(cries)*. What can I tell you, I miss him. In the beginning, I was in shock, I was ill. They took me to the hospital, they thought that I had cancer. I was in Belinson Hospital for a month—they didn't find cancer—until I got tired of it. I told them: "Look, this is like being in prison for no reason. I was in prison for a reason. Let me go home with the good or the bad, I will live through it peacefully." I started thinking. They [Tamar and Ya'acov] weren't working yet, they had nothing. They had an apartment, we bought it together, his parents and we. I went to work, I worked until the outbreak of the Yom Kippur War. And then I began being sick again. So I didn't work from Yom Kippur through Passover. I went somewhere, I said that I knew how to embroider well, how to patch things well, and that I am good with my hands. I worked there for five years. Look, I did everything for them, and until my dying day I will do everything for them. I have no friends. Since my husband became ill, he began being jealous. I couldn't go anywhere, couldn't move. He kicked out whoever came over. Aside from that, in Israel, there is no emotion here. Maybe there is in the kibbutz, I don't know. Even Tamar, who is a very good daughter, has no feelings. I don't know why, and I remained alone. I don't even want to think about living with her now. Tell me, should I go and live in an old-age home? Tell me, honestly. [Anya had broken her hip].

Bosmat: "My grandfather lives in an old-age home and he is very happy."

How old is he?

"Over eighty."

Oh, I am seventy. Aside from that, is he as lucid as I am? Normal? I read books.

"You said that tomorrow is your parents' memorial. Why on Holocaust Day?"

On the day, on the last day of Passover, they took them out of their homes and brought them to Sobibor.

"How did you find out about it?"

I was there, I went back, I went to Sobibor. They brought them there in 1942. There was an action where they took out all of the Jews from the town and they brought them to Sobibor. After the war, I went back home and I was in Lodz. I sold our piece of land where our house was and with the goy I went to Sobibor. And I know, the goyim told us, the exact day, the exact hour. Aside from that, I have a cousin who stayed in K. She told me.

"How long were you in contact with your parents?"

Until 'forty-one, when the war broke out with the Russians. I was in touch with them during the first year. After that, the contact was broken, then I came back, then I found the land that I had left. I have no one in the world.

Anya continues her monologue, talking about her last fall, how she suffers because of her daughter's in-laws, and her fear of the old-age home.

"Do you remember the holidays at home? Tell me about a holiday."

Do I remember? (*Anya becomes very excited. She cries a little and breathes heavily.*) Child, on Hanukkah, we made *schmaltz* for Passover. Do you know what *schmaltz* is? It is grease from the chickens, not from chickens, from the goose. We would watch over the attic inside, it was closed until Passover. We made wine from raisins, but we arranged it so that, Heaven forbid, the goy shouldn't see the wine. If not, then it wouldn't be kosher for Passover. We didn't buy matzos, we baked them. We didn't turn the dough, you don't turn it from both sides, only from one side, on very clean boards. And the orthodox don't take during the last days or during the middle, only early in the morning. We took it early in the morning and we put the matzos into a big sheet, we put it in the middle and it was closed since we didn't have matzoth meal. And in such a kosher house, we didn't eat rice or peas, what else didn't we eat? We didn't even eat cheese, only milk. Everything was different, on Passover eve everything was Jewish. In my house on Passover eve, we took out everything, we brought in a man and he straightened up the whole house. Every bed was very clean, he cleaned the boards, the sheets, we aired out the straw mattresses and everything was very clean. Later on, the table, I, father, my sister, my brother. No, no strangers, just the close family. We sat around the table, everyone had a Haggadah. We didn't sing, no, we just read the Haggadah. The four questions, my brother asked the four questions. He was the only son and Passover was the holiest day, that was Passover.

I can't go to a seder where they (pretends she is clapping her hands), that isn't Passover for me. And Shabbat was Shabbat, not like here. My father read, he sat and read, we went for walks. Then we were freer, but on Shabbat, [our hair was in] braids. We cleaned on Fridays with scarves on our heads. I fought against that, I didn't like it. I was twenty-one, I started to fight: Why do I have to wear a scarf on my head? Can't I clean with my hair worn like a normal person? I had long hair, so what? But on Yom Kippur, our entire town was dark, we didn't turn on any lights, we only lit candles. Little children stayed at home. Every woman, sick or healthy, fasted. The synagogue was full, completely full. Men with shoes and white socks sat and prayed all night long. That was our holiday in K.

I can't stand it here. I have a daughter of a friend, she can't stand it when I am alone at my house on holidays. I tried, I came back, I wanted, it's not a seder. They talked and talked and chatted and ate: that is not a seder for me. I said: "Fania, we are finished, don't invite me any more." So during that seder I cried at home. I will never go to an old-age home, I have no choice, so I suffer. But if she was only a little, if she [Tamar] loved me. I can't say, I say that it is, all mothers nowadays say the same thing. Would I have left my mother alone and gone to my husband's brother? Never, never. My husband was sick and every year he went to a sanitarium. He suffered, he would come home in the middle, but I never left Tamar alone. But, she has no feeling, she has no feeling. But, I will tell you that those young people, when the old like me stay in one place and don't move, they don't need us. I have nothing left in life other than Tamar. I have nothing left.

"And your granddaughters?"

I love my granddaughters, I am crazy about them. Dafna has me very worried. She is too fragile, I am very worried about her. She is smart and gentle. She suffered, Ya'acov told me. So I asked her, [she said,] "Grandma, we don't have to talk about that." Idit is completely different.

Anya quickly returns to talking about herself, about her neighbors, and about how difficult it is to clean the stairwell. I make another attempt: "Do you want to talk about your first husband?"

I will tell you about him only briefly. I was thirteen when a friend of my brother's came over when I was sleeping at my grandmother's house. My grandmother was going to America and so my parents went with her to Warsaw. I was sleeping, they came over at twelve, but I felt that someone had come in. They both came in and the boy said: "She will be my wife." My brother said: "What, she is only thirteen years old?" "I have time, I will wait." He was twenty-three, there was a difference of ten years. That's the way it was. He was waiting for me, he was a Communist, his parents didn't want me because I wasn't rich. And my parents didn't want him because he was like a goy. We weren't together for very long because the war broke out. We met again in Russia, we were [together] a little bit longer, not for a long time. I had a son and the son died on me . . . later on, he died in the war. I got the documents from the Red Army and that is all. I looked for him, I waited for him, I was in Lodz for nine months, there were messages on the walls. Everywhere I thought, when we met the last time, we said . . . if we meet again and we don't agree about things, that will be all right too as long as we know that we are both alive. He didn't remain alive. If he had, he knew where to find me. He didn't—I have erased it from my life. I didn't get married because I loved him. I wanted children, I got married because I wanted children. Now, finish [your tea] and I will show you the book and the pictures *(whispers)*, but it's a secret. I don't want anybody to know that I had a husband. The pictures were left at my uncle's home in America. Here, in Israel *(shows me the pictures)*, Tamar heard about it a lot, there weren't secrets between us. I am not like other parents, I didn't keep secrets *(talking while she looks at the pictures)*. Did you see me with those braids? They cut them here, they grew and now I don't have them anymore. I don't want to hear about it, I don't even want to look at it, it's over. Why should I? But I have a lot more pictures, I have a lot more.

The man in Tashkent was right: Anya had been a beautiful young woman. She brings me back to reality by asking me if I am hungry and if I have my own car. When she discovers that I am traveling by bus, she accompanies me, walking and limping, to the bus stop and waits with me until the bus arrives. When it comes, the driver knows her, says hello warmly, and identifies me as her granddaughter. Neither of us tells him that he is mistaken, but we look at one another with embarrassment. I part from her warmly and, after a few seconds, can no longer see her bent figure.

On the bus, I hear the news on Israeli radio: the index rose by two and two-tenths percent. The Likud ministers blame the economic problems on the Labor Party while the Labor Party blames the Likud ... An idea comes to mind: we need this nonsense in order not to pay attention to Anya's words, "Why didn't they want to hear about what hurt me?" For a moment, I want to go back to Anya and give her a big hug that would drain away all the loss and all the pain she has suffered in her life. Would it help her if I were to listen to her for another hundred hours? Isn't that all she is asking for?

The interview with Anya is exceptional for a number of reasons. To begin with, it includes a relatively wide-ranging description of three periods (before, during, and after the Holocaust) that does not appear in most of the interviews with the first generation. Most of the survivors focused on the description of one period, the one that is most significant to them, and it is this one they tend to describe to a great extent. It may be before the Holocaust, during the Holocaust itself, or afterward (Rosenthal, 1993). However, as we have seen, the amount of description is not always equal to its importance. For Genia and Ze'ev, life during the Holocaust colored their narratives of the periods preceding and following it. In contrast, Olga describes the war in great detail, but in her eyes, rebuilding her life in Israel is more important. Anya describes all three periods in detail. What does this reveal about her biography reconstruction?

Another aspect of the same issue is the fact that Anya tends to document small details that make it difficult to clarify the central theme behind them. On the one hand, Anya amazes us with her ability to remember the color of the dress she had on when the war broke out, or the blouse and skirt she was wearing when she was walking with her aunt on September 9,

1939, toward her home. On the other hand, these details "dilute" the trauma of parts of her story by diverting attention from the feelings that accompany them. This is true for both the storyteller and the listener. Feelings of being flooded or choked, of reluctance to hear the stories, occurred more than once. Does this help Anya omit those "things that one need not talk about"? Do they serve her need to create an emotional break with the past?

Although Anya tends to talk about peripheral details, her speech is full of feeling. There are several points during the interview when she becomes emotional as she talks about things that happened, when she thinks about them deeply, or when she tries to deny them. Paradoxically, however, this can have a distancing effect on the listener. It is difficult to understand everything she may be conveying. During the interview itself, her "orders" and direct questions to Bosmat ("Drink already," or "Are you tired? Are you cold?") make this point more acutely: on the one hand, she displays interest and closeness, on the other, the impersonal approach of "a good host."

Most of Anya's stories are not narratives; they are arguments, as if she is having an ongoing dispute with an invisible opponent: Who from her family rode in the wagon and who walked behind? Was it the Jews or the Germans who stole their money? What was the name of that town in Ukraine? In addition, at times she gestures and says: "It does not matter." To whom does it not matter? There are a number of ways of understanding the function these arguments serve. They are part of an internal dialogue: they keep alive the things she is perhaps afraid of forgetting. As she remarks toward the end of the interview, "These are dead things."

Or perhaps, she has told of them so many times, in so many different ways, she is no longer sure herself what really happened. But her stories also serve as an external monologue, an attempt to *justify to her parents* what happened and why she did what she did at each stage, especially after she had left (in her mind, deserted) them. When she left Poland to follow her friend (and Communist convictions) to Russia, it was the family bond that was broken, never to be restored again. Along with her severe self-judgment, Anya also judges herself in relation to the public argument in Israel, which looks for justifications and explanations from the living to the dead. Her discourse—the details, arguments and strong emotion of her life story—leaves her very lonely: no one can rescue her from reproaching herself. "I have no one in the world," she says, and means precisely this.

As she builds her story, Anya examines herself through a magnifying glass: What did she understand then? What does she understand today? What was the truth? "Today, we do not understand what we did [then]," or "To this day, I don't understand." When she tells of her escape in Russia, she says three times: "We were liberated from our work in the forest," but adds: "It wasn't the truth, but there was no choice." Years later, she is still apologizing. On the one hand, she says: "It is impossible to explain what it was like," when she describes the burning of the synagogue and the killing. On the other, she also says: "I have forgotten a great deal, but [not] what I saw" when she talks about the proud, dignified butcher who was taken to his death by the Germans.

Part of Anya's self-imposed injunction to describe precisely what happened before, during, and after the Holocaust is related to her tendency "to produce evidence" for her stories. As she mentions at the very beginning of the interview, "There is a book [of Holocaust survivors from her town], I will bring it to you in a moment to look at." She also mentions this in relation to her letters and photographs. All the places in the interview that include the mention of photographs are connected to memories of her family: family members who died in the Holocaust, the pretty hair she had as a child, the synagogue, the goy's skirt, even the leveled earth that remained where her house had once stood. Is this evidence necessary in order to assure us that her stories are not a figment of her imagination, and herself that the facts are as she states them and not otherwise?

Bosmat has already remarked on Anya's finely detailed memory of her life with her family, especially from the first days of the war until her escape to Russia. Beyond her desire to preserve in her own mind the family framework that had been lost forever, this description also indicates how self-centered is Anya's thinking. She holds herself responsible for all that happened around her (Genia also felt this sense of responsibility). However, for Anya it encompasses an unusual combination of helplessness and creativity—perhaps an expression of her fear and her hope. In this way, Anya presents the two facets of herself that also prevailed after her flight: the "ten fingers" that saved her life, and the fact that she has "no one left in the world." If only initiative and control had been important, how would she be able to account for the loss of the rest of her family? If helplessness, how can she account for the fact that she survived innumerable threatening situations? Both of these feelings are in conflict with one another, a conflict that prevents Anya from being at peace with herself. This conflict is difficult to handle, especially in light of her feelings that her suffering was—and is—illegitimate according to the postwar survivors' "scale of suffering" (this will be mentioned in the interview that follows with Anya's daughter, Tamar).

Before the war broke out, Anya knew that her mother was the breadwinner and her father was busy with his studies of the Torah. At some point, her father tried to become an accountant (as did her husband in Israel), but "the Book" is "his life." Anya learns to sew, to embroider, to work in the printing shop, and does any job that comes along. When the war begins, Anya appears to be an assertive person. During a bomb attack, she crawls to look for her lost brother. She brings potatoes ("real big ones") and bread ("two very big loaves"). She manages with the Germans (she pretends that she is thirty-five years old and a mother of four), and she confronts the Christians when she goes back to her village. It is Anya who goes between the villages bringing food and news of the family. She is younger—unmarried, with no children—and so is more mobile than the rest. Even after she escapes to Russia, the old clothes she left behind help her family: they sold them and now "they have bread."

There are other descriptions, however, which portray Anya as soft and helpless. During the confusion of the war, there is one especially touching moment: "Friday night, we were all tired. The children slept on the straw. And I sat in front of Father and said: 'What will our end be?' Father said: 'Don't worry, we know the Germans, everything will be fine.'" Her meeting with her brother after a terrible night of killing also has this softness: he combs her hair and they hug one another. In contrast to these descriptions of her father and brother, Anya presents her sick mother as the realistic one: "And my mother understood that it would be my end. And she [said]: 'Start running away, run away! There is nothing for you to do here.'" Overnight, Anya changes from being the "small, short one" to the "tall one," someone who is in charge of her own survival.

On the surface, Anya's family is the center of her life, then as well as now, as is Olga's. "Who throws away parents?" she says, unwilling to go to eastern Russia until she hears from them. What Anya does not say, however, is whether she felt guilty for leaving them behind. We learn about it only indirectly through her description of (which may also be a projection onto) Tamar: "Would I have left my mother alone and gone [to the seder] to my husband's brother? She has no feeling." Anya allows only her family to help her in her hour of need. She refuses those who offer help when she is in Israel and abroad and gives consent only to her family, who give her money to buy an apartment, a refrigerator, and a washing machine. But she also focuses in on her family when she argues that there is "evil under good." She says of her sick husband, "he was evil."

Unlike Olga's, Anya's view of her family does not help her maintain a positive feeling toward them or toward herself. She decides they cannot relieve her burden. An early sign of this guilt is her prewar wish, as a Communist, to escape from home with "her boyfriend," a wish that did not become a reality due to her mother's illness and the outbreak of the war. After all, her parents rejected him because he "was like a goy" (meaning secular), just as his family rejected her because she "was not rich." But this feeling of being left alone ripens only when Anya reaches her uncle in Haifa at the end of her wanderings. Then she is in despair: "Why didn't they want to hear about what hurt me? Why didn't they want to understand that I left a sick mother, a religious father, a gentle brother. They didn't want to hear about it ... I kept it in my heart." Did her loneliness begin then, when she realized that there was no one left to support her emotionally, to help her cope with her pain and guilt?

Anya's stories, like Olga's, cover up other untold stories. She has hidden the death of her child away in the deep recesses of her mind. There is even a moment when it is not clear whether there was a baby that died. Perhaps it was only a miscarriage? She also mentioned it when she talked about the abortion she had after Tamar, and once when she said: "I had a son, and the son died on me," when she is talking about the death of her first husband in Russia. She does not say what caused the baby's death, as if asking the question, Am I normal, how could I go on living after my baby died, after I left my parents and siblings? In a distant echo to this question, Anya responds when Bosmat tells her about her grandfather in the old-age home: "Aside from that, is he as lucid as I am? Normal? I read books." She also says: "I didn't have a dress, I didn't have a life, I only wanted to have a book." That is to say, as long as she is a learned person (like her father) there is proof that she is sane. Only then can she find meaning in her independent existence.

Tamar

"It is difficult for her to acknowledge that I am a separate person"

I (Dan) have known Tamar for seven years, ever since I left the kibbutz. We met in a professional context and afterward discovered that we were neighbors—somehow it is possible to live next to people for years without knowing their life stories. During our work together I had an inner feeling about Tamar, that she had a femininity and an artistic sensitivity she denied. However, my wife asserts, and to a certain extent it is true, that this is my problem: in every woman I like I find something of value that she herself is unaware of. Despite my acquaintance, Bosmat and I were somewhat wary of meeting Tamar because of Anya's description of her ("she has no feeling"). We tried to imagine how Tamar, as an only child, deals with her mother's stories ("I am not like other parents, I didn't make a secret of it"). Did she rebel against her mother, as Tzipke did? Did she devalue her own life story, as Hannah did? Perhaps she has tried to focus on her Israeli identity, like Dina in her continuation of Olga's story? When we meet for the interview, there is a simultaneous feeling of embarrassment: we know and do not know each other. I express my embarrassment through my need to eat something. Tamar expresses it by taking care of her dog: Should she let him out? Should she bring him in? Should she ask one of her daughters to take care of him? These questions run through most of the interview. Tamar begins as if she has prepared a lecture ahead of time.

I think it's like this. I was born in 1951 in Tel Aviv. My mother, my parents were Holocaust survivors, and I will tell you more about that because my mother was born in 1915 and my father was born seven years before her. She came from a town in Poland and arrived in Israel after she was saved and was in Russia. I am not completely sure about her travels and the technical details. She was on the immigrant ship *Theodore Herzl* that was captured and she was in Cyprus when the State "broke out." She came to Israel, she had quite a large family here, uncles and cousins, but she is the only one from her family in Poland who remained alive, from the entire side of her family *(sigh)*. My mother was already a widow, and . . . she lost a baby in Russia.

My father had a similar story. He was an old bachelor, his parents were already in Israel, as well as his brothers and his sister's son. He was very close to immigration before the war broke out. He waited for a certificate, he was close to the border, and somehow he just missed getting out. He was a soldier in the Polish army. When the war began, he was still involved in some activity, it was chaotic, Poland was conquered in about two days, and he was afraid because he was a Polish soldier. It wasn't so clear what was going to happen, so he escaped to Russia and he managed there pretty well from the very beginning. I think he was a miller. I don't really know about what he went through, but I didn't hear terrible stories of suffering, hunger, or deprivation [from him] like I heard from my mother. He also boarded an immigrant ship whose name I have forgotten, was captured [by the British], and got to Cyprus. I have pictures of my mother from Cyprus and pictures of him from there, but they didn't know each other then. They met here in Israel, in Tel Aviv, and they got married through his brother, whose wife was from the same town as my mother, and they got them acquainted, I guess. They got married at a relatively late age, and when I was born, after my mother had already had a number of miscarriages, one or two, and also afterwards she had . . . due to her age and not only due to her age, her health as well as what she went through. That is the simple story, I was the only child who remained from all of her pregnancies.

Tamar speaks as if she is delivering a report, that is, without emotional involvement. Every now and then, mixed in with her monotone, there is an outpouring of irony: the State "broke out," her father didn't undergo "terrible" experiences like her mother.

When I was born, we lived on Eilat Street. Do you know where that is? We had a sort of hut on the roof and we lived there. I remember a few pictures from the roof: down below there were all kinds of carpentry shops and tin workers, craftsmen of a sort. Now I am not sure what I remember and what my mother told me. My father had a vegetable store in Jaffa *(laughs)*, and according to my mother, and since I know my father it makes sense, he had a partner who cheated him all the time, and he therefore remained very poor. Finally he left and worked as a cashier for a wholesale vegetable store. A cashier and an accountant, he was expert in that field. He was simply a wasted talent, he had been a yeshiva student, he came to Israel knowing a high level of Hebrew and writing, but he was *(ironic laughter)*, I think he was a person who had no ability whatsoever to learn the rules and manage in the reality here. His ideal for many years was to work as a clerk for the Tel Aviv municipality. He once told me that he missed that opportunity.

When I was three they moved to a small neighborhood, somewhere between Givatayim and Yad Eliyahu, a very small neighborhood, tiny, an apartment with two rooms that were built at the time when a lot of immigrants arrived and there was a need to make room for all of them. In the beginning, the neighborhood was very good because a lot of Austrians, Hungarians, and Poles lived there. Even Ephraim Kishon lived there, as well as many people from the Liberal party. After a few years, some of them got settled and left the neighborhood. That is, it began as a very high quality neighborhood, but of course, many moved on and it became a small, peripheral neighborhood. In a certain way, it was fun living there because I actually grew up close to the center of Tel Aviv. To this day, I feel as if I am from Tel Aviv rather than from Beer-Sheva. And I went to school there and I had an organized and settled way of life, very conservative. I was in the same elementary school for eight years, with the same children and friends. Even before that I spent three years in the same nursery school with the same children *(turns to Bosmat).*

I don't know what generation you belong to, where to place myself, but ah—it was a period, from my point of view, it was one of the most important periods in my life. How can I explain it to you . . . there was also the matter of good high schools, before the comprehensive method, and the children were thrown out [for not being good enough students]. That is, our high school was very strict and it suited me, I had a very good time there. And I had a social life that was very . . . there were things that were difficult for me during adolescence like . . . but ahh . . . I also enjoyed the studies a lot, as well as the friendships and, in the end, it was there that I met my husband. I still have friends from that time.

Even though Tamar continues to talk without a pause, like Anya, her words become more and more "sticky." Every second word is "ahh," as if she is trying to say and not say something at the same time. I have the feeling that she is wondering how we are understanding her words, and mostly, what impression Bosmat is getting of her.

So, during the last three years I majored in biology and that's it. Ahh, at home I was always, I think, a very good girl and it was only when I was a teenager that I, I killed my mother, I made terrible troubles for her, especially . . .

"What, for example?" (Tamar laughs).

Okay, so I yelled at her, and I hated her, and I didn't like going places with her and . . . I think that we would be walking along the street and I felt great embarrassment that she was with me, and that she represented me, that she was my mother, and I couldn't stand the fact that she was proud of me, that I was her daughter. All kinds of things like that.

"Did you get over that at some point?"

Oh no, I don't think that it is over. That is, I have a hard time with her *(sighs while speaking)*, I don't know whether it has to do with me or with her, she is just a difficult person. She is a very hard woman. I think that if I look at it from a distance, she went through some emotional crisis, an emotional crisis due to what she went through there. I don't think she was an easy person from the beginning. What she went through there turned her into a more difficult person.

"Can you give me a concrete example?" Tamar hesitates for a moment, choosing her words carefully.

I think that she has a tendency to be a glutton. It is hard for me to give you a big story, I think about the part that, for example, that to this day, the story of the sanctity of food for children [is important]—"they should eat." To this day, she can tell me suddenly, while we are having a telephone conversation, after she has been here a hundred times and she knows that . . . I will never . . . my family complains about the way that I fill the refrigerator. My freezers are always overflowing with cooked and un-cooked food. For example, when I went away for three weeks in September, I organized the house, so that even if I had been away for half a year, there would have been hot meals for lunch every day. From that point of view, I don't think that my mother has reached my little finger, but to this day, she picks up the phone and asks whether the children ate something, after all, they don't eat here like they should. I think that it is difficult for her to acknowledge *(excited)* that . . . that I am a grown-up and a separate person.

For example, when we were a young couple, like most parents, my parents also helped us out here and there financially. But those days passed long ago. Can you imagine that my parents helped me build this house? *(looks at us to see if we understand how absurd this is)*. And, to this day, she is capable of going and telling my daughters that the only thing we have is the money she gave us. And not only that, there was also a time when she went and told that to the neighbors! *(angry)*. What sort of behavior is that?! My hair would stand on end. Aside from the wild ex-aggeration, it is the sort of thing that makes me feel worthless. To this day, she has the feeling that I am dependent on her and that I am incapable of managing on my own. After all, it is clear that it's just not true! It's clear that it doesn't really exist. Things like that annoy me *(sighs)*.

"It makes me feel worthless." For the first time in the interview, Tamar is angry. I wonder what power Anya still has over her daughter, and how Tamar abets this "magical" power.

I always have to be on standby. If we have been getting along nicely for a while, she will exploit it: "It was nice, so come over, come over I will begin to swallow you up, and I will begin telling you what to do." In the beginning, she will do it somewhat gently because we are still getting along, but later on, she will start telling me what to do and what she thinks. She will begin managing me and taking charge of my children. I remember during the first few years of my marriage, Ya'acov would say that if something was to happen to him, my mother would come and take charge of me and my children. Just the fantasy of that happening would finish me. Of course it's clear that I wouldn't let that happen—never. Now, she can be very aggressive and she can do terrible things. She is not a stupid woman and when you catch her when she is in the right mood, you can also talk with her. She doesn't live with too many denials. She can talk about things, about death, the Holocaust, in a very direct manner, to the point, and you can make sense of it.

Tamar is attempting to soften the hard picture of her mother she has painted.

I am trying to think about all kinds of things that she does which are very hard for me to bear. I won't tell you about the fact that she uses emotional blackmail. You can open up any book about the typical Polish mother, like "I will only rest in my grave," things that people make fun of, but it happens all of the time with her. Even when we were there for the holiday, she said to me: "Next year, if I will still be alive, I will do this and that; next year, if I will still be alive, I will do so and so." So I said to her: "Look . . . after all, it is clear that if you won't be alive, you won't be able to do it." Today it makes me laugh, but it is terrible and it has gone on for so many years! There were years that I enjoyed it. For example, my mother always gave me the feeling that, night or day, whenever I needed her, she would be on call. That is, if I want a cup of cocoa in the middle of the night, or a bowl of soup, she would go and make it for me. That is, to feed the child or to worry that she is warm when she is ill, is the most important thing in life. For many years there was a myth in our home that she didn't sleep! She didn't need to sleep, or that she didn't eat, or that she ate only apples . . . my father worked for a wholesale market and he would bring home fruits and vegetables for free, so . . .

Slowly, I begin to understand how much energy Tamar invests in her relationship with her mother. I look for relief. "You talked about your mother but you barely mentioned your father."

Okay *(a moment of sadness)*. My father was very quiet and introverted. He didn't talk a lot and was wrapped up in himself. I don't think they were very close. There wasn't a big love there, they also tended to fight. I blamed my mother for most of those things. Not that I think that he was an easy person or a saint, I—I don't think that they were suited to one another. He was the kind of person, externally, he seemed a very easygoing kind of man who didn't get into conflicts, unassertive. My mother had all kinds of outbursts at different times and . . . harsh complaints. Perhaps— I don't know if I could live with a person like my father. He really wasn't much of a support or protection. But I think that a big part of it came from her, from her dissatisfaction.

In fact, most of his life was coming home from work and reading the newspaper. He would work very early hours because the market opens and closes early. He had many books related to the Bible. It is strange, because he didn't live the life of a religious man, even though he finished his yeshiva studies, but that is what he loved, reading. He had a few friends and he would go and meet them every now and then and they would listen to the Yiddish programs on the radio. I didn't have very deep discussions with my father. He spoiled me and he was nice to me, but the one who really took it upon herself to raise me was my mother . . . I don't believe that he changed my diapers when I was a baby or things like that. My mother brought me up, both me and the house were under her complete supervision. She didn't even let him wash out a cup. She said that he didn't do it right. My mother washes out cups in a terrible manner herself, so that it has nothing to do with the actual level of cleanliness *(laughs)*.

I also think that somehow the whole story of the war "diminished" him. I remember parts of it, the way people related to him who knew him before, that he had been a man with a wonderful sense of humor, much more sociable and open before the war. My uncle told me about him as a child, that my father was his mother's beloved child, out of a gigantic group of children. He was shy and introverted and I think that, to some extent, he remained so. He also got married at a late age. My father's mother died in Israel, he was in Russia or Cyprus, and ... one of the amazing things to think about is that his father died when I was one year old. It amazes me to think about it. I live with such a great feeling of emptiness, of not having grandparents, and here, for a whole year I had a grandfather. It just seems to me to be something not ... *(agitated)* and he lived with the strong wish to meet his mother when he came to Israel, but she was already dead. I don't know. On the other hand, perhaps that is what enabled him to marry at all.

The war "diminished" him—an odd expression. The Tamar who talks about her father is different from the Tamar who talks about her mother. Even if there is evidence of a continuous inner dialogue, Tamar is qualitatively more emotional.

Good friends of my parents lived in Haifa, they were childless and they were the same age [as my parents]. He was my father's age from a small town and his name was Ya'acov and his wife was older than him. She was Romanian and they met in Russia. They were very close and they would bring up all kinds of memories. There were pieces of past experiences of my mother's, all kinds of memories—Tashkent—all kinds of out of the way places in Russia. Now, the stories on television about the places that are waking up in Russia, I remembered that my parents were in places like Uzbekistan, I don't remember anymore the names of all those strange places that they were, when they were hiding there. These were stories that I would hear from these friends.

My father had two brothers in Israel *(she turns to us suddenly)*—are you interested in hearing about this? His youngest brother immigrated a few years before him, he was thought to be the handsome and stupid one. He was in the police. He was a very simple man and I think that he was very superficial, that is, as if he was Israeli. I don't think that he was a deep person, that you could hear wise things from him. The older brother in the family was seven years older than my father. He was also becoming a rabbi, he was thought to be a very learned man. He and his wife didn't have any children because of the blood [Rh negative] that she had. She was pregnant nine times and all the babies died one after another. It was a terrible tragedy. He was like my father. They had a common language, they had a similar education and a similar background. He also didn't succeed from an economic standpoint, like my father. He had a store and he didn't succeed in ever selling one pair of shoes, it was amazing. He died when I was fifteen.

The younger brother, who was "handsome and stupid," was the first one to immigrate; "Israeli" equals "superficial." Is Tamar presenting her own preferences or her father's? "Do you have a memory of you doing something with your father?"

(Sigh) Do I have a memory of doing something with my father? I always remember that they spoiled me on Saturday mornings, especially my father. They would bring me an omelet in bed and always ask, he would ask me what I want and he would make me a special treat for breakfast. From that point of view, it was fun.

Tamar has difficulty addressing her father in the singular, even when describing how he spoiled her. "Did your father observe Shabbat?"

Look, my parents didn't travel on Shabbat because they didn't have a car. They didn't really observe Shabbat, but on the holidays my father went to services at the synagogue and our kitchen was separated into milk and meat, because the family from Haifa was very religious. It is interesting to hear what mother told you *(she turns to Bosmat)*. I think that her stories change now and then, but I don't know in which direction. Anyway, I understand from her stories that she was a very active Communist and that when the war broke out, she was twenty-four, her boyfriend was in Russia, he got away quickly and she was supposed to join him. I remember some description of hers that she already had her trousseau, which she had embroidered herself during that time, ready in suitcases. My mother is very talented with her hands, she embroiders and knits, and she has very good hands for things like that. But she sews terribly and all during my childhood, she sewed me dresses that were simply horrendous in an awful Polish style. But in embroidery and knitting, she is wonderful.

I remember that we went to Haifa when I was a little girl and she told me about each and every dress, dresses she left there, and later on, when she ran away, they remained, and her family managed to live off them. So she intended to join him [her boyfriend] and she joined him and they got married there, and when she came to Israel . . . in Israel she was no longer a Communist. By the way, to this day I don't know how my parents vote. Of all the terrible things that were talked about in my house, there were never, never discussions about how one votes and whom one votes for. That's a bit funny, isn't it?

Tamar goes back to talking about her mother without noticing that she is doing so. I (Bosmat) think to myself, it isn't only the dresses that Anya has left behind.

I understood that her husband was recruited into the Russian army, into the Red Army, and he was killed. A lot of people were killed and . . . she remained with a baby and when he was two years old he died. Not too long ago she told it to the girls and I listened in. They went to some *kolkhoz,* some group of people, and they worked there in agriculture. They conscripted the husbands and only the girls remained, but in that story her baby didn't appear either. So, I don't know whether that was before or after he died.

"Did she always tell you stories like those?"

Yes, always! If you ask me, in my opinion she overdid it. There are homes where they don't talk about it. I knew people in all different kinds of stages and they said: "We didn't know what the parents went through." Today I think that she was obsessive about it, she was too pushy, and she didn't let us develop our own opinions. Everything was in the shadow of those events.

"Did your father also talk?"

(Sighs) My father told me very little, but in general, he wasn't a big talker. He was less emotional and less involved. And . . . I think that he was more—he was psychologically healthier and he was organized. I think that he also lost fewer close family members. He didn't lose a wife, he didn't lose a child. That is to say, he lost some brothers and the families of his brothers, but somehow it seems different to me. My mother was very close to her parents, to this day she doesn't . . . during adolescence a person needs to develop and to begin relating to one's parents in a more realistic way. I don't think she went through that stage, because her parents to this day [serve as] some sort of model, some sort of ideal for her.

Tamar gives a big sigh. Her father is healthier because he lost less and her mother is unrealistic because she was very close to those she left and lost. For the first time, it would seem that Tamar is close to saying she is unable to take in her mother's pain.

So, if we go back to Shabbat, during those days in Israel, Shabbat was more like Shabbat. There wasn't television and more people went to synagogue, there weren't cars. And it was part of the experience of the neighborhood. But with us, I don't think that we ever had happy holidays. It's true that we were never alone on Passover, we always went to family. My father had two cousins that had come from a small town close to his. We got along very nicely with them, they didn't live far away. One was very religious and they had wonderful seders, really religious and beautiful. A few times my parents also invited people and we read the entire Haggadah and it was like it should be. But, somehow it doesn't bring out a feeling of happiness, I don't have memories of real joy. To this day, I have some flaw when it comes to holidays. It's true that over the years I have begun organizing more holiday dinners, and we go through all of the rituals, but somehow, I am not really happy. I remember a lot of Passover eves: even if we got together in big gatherings, we were a marginal family. That is to say, we were never strong in our own right, only with other people. I had the feeling that we were a very small family and in the wider family circle we were always on the periphery. There were other people who were closer. Sometimes you see brothers who are really like brothers, for example, my father's two cousins. They were very close, they went through Auschwitz together and all that.

We were a very small family unit. It's strange, because I have a lot of family. I am not only talking about my father's side. My mother has cousins and they have lots of children in America and in Israel. In my childhood we even met a lot. But I don't keep in touch, it's been years since I've gone to their weddings and celebrations. They are very nice and successful people. It's not that I can say, "What a disgusting family and I don't want any contact with them." They are nice, cultured, intelligent people. It might be that I don't feel like I really belong to them . . . and perhaps, also, that if I come there is always my mother there in the background.

When I look at it through the eyes of an adult, I have the feeling that we were somewhat deprived. That is to say, they were already Israeli and they fought in the War of Independence and they settled in the country and it is somewhat like the movie with Gila Almagor with her mother, *Avia's Summer*. Okay, so my mother wasn't completely crazy, right? But somewhere, she was a diaspora figure, she didn't fit in, and I think that her stories went that way. That is, she was young in Poland and she was thought of as being a very talented girl, very pretty and successful, and when she came back from Russia, she came back half a person *(sighs and looks at Bosmat)*. She also got old quickly. There are pictures of when I was a baby and she still looked all right, but her hair turned white very early, she got wrinkled, and her appearance became unimportant to her. She turned into a person who didn't take good care of herself, she never used creams or [wore nice] clothes. You could not learn femininity from her. That is, the house needed to be clean, and one's clothes had to be aesthetic, and the sheets were always white, but . . . once we went to the Carmel market and one of the shopkeepers knew her. He was with her in Cyprus and he began telling me: "How nice you look, you should know how your mother looked at your age, what a beautiful woman she was, how wonderful she was." People were amazed at what has happened to her, she simply underwent some sort of metamorphosis.

"We were never strong in our own right" and *"you could not learn femininity from her." These are strong statements Tamar is using to define her loneliness. "Did you have objects in your house from Poland?"*

Nothing was left, nothing was left. My mother said that she came, her house was in ruins. They destroyed the houses and they ploughed everything under. Now, there were a lot of pictures, there were pictures, because they sent them to their uncles in Israel and America. So my mother took them and made copies. But there weren't any real things left. Her grandmother, my mother's grandmother who died in Israel, when my mother was in Cyprus, at the age of eighty-four, my mother's grandmother had a number of children. There were a few that remained in Poland and one of them was my mother's mother. All of them and their children were murdered. There was a group of boys, uncles who went to America, and they succeeded more or less, and there was an uncle who immigrated to Israel, a one and only uncle, this is the uncle they sat Shiva for when he arrived in Israel.[1] He went to study carpentry and that was thought of as being terrible. He was a carpenter and for many years I had a cabinet he made.

Now, when the war broke out, Grandmother was already a widow, she visited all her sons, and she was in Israel then. So she was here and later my mother wrote to her from Cyprus. She loved her grandmother very much. There, everyone was very tall and red-haired, and some of their children are like that. One moment, how did I start talking about Grandmother? *("I had asked you about objects.")* So when she died, she inherited diamond earrings and all kinds of things like that. The uncle from America, when he came to Israel a short while after my mother immigrated and they were very excited about that . . . someone from the family survived, and they offered my mother the earrings. According to her, and you need to censor her stories, I don't know, they offered her the diamonds. But she said that she had lost all she had in the war and that she didn't need any diamonds. She really didn't get dressed up all those years.

"Did she try to have more children after you?"

She was pregnant at least twice after me. I remember at least one of them, I have a very foggy memory about being in a hospital where she must have been after a miscarriage. There was some story, I don't remember any of it, that she was pregnant, I was about a year old, and she ran after me and fell, and as a result the baby died. Her description was very dramatic and she felt the need to tell it to me at a young age in great detail. It's very strange that I don't feel guilty, but according to her story I killed my brother, that's the story more or less. The description was very dramatic, because it turned out that it was supposed to be a boy. It must have had some special meaning for them—that it was a boy. I never, the issue never really bothered me, and she really, she said that she wanted to commit suicide, then she almost wanted to jump out of the window *(excited)*. Okay, I am talking about it very coldly, but I am still quite angry with her. I don't think that it is the kind of thing with which you bring up a child, all kinds of awful accusations like that. It must have been a time when people allowed themselves to say whatever came into their heads to their children at every stage and in every situation. They told me: "It must be very hard for you to be an only child," as if I could do something about it. The truth is that I enjoyed being an only child very much. It was clear to me that their [my parents'] resources were very limited, by all means, and if I had needed to share them with someone else, it would have been very uncomfortable for me. I had a very egotistic and pragmatic approach. Later on, it became more difficult. When my father died, my mother became a burden, and if there had been someone else, then there would be someone to share it with *(sighs)*.

All in all, my mother has a monopoly: *a)* a monopoly on the Holocaust; and *b)* a monopoly on death, the death of her entire family. Since my father died, she also has a monopoly on his death. She also has a monopoly on her death, and to some extent it leaves me in the situation of either being obedient and led like a lamb to the slaughter or of being defiant and distant and terrible. There are moments when I am successful at being with her. But I think that I only went with her to the cemetery to my father's memorial service once or twice. It's a whole world she is busy with, I am outside of that world.

I try to imagine what it is like to grow up near a mother who has a "monopoly on death." "We were talking about objects. Were there things that came through your father's home?"

(Excited) Oy, that is a story, it drives me crazy because I just discovered it last time I was visiting my mother. In the same way that there is a picture of my mother's parents hanging on the wall, there was a picture of my father's parents. The last time when I went with my girls, the picture wasn't on the wall. It turns out that she gave it to my cousin. I yelled at her, how mad I got, what nerve, "It was a picture of Father's parents!" I told her: "How are you depriving me of my inheritance from my father?" And she said: "Why do you need that picture?" *(Very angry)* Who gives her the right? *(Turns to Bosmat)* You see, that is an example of no boundaries, of being transparent. How could she do such a thing? *(very agitated).*

My father's relatives died and they left a few things and my aunt took them. Among the things left were a pair of candlesticks, silver candlesticks this big *(shows a height of about a foot and a half)* with filigree like in the books, beautiful. I can only covet them, but I don't have any real right, because I didn't have any connection to her. That is, I got none of those things. I think that my father, it wasn't important for him at all, he didn't fight and he didn't demand and I guess that they had no meaning for my mother. It didn't occur to them that I wanted something for myself, they were completely unaware of that *(angered),* and the fact that she gave away the picture that was hanging on the wall just burns me up, finishes me off. There isn't another picture like that.

"When you compare your story to Ya'acov's, what do you see?"

First of all, Ya'acov's mother talked very little. I think that Ya'acov really didn't know a lot about his background. That is to say, he knew a little about the way that his mother was saved and that she was in a *kolkhoz* in Russia. His father, it seems, did talk and Ya'acov didn't really understand it, because some of the stories that his father told him didn't fit into his picture *(sighs).* But I also don't think that my parents always talked to me about it. When people ask me, I tell [them], but it isn't a subject I talk about with the children or with Ya'acov. It is known, it exists, I think that one of the good things for the children of the second generation, my friends are like that, we don't need to talk about it a lot, we were pretty much aware of what those things meant. There are codes . . . there is a feeling of sharing a common fate. My friends from childhood, each one had a story, and we all knew the stories. For example, a woman and a man lived downstairs who didn't have any children, and there were stories that she was one of those Mengele had done experiments on and, therefore, she was barren. People with numbers on their arms were a natural part of my childhood. When we were adults, we began talking about it. For example, I have a very good girlfriend from high school and we met not too long ago. And then she told me a more detailed story about how her mother was saved and how the gentile hid her and how later on she found work with those goyim. She made them into one of the Righteous Gentiles[2] and she brought them to Israel, all kinds of fascinating things like that. I think that all of my friends knew exactly what town their parents came from, and they knew the names of the streets in those towns even though they had never been there. The truth is that I don't really know the name of the street. I know the towns, because they were very tiny towns that only had one main street. The truth is that for a while I have had the idea of going to Poland and now it has become a real possibility, but I don't know whether in the end it will come about because of all kinds of reasons.

"Will you go alone?"

(Sighs) I have a plan to go with a friend perhaps, it depends on a lot of things, I don't know whether it will actually happen. There was a group from the university and I went and looked at all of the details. It seemed to be not for me whatsoever, it involves youth and a lot of people. I decided not to go with them, I don't know.

"How do your daughters react to Grandmother and to her stories?"

They are interested and they respond with interest and with care. It isn't the most important thing for them, they are willing to participate, but I don't know. The truth is that I have already met children who have an interest in it to a greater extent. Look, Idit was in Poland, for example, and before she was in Poland they had a series of workshops and very nice things. The trip was very emotional and special, and she returned with a lot of experiences. But I don't see that it was as important for them as it is for me and my girlfriends. And I don't think that they are very different from other youth. I don't talk to my daughters about it, there are many things that I don't talk to them about. I think that I am quite a closed mother when it comes to personal matters. And also, in the last few years, I have put it into a different perspective in my life. It is less dominant, I hope.

Tamar gives a smile of hope. Bosmat answers warmly: "This interview was very interesting."

I have a feeling that the interview was brief, you know? It was even somewhat superficial. It was more on the level of facts and the things on the level about how you live with it on the day-to-day basis, but where are the fantasies, where are all the dreams, where are all the things that are connected to the inner world? I didn't initiate it, I didn't talk about those things, because it is difficult to bring it out in that way. It was, it's a bit, it's fragmentary.

Bosmat and I go out into the fresh summer air of the desert. It is already dark and the lights of the small houses in the neighborhood are lit. Two children are playing ball, and a dog is running around underfoot. We walk without speaking. We both feel the need, after all these words, to listen to the surrounding silence, to sort out our feelings. What can one say after such an interview? We entered Tamar's house with some apprehension, and now we feel a heaviness as we walk. I accompany Bosmat to the bus and we part with a hug. "You can feel that she is already getting larger," I say to myself with a smile and add, with some concern, "Did Bosmat's baby hear what was said to its mother in this interview?"

Tamar is almost without a life story of her own, if we define "story" as a narrative with a plot that has a beginning, a middle, and an end. She is engaged in a sort of dialogue, an inner struggle that has no beginning or end; it is a continuous flow of words. In every part of the interview we run into the "invisible opponent," just as we did in the interview with her mother, Anya. And even though Tamar is a very intelligent and educated woman, she speaks in a simple manner. In editing, we have taken out frequent recurrences of "ah" and "that is," repeated expressions, and instances where a sentence remains unfinished. Does she speak this way "as if" to say: "I am unworthy"? Perhaps she is imitating her mother's poor Hebrew? In addition, Tamar uses words that are full of irony, even somewhat aggressive: the State "broke out," her father "missed" immigrating before the war. These expressions convey the feeling of an adolescent struggling for independence, as if Tamar were imitating the style of one of her daughters.

The manifest part of her story is almost self-evident: it is her ongoing struggle for separation from her mother, her anger over the mother who "swallows" her, who gives her the feeling that she is "worthless." Is it her mother who cannot see in Tamar "a separate and independent person" or is it Tamar's lack of self-legitimacy, the struggle of a child growing up with no clear boundaries between her overprotective mother and herself? During adolescence, Tamar was embarrassed about walking along the street with her mother because she was "irrelevant": she didn't speak Hebrew, she told people unpleasant things to their faces, she was a troublemaker. Anya even accused her of killing her brother (the fetus) by causing her mother's fall and miscarriage. In a way, Tamar's struggle reminds us of Tzipke's. However, Tamar is less reflective than Tzipke. Her narrative is constructed around her failure to become independent rather than her success.

The conflict has not yet been resolved: Tamar has not worked it through. Anya still bothers her on the telephone with questions about whether there is enough food in the refrigerator for the children, "who don't eat like they should." Anya embarrasses her by telling her neighbors that *she* provided the money for Tamar and Ya'acov's home. Anya gives her cousin the only remaining photograph of Tamar's paternal grandparents. After this list of betrayals Tamar adds that one needs to be wary of her mother, who knows how to provide the illusion of being nice in order to strike again from an unexpected direction. Tamar portrays Anya as having almost supernatural powers: she is known not to need sleep or food ("She only eats apples"). And if that is not enough, Ya'acov adds his own fantasy: if something was to happen to him, her mother would come and "take charge of me and my children."

There is no way to make sense of the magical power Anya has in Tamar's eyes without feeling Tamar's keen admiration for her mother, which coexists with her anger and frustration: How Anya coped with starvation in Russia, with the loss of her husband and baby, her parents and siblings. How she saved herself by her own hands. How she coped later on with her second husband (Tamar's father), who was "unsuccessful," with his sickness and death, and more recently, with her broken hip. Moreover, "she always was there for me" when Tamar was a child. "It was she who really raised me," as opposed to a father who spoiled her but never washed a cup at home.

The manifest part of Tamar's narrative, her inner conflict, continues through the whole interview, no matter what subject is under discussion. Despite her awareness of this problem, she is, in her forties, still totally paralyzed by it. Why hasn't she developed a way of handling it as Tzipke or Hannah did, by finding ways of living as a separate person? This brings us to a less obvious aspect of her narrative: the feelings of inferiority and marginality Tamar has absorbed, which to us seem only partially related to her mother.

Let us look more closely at how Tamar conveyed these feelings. She begins the interview with the expression "I think it's like this" and continues with a description of their neighborhood, which was on the outskirts of Tel Aviv. People like Ephraim Kishon, who lived there in the beginning, left early on. While trying to discover for herself what she was good at, Tamar said (in sections of the interview not presented here) that she tried "to learn a lot of things not on a deep level, not like medicine or painting," which "entails depth or personal expression." The town of Arad for her had been a wonderful change: she and Ya'acov distanced themselves physically from their parents. Both were free and they traveled a lot. Still, even then she felt like "a young and frustrated mother." In her professional work in the army, she faced difficulties and pressures, but she could not imagine "that there is a [professional] life [alternative] outside of this workplace." At the end of the interview, she feels she has missed important things: "It was . . . somewhat superficial . . . where are the fantasies . . . all the dreams . . . the inner world . . . things . . . it is difficult to bring out." For us, these are the very things Tamar has difficulty allowing herself to feel and express, not only those she has not been able to touch on in the interview context.

Tamar's feeling of marginality began in her family. Her parents were married through matchmaking, "not due to love." They were successful and beautiful before the war came and ruined everything. Her father was a smart student, on his way to becoming a rabbi. In Israel he became an unsuccessful accountant. Her mother had been a beautiful and active woman. In Israel, she very quickly lost her looks and no longer took care of herself, as if in a constant state of mourning. As Tamar remarks: "She has a monopoly on the Holocaust and on death." In a symbolic way, Tamar's mother refused to accept the diamond earrings, an inheritance from her beloved grandmother, because "she had lost all she had [there] in the war and ... she didn't need any diamonds." If it is possible to localize the overall influence of the Holocaust, it is in the feeling of worthlessness Tamar has internalized through her parents' relationship after the war, the loss of their closest family members, and their immigration to Israel.

This pattern has also emerged in relation to the wider family circle in which, Tamar says, "We were a marginal family, we weren't strong in our own right." She and her parents were not associated with the "real" experiences of either "there" or "here," experiences that have brought other family members closer together. Social legitimization was given only to those who went through "real pain," like Auschwitz, "real heroism," like the War of Independence, or "real joy and belief," like her orthodox relatives. Tamar can claim nothing of her own on this "scale of suffering." We note that there was no "real closeness" between her parents and their relatives, unlike the relationship that her cousins "who went through Auschwitz together" had. Her parents did not feel that they were "Israelis" like those relatives who had arrived in the country earlier and participated in the War of Independence. In addition, they didn't have "real holiday joy" like the religious branch of the family, which had "really wonderful [Passover] seders." Her parents, the secular "Asiatics," always fell between the widening cracks in her family (Auschwitz, Israeli, orthodox), and Tamar is still falling with them into those same cracks because she cannot dissociate herself from these "scales of suffering."

In a way, Tamar expresses her own alienation from life in Israel. It is an echo of the things that she has said about that part of her mother's family that settled in America and "managed quite well," as opposed to her mother's uncle, who came to Israel before the war and only became a carpenter. Her father's brother, "the young and stupid one," immigrated to Israel first. It is a sort of diaspora, pre-Holocaust way of thinking among her family members, looking down upon life in Israel. Perhaps there is still a hidden yearning in Tamar's inner thoughts for another time and place.

In this sense too, it is worthwhile to compare Tamar's interview with that of Dina. They live in two very different worlds, even though they are from the same background (they were born in Israel to Polish parents) and about the same age. Dina, following in Olga's footsteps, is an Israeli through and through. She sees herself as creating her reality through her actions, while accepting the local behavioral norms. She builds her feelings of worth, as well as her sense of security, around them. Tamar, who from an objective standpoint has not done any less in her life, feels alienated from the local reality. She feels close only to daughters of other Holocaust survivors, who comprised her childhood social environment and with whom she still meets and shares her experiences and feelings.

We set up a date with Dafna and Idit, Ya'acov and Tamar's older daughters. Dafna is serving in the army—she joined on the same day and in the same place as my daughter—and Idit is in her senior year at the local high school. I wonder how well Dafna and Idit have succeeded in constructing the narrative of their own life stories, their feelings of belonging, femininity, and Israeliness. Have they achieved it by rejecting their grandmother and fighting with Tamar, who sees herself as "a quite closed mother"? Or have they managed to accept their grandmother and their mother in a different way?

Dafna

"I want to do things on my own, to form my own opinion"

I (Dan) have known Dafna for some while. When we lived in Beer-Sheva, she was our babysitter. When Dafna would come to baby-sit, her brown eyes, quiet and sad, would light up when she saw the children. My son Haran loved her. He was always overjoyed when we told him: "Dafna is coming to stay with you while we go out." When I took her home, she was always happy to talk to me, but never about herself or how she saw her own life.

When we sit down to begin the interview, Dafna decides to tell me that she has been in therapy and wants to know how an interview differs from a therapy session. The question makes me somewhat uncomfortable—does Dafna identify me with her therapist? I try to explain how I view the difference: "I will only listen to your story, I will not try to intervene or help you with your problems." When I turn on the tape recorder, she smiles at me and begins talking as if we are "on the air."

It's as if I was born, I don't know what happened until Idit was born—
I was about a year old *(laughs)*. It was fun having a sister and a friend,
because she was always my friend, but I also felt that she had usurped my
place. She invested so much in our parents and all of that and I was exactly
the opposite. In fact, Mother invested a lot of years in me, but later on, I
invested more in her than the other way around. Still, Idit was mostly
with Daddy. She was more of the good girl and the helpful one, and I was
the one who would get nervous and angry easily. We lived in Arad up to
the second grade, but I don't remember, and later on we moved to Dimona. I had good girlfriends outside of home and I fit in well in school
(five-second pause). When we moved to Beer-Sheva, it was harder for me
to fit in. Actually, I didn't mind leaving Dimona as much as I minded
leaving Arad. But, anyway, of all the family, I took the move the hardest.
I saw all kinds of children that were accepted and I felt inferior. Idit,
however, fit quite nicely into the new neighborhood. Somehow, I let my
feelings of inferiority develop and I didn't know how to control them. It
sounds as if I am pinning all of my problems on Idit, but it's not that way
exactly. I am responsible for my own problems.

In the tenth grade, I had girlfriends but I didn't feel that I loved them,
really. There was a very big wish to succeed and I didn't feel comfortable
with it. At the end of the tenth grade, I had a boyfriend for a few months
and when it ended, it was a sort of blow for me, I didn't know what to
do with myself. I almost never left home, I talked to my father. I had a
crisis, I didn't have the desire to meet people, it was he who helped me,
with his help I held myself together. My mother didn't have the patience
for all of my problems. Perhaps she was willing to help, but she wanted
me to take care of myself and all that. So, then I started going to therapy.
All in all, I think that the crisis brought me closer to my family.

*It is difficult for Dafna to talk about the crisis she went through, but she
continues describing it in detail. She does not seem able to find a way to
move beyond it. After a while, I look for a subject that will perhaps be more
"neutral": "Were you close to your grandmother and grandfather?"*

I think that Idit accepted them more, Grandma and Grandpa. I don't
know whether she loves them more, but she took it upon herself to be
their granddaughter more than I did. For example, she loves Grandma's
cooking, it's Polish cooking. I don't like most of the food that she makes.

"Are you talking about Grandma Anya?"

Yes, she is easier to love than Father's mother. She gives love. Perhaps it is difficult for those who have to live with her to get along with her, but I didn't have to live with her. It's easy to love her because she gives hugs and kisses and she makes you feel that she loves you. She is also very generous—she loves to give a lot of things. Perhaps she feels in competition with my father's mother a bit; she doesn't like her. Today, I am not afraid to argue with her either. Anyway, she would take us to the playground and give us candy bars. They would also give us good food to eat. I would go visit her with Idit. She still talks about my grandfather and she cries over the fact that he died. She is definitely ready to talk about him today more than she did earlier. I remember that she told us that she had been married during the war, that she had a baby, and that she also brought up her niece, who was like a daughter to her. Her mother told her to leave home in order to escape, because Grandma was a Communist. It was she who went out to get food, but toward the end, it was enough for only one day. She doesn't know who took care of that after she escaped. Today, I know basically what happened, but I still hear about things that I didn't know about before, mostly the part before Russia.

"She gives love." I feel a warmth about Anya that has not been reported before.

"How did you take those stories as a child?"

As a child I don't think that I took them hard. I would hear about them in small bits and pieces that were well filtered. There was only one time that I remember that she spoke for about four or five hours and that was too much. I wanted to leave, but I know that I didn't. And I remember that afterwards I cried for a long time *(ten-second pause).*

"And your grandmother and grandfather on your father's side?"

When my family goes to visit them, I love to go and be where they live, I have a lot of memories from there. But I will never go visit by myself. I take the initiative more with Anya. I don't feel so close to my grandmother on my father's side. She pretty much lives in a way that is comfortable for her. I really don't know much about her. I know that there was a period when she and her sisters lived in Russia or in Ukraine. They escaped, wandered around all of Russia, perhaps they suffered from poverty and starvation, it must have been traumatic for her. Grandfather would talk, I didn't understand everything. But I won't exactly push to ask him—I feel no need to go to him. He wants it to be like when I was little. Perhaps I am also afraid that I will feel sad and begin to cry again. He would tell me how he beat the Germans by throwing sand into their eyes and all kinds of stories like that. Grandma would also stop him in the middle. I rarely go visit them, I don't feel very safe with them *(hesitates)*.

She [grandmother on father's side] is absorbed in herself and she destroys everything around her. She is not the most active person in the world—she doesn't try to do anything with herself. So, I keep at a distance. I think that Mor was less influenced, they didn't dare try with her. Idit and I—we were more affected. Mother was also partly responsible, she rarely pushed us to do things on our own, and she watched over us the way her mother watched over her. Perhaps when we were little, it didn't bother me so much, but as an adolescent it bothered me a lot: I want to do things on my own, to form my own opinion about what and how to do things. From that point of view my father—he invested a lot of time in us, he is different in that way from other fathers. Perhaps it is because his parents invested less in him? He also knows how to tell us how he is feeling. My mother doesn't know how to do that, she is more closed. And in contrast to my father, my uncle [his brother] is a fairly closed person, even though they invested a lot in their children. They had a lot of games at home, but it's different than it is with us, I don't know how to explain it exactly.

Dafna takes a break, as if she has shown me around her cellar and now she wants to leave it. "What do you do on holidays?"

On Passover we go to our uncle's. It is a pretty boring holiday. That is, it's fun being with our cousins and it's fun being in Tel Aviv. But the holiday itself is celebrated because we have to celebrate it, there really aren't any special experiences. My aunt's relatives also participate. My mother's mother never agreed to come there for the seder. She had some sort of quarrel with them. In fact, I don't have any desire to celebrate with them, I only go because I feel it's my duty. I prefer the day-to-day over the holidays. At Dudu's house, my boyfriend, they really have happy holidays. His father's family comes from Morocco and there they really celebrate. Also at my girlfriend's house, her father is from Romania, it is happier. There are also more people there.

"Do you recall any legends or stories in your family?"

In Yiddish, legends that my mother and father told. They heard them from my grandmother. They would read and translate them for us at bedtime. I remember a story about a monster with a braid. And one of Grandma's stories about a boy that chewed and chewed. All kinds of stories like that. When we were little, mother would tell us a story about people from China, beautiful stories. As a child, I remember that I had two books of fairy tales that I loved very much. I loved stories about children who had things happening to them, without their doing anything, without any effort on their part. Today I am interested in psychology. A little while ago I read a book on Zen and the art of motorcycle maintenance. That put me in the mood to learn about taking care of a motorcycle . . . to find something to do. I also read books about the Holocaust, especially when I was around fourteen. I have a picture in my head of *musselmen*, it's a horrible picture. I have a recurrent dream: It is something, the Nazis are coming to take me, I ask them to have pity on me, a sort of daydream. I try to fight, to rescue myself. I cannot decide whether to run away or to fight and protect my sisters. I am sure that it is due to the films I have seen. It's sort of a recurrent dream that comes back to me. I know it has to do with the Holocaust.

Dafna moves uncomfortably in her chair. I ask her if she wants to go on and she smiles with a feeling of relief and says simply: "No." Perhaps it is difficult for her to continue to talk because of our previous acquaintance or because she identifies me as a therapist and wants to discuss different matters than the ones I am interested in.

Idit

"The most important thing is myself"

When Idit enters my house for the interview, I immediately feel the difference between her and her elder sister. Idit has an athlete's body and a firm handshake. There is almost none of the embarrassment of a first meeting, at least nothing that is obvious. Idit speaks with a sense of assurance and without pause; it is difficult to stop her. "I can talk about myself for hours," she tells me right at the beginning. Her story is a long one about social ties: boyfriends, girlfriends, her parents, and her older sister. She presents her wish to be wanted by everyone, to have intertwined relationships of love and hate. Her family is her beginning and her end point.

"When you think about family, whom do you include?"
Father, Mother, Dafna, Mor, and me.
"Not your grandparents?"
No, of course not. There is more family on my father's side, his brother's family, that I don't know at all. They are, they lived in America for a few years, and in my opinion, they should have stayed there. They have such Polish customs, to say the right thing at the right time, to wear the right thing, to put their hair in the right way: *(imitating)* "How good it is to see that you put on weight" and "You look so feminine now." It is so disgusting, I really hate them. I have nothing to do with them, my father says he does not accept my reaction, that it doesn't matter to him; rightly so, because it is his brother, it is his family. But he knows that it really doesn't work. Family—so what? For him it's important. We talked about it when we were there for Passover. I like them less and less. Then he agreed and said that when we are older, perhaps we will pay less attention to other aspects of reality and more attention to relationships.

After I went to Poland I thought that when I grow up, perhaps I will want to live close to my parents. I don't want to travel so much. I prefer that everyone will live close to one another and that we will celebrate the holidays together and perhaps even more than that.

"How do you celebrate holidays in your family today?"
In a very non-Jewish and nontraditional way. It gets less and less traditional over the years. We are not, we are very secular. That is, I know that tradition is not connected necessarily to Zionism, but something is wrong with us, it's like "dinner with candles." My grandfather, Anya's husband, was religious. His father was a very important rabbi or something like that. On Father's side they were completely secular. We are influenced by my father, I think. But my mother didn't live with religious people either, she came from a Communist background, she didn't really try ... but we have a different tradition of celebrating, of developing an intimate closeness, of belonging. Holidays are vacations, fun meals, trips to Tel Aviv. Once, Dafna and I were sick and we didn't go to Tel Aviv, we only went out to eat in the city and that was fun too. But all in all, I am sorry ... perhaps when I get married my husband will want to keep up traditions, it depends, perhaps I will observe Shabbat—lighting candles and meat meals in the evening. We are really lacking in things like that, we don't have any strong foundation that holds us up. It's a shame because

perhaps one day, if we need it, we won't have it. Let's say that one day one of us goes abroad to live, and then it will be a shame if there isn't something strong like that to hold us together. But today I feel no need for it.

"You brought up your trip to Poland. Perhaps you can tell me more about it."

I will talk a little about the Holocaust, because for me, it is connected to my trip to Poland. The subject frightens me a lot, it frightens me to death. I don't know if it is connected to my family. When my grandmother holds me and cries—she scares me to death. I think that when I was little, I loved her very much. But now my relationship to Anya—I have no relationship to her. Out of sight—out of mind. It's that way also with my grandmother and grandfather on my father's side. I am a terrible grand-daughter, it's sort of laziness. She is alone, she lives alone. I sometimes think that I need to do something about it, but I prefer living with guilt feelings and going about my day-to-day life without thinking about her all of the time. Once a week—a telephone call, how are you? Or, when she comes to visit, to give her a kiss and that's all.

So when it comes to the Holocaust, it is terribly, terribly frightening, it is the subject that haunts me. It is the most frightening topic—ghosts, devils, black forces. I can't say how much it exists or doesn't exist, but I am afraid. It is part of my fear: the Holocaust. It is as if, like they show on television during the memorial days, all of those corpses and all of that. On the one hand, I think that horror movies are very compelling. I once saw one and I couldn't sleep for two weeks afterward. I realized it and I stopped; it isn't good for me. I simply broke myself off from it. I don't see things, I don't think about it and don't read books about it because it frightens me terribly, terribly. Really, books that I would read disturbed me very much, so I can't do it anymore. It isn't pleasant for me to think about, so I gave it up and that's that. I feel some ideological commitment, I know. The most important thing is myself, that is, what I feel and if it makes me feel good or bad or whether people love me or not, things like that. It is as if the ideological matter isn't strong enough to make me deal with it, really. I don't, I have a very hard time with ceremonies on memorial days.

"Do you know what your relatives went through during the Holocaust?"

Yes, I know a lot about the Holocaust. To begin with, from the historical point of view with the preparations for the trip to Poland, I really know a lot about that. And also from an emotional standpoint, I understood a lot.

"Did you understand from what your grandmothers and grandfather told you?"

No, not so much.

"So how did you find out?"

There were a lot of times when I asked, single moments. And at some point I would stop. I once asked my grandmother when I worked on my roots project in school. At the end, I never did it, the project annoyed me, everything was connected to the Holocaust. And I don't know, there were all kinds of times when I was—not because of the emotions, because of the thought—why am I not curious about it? Of course it interests me: I would ask. I would ask, and then all of a sudden it would stop interesting me, in the middle of asking, or something like that. It is always vague for me, their stories are always very unclear to me. It's really a part here and a part there, a gigantic jump like that. It seems like a terrible nightmare, what had happened on my mother's side . . . I don't know too much about what happened on my father's side. Once, my father told me things about his father that gave me the feeling there was something very dark there. But he didn't really talk about himself, never. I only know that my grandfather is a Holocaust survivor, that he was in hiding and experienced his brother's and father's death. But the one I really see as a typical "Holocaust survivor" is Anya. You met her, do you know why? Do you understand? It's a kind of character! I can't explain it; it comes across through her Polishness and her "survivorness" *(nervous laughter).* It is expressed in her suspiciousness, in everything. It scares me, because I am afraid that one day I will be an old woman like her. The way she looks with her bent shoulders, I don't want to look like that. Perhaps because of that I think that I will want to grow old on a kibbutz. There they have an Israeli atmosphere, flowers and care.

I recall that I have already heard a similar positive reference to the kibbutz in Anya's narrative.

So that's it, it is a subject that I don't think about and barely talk about. And there are all kinds of poems, songs about Holocaust Day, that stick in my mind and don't go away. But trying to remember them, I forget them. They are beautiful songs, I think, in the poetic sense. And I always run away from them in a hysterical way. I think about it now—I get frightened. There was one Holocaust Day, I remember, after the ceremony of Memorial Day, and I couldn't remain upstairs [in the house], all alone in the dark, and I needed to go downstairs to the living room, where my whole family was. I was really afraid to be there alone where they could hunt me.

"But trying to remember them, I forget them." What a wonderful expression.

All of that isn't really connected to the subject of Poland. It is a part of a hollowness in me, which I don't touch. I really didn't think about it. The trip to Poland was much more realistic: there was a trip and there was a kind of a competition in school. And the first thing was that whenever there is a competition, I run for it, that's the way it is. It's something that I approached logically: it is something that is very interesting to do. It would be a shame to miss out on a trip abroad. And my parents will give their consent because it is important. It's a shame to give it up, curiosity and all that. So I went for it and got into the delegation. It was a practical matter. My girlfriend also was elected. From a social standpoint, the framework, to be together for a week in Poland, was a highlight. And part of it was connected to going abroad, the experience. I like adventures—if I have the opportunity and if it is arranged for me.

We went and . . . one thing is that it was very sad. On the other hand, I was always wrapped up in myself, I had all kinds of emotional upheavals that were connected to the social framework. Perhaps I was influenced by what I saw, but I wasn't conscious of it. I don't think that I repressed the matter. You know what—perhaps it isn't good that I went at all. It's good that I went, but perhaps not, from the standpoint that I didn't get everything out of it that I could. Because there were a lot of things going on at the same time. Perhaps I will need to go when I am ready to go for a more deep experience. So, among other things, I was in Poland. I didn't define things for myself and I didn't think about it. It bothered me very much that for the entire week I didn't even cry once. We were in lots of places, we were in Auschwitz, Treblinka, and Majdanek. I don't remember anymore . . . we even had a free day in Kraków: we went shopping and things like that. My good friend and I slept in the same room. We had fun, we would play, have a good time and enjoy everything that you can in a strange country. To some extent, it could be that someone else took the responsibility of taking us from here to there so we had a good time. It wasn't insulting though, let's say that we were respectful. But I think that I didn't get out of the trip to Poland what I could have gotten. It was an experience: I came back—I said that it was fun. As to the Holocaust, I don't think I can exhaust the subject in a week's trip like that—perhaps it is possible. Yes, to see the terrible places, that is possible. Perhaps I should have gone to the places where my grandparents lived and to feel what their life has been like.

"Did they know that you went? Did they say anything?"

Yes, my grandmother wanted to talk to me about it, but we didn't get the chance. Perhaps I evaded it, I don't know.

"Are you talking about Grandma Anya?"

Yes. All of these things dissolved in my opinion. If I dare to think about it one day, then I will specifically bring myself there. It was shocking and I couldn't cry. I think that I wanted to but I was so tired. I couldn't even bring myself to almost cry. It is something that I had such a hard time with, from trying so hard, but I tried to press inside. It was when we were in Auschwitz, I saw children's clothes through the glass. I held myself, I almost cried, I thought about how these clothes could fit my sister Mor, that she could have been here, and then it was hard for me. It was the only thing that really moved me. There were people who were in a worse state than I was, those that were moved all the time. Perhaps I could have gotten a hundred times more out of it emotionally, I am not sure that I wanted to. This is the first time that I am really thinking of it, I think that I ran away from it. It is a sort of black power. Do you understand?

I think I do understand, but I also feel angry at those who organize such youth delegations to Poland, trying to nationalize their emotions. Does such a trip help them work through the past—or get stuck in its vicious circle? And why take her in a delegation and not with her family? I get caught up in my own thoughts and forget Idit, who is looking for a way to end the interview.

Dafna and Idit are very different: Dafna is fragile. She uses words with care and defines things exactly. She is very conscious of her problems and of the emotional crisis she has experienced. She says: "I loved stories about children who had things happening to them, without their doing anything, without any effort on their part." Perhaps this is how she characterizes herself. Idit, in contrast, is energetic. She fights for her place in society and uses words in a grand manner, defining things in an overly critical tone. Talking about Ya'acov's brother's family, for example, she says: "They have such Polish customs . . . It is so disgusting, I really hate them."

Aside from these differences, there are some common points in their narratives. The interviews reveal a lot of fear, verbal and nonverbal, which hampers both sisters' capacity to tell their story. Like Anya and Tamar, they have the same tendency to use argument to handle their overt or covert fear. In both interviews we sense a need for family success, perhaps as external proof of having overcome the still-existent shadows of the past. However, while for Dafna it introduces a feeling of inferiority and loss, for Idit the urge to succeed inspires conflict and competition.

Both sisters perceive their father as the one who calms them down. He is the one who listens to them during adolescence, an age when girls usually have difficulty separating themselves from their mothers. They describe Ya'acov as a father who is "different from other fathers," who "knows how to tell us about what he is feeling," in comparison to Tamar, whom they perceive as closed and distant. We cannot know whether this is so or whether it simply expresses their adolescent point of view. Both sisters hint at an earlier warmth and intimacy with their mother (Chinese fairy tales, holding hands), but we also find a growing detachment, which develops with time and age. Dafna reflects on her mother's difficulty in helping her develop her own "independent" path. She states very clearly, "Mother also was . . . responsible, she rarely pushed us to do things on our own, and she watched over us the way her mother watched over her."

Dafna's and Idit's relationship with their grandmothers deserves special attention. Dafna sees her grandmother as a woman who is "easier to love than my father's mother. She gives love . . . it's easy to love her because . . . she makes you feel that she loves you." Dafna is aware of the fact that "it is difficult for those who have to live with her." But she has gained her own independence: "Today, I am not afraid to argue with her." In contrast, Grandma Anya frightens Idit "when she holds me and cries." Idit prefers to distance herself from Anya, even to feel guilty over the fact that she is a "bad granddaughter," so that she can "live her own day-to-day life." If she would get closer to Anya, would her liveliness be hampered? We don't know, but that is the fear Idit expresses when she says: "It scares me, because I am afraid that one day I will be an old woman like her."

What for Idit is frightening and repellent is for Dafna an expression of love. Perhaps it is with the help of this love that Dafna has internalized Anya's story and her pain. She provides details about Anya that Idit describes as "vague" stories: the fact, for example, that Anya was married during the war and that she had a baby and also a niece "who was like a daughter to her," and that her mother ordered her to escape from the Germans. She tells us how Anya worried about bringing the family food, "but toward the end it was enough for only one day." Even though Dafna does not say so, it is possible to feel how touched she was by these stories. Dafna notes that she heard the stories in "small bits and pieces that were well filtered." There was only one time that "I wanted to leave, but I know that I didn't. And I remember that afterwards I cried for a long time." Perhaps Dafna's transparency in her relationship with her grandmother is what frightens Idit, who prefers "not to think about it."

Dafna and Idit are split in their feelings toward their two grandmothers. It is interesting that Dafna expresses her feelings toward her father's mother in almost the exact words Idit uses to describe her feelings toward Anya. Dafna says, "She is absorbed in herself and she destroys everything around her . . . she doesn't try to do anything with herself. So, I keep at a distance."

Idit draws the boundary of her family around "Father, Mother, Dafna, Mor, and me." The family is an anchor of security for both of them: Dafna turns to her family in her emotional crisis, Idit when she is afraid on Holocaust Day. But they both realize the limits of this security, the areas that are still fragile. The hidden sadness of the past emerges especially during family festivities and on holidays. Dafna, like Idit, expresses a longing for a holiday that is "celebrated not only to fulfill an obligation," a holiday "that is full of happiness," as in her boyfriend's family, which is from Morocco, or her girlfriend's Romanian family. There is more than a clue in Dafna's unwillingness to participate in the seder. She echoes Tamar's words in saying: "In fact, I don't have any desire to celebrate . . . I go only because I feel it's my duty," to the point that "I prefer the day-to-day over the holidays." Idit defines the importance of tradition and the lack of tradition in her family: "We are really lacking in things like that, we don't have any strong foundation that holds us up. It's a shame because perhaps one day, if we need it, we won't have it."

Both Dafna and Idit are frightened by the Holocaust. However, compared to her sister, Dafna uses fewer words to describe it. She has a recurring dream: the Nazis are coming to take her away. She cannot decide whether to run away or fight back and protect her sisters: "I know it has to do with the Holocaust." Dafna is well aware of the fragility of the border between "then" and "now," between "there" and "here." She reached the threshold of an emotional crisis, but returned strengthened "with the need to develop her own opinion." Is it in reaction to this fragility that Idit has built herself the defense of appearing strong and competitive? There is no point in trying to decide who is stronger, Dafna in her open fragility or Idit in her strong repression. Each one has chosen her own way of dealing with this difficulty. As often happens between sisters who are close in age and share the same family hardship, the path chosen by one becomes a mirror image of the other.

Are the biographical reconstructions of Dafna and Idit an outcome of the burdens of the past that have not been worked through by Anya and Tamar? Did they both react to the past, transmitted in the form of fear—with little hope—into their present-day life? This is difficult to answer. Each one has "adopted" a different grandmother as the model of what they are afraid of. Their two grandmothers symbolize an aspect of the past that Dafna and Idit fear will be transmitted to them. This intergenerational predicament is reinforced by Tamar, who has not succeeded in navigating her way between her mother and her daughters. According to Dafna, "She tried to watch over us like her mother watched over her." Idit talks about her mother's "Polishness," about her being "closed." And both of them have absorbed the feeling of the "loss of belonging" that Anya and Tamar have also expressed in their narratives.

We cannot conclude this chapter without considering the different ways that Orit Anisevitch and Idit Segal perceive their grandmothers and the possible link between this perception and how they summarized their trips to Poland. The difference is almost as great as that between the Native American myth of old age (the wise elders sitting in the center of the village in rocking chairs while the young come to listen to their advice) and the Eskimo myth (the elderly become a burden to the community and go to die alone in the snow): "out of sight—out of mind," as Idit says. Orit, who went with Olga to Warsaw, absorbed through her grand-mother what had happened and reexamined how it relates to her present perspective on the family. Idit went to Poland as part of a delegation, a result of her social competitiveness, and found out how unready she was to confront the family's Polish past and its connection to her present reality.

Orit Anisevitch represents those in the third generation who have been released from fear. They can examine the past out of personal curiosity and develop a psychological security beyond the physical security the older generations have achieved. Dafna and Idit, however, express the fear and insecurity that has not been worked through, so that the traumatic past controls the future and fear controls hope.

The Loss of Family Bonds from Generation to Generation

Anya lost everything as a result of the Holocaust: a husband and baby, parents, a brother and sister, an orthodox Jewish home, a language, a belief in Communism, and a sense of home, hope, and security. In con-trast, Olga tried to develop a new sense of hope and security in spite of what she had lost by letting go of the world she had before the war. Anya is still deeply connected to the past from which she was torn by the Ho-locaust. What is the magnet that ties her to the past as if to a point on a map of a country that no longer exists? Anya has not confronted this question, she has only reacted to it.

It is difficult to clarify the ongoing power of what was lost forever in Anya's life without taking into account the fact that, before the war, she was in the process of giving up her family and Jewish tradition for the sake of the new relationship with her boyfriend and their joint belief in Communism. These developments stood in direct opposition to the values and tradition her home had represented. Symbolically, Anya had already prepared a suitcase to run away when she found out that her mother was ill. It was rather an untimely coincidence that the war also broke out. Now her hidden plan turned against her: she was forced to escape and leave her family because of her Communist leanings.

For the duration of the war, Anya was caught in a conflict about where she belonged. Instead of gradually moving from her religious Jewish family background to the new Communist ideology, she was forced to break from the former, and eventually also from the latter. Her mother's illness created the initial dilemma—to stay or to leave? If not for the war, perhaps she might have succeeded in mourning and slowly separating from the family background she had decided to break away from. However, the Holocaust and the death of her friend merged the two levels of separation, the desired and the forced, into one final, irreversible tragedy. By the end of the war, there was nothing left. To this day, she is still dealing with the loss of a feeling of belonging.

Breaking away leaves an open question: where do I really belong? In a certain sense, her total loss brought Anya back to her memories of her original family, although not to their religious belief. One could see it as a compromise (meaning "I remained faithful to people but not to their beliefs"). In her interview, however, Anya gives no suggestion of acceptance or compromise. Indeed, the opposite is true. She is constantly justifying herself. Perhaps in this way she is expressing her lack of self-acceptance. Her forced stay in Russia, the death of her husband and their son, the loss of everything she had left behind, countered her original sense of belonging to Communism. Tamar says that her mother "was no longer a Communist" when she immigrated to Israel, and Anya says: "I erased it from my life," referring to both the loss of her first husband and their mutual belief.

It is as if Anya is reacting to two magnets simultaneously. According to the visible compass, she moves forward: she remarries, she has Tamar, she tries to get acclimated to Israel and become active in her new environment. But according to the hidden compass, she continues to cling to the past. Over the years, Anya has tried to paint the past as "prettier" (as Tamar notes: "She didn't get over the adolescent stage with her family").

On a practical level, Anya has invested a great deal in rebuilding her life in Israel: in her daughter, in her sick husband, and in her home. For Ze'ev and Olga, this was a source of hopefulness and strength that helped them move beyond the painful past. However, for Anya, her present-day reality has not helped her neutralize the intensity of the hidden compass geared to "there" and "then." The power of Anya's past, which has a shadow existence behind present-day reality, acts as an "untold story." We saw how Olga, who also had an "untold story," succeeded in achieving a new sense of hopefulness and belonging, while expressing open anger toward her father. But Anya does not feel anger toward her parents; she feels only guilt and a terrible longing for their lost support and warmth.

Just as Dina internalized the power of Olga's emphasis on the here and now, Tamar has internalized the ongoing struggle between the two poles in her mother's life. The relative advantage is on Dina's side; her internalization is much more functional from the point of view of acclimation to the norms of Israeli society. Tamar's internalization has created new problems of social acclimation. The feeling of being on the periphery (in relation to orthodox Jews, to Auschwitz survivors, and to heroes of the War of Independence) has caused her to feel inferior; she has internalized the cruel "scale of suffering" that existed among Holocaust survivors, and in Israeli society as a whole, in the fifties and sixties. Tamar did not wish to continue her mother's alienation from the Israeli reality, but in trying to negotiate between her admiration for her mother and her anger toward her, Tamar's conflict has brought her closer to her mother's alienation rather than further away. In this way, Anya has transferred her own alienation to her daughter, and Tamar has built anew her sense of not belonging to a supportive social or family framework.

Dafna and Idit were exposed to their mother's conflict, added to that of their grandparents' generation. Indeed, the times, as well as their economic situation and the social norms, have changed. But unlike Orit, the Segal girls still suffer from a strong feeling of marginality in relation to other young people their age. Dafna expresses it in words, and one can sense it from Idit's endless struggle for social acknowledgment. The question of their social standing obligates them to invest their resources from a very young age in overcoming their inferior position. Their styles are different: Dafna tends to observe, like Ganit, and even to retreat into herself, while Idit fights back vigorously. But we do not find in either of their narratives what we found in the interview with Orit and Yoav: the fun of present-day experiences as reality unfolds, bringing with it the possibility of new questions about what remains unresolved from the past.

The three generations of women in the Anisevitch and Segal families help us clarify several matters: first, they illustrate how difficult it was to become an adult woman, a mother, and a daughter in these families. This could be true without the Holocaust—if we take into account the processes of emigration and immigration, and of building a new Israeli society—however, the Holocaust made it much more difficult. Evidence of this emerged in the interviews with Dafna and Idit—they were in great need of strength and power. They continue to see softness as a sign of weakness, not only in their own eyes but also in the eyes of their society.

Second, the passing of experience from one generation to another could potentially open up new psychological possibilities for working through the wounds of the past. But that is not always what happened. In the Anisevitch family, a process of intergenerationally working through the past started only with granddaughter Orit's trip to Poland and the new insights she gained out of this trip. In the Segal family, even in the third generation, we can still see signs of a fear that has not been worked through. Although we will never be able to assert that it happened "because of the Holocaust," we believe it provided a sense of finality and irreversibility to the difficulties that already existed in these families, and within and between these women.

Third, we have not discussed the possible influences of grandfathers and fathers—members of the first and second generations—on the grandchildren's ability to work through the Holocaust. They, too, can open up new possibilities for coming to terms with the past through the support they give their spouses and the legitimate alternatives they create for their children (as, for example, in the case of Ya'acov). At the same time, the fathers can also repress some of these possibilities by ignoring the difficulties faced by their wives, as in Tzipke's case, or by failing to create significant new ways to refer to the present and the past.

Finally, it is important to remember that the interview presents a snapshot of the situation tied to one time and place. It is still possible that these processes will proceed and that their relative rhythm will change. The granddaughters will grow up and become mothers in their own right; then at last they may start to confront what they could not during their adolescence. We have learned from Tzipke Belinsky's and Hannah Lerman's stories that families do change over time. It is indeed possible that if we meet Dina and Orit, Tamar, Dafna, and Idit ten years from now, we may well find that they are in a very different place.

5

THE GUETTAS

Under Occupation in Libya

with Noga Gil'ad

Laura is a member of the same generation as Genia, Ze'ev, Olga, and Anya. We have no exact date for her birth, but according to our estimates, she was probably born in about 1915 in Tripoli, Libya, which was then under Italian rule. The rise of the Fascist party in Libya under the auspices of the Libyan government was not generally accompanied by persecution of the Jews. Only in 1940, when the politician Italo Balbo was killed in a plane accident, did the situation worsen. In effect, the Tripolian Jews suffered more from the Arab riots under British rule than they did under the fascist Italian and German regimes (Gutman, 1990).

How does Laura's life story reflect the outside world, in comparison to the other first-generation members, who experienced the Holocaust more directly? Laura tells her story today from within the perspective of her life in Israel. Will this cause her to emphasize the Israeli context of her life rather than the Libyan years before, during, and after the war?

Laura herself knows a great deal about human suffering. Her father died of a heart attack when she was nine, and during the war, her younger brother, whom she loved very much, died of typhus. After she immigrated to Israel, her little daughter, Miriam, died, and a few years later, her husband died of a heart attack. Yet through all of this, the framework of Laura's family was not destroyed—not in the way it was among European Jews. How will this combination of personal losses with an ongoing family framework affect her life story? How will it be expressed in those of her son and granddaughter?

GUETTA FAMILY CHRONOLOGY

1915?   Laura is born in Tripoli, the eldest in a family that eventually includes two more girls and three boys. [Laura refers to time in terms of her own age rather than a calendar date.]

1924?   When Laura is nine, her father dies of a heart attack after being accused of stealing.

1925?   At ten, Laura moves in with her aunt.

1927?   At twelve, Laura finishes school. Six months later, she becomes engaged to her cousin, Chalfo.

1931?   At sixteen, Laura marries Chalfo. Reuven, their first son, is born.

1940   The war: Bombs fall on Tripoli. Laura escapes to Garian, in the mountains. Vittorio-David, her second son, is born there. She is twenty-five.

1944?   Toward the end of the war, Laura gives birth to a daughter, Miriam. She returns to her mother-in-law's house. Her youngest brother dies of typhus at her mother's house.

1945   The Arabs attack the Jews; the British intervene. Reuven immigrates to Israel.

1948   The family leaves Tripoli for Italy and from there immigrates to Israel, where they live in a *ma'abara* (make-shift housing). Miriam falls and later dies in the hospital. They move to permanent housing.

1956   Vittorio leaves school at age fourteen and goes to work in the construction business.

1960   Chalfo dies of a heart attack. Vittorio postpones his army service because of his father's death. A year later, he enlists. Shortly after his discharge he marries but divorces within a year. Some time later, he marries Paula. Two years after the wedding, Paula has a miscarriage.

1972   Liat, a daughter, is born to Vittorio and Paula. After several years of a debilitating illness, Vittorio returns to work.

1973   David is born. Vittorio and Paula move to Ashdod. The economic recession hurts Vittorio's business.

1984   Laura visits Italy and meets a family member who went through the Holocaust. Vittorio and Paula move to a house they are building in Savyon. Vittorio becomes a construction contractor.

1987   There is a recession in the construction industry. Vittorio becomes a meat salesman.

1989   Amaliya, one of Dan Bar-On's students, interviews Laura, Vittorio and Paula, and Liat.

Laura

"My life before was a totally different kind of life"

Laura opens the door wide and invites me [Amaliya] in. I am surprised at her height and her cared-for appearance. Only her face, which is lined with fine wrinkles, and perhaps also her slippers, suggest that she is old. Her way of talking, her warm eyes, and her melodic intonation are youthful. She serves me mint tea in an almost aristocratic manner. The serving dishes are perfectly matched. Laura does not need an opening cue from me. Her words flow easily.

Really, life beforehand was totally different, today life is totally different. Like the difference between day and night. How we grew up six children with my mother, and my father had a heart condition. I was seven, he had a heart condition. He once bought a stolen rug. He didn't know that it was stolen. He was a religious man and also very respected, and all of a sudden, on Rosh Hashanah, the police came to the synagogue and took him away. He had a heart attack and then it continued. I was seven or eight, there were difficult nights at mother's house. And then, when I was nine, I became orphaned. I had a brother who was six months old. I would go from house to house—who will nurse him? We grew up without a father, and my mother looked for someone in the Jewish community who would take care of the property that he had left and who would take care of the orphans. Someone who would give her a living so that she could make a living and find husbands for her daughters. We found somebody good, loyal and good. He would come by every evening to talk to my mother. My father left four apartments that were being rented out. And my mother said: "We will keep them for the girls when we marry them off." That's the way it was. Boys don't go out with girls who don't have apartments. It is the girl's honor. My mother tells me all of her problems, that she is sad about her husband. She was a young woman of thirty-four. And I was so attached to her and very emotional. She would begin telling me her story and I would start to cry, grab onto her leg, and fall asleep.

Now, the man that came over to my mother's house and sees me in this state, says to me: "Get up." One day, two days, a night, two nights, he says: "You will no longer stay with your mother. Everyone goes out to have a good time, to walk around, to play in the street. You hang onto your mother and cry. Come home with me." He took me to his home, he has a daughter who was almost my age, and there I forgot half of my mother's troubles. I began laughing, jumping, and I came home from school with their daughter, Victoria. She had two children that fell ill with German measles. I see meat on the sink and that woman isn't moving, she is not in the mood. I tell her: "Look, we've come back from school. There is nothing to eat." "Do you want to do me a favor? Make them something. Here is the meat on the sink." "I can't reach the faucet." She says to me: "Take a chair, there is a little chair." I would get on the chair, wash, make, keep kosher, whatever she told me to do, I listen to her. I would go up and get down, I was like a devil. When my father was still alive, my mother would send me to the market with his food. I would walk there in five minutes and walk back in five minutes. I was like a devil. I would fight life.

"I was like a devil. I would fight life." Laura is completely absorbed in the difficult days after the death of her father. She is still caught somewhere between her mother's sadness and her own happiness, even mixing tenses while she is talking.

Our guardian said one day: "Take her for your son." I hear this word, they will take me for their son? What do they think, and I begin: "I don't want to get married." They all sit around chatting, they sit on the floor. There are high pillows on the floor made from *jelod* [sheepskin]. We are all sitting in the living room and he begins to tell her, I was twelve, twelve and a half: "Take her for your son." And my sister-in-law says: "You won't leave the house. We won't leave you. You belong to us, we won't leave you." I saw such a nice character. She was quick, nice, and smart. This business went on for three-and-a-half years *(sighs)*. Once, there were marriages without love. There were only arranged marriages. It's different today. Today, you can bring the best person: "No, I will take the man I love." Once, it wasn't like that . . . and I didn't want [to get married]. I cried and I was angry with my life for nights. And my boy [said]: "You don't want?" and I told him: "No." He said: "Laura, you will see that you will have a nice house, a good home, rich people, you will be respected and everything else." He convinced me.

But, there were always tears, night and day. They separated me from my parents, my studies, from school. The night of the wedding I cried until morning. I wanted "Mama, Mama." I didn't manage without my mother. I was fourteen and a half! He was a good man, though, but I entered a strange family. I would go visit my mother every Shabbat for the entire day. Today marriages are completely different. Today marriages are based on love, on meetings. Once, they would bring you [to the boy]. Take him and be quiet. That was that. The girl was always under her mother's pressure. "And be respectful of your husband's parents so that they won't bring you trouble. You have no father. I don't want to hear any problems from you. Whatever they tell you, say yes."

We had a good life, we got used to one another. We didn't suffer, we gave up a lot. But then, we got used to it and we had it good. It was good. And that's the way it once was. Today, it's not like that. There is social security, you live alone, you develop on your own, friends, today there is no one without friends. Once the children were left to their parents and the parents guided them in the way that they knew. But it wasn't so bad for us because we were brought up well.

Laura goes back and forth between then and now, there and here, between "today things are different" and "we gave up a lot, but . . . we got used to it and . . . it was good."

My mother's house was religious. On Shabbat I would bend down to pick up a piece of paper, I was a little girl, my father would say: "Put it back, it is forbidden to bend down." I would throw it down. Whoever wasn't religious was not Jewish. Here, I heard of a free Jew, a religious Jew. Then all of the Jews were religious. There were no exceptions. Whoever wasn't religious, wasn't a Jew. Everyone [went] to the synagogue, at age three, with a skullcap and to the synagogue, everyone, a father and his sons. The woman is a good housekeeper. A woman is at home, a man outside. Today, life is different. Today, women work outside. She hears, she develops *(sighs)*.

And that's the way I was brought up. I lived with my mother-in-law for ten years. I had my first son. Afterwards, the war came. We escaped to the mountains and I had the second child ten years later. Thank God, I brought up two sons and later on, a daughter. But my marriage, I don't know what marriage is at all, I don't know. Tell a baby what marriage is. Will he answer you?! That's the way I was. They throw you into it and [you] give birth alone after a little while. Today, a girl of ten or of eight knows what happens. On television, everything, everything is out in the open. Once it wasn't like that, everything was a secret. You study in school, you embroider, you sew. The business of a sex life is a secret—everything is covered up. Nobody knows. Today a girl that gets married knows everything.

Today I feel what my mother suffered. When I became a widow . . . I felt, I saw what she would do, things that no one would do. She cries every day, she was not quiet. The house was closed, nobody comes to the door. Thank heavens that now there is a husband at least. I have sons and they have a good life. But, it's an important word, that I felt my mother's pain after I became a widow. Look how much a person suffers: no work, no money, desperation at home. We suffered, we did any available job. I ran off to work at four o'clock in the morning. I worked in the cultural center, it was a big auditorium to clean, benches to move. It wasn't nice doing dirty work. I would go home at seven o'clock in the morning so that no one would see me. In order to bring home a salary and bring up my son Vittorio and . . . in order to make a living I was both a man and a woman. No husband, I was a woman and a man. And I did things that I didn't think I would do. We did them in order not to ask anybody for anything. Not to need anybody, to [live] with respect. We went out wearing gloves, a nice shoe, but we worked. So nobody would feel, so no one would say anything.

I am not always successful in keeping track of when Laura is talking about her childhood difficulties in Libya and when she is talking about her life in Israel. Perhaps there are no boundaries of time and place when we don't "ask anybody for anything . . . to [live] with respect."

Here, in Israel, it is not a disgrace. Abroad, a woman would die of starvation before she would do dirty work. But here, in our country, we do it. I see a lot of women in Israel—her husband is a doctor and she does all kind of work. Why? "My husband doesn't make enough. He is an intern, he is studying." A house, a mortgage, they do everything. There I had a maid, I never opened the door. If someone knocks, my husband says: "Don't go. Here, she is opening the door. You don't have to open the door." I live with my second husband. He has a lot of children. I take care of all of them, they come on Shabbat, I receive them nicely. Bring me a woman of a hundred and I am suited to her. Bring me a girl of fourteen and I can live with her. I can manage with every age, I can adapt. That's the way I was born. No . . . not as something, as a person who is clever and knows how to manage, who can manage with everybody. I am not sly, I have no slyness. I speak honestly and openly. But, in my head, I have a brain.

Laura looks at me and we both laugh out loud. What an outburst of happiness after a description of hardship and of the differences between "there and here."

I had a very nice doctor at King George [a street in Tel Aviv]. I went to him a number of times, to the gynecologist. He told me: "Laura, it's a shame that you have to come in [to my office]. I heard so much laughter when you were outside [in the waiting room]. When you leave, they'll start fighting. I have no one who will entertain them." You don't need to make a big deal out of everything. Even between good families and worse ones, you don't have to take the worse ones. *(Looks at me)* There is something good and something bad, remember only the good. Pick up the phone, ask, visit, do something so that the family will feel that you exist, that they live together. I don't like to act like my sister, she cuts herself off from everyone. I pick up the phone to Italy, I pick up the phone to the *moshav.*

The same night that my mother gave birth and they told her: "Congratulations"—my father wanted a good sign, "a child is a good sign." A boy is a good sign, a boy. And a daughter: "You should have good luck." I didn't know Hebrew—from that same night onward I said: "Ah, now I know what a good sign is, what congratulations is." I was four years old. Really, I remember my mother giving birth to my sister and my father didn't take it well, a third daughter! He was religious and he read the Bible, he knew Hebrew, he knew what a good sign was, and I did not know. My mother, every Sunday and Tuesday evening gives everyone a bath, washes their hair, washes them and puts them in bed. I would help my mother a lot. I came home from school and tell her: "Mommy, I want to eat." She says: "What? Who comes home from school to eat? Who told you that? If you are hungry, wait a bit."

My children were hungry, I get up . . . I brought up my children differently, not like the way my mother raised us. My mother was strong and suffered a lot in her lifetime. She had a strong character in order to bear the suffering that she had. She would go, buy, bring, cut, light the stove, fry, cook, and bring. My mother was not happy, she was a widow at a young age, at the age of thirty-four. And I was the first, I undertook all of the jobs that my mother did, all of the jobs. I cooked, I prepared things, I did the dishes. Ah, I studied. I studied until midnight. All of a sudden I see the electricity go off, there is no electricity. "You want to be a lawyer or a professor? Sleep! You are as thin as a stick. You have studied enough. I want you to go to sleep now." "Oy, I haven't finished, I'm in the middle of my homework." Why? Because in the middle of the day, I help my mother. Today, you turn the electricity back on. It wasn't like that with her: "Go to sleep." In the morning in the window, I see that it is five o'clock, I see a little light, I finished my lessons. I am frightened of the teacher, that I will be the worst one. I want to be the best. I always wanted to be the first child to raise a hand. And I go over all of the lessons, I go to school everything is perfect. I get up early, I finish everything. When the teacher passed me on to the next grade, she passed on the message: "Take care of her. She is a good example. She is a light for others. You have what to teach."

Laura is proud of herself. Her tone of voice and her intonation indicate her swing back into her memories.

And I went through my pressured life, but with pleasure, without being spoiled. Today there is spoiling, I, I wasn't spoiled by anyone. Only by my husband, never by my mother. My mother would suffer, she was in the middle of problems. How could she spoil me? Today, even when a mother has problems, she spoils her children, right?! It was different with us. Everything that she said, I need to listen, to help her, to put myself into everything. In my studies, too. In the dark she brought us to a seamstress in order to learn how to sew so that we wouldn't wander the streets. So that she would take care of us. That's it, we had a hard childhood.

Laura sighs and offers me another cup of tea. I ask: "Were you only three daughters?"

No, of course. My mother, after the girls, gave birth to three sons. I once came home from school and I saw that my mother was sick. She was throwing up in bed, all over the room. I asked her, I am the eldest. She says to me: "I took some strong medicine so that I would get rid of the daughters and bring sons. I took deathly medicine. Either death or sons." I am afraid that she will die, afraid that she will be sicker, and I take care of her day and night. She got better, got up, and stopped vomiting. Afterwards, she gave birth to three sons. After the medicine that almost killed her. And . . . my father left the last one when he was six months old. What a flower he was, he was bright with blue eyes. I would take him from the morning to evening, walk around with him: "Where is a woman who can nurse him?" I asked and cried. He was heavy and I was thin, I could barely pick him up. Everyone would say: "What a poor girl she is. The way she walks around with the child." Today, when a child cries, his mother doesn't nurse him. There is a milk bottle, there are bottles. Boil a bottle and give the pacifier. Then no, I would walk around for days in order to save him, so that he wouldn't be hungry, so that nothing would happen to him. And we saved him, until he was twenty, when the typhus came and took him. He was a good boy, a really good boy.

Laura is crying and I feel her sorrow over the death of her little brother, the one she raised as a "mother."

Up till then we were three girls. It was a pleasure, believe me, at home seeing how Mother washed and dressed us. A pleasure, I tell you, to raise girls. It is more interesting than boys. I swear to you. A lot more interesting. In everything. In clothing. And the girl that you do nice things for, you enjoy her more. She admires you more . . . closer to her mother. A daughter that I stroke and give two kisses to, she hugs you right away. She is loyal. We were three girls, it was a pleasure. All of the boys studied the Torah. The little one was something, he was like a flower. He was beautiful and smart. My mother would praise him and she had what to praise. He was like the sun in the whole family. He was a good person. It wasn't enough that he had an easy nature, he was also good, and smart, and learned, and handsome, and everything. He was really something. I would watch over him every day, to see him—did he eat or not. "A woman was born to work in the house," my mother said. "He was born to study the Torah." Not today. Girls go to school, then they didn't. Separate was separate.

In the morning I would buy sweat pants, I had a little money that I saved from money that my uncles gave me. And I would go to school to work out early in the morning. My mother would see me sometimes, one just like that. "What are you doing at school?" "I am working out." "No, girls no. It is forbidden. Who said you could work out? We don't work out!" "Leave me alone, I like to be boisterous, there is a fire in my body. I run around, run and jump. It gives me pleasure." She tells me: "No! Not you." I leave the pants, my mother doesn't want it, she doesn't want it.

And we had a big church. They would bring all of the important dead there, downstairs. Everything was clean and shiny, there were stained glass windows. Once a month, they would take us on outings from school. There you would go and see a writer, a learned person. The Italians made Libya a Christian country. I also had Christian girlfriends, I would go visit them, they would come visit me. Now, when I came home from school I had a little freedom from my mother, two hours a day. She gives me an hour and a half to play and to come back and help her. There was a hillside that was completely covered with grass and it was covered with leaves and it was completely green. I would roll from the top to the bottom. There is a kind of sidewalk—you reach it. Once I didn't reach it, I fell down all the way. Oy, I got such blows to my head, to my body, and I am afraid to tell my mother. We will get more: "Why are you being so boisterous? Who told you to act like that?!"

A person who is born to be quick. It's the character given by God. Born to love people, I love people. I love company, love whoever comes to visit, I don't like a quiet house. Everyone is born with their own nature. But to suffer in life or not to suffer, that is everyone and their luck. We saw better days and worse days. What can I tell you? We were six children in my mother's house and she was a widow and she always kept us clean, always taken care of. Exactly like we should be. Nice. She was alone, but each one of us took care of ourselves. And especially me the eldest. The eldest one is given tasks, to watch over the others. My mother took good care of us, she was a wonderful woman, a wonderful housekeeper. She took care of six without a father, each one of us was raised better than the next. She married us off well. She made great efforts. Even though she was strong, she was right, I justify her. With six without a father, you don't need to give everyone what they want. We were disciplined for our own good, everything for our own good. You think that when you grow up, you want to see Paradise. No, Paradise is a small world, with its own beliefs, with mother's hugs. With family love. With kind treatment. We are all together, bed next to bed, hitting each other at night, playing together. When I see children: "Oy, how nice, how I was," I remember.

Laura speaks with her hands, filling up the room with her gestures. She makes an apt distinction between being "born with [one's] own nature," which cannot be changed, and "to suffer or not to suffer," which is a matter of changing luck. "*Can you tell me a little more about what it was like when you got married?*"

I lived my life under control. On Shabbat, when I want to see my parents, my sisters, what does the woman want?! To be with her mother, her sisters. That is her pleasure. My mother-in-law says: "No, your sister-in-law is coming over today. It's not nice to leave." I was dressed, coat, I throw it all down, I sit down. My mother says: "Don't bring me problems. Live in harmony. I want to see you happy. Give in a little. Live peacefully and your husband will respect." Actually, my husband wanted us to go out. I tell him: "No. I want you to get along with your parents. Your sister is coming, it's not nice for me to go out." I lived with my mother-in-law for ten years. We never had a fight. Whatever she wanted . . . I call her "mother" with all my heart, like a real mother. I loved her, I grew up with her. She taught me how to cook, she taught me. I know, but she still taught me how to progress. And my husband was good. I have nothing to say, a man of gold and I lived with them for ten years. When we parted, I didn't want to move far away. In the war in 'forty [World War II] we ran away from the bombing. When we got back, I say: "Only near my mother-in-law, wherever she lives, I [will live] near her." I got used to them and they are good people. Look, I am that type of person. Wherever you put me, I have love. I love to go out, to do things. Every evening my brothers-in-law come to see me before they visit their mother. They come to me, to my house.

I was the first daughter-in-law and I always remained the first. During holidays, there were six sons and six daughters-in-law, and each one brought their maid. There were big holidays. My husband's father would bring the food in wagons, in wagons, he would bring vegetables. And we were . . . the holidays were happy, a big house, full of good things. We were six daughters-in-law, we never fought with one another. We were never angry with one another, we didn't know what anger was. Abroad, in Tripoli, there were no quarrels. I never saw a fight with each other. Here, I see it. Here, I see it, and it is not interesting at all. There is nothing better than a quiet life where one respects the other. That is happiness, when one respects the other.

"*What did you do during the period of the war, the war of 'forty?*"
We escaped from home.

"Could you escape?"

My husband had a store, he closed it. He needed to sell material in Ponti, and we escaped to Garian. It's like from here to Eilat. From Tripoli to Garian—from here to Eilat. And Chalfo, my husband, needs to sell, he would spend Shabbat with me. I had two children, Reuven who was ten and Vittorio the baby, a baby was born and Chalfo came to spend Shabbat with me. On Monday, he takes a taxi to his store, three days in the city and sleeps at his mother's house. But I worry about him. Why? Because they are bombing the city. But where I lived, there weren't bombings. The entire Italian army was in Garian, an Italian city, completely Christian. The whole army was there and it was full of villas. And each villa is covered with green, so that the army won't see it. And we lived there. My husband had a lot of money then, he made a good living. And I also had a maid there, we rented a house. And I raised Vittorio there for three years, my second son, I gave birth to him after ten years. We had a good life in Garian. It is a small city. Up on top, a big mountain. When there is thunder, you look up at the sky and you see the electric threads in the sky. We were high up and we saw everything. You see it, you see the sky lighting up. And we enjoyed three years.

Sometimes, in the morning, I open up the door to the house, I want to go out—I can't because of the ice. I begin calling the neighbor: "Sago, come here." He takes the shovel and makes me a pathway to walk on comfortably. You open up a faucet, there is no water because of the cold. You take the ice, you put it in a bucket, you put it on the stove to wash your face. Vittorio was a baby, he was born there. At two months old, three months, I was new there. And you warm the ice in order to wash your face and to cook. The stove is lit and the baby is near me, I am happy, I had a child after ten years, it made me happy. And the bombs, what do I care? I am happy with what I have.

On Laura's radiant face, I can still see how happy she was that she gave birth to Vittorio ten years after her first son. It is difficult to think about what was going on in Europe when Laura was enjoying her life in Garian.

I stayed there for three years. In the summertime, there was great entertainment. It was something. You go for a walk, you go to a café, you go for a walk with the baby in his stroller. And . . . only during the three days when my husband isn't there, we are all unhappy, we aren't in a good mood. It is hard for a mother by herself with two children. During a war and that . . . we don't have a war within the city, we only hear the bombs, but they don't reach us. Once I was in Colina Varda. There you hear them more. Then we realized that I was to give birth, we were afraid. I was often afraid. He took me further away, to Garian. In Garian, you have all of the wealthy people who want to guard their health and their peace of mind, in Garian.

I would get up, nurse Vittorio, and . . . turn on the electricity, no electricity. That was in a bombardment of Tripoli, they turned off our electricity. They were afraid that they would hit the soldiers, and I began to worry and I worried until the morning. There is light at five o'clock in the morning and I go out into the streets to hear what happened yesterday. There is no telephone, there is nothing. They tell me: "Yes, there was an unusual night, so many people were killed there!" And I wait. "I wish Mother would come, look how beautiful, here you don't feel a thing."

And we lived like that for three years. If you didn't have money and you couldn't get out, you suffered, you stayed in your house. For example, here if there will be, God forbid, a war, we are all in the same boat. You don't have a rich one going away and a poor one staying. We all stay in homes, all of us. The rich are like the poor. But there it was different. Whoever was rich had where to run to. We worried about others, we weren't quiet. Why? Because a man has to worry about others, not only about himself. We worried about others and . . . people got hurt. That's the way life is. Some is suffering, some is pleasure, some is laughter and entertainment, some is quiet. That is the way life is for a person until the day he dies.

When the war ended, I went back, my brother died from typhus, I couldn't stand any more, Mother was in a bad state, I said: "I must be near my mother." The war ended, so we went back to the city. My house is closed, it is full of all the furniture, everything. We went back. Everyone who was far away came back.

"How did your mother, sisters, and brothers manage during the war?"

They managed fine. In the war, everyone escaped. Not as far away as Garian, like I did. They left the city for the outlying areas. There, the rich had built themselves small villas and everyone escaped. Fifteen or twenty miles, they escaped. My mother escaped with them. I rented a house for my mother. I remained for a while until I said: "I want to leave. Pregnancy like this after ten years, I am afraid that something will happen to my pregnancy. Whatever we can take with us, I don't care, the main thing is to get away from here." There isn't too much danger, there is only a little bit of danger. I left my mother in an apartment that I rented and I went further away to Garian.

Laura is now tense and I ask myself whether she is still struggling over her fears about her pregnancy with Vittorio or whether it is her feeling that she left her mother behind and too close to danger.

"Who lived with your mother?"

In the beginning, my sister Julianna lived with my mother. Afterwards, her husband found her a place and my mother remained with my brother Daniel, only with Daniel. My mother was full of energy. Every day she would look, is there a bomb or not, go down to the city, look at her house. People tell her: "You are not afraid." She says: "No. I sleep here at night, but in the daytime, I want to be near my house." Afterwards, the boy died on her. War killed him. He got typhus, once there was an illness like that. He was twenty, like my brother's son who died at that age too. Not the same disease, but the same age. She ended her life in suffering. She didn't enjoy life *(cries)*.

I've seen good things. We suffered, but part of life has been good. My daughter died here in Israel, my husband died here in Israel. I suffered a lot. I had a modest life, but I enjoyed a good life abroad. And when my brother died, my mother suffered very much. She suffered a lot during the war of 'forty. She was left alone. When the war ended, we went back to the city.

"The Italians didn't arrest the Jews? The Germans, the Italians?"

The Germans arrived and they didn't hurt us. Before the war started, I lived in the city center, like Dizengoff center here, in Tel Aviv. I am on the porch, we had a porch that was maybe sixty feet long, we had a beautiful house, a luxurious one. On the porch, I heard that the Germans are here. I bend down, I see some men from my porch, handsome men. Each one looks better than the next, a real light. They are speaking German. And my husband says to me: "I hope that they won't do anything to us here." I said: "Why?" He says: "What they did in Germany? What they started in Italy? They have now come here to us, but they don't talk about the bad things at all. They are only here for business." We made money off of them, they behaved well, they didn't start up with us. Nazism—no, no, they didn't start at all. They came to us already after the end of their show there. At the end of the murdering and the other things. They didn't do anything to us, they only had business dealings. From my porch, I hear the German language every evening.

Now that they found oil there, my husband and I would drink coffee on Saturday night. A nice place, interesting, everyone there was German. Tables and tables. Coffee, a piece of cake, speaking German. I say to my husband: "I am afraid." He tells me: "Don't be afraid. You know how good they are to us? Meanwhile, we will take care, we are doing all right with them." They came only for business reasons. In Italy they did [evil things], in Germany they did [evil things]. With us—none.

Laura moves uncomfortably in her chair. She knows what "their show" was like in Europe (and it was not over when the Germans appeared in Tripoli). Is it hard for her to connect that to the handsome men who came to Tripoli to do business?

We lived under the British rule . . . I'll tell you the truth, then we really suffered. We had riots twice. We had riots in 'forty-five, 'forty-seven. It was terrible. They released the Arabs. They came from the villages "to kill the Jews." And they knock on the doors, the houses of Jews. In the ghetto, they didn't manage to kill anyone. Why? Because all of the Jews were heroes and didn't let them in. They closed them off at the border and they left. And the people from up above, a bucket of hot water, boiling water, they didn't let the Arabs into the Jewish ghetto. In our neighborhood [outside the ghetto], we were a building with nine apartments, four Jews and five Christians. The Christians pointed out the Jews' apartments. There were also Christians that hid us. There were good Christians and bad Christians.

In the beginning, when the British came, we were very happy. Why? Because it was Mussolini with Hitler, right? We were afraid that they would do to us in Tripoli what they did in Italy, Germany, Bulgaria. Like they did everywhere. When Mussolini was in power we suffered a lot. At the end. In the beginning, we had it good. He taught us in school, how to eat with two forks, how to go to the Lido, how to be modern. Cafés, luxury, wealth, education, discipline. We learned everything from the Italians. And later on, when he started up with Hitler, we became afraid that he might harm us.

So when the English came, I was outside the city. Suddenly, one Saturday I am sitting and I hear the English language. Wow, the English have arrived, I suppose! Why, I knew they would come. For three days, the Italians opened up all of their army warehouses. Clothes and food and undershirts and blankets and underwear and nice shirts, everything was open. And we see that crates are literally falling onto the road. They were afraid that the Arabs would riot against the Jews. The Italians, the government opened up their warehouses to them. "Be busy with that, but don't start up with the Jews or with the Christians."

The Italians left, the English had not yet arrived. What will be? We were scared to death. We were frightened of the riots. Perhaps the Arabs will be set on us. Fear of the Arabs is worse than everything else. And we didn't have . . . we don't know what the end will bring. I would stand on the road and see . . . Arabs dragging, dragging boxes. Full wagons, I saw such anarchy—there was no one there. There was no government—there was anarchy. That was Wednesday, Thursday, Friday. On Saturday we are sitting around. I like to get up early on Saturday, I always get up early, the air is nicer. I hear English beneath my window. I opened up the window and I saw English soldiers. They began singing and dancing. My husband: "Come here. Everything is finished . . . the English have come." I let them into my house, we made them drinks, we gave them food. We didn't know their language, we [spoke with our] hands. We spoke Italian, they spoke English, it was a nice day. We were liberated, we weren't afraid. Now there is a state.

One day I am sitting around . . . no not one day, one night. It was eight o'clock at night, and somebody came from the kitchen window, knocked on the glass. I said: "Who is it?" I see a black man. "What do you want?" I asked him in Italian. He says to me: "Are there women here?" People started knocking on the door. The maid who was washing dishes ran away. She was afraid. I see a black man standing there and he doesn't want to move. We said: "No. There are no women." We had a big dog. He barks and barks. I say: "Bark, there is someone there." I saw that the entire garden, there was a big garden, was full of soldiers. He was barking at them. We said: "No, there are no women here." He ran away. I did not sleep quietly. I said: "I am afraid that he will come back and bring a group with him."

At six in the morning, I hear shots. And I say to my husband: "Do you hear that? Shots. Are they strong?" He said: "Go back to sleep. Nothing is happening. They are getting up early to get themselves some birds. Go back to sleep." At ten o'clock, the house is closed and the neighbor knocks on the door. I don't want to open it up. I am afraid. She tells me: "Open the door, don't be afraid, it's your neighbor." I opened up the door, she was bruised all over, her clothes were ripped. She told me: "You didn't see last night?" "What happened?" She said: "The villa across the way, the negroes came, they drank, we gave them food. We say that the English are good, we entertained them. After we served them food they wanted women. The women did not agree under any circumstances to go to bed with them. They forced them, they tore their clothes, they forced them into bed. And the men are looking and screaming and they are getting beaten. Some went with the women and some stayed to beat the men. What a night. Didn't you know?"

That same day I said to my husband: "Today I am going back to the city. The war is over, the English have come. Devils have been released on us now, in villas that are far away from the cities. They were released. They will want to come to knock on our doors every day. Soldiers want women, they have no women. We are going home today!" My house, I have a house there, a house in the center of the city. We brought the car and filled it, and I said to him: "Let's go, let's escape. Perhaps they will come here tonight." I was young and I didn't want to stay there. We left the villa. We didn't sell it . . . we didn't take anything from it. We built it close to my mother after we got back from Garian and we left it behind. To this day we don't know who took it, two acres of land, we left it all behind. In the end, the British were not good to us. They allowed the riots. They tortured us in 'forty-five and again in 'forty-seven. We looked for ways to come to Israel. We wanted quiet, we didn't want to be afraid. Not of the British, not of the Arabs. We wanted our own state.

"Did only the Jews suffer when the British came?"

It was only against the Jews. They knock on the door. A Christian woman opens it up. "Are you a Jew?" "No, I am Christian." They go away. "A Jew?" They enter, they take the gold and they butcher their children, they butcher her. Only against the Jews, all of the troubles were against the Jews. Wherever we go, they are behind us. Arabs are bastards. We were afraid of them there, we are afraid of them here. We don't trust them. We forgot our fear when we came here. Now, the fear has returned.

And we don't know what the end will be . . . there will be a good end, I hope. And they always wanted, they always persecuted us. Always. The English freed them against the Jews.

"When did you immigrate to Israel?"

We immigrated in the year 'forty-nine. In the beginning . . . my son Reuven escaped via Italy. He went there to study. And they brought him from Italy to Israel. And I can't live without Reuven. I sat for three months without Reuven. I went crazy. And as soon as they began taking out passports and the business started loosening up, we were among the first to escape. We came here. We thought [that it would be] different. No work, no house, we left everything behind, we left all of our wealth. As soon as we arrived they say: "What does your husband do?" I say to them: "My husband is a merchant." "No, here he can't be a merchant." We brought a few bolts of material from abroad, silk from his store. Reuven would go, my son would go to Dizengoff to sell pure silk. He would sell it for peanuts. We didn't know, we didn't know where to sell or how to live.

I left my husband in Italy. Why? Because my husband had some problem with his nose and they wanted to operate on it, he had something on the skin. They told me: "They will take better care of him here, you go ahead." And I came for Reuven. I didn't want to leave him. I said: "My husband will wait here for a month or two. I want to see Reuven." And when we arrived, there was no house and no work. They gave us tents. We suffered. One evening, the tent blew away with the wind. We were under the open sky, there was wind and rain. We didn't have a bathroom. You walked with boots in the mud, you came back without the boots. Oy, the way we lived, God forbid.

Do you know what a person is like without a house? Or without work? Lost. We didn't know what to do, where to turn. We didn't speak the language . . . even if you wanted to rent a place, they reject you. They throw you out of the office and you don't even know where you are. Nowadays, when immigrants come, they get an apartment, they are given money in their hands . . . once they didn't even leave us with a coin in our hand. Even when I wanted to buy milk, I didn't have any money for my daughter. My daughter died from suffering, from torture, from lack of food, from lack of a home *(cries)*. She was a year old. And we didn't know where to turn. Even when you turn for help, they talk, they don't answer you, they don't pay attention that you are speaking *(sobbing)*.

There was anarchy then, real anarchy. I was tortured, I lost weight, nobody noticed. Whoever died, died. Whoever lived, lived. The child . . . she suffered a lot. There wasn't food, there was no house. Nothing. My poor child died from suffering. And my husband, they gave him such hard work, on top of a high mountain. Two weeks out of every two to three months. They barely paid him. And I needed to manage with this low salary until more work would come along. And . . . he developed a weak heart. What can I tell you?! Life was hard. The absorption of the immigrants was very bad, not like today. When I see that they bring them, and they worry about them and they prepare things for them and they give them money in their hands . . . they get a room in the Mezkaz Klita [absorption center]. And we live underneath the stars and we don't have a bathroom or anything. I would go to the bathroom, I can't tell you what horrors I saw. I couldn't go in. I would vomit every day. Suffering, suffering, suffering. We performed a good deed when we came, we sinned, I don't know.

"We performed a good deed when we came, we sinned, I don't know." The good deed and the sin are mixed up in Laura's mind when she thinks about how she missed her son Reuven and feels guilty over Miriam's death.

Later on, they gave us an apartment and things began changing a little. When my husband died, they gave me work in the library, in the auditorium, a big lounge to keep quiet and to take care of. And things started changing a little. My sister Julianna didn't suffer like that. Why? Because those who came a few months earlier were given Arab houses. Her husband is cleverer than others. My husband is more naive. That one immediately began looking with his wife and children. They found an empty apartment, with a garden, they went in and settled there and no one evicted them.

He wrote us letters, come look for an apartment. We came—we didn't find anything. We looked a lot—nothing. Only the tent that they gave us in Beer Tuviya. The tent there, the life there. Under a tent, that's what the government gives. But Julianna's husband managed quite nicely and he didn't suffer. He had a garden, he planted there, he made food. He was clever, he knew how to work. He brought a goat for milk. He did everything, but we remained under the government's care. Whatever they gave us—we got. We didn't know what a *moshav* [cooperative settlement] was. Afterwards I was sorry. I said, if I had gone to the *moshav*, life would have been better. They told me: "Do you want a *moshav* or do you want to wait for an apartment?" I said: "No. I'll wait for an apartment." I got an apartment two years later. But those who went to the *moshav* got a house right away. They gave us an apartment, but what about work? In the *moshav*, you have both a house and work. In the city there is no work. An apartment, you need to pay rent every month. Why? Because we didn't bring money with us, we left it all behind. Until today, all of our property is still there. Everything that we built and did all remained for Qaddafi. If we had brought [it with us], we would have had a good life. We wanted to see Israel. For us, Israel was a very big thing. We wanted to come, and we came, thank God.

"What did Reuven do in Israel?"

Reuven, as soon as I saw him, I asked him to learn a profession, so that he could have his own future. And we asked around and they said: "Send him to what-do-you-call-it books so that he will learn to be a book binder." I sent him to study. He studied for a few weeks and he told me: "Mother, the work is boring. I don't want to work there any more. It's not for me at all, I don't want it." "Okay," I told him, "you know what you can study? Learn plumbing, that's a job that, with time, you can become a contractor." And what I said is exactly what happened. There is a man from Tripoli, a neighbor, who was a plumbing contractor. I see his house, how wealthy he is, how his wife is dressed, how their children are dressed, I say: "I want to see you looking like him."

We asked where you learn plumbing and they gave us an address. Someone, a good man. He learned how to be a plumber almost for free. When he finished and he knew that he had a job, he gave me his salary. We moved to an apartment and he helped us at home. He was the bread-winner. His father didn't have a job, and a while later, just as I said, he became a contractor and Vittorio went to work with him. He hired his brother to work with him and help him. And he also saw that they were managing well, thank God, there is building going on in the country and he became a partner with another and they were independent. Thank God, they had a good life. The situation changed and the children managed and everything went well and we forgot the bad times and remember the good ones.

That relaxes me. What I had decided abroad, I saw here. Even when I was abroad, he would send me a letter every day. I tell him: "Reuven, be careful. I only want you to be a plumber." I wanted to see him become an independent contractor. And he would send me letters, I would cry when I read them. It hurt me that he was so far away. There were ten years between him and his brother and I bore him when I was very young and I loved him very much. We are very close. I tell him: "I only want to see you become a contractor. Take care of yourself." And in the end, he made good money, he progressed, he married off his children, and he had everything he wanted. He was a much better contractor than the Rasco Company. And the two brothers worked together. That's Israel, you need a little bit of patience and afterwards, you progress. In the beginning you suffer and then the pain goes and things go well *(looks at me, proudly)*.

In the Italian school, [it was] "Colo Reuven and Shimon Vittorio." And there would be Christian children who would go outside. We lived with the Christians. When the children go out to play, they need a name that is acceptable. Because they don't differentiate between Jews and Christians. Everyone has culture, everyone goes to school, everyone is dressed nicely, and there was no difference between them whatsoever. All are children of the state. All of the children are beautiful, dressed nicely. They study together. Now, every now and then my husband's father passes by and says: "Why are you sending him to the kindergarten? I passed by there and I saw through the window that he is praying with the Christians toward the Madonna and toward Jesus." I told him: "Really?" I said: "Okay, I will go to the teacher and talk to her." I went to the teacher and I said: "Look, all of the children who are here, are all of them Christian?" She said: "No, of course not. There are Jews, there are Christians, we live in the same neighborhoods." I tell her: "Look. My father-in-law passed by and saw my son praying like the Christians. We have different prayers. We don't have a Saint Marie. We only pray to God." "What will we do with him?" I told her: "Look, how many Jews do you have?" I saw that by the ... they would wear a white tunic with embroidery [the child's name embroidered on it]. I read a few of the children's names that were Jewish. I know which names are Jewish. I told her: "Leave all of these alone in a different room. Let your Christians pray to Jesus and be careful with mine. My father-in-law is religious and we are religious, we don't have anything to do with another religion." She says to me: "Why not?

I don't want to sin. It's also forbidden for me to do that. I am also religious."

They were good people, good people. I don't have anything else to say. We didn't see bad things from them, only good. You know, during the riots my mother-in-law went to her neighbor's house and she escaped over their roof. They gave her a ladder, she went up and down. She was there for a week. When someone would knock at the door and ask: "Are there Jews here?" "What do you mean? Of course, there aren't any Jews here?! I am a Christian and I don't hide Jews." And they come, not six or seven, but sixty to seventy from the villages in order to kill Jews. She tells them: "No, I don't have any Jews here. You can come in and see." She gives them a sense of security that they can come in. They don't enter. They go away. We escaped from the Arabs. Their son is bad. He would go to the riots, steal, kill, and come back. And his mother loved me so much. She tells me: "Only you are my daughter." There were cultured Arabs, ones that studied in the university. But their son was anti-Jewish, anti-Israeli, he hated the Jews. Their son, not the mother. There were good relations between us. I would bake a cake—send them a full platter. They would call me from the roof, I go down and go to them, drink a cup of tea. She tells me: "You are our daughter. You don't raise your nose up like the other Jews who make money. You sit on the floor like us. You are not stuck-up, you are our daughter."

Once Vittorio was little, about four and a half or five. On Sunday the maid made coffee, a full pot, brought it to the table, starts pouring for the children, the entire pot, maybe a liter and a half, on the foot. He was wearing a woolen sock, it was winter. He began screaming, I pulled off the sock, the skin was burned. "Laura, Laura. What happened?" I tell her: "Come look. I am going to the hospital." She says: "No. I am coming. Don't go to the hospital. One moment." She came and looked at him. She said: "Bring me eggs, boil them, throw away the white." She put the yolks in a frying pan on the stove, she mashed them until they became oil, a piece of black gum remained inside. She took a piece of cotton and a match. She put one inside the other and put it on his leg. He wore shoes after four days. She made his skin like new. "What's better, the hospital or me?" After four days, he had new skin. I tell you, there is no medicine like that, like natural medicine. If I had taken him to the hospital, it would have taken a month, a month and a half. She was just like a mother, she was a beautiful woman. She wore beautiful clothes and had a cultured home.

And when the riots began, she called me. I went down with my children and went in. We hid in a closed room, and I was afraid of their son because he was a murderer. And I say to her: "What can I do, I am afraid of Achmed." She [said]: "I don't let him. He won't touch you and he won't bring anyone in here. Put the children in the closet. You are my daughter. How would I ever let him touch you!" And after three or four days the whole thing passed. They put up notices that it was forbidden to touch the Jews. But the son saw us, he wanted to kill us. But he couldn't do anything, because he respected his mother and his father. His mother and father were good to us. And we were good to them. Look how good it is to be a good person. In the hour of need, you find the good in him immediately. "Achmed, this is our daughter. Achmed, don't frighten her." He tells me stories and frightens me. "You Jews. All you can say is our Palestine, our Palestine." She tells him: "Achmed, don't frighten her. Leave her alone. She doesn't say that she wants Palestine. She wants to stay here. She belongs in Tripoli. She is not going anywhere." He says: "You Jews, if we say that we will butcher you, you become afraid. But if I don't touch you, you want to go to Palestine." And a miracle saved us. And later on, when I wanted to immigrate, I didn't talk and I didn't say a word. I closed the door and a taxi took me to the airport. I was afraid because they always gave me trust and I loved them. I loved their city. Whoever wanted to go to Palestine went against them. They are against us, like today.

"In Tripoli did you hear what was going on in Europe during the war?"

Of course. We fasted. My husband goes to pray in the morning, he goes to the synagogue, we would only pray in the synagogue, every morning. And he comes and says (when I was pregnant with Vittorio): "Do me a favor and light candles today for the Jews." I ask him: "Why?" He says: "The Jews of Europe, butchering and burning. Children and adults, today is a day of fasting. Fast." If we fasted, it had significance. Today, if you fast, it doesn't mean anything. But in Tripoli, everyone would fast. They would say it was a day to fast, I would fast. "I am going to fast and so are you." I fast. And I light [candles]. "What happened?" "In Europe, there is Hell. They take children on trains and they burn them in the oven." And, aside from that, a cousin of mine, with his wife from England, lived near my mother. I would go to my mother's house before the war, they wanted to help her escape, and not to stay there. We knew there was going to be a war and we were afraid. The English shouldn't stay. They were helped to escape. Where did they send them to? To Germany where there was murder. They took perhaps three hundred people from Tripoli. All of them with English passports. They took them to Germany. From the morning until the evening, there was the smell of people burning in the ovens. She says: "From the morning until the evening, you smell fire. They gave us better portions. We ate bread more or less, because of our passports." She says: "The others were, what can I say, no one should see such situations."

Every day we buy a newspaper and bring it home. It told about exactly what was happening in Germany. We read about it in the papers. We heard about it in the services at the synagogue. It was a civilized place where we lived, it wasn't primitive. It was a civilized country, newspapers, swimsuits, Lido, cafés, fashion, luxury, modern, maxi, mini, all of it. It was like here.

"Did the Italians talk about the murder of the Jews?"

Yes. During the Italian regime, we would read. We would get the newspaper delivered to our home.

"And you—what did the Jews do?"

They took it to heart, they would fast and light candles. They would also pray every day in the synagogue. And there wasn't a house that wouldn't light candles and that didn't pray to God. There were sermons in the synagogue. "Fast, great decrees are being made about Germany. They are taking children away from their mothers. They are cutting them and burning them."

I once saw in a movie, there was a mother with two children. A German officer came and said: "Are these your children? The little one is cute." He grabbed the little girl, and she said: "Leave her alone." He said: "No, this one is for me." The girl was crying. Afterwards, he took the big one from her and gave her a kick and knocked her down. He took both of the girls and left. Two girls from a mother, I saw that on television. They suffered a lot. From that suffering, God gave us our own country. And why did they suffer like that? Why? Nobody knows. Their suffering was very great, it is remembered until today, you know on that memorial day

... Holocaust Day. Why did God bring the Jews so much suffering? I don't know, I don't know till this day.

"Did you meet people in Israel who went through the Holocaust?"

Yes, of course. My cousin was in the Holocaust. She was young. Her mother tells me. I saw her in Italy six years ago. Today she lives in Italy. And I went in and ... they began talking. I told her: "What happened when the Germans were there?" Then she told me: "Yes, how we suffered. But as much as we suffered, they didn't hurt us as much as they hurt the others. We heard noise, we smelled things. We saw people running, they looked like they were suffering, like they were being tortured. We were closed in the camp. They brought us food, women by themselves and men by themselves. We suffered but they didn't think about killing us. One out of three hundred died from rotten food. We never thought that we would live and make it to our own home, to our place, once again, live with the entire family, live with the husband. We didn't think about it. And we returned, but we suffered terrible things there." Three years of torture. They took them from Tripoli and put them into camps. She says: "Everything was frightening. Huts, wire, everything was closed. The army was in charge of us. Every day it was hot like in Hell. Either cold or hot and we were tortured. But they were unfortunate, the ones burned in the ovens, the ones butchered. Not us." They were afraid to touch them because they were English refugees. They took care of them.

Here, we were together in the same tents with survivors. Afterwards, they brought us together to Amidar. And to this day the ones from Amidar they are moving away from here, they tell me: "Hello, Mrs. Guetta." We lived together in the tents, in the huts. Most of the nice people were Bulgarians. Really. They have a Bulgarian neighborhood. There is a street between us of only ten meters. And I was their friend; they would come visit me and I would go visit them. One had a vegetable stand, another one a grocery store. You know, they came without work; everyone took a crate, made a scale, and began. One sold vegetables, another a grocery store, a few cookies. They made enough to live on. They come at night, we would all wash up, sit in the garden, get dressed, have fun, laugh. They would come visit me. What did I have to give them? Black sunflower seeds and an orange. That's all there was, I had nothing better. There was no money. Even if you wanted to buy, there wasn't any. But we were happy;

we opened our door every evening. When you left your door open, no one came in. There weren't any thefts, no hashish, no murders, no bad culture. Everything cost less and was more enjoyable. Now, there's more money and there is less fun.

Laura ends with another moral, like those interwoven throughout the interview. Even after I turn off the tape recorder, she continues to describe more and more details from her life, about her suffering, about the things she liked and the lessons of her life. She doesn't let me leave the house without giving me a large package of food and without asking me a number of personal questions: Do I have a boyfriend and is there anything she can do about finding me one?

[Dan Bar-On and Noga Gil'ad:] Laura has a complete life story to tell. External events touched her life only after the war, when the British took over and the riots against the Jews began. The continuity of the family framework is part and parcel of her biographical reconstruction. Although Laura's life was not easy, especially the immigration to Israel, and she suffered severe and very painful losses (her father and her little brother, her daughter and her husband), these did not disrupt the centrality and continuity of the family in her narrative reconstruction, nor did they diminish her capacity for hopefulness and joy.

Laura's language is rich and full of images. She frequently uses present-tense verbs, which give one the feeling of "here and now." Her opening sentence provides the nucleus of her life story: "life beforehand" and "life today" are totally different. However, Laura is not referring only to the transition from Libya to Israel. She sees the turning point in her life as her father's illness and death when she was nine years old. Because she was the oldest in the family, her short childhood ended and her life as a woman began, a life full of hardships. These events remind us of Genia's turning point (her mother's death), but Genia's and Laura's reconstructions of these events in their life stories are very different. For Genia, this loss marked the beginning of her family's destruction and the end of any positive meaning in motherhood. For Laura, however, it was the beginning of life as a mature woman and mother.

Laura learns very early that men die and women continue to carry the burden. When her father was ill, she helped her mother raise the other children and did the housework ("I was like a devil"). When her father dies, she looks for a wet nurse for her brother, a six-month-old baby. A partner to her mother's suffering, she describes how she falls asleep, crying at her mother's feet. As a result of her guardian's intervention, she moves into her uncle's home. It is unclear whether he had already intended to arrange her marriage or whether the idea developed while she was living with him. Laura describes the move with mixed feelings: On the one hand, the move allowed her to laugh, to go out, to be a child again, to learn to be a woman from her mother-in-law, whom she loved like a mother. But on the other, Laura did not want to be separated from her own mother and perhaps even felt guilty about leaving her, and her sisters and brothers, alone. Laura does not express this feeling of guilt directly; it can only be read between the lines. It surfaces later, when she is already married and busy raising her younger son in Garian. It is then that her youngest brother died of typhus while staying with their mother.

A large portion of Laura's biographical narrative is devoted to her difficulty over her identity as a woman. As a young child of four she learns that her father prefers boys over girls (a "good sign"). Later on, she sees her mother almost commit suicide by taking something that was supposed to help her give birth to sons. She learns the absolute difference between women's and men's roles when her mother forbids her to work out at school. Laura speaks of her body's need to be active because "a person is born to be quick." However, it does not help; her mother refuses and she has to stop.

By then, Laura is already living at her aunt's house. It is not clear to her whether this disagreement occurred with her own mother or with her aunt/mother-in-law, whom she loved like a "real mother" and who raised her from the age of ten. Afterwards, Laura describes a quarrel she had with her mother (her aunt?) over the right to study at night. Her mother does not think much of her studies, because a woman's place is in the kitchen, near her husband. For Laura, however, it is important to be the best in school, to excel in her studies. Her formal schooling ends at the age of twelve, and Laura soon marries and gives birth to Reuven.

In her reconstruction of these events, Laura's ambivalence about her independence as a woman surfaces. Laura wonders: Are the ways of the past good or bad? On the one hand, she says: "I had barely been born," "I didn't know what marriage was," things "that today every girl of eight or ten knows." On the other, she admires the past: her mother gave everyone a home, and her mother-in-law/aunt taught her everything she knew and related to her as the best of her daughters-in-law. When Laura talks about the differences between *here* and *there,* the past and the present, she expresses this ambivalence: "Here, in Israel, it [dirty work] is not a disgrace ... we do it." That is, today women have more independence, but it eats into their self-respect. Laura has found a solution; she manages well with everyone. Her gynecologist has told her: "I heard so much laughter when you were outside [in the waiting room]." In this way, Laura has claimed both independence and a central role in her family for herself; she does not remain distant and alienated like her sister.

In some ways, Laura reminds us of Olga. Like her, she has learned to move ahead "rebuilding life" without giving in to suffering. She moved from her mother's house to her aunt's after the death of her father, from Tripoli to Garian when she was pregnant with her second child during the war, and then back to Tripoli when the riots began. Afterwards, following in the footsteps of her older son, she moved to Israel via Italy. In every move, she notes her fear and the hardships they endured, but she maintains her hope for a better life. One of her hopes materializes when her two sons become building contractors, something she wished for them while she was still living in Tripoli.

In contrast to Olga, however, Laura did not lose most of her family in the Holocaust. Perhaps it is this difference that allows her to reveal herself without fear and, especially, without anger. She accepted her parents' religious identity ("whoever wasn't religious, wasn't a Jew"), as well as her Christian neighbors and the Italian fascists (they taught us "how to eat with two forks"), who gave the Jews a feeling of relative security. She appreciated her Arab neighbor, who came to her aid when she was endangered. She even perceived the Germans, whom they "did business" with, in a positive light. Only the "English" elicit her anger. They not only frightened her, they also disappointed her expectations by "releasing the Arabs" to riot against her people.

Until the war, Laura does not mention any dates. She mentions only her age in association with various events in the family life cycle, so we have no way of knowing her exact birth date. In our opinion, this is not a coincidence. It is as if she is saying: "Until 1940, external events did not affect my life story." During that year, however, world events in general, and in Tripoli specifically, forced themselves in. From that moment, the important dates in her personal life become intertwined with those of particular external events. But even then, she perceives the outside world as simply a thin layer around her personal and family narrative.

Laura was looking for tranquillity so that she could give birth to her second son away from the bombs. She immigrated to Israel, more out of longing for her older son, Reuven, than out of a belief in Zionist ideology. Even when she tells what she knew about the Holocaust (in response to Amaliya's questions), her description is detached, a less overt form of fearfulness: we fasted, lit candles, read newspapers—proof that we lived in a civilized country where one knows what is going on in the world. Later, she lived in the same neighborhood in Israel with survivors. From a cousin who was in Bergen-Belsen, she heard for the first time, and only six years ago, of the hardships in the camp.

The influence of external events on Laura's life intensifies when she begins to describe in great detail the suffering and the humiliation she encountered when she immigrated to Israel. Here, reality invades her own story. Her suffering is not only personal, not only connected to her family, it is *collective*. At the same time, any effect the Israeli experience might have had on her perspective on life in Libya is conspicuously absent. If we expect that Israeli values will "color" the way she related to the Italian fascists and the Germans, perhaps even to the Christians and Arabs, we do not find it in Laura's story. Only the negative attitudes she expresses toward the rioting Arabs suggest any such after-the-fact "coloring" ("When we arrived here, we forgot that fear. Now the fear has returned"). We wonder if this thinking will become more overt when we listen to Vittorio and Liat.

Vittorio

"I came to Israel and fit in with all the Sabras"

I meet Vittorio at the entrance to his house in Savyon (one of Tel Aviv's more prosperous suburbs) resting in his hammock. When he gets up, I notice that he is dressed meticulously, like his mother. His big eyes, his warm look and smile, also remind me of her. He brings me into the house while giving me detailed explanations about which carpenter built each cabinet and stained glass window and how they did it. Inside, everything is arranged beautifully and perfectly. When he heads into the kitchen, I notice that he is going a bit bald and gray, a small detail that gives away his age, forty-four according to his mother's arithmetic. His wife, Paula, joins us for the first few minutes. Vittorio, like his mother, does not need any introduction.

Okay, I still remember my childhood in Libya. Does it interest you? I remember myself at age six or seven. I think that I studied for one year in Libya, finished one year of school there. My father worked, he sold material, he was affluent. We had a maid. She would take me to school every morning, but I didn't want her to hold my hand. The situation was that she would walk close to the edge of the sidewalk and I would walk close to the stores until we reached the school. That was the way it was every day—in the morning she would take me and in the afternoon she would bring me home. And . . . we lived in the city center. There wasn't room to move, to go down to the street and play.

Vittorio stops for a moment and Paula joins in on her own initiative.

We were also house children from an early age. You don't go out to play in the streets. Only people, simpler people, are allowed to play in the streets. We, the children of good families, were forbidden. We were very spoiled. We always had a servant at home who did all of the housework. We came home from school and everything was ready. I would give him my school bag and send him away so that he wouldn't come with me. I was embarrassed. He was unfortunate, he would walk a kilometer behind me carrying my bag. We went to a Christian Italian school. I was in that school from kindergarten. So, of course, you don't have only Jewish friends. In a society like that, with Christians and . . . but no . . . we didn't feel like outsiders.

We didn't have anything to do with the Arabs. There weren't any Arabs who went to my school. They had their own school. We had an Italian government school. From first grade through high school we weren't afraid of the Arabs. I was born after all of the big riots of 'forty-five and 'forty-eight, after the establishment of the State [of Israel]. So by then . . . we really didn't feel fear, even during the Six-Day War when we were shut up in the house for three weeks. We could have gotten out and left for Israel immediately, there wasn't any problem. But since my uncles couldn't leave, my mother didn't want to go. She wanted to send us ahead and she would remain, but who would agree to such a thing? Then, when my uncle left, we left a few days later. My two uncles and my grandmother left. As soon as we phoned the embassy, they came and took us and we left!

Paula leaves us for the kitchen, while Vittorio continues his story.

We came to Israel and we were thrown into transit camps right away, put into tents. During that time we became street children. We would go to school, we didn't learn anything, we didn't do anything. In the beginning we went to an Agudat Yisrael [Ashkenazi or orthodox] school with a small *tallith* [men's prayer shawl]. Then our parents took us to religious schools, they wanted religion. Half of a lesson was devoted to praying, two hours you spend praying. You go home and do some homework, you go out into the streets and you play with a hoop, with a pot and a cover. It served as a . . . like a steering wheel.

And that's the way we lived in the transit camp. I also remember the period when my sister got sick. I don't know whether or not my mother brought up the subject, my sister was either four or five. I remember the day she fell, I think from a porch like this one, there was a descent of eight inches or so. She fell and broke her back. She was very sick for a long time at home and there wasn't anyone who could take care of her. The hospital at Tel Hashomer existed, but they didn't want to admit her. When they did admit her, it was too late. It was me who took her to the hospital, I brought her there. She was there for three days before she died. And that's how we were brought up in the transit camp *(sighs)*.

Slowly, slowly we moved to . . . permanent housing, without electricity or a sewage system, under very difficult conditions there as well. Our neighbors, we had neighbors who were Holocaust survivors. For them it was deluxe. After we understood what they went through, it was really easy for them. I mean, after what they went through in the concentration camps. We sat there without electricity, without a sewage system. It didn't bother them. It was the time of austerity, there was no meat, fish, fruit. Everything was rationed. They rationed things once a month. Clothing was also bought with coupons that they gave us.

"For them it was deluxe." I had never thought that way about the transit camps, the Holocaust survivors, and the North African immigrants.

And that's how it was during my elementary school. I was never an excellent student, I was always the one who bothered others, until the age of thirteen or fourteen, when I left school before the end of the school year. I left to go to work in the construction business, to learn a profession, to become a plumber. Later on, I went to evening school to make up the two years that I was missing. I wasn't the only one. There were a lot of kids who did that. It's not like today. I think that four or five from my class made it to high school. The rest didn't . . . they didn't get there. We finished elementary school and we went to learn a profession, welding or construction or garage work, it's not like today. Today, to do any little job they demand at least ten years of school, twelve years of school.

So I worked in construction, I helped to support the household. My father worked hard, he always suffered, he was sick, and he could barely make a living. With help from the party [the ruling Labor party], they fixed him up with some work twice a week. Two days a week he worked permanently in the City Hall. But then one day he got a blood clot in his brain. They took him to the hospital when he was very ill. After that, it was very difficult to look at him. He was covered with a type of curtain for three weeks, his entire shape was distorted.

Vittorio's face expresses pain at this memory of his father, yet the tone of voice in which he describes these difficult things—the illness and the death of his sister and his father—is smooth, as if he is glossing over his feelings.

I continued living at home, alone with my mother, because my brother had meanwhile gotten married. And they helped me with my army service, they gave me a year off because my father had died. However, when I went into the army, I had to leave my mother alone at home. None of my requests to serve close to home were granted. When they wanted to transfer me, only a few months were left of my army service, it wasn't worthwhile anymore. My mother knew how to manage, she rented out the rooms to students. Students came and went, she would rent them rooms, sit with them, prepare everything for them. And so during vacations, I would come and befriend them, these students. And from that, I began dating seriously one of the women students.

And so we were dating seriously for a while, and I didn't want to continue, her parents didn't want me to either, we weren't suited for one another. She, she already had her master's degree from the university and I . . . barely [finished] elementary school. I thought to break it off, but she didn't want to. And I, out of respect, was embarrassed to ahh . . . send her away. Because I thought, to this day I believe that she deserved someone better than me. Somebody on her level, with her education. Forget about the everyday behavior, I wasn't her equal in other things. I tried so hard to explain it to her, to talk to her very gently, like a sister. It didn't help. Until one day she decided to leave Israel. I was very happy and hoped that it would be good for her. Till this day, I want the best for her. I felt bad for her, because she didn't do anything bad. Then she left Israel. I was happy, I thought that she would manage abroad, it will end, it will be for the best. And then, I think after two weeks or three, I began getting letters again that she wants to come back and that we should continue to see one another. And, of course, that didn't put me in a good mood. And then suddenly, a short while later, perhaps after a month and a half, she came back to Israel.

I didn't even go to the airport to welcome her. I wanted to cut off the contact, maybe she would get hurt. It will help if we break up. I didn't go to the airport. Of course, my mother wanted me to go get her. She said: "I don't have a daughter—my daughter died—she is my daughter." The relations between them were fantastic. I also admire her to this day. Of course, my mother went to visit her. I began to hear stories about how disappointed she was that I didn't come. It didn't help me and I went to see her and that was that. I tried to explain and it didn't work.

And then one evening my uncle (may his name be for a blessing) came and I had great respect for this uncle. To this day, I admire that man. He had a special wisdom. And he and my mother pressured me into taking this step, into marrying her. And I knew that nothing would come of that, it is not possible. It's impossible to marry such a person. But, I didn't have a choice. I didn't want to insult her and tell her to leave me alone and also due to the pressure at home—we got married. And, of course, after the wedding, she saw immediately after the wedding, it didn't work. So then she immediately left home. And we were divorced within one year. I went through a difficult time with her, I didn't have a job then, it was during the recession. She supported me financially. She always worked, she was a teacher. Then, the recession didn't affect the teachers, they worked in the schools and they also gave private lessons. It was good for them. That's all.

I recall that Laura's marriage was against her wishes. I am amazed at Vittorio's openness—to tell me right away about the failure of his first marriage, the marriage his mother wanted because "I don't have a daughter... she is my daughter."

So one day my mother goes to the airport to greet one of the students, someone else, who had spent a long time abroad. They were like her own daughters. So she would go and meet them at the airport. She comes back and tells me: "Imagine who came from abroad?" How can I guess who came? "Guess." "I can't guess." She says: "Your cousin, Paula." I remembered her mother from my childhood abroad. I didn't know what her daughter looked like. I also remembered her father. And I was happy, my cousin comes to Israel. I saw her and she was an impressive-looking girl. She began turning my head, to the other side. After all, the story there was all over, it didn't work. I think that I already got a divorce.

And so she arrived in Israel as a new immigrant, and she is now my wife. After a while, I met her at my brother's house and we got to know one another. We began dating, I was missing it, do you understand? Everything that had been, was reversed. I had a great love. It's that way till this day, nothing has changed. I also loved my uncle's family and her mother. They receive people very nicely and I moved in with them even before we were married. Not like the way that people live together, of course. Everyone had their own room. People live together, I know. Many try to live together. And that's the way that we lived together. I lived in her parent's house and then we got married. Everything was fine and good. I worked as a building contractor. We had an apartment, we were more or less set up. And then the problems began. I got very sick. I became . . . depressed. One day I came home and I felt that something wasn't, how can I describe it, wasn't right in my head. You don't know what you are doing. You do something and you don't think that you've done it. You go to check whether you really put it in its place or not.

Vittorio's voice becomes very shaky. Although he describes his physical and mental illness with amazing openness, it seems difficult for him to recall it.

Paula is good when things like this happen. Immediately, she started phoning doctors and professors. She made an appointment with one of the experts in the country and he discovered that I had that illness. I needed to be admitted into the hospital immediately and I was admitted into Tel Hashomer [general hospital]. My wife, the things that she did for me then, nobody would believe it. All of the cases that were with me in the hospital, cases like that, ended up divorced. In a situation like that it is difficult for a woman to support her husband. Most of the patients that were with me, the young and the old, were abandoned. My wife would appear every morning at seven o'clock. She would stay until twelve o'clock, until I would fall asleep and then she would go. The doctors would send her away: "Go home." Nothing helped. My mother and her mother as well, of course. Her mother left her family, her children, she had five more children at home. At six o'clock in the morning they were already on their way to Tel Hashomer. Every morning for a period of six months while I was in the hospital. There were ups and downs in my illness.

This story went on for three years. The sickness with its ups and downs, with difficult problems at home. With all that my wife supported me so much when I was in the hospital, she was exactly the opposite at home. She . . . she didn't understand the situation. I don't think that they explained it to her exactly in the hospital . . . how she needed to behave with me. I was a sick man and I lay at home for another two-and-a-half years without working. Luckily, I had money to live off. We got to very hard times, my wife and me. Fights, we would fight over everything. Such fears, three very hard years. I think that we didn't get a divorce because she was my cousin. I don't know why, we were embarrassed. After all, I had already been divorced once.

When I think about it, I understand what happened. For example, I was unable to go and get washed. It was the illness. The person becomes just a thing. He can't do anything, he can't function. To lie around for three years, like an idiot, unable to do anything. To move that from here to there, I want to move it, but I can't. My brain doesn't give me the order to do it. She didn't understand these things. Then we fought about everything. "Get up and get washed. Why are you lying on the bed with your shoes on like a corpse." I couldn't. Both of us discovered it when it was over and things went back the way they were before. Then we discovered it. She was consulted, things like that, they spoke to her many times, but I guess at that point they didn't instruct her. It was a very difficult time.

I wonder whether Paula did not understand or whether it was her way of encouraging him. I am curious to know whether in the records of his illness it is written that his grandfather, father, sister, and uncle died from illnesses, and whether this affected him.

And . . . good, after three years I slowly began returning to work. Liat was born. Before Liat was born, my wife had a breakdown, she had a miscarriage. David was born a year after Liat and slowly life got back to normal. I returned to work. Of course, my wife stopped working. The children were born and we went back to our old way of life, the same love that we had before we got married. Life began to be normal again. I wanted to move to a larger apartment. How to do that? My wife didn't want to leave Ramat Gan. But my budget didn't allow buying a larger apartment in Ramat Gan. Then I had no money to buy a big apartment. I came and said: "Look, I'm buying an apartment as an investment in Ashdod. We will invest our money." "But I won't live there." I told her: "You won't live there, it's only for investment purposes, don't worry." I always wanted to have my own house. So, I bought a house in Ashdod, but I planned to sell it one day and to move to a private house in Ramat Gan. I bought an apartment without her seeing, an investment, as it were.

And one day I said: "Look Paula, we need to move to Ashdod." "Why?" I told her: "With money that I had, I bought an apartment in Ashdod and a plot of land in Savyon." I needed to sell my apartment in Ramat Gan so that I would have the money. Paula took it very hard. My mother, too. She would visit us every day, sometimes twice a day. I will never forget the day that we moved to Ashdod, the tears in her eyes. For her, Ashdod was the end of the world. Afterwards, we needed to move from Ashdod to Savyon, indeed with a lot of happiness, but she also cried then. She got attached to the neighbors, to the place. It was again hard for her.

I am surprised at the importance Vittorio is giving to his wife's feelings, which is unusual according to my stereotype of North African men. At the same time, I can feel the pressure he was under to climb the socioeconomic ladder.

We had four wonderful years in Ashdod. Things went well in every respect. From an economic standpoint, from all aspects, we had four fantastic years. Until the economic reform, Erlich's period [a finance minister in Begin's government]. At work, I lost money instead of making money and I was also in the middle of building my house in Savyon. We didn't have money to send our son to the nursery school. And my wife is the type who is willing to live in one room as long as she does so in style. I am ready to give up on things in order to have my own house. Not her. She manages with one room, but she doesn't want them to send her son home because we didn't pay. And once again, it was hard, very hard. In the end, we moved here, without a kitchen, without a fence, like we were camping out. With a child, we had Zvi, he was one year old, he would crawl down the stairs without a railing. Neighbors would come over to say congratulations, to meet us and I was ashamed to show them the [unfinished] house. We began living here without a kitchen.

Who came to live here? Rich people. The poor, like me, don't come here. Everyone was settled, with new cars, with trips abroad, everything completely paid for. We got to that stage slowly over the years. We lived here for a year without a kitchen, that was very hard. I changed from being a plumber to being a building contractor. According to the forecasts, it was supposed to be a very serious business, with a high income. But in reality, it wasn't so. You see, in our country, we are once again moving into a good period for building, but that too will end. Then I went into the business during a good period, but I got in very close to the end. I hadn't managed to work for half a year or a year and there began to be cutbacks in building, until not many years ago. I sat in the house for two years until I found the work that I do today as a salesman for meat products. So, in general, I have told you everything up to today. What else?

I am surprised by Vittorio's quick ending. "Can you tell me a little more about your childhood in Tripoli?"

I can't tell you a lot about Tripoli because we were shut up in the house. It's not like here in Israel, where we were out on the streets. In Tripoli, you don't have children who are out on the streets—street children. Such a thing didn't exist in Tripoli like it does here, children running outside to play for good or bad. Abroad, there was no such thing for us. A child goes to school or to nursery school, goes with his mother to his grandmother's, to his aunt's, but not more than that. During that time, that's what it was like. I don't remember there being something other than that. Anyway, not where we lived. Because we lived in the center of the city. There were a lot of cars sandwiched in, a busy street. It wasn't an area with gardens and playgrounds or things like that. And the parents, too, during that time, never worried about taking their children to places like that in order to keep them busy. That's what it was like in Tripoli, from the perspective of a child.

"Can you describe your life a bit more? What did you do?"

Look, in the morning my father went out like a king. He would leave the house with a boy walking after him, he would take him to the market. The Arab boy had a kind of basket on his back. My father put in the basket whatever he wanted to take with him. Every day he would buy fresh fruit, vegetables, meat, and fish. He would buy food every day because we didn't have a refrigerator at home. He would buy large quantities of fruit and vegetables and meat and fish every day. And, of course, he would send the Arab home at ten o'clock and he would set it out there. They would cut the meat into strips, dry it in the sun with a lot of salt. You had to be more careful with the fish. Every day they went out and bought fresh food. Father would come home and my mother would yell: "What did you do? Who needs this? Yesterday, you brought home a fish that weighed three kilo and also today. Who is going to eat it?" He said: "It doesn't matter, make it. If you don't, we'll throw it away." He would sometimes spoil me and take me with him to the market to buy a pigeon or a chicken. I would bring it home and tie it to the leg of the table. My mother would make a lot of noise until they would butcher the chicken.

That's what I remember from Tripoli. Every now and then I would go with my father to the synagogue. It was an honor for me. They would put me on the Ark. Abroad, there were very fancy synagogues. There aren't any like that here. They were very rich. It was a synagogue that he established. He was the *gabai* [usher], it's passed down from father to son. So, I would go with him there and he would put me on the Ark. For me, it was a punishment. I never liked that, to this day. On Yom Kippur, I only go for the last half hour. I believe in religion, but I don't think that you have to sit there all day and to go over the same prayers. Look at it once. The same thing: "We sinned in front of you." Why do you have to read that a million times? I say once: "We sinned in front of you," ask forgiveness, and that's the end of the story. Why do you have to sit there for hours and go over the same thing for the entire day? Do you understand? In my opinion, if they would cut down this prayer to ten minutes, then many people would come to pray. I would.

Vittorio gives a mischievous child's smile. He is testing me to see my reaction. I laugh.

I remember Grandma's house. It was a very rich house. It's a house that you go up a few stairs and you go in the door and afterwards there is a living room as big as a hall. A hall where they have parties; it's really as big as a hall. And this hall is full of many rooms, big doors and ceilings about twelve feet high. In the middle of the hall there is a safe, like in a bank, and there they kept all of the things made of gold and silver. A number of servants and maids worked there. They were really unfortunate, they would work only for their food and some nice dress for the holidays. They almost worked for free. And when she finishes doing that type of work at age twenty or twenty-five, she gets married. Those kinds of families always had six or seven girls, I don't know why. One woman brings her sister and it goes on that way from generation to generation.

We would sit with Grandpa at a table that was thirty or forty feet long. Of course, first the men would be honored, they would be served first. The women didn't always sit at the table. They might sit in the kitchen and eat by themselves. Do you understand? That's how it was in a very rich household. It's impossible to describe, it's something very, very different. You don't see things like that in Israel. I remember all the silverware, all the dishes. Not the dishes, but the full service. Everything was made of silver. It was something very, very expensive. That's on my father's side. On my mother's side, there was a house in the ghetto, an old house, like you see here in Jaffa. When you climb the stairs, you barely reach the top. When we would meet, my cousins and me, we would bring up the water in a bucket, if you know how to do that. There was a well there that would fill up in the winter, I guess. And whenever we went there that was our game, to fill up the bucket with water. We would let the bucket down and bring it back up full. We would say to Grandma: "Where is the *gish?*" *Gish* is the junk. She would take out a gigantic drawer that was full of screws, broken locks, and all kinds of other things that were broken, pieces of broken metal, and that was the Lego that was there. We would sit down and try to put it together, we would play. When we would finish, we would pick up the junk. Every piece of junk from the house would be put into that big drawer that weighed a lot because it was full of metal. That's when I was three or four. We would sit around it and play. And a flock of goats with bells would pass by and we would go down and ask for milk. He would grab one of the goats and milk it. He would bring you the milk to your house. That was the difference between the classes in Libya, between the rich people who lived in the city and the ones who were not as rich and lived in the ghetto. There, everyone was Jewish.

Does the house in Savyon symbolize the richness of his grandfather's house? Are his openness and his mischievousness rooted in the happiness of his mother's house, with the bucket from the well, the drawer full of junk, and the goats' milk? Vittorio's thoughts also wander from Libya to Israel.

Here in Israel, I made trouble like no one else had. I broke the door to the classroom. Why? I remember that I was in school and you could do whatever you wanted to because the teacher couldn't control the class. So every time she would kick me out of class, I would take stones like this, boom. That's the way I finished off the door to the school. I made a hole over two feet wide in it. I did that all the time. And they never expelled me for three days. The next day I would go back to school. That was then the system in Israel.

Over the years I changed for the better. But I remember that it was a difficult period. I remember that the shoes were small, they would cut them to make room for my toes. We wore them like that in winter too because we didn't have the money to buy new ones. It's that simple. Even someone who had the money couldn't buy, because there were coupons for shoes. I'm talking about the fifties, it was during the time of [the finance minister] Dov Yosef, what's called the time of austerity. I look at the children today with all of those things like Levis. Who had things like that then? There was barely food. But my mother always knew how to manage. She raised chickens and turkeys in the garden, I don't know if she told you, and we lived off of that. She would sell them and that's the way we barely managed.

I came to Israel, I fit in with the Sabras. My mother had her views from the old country, to watch over, to keep the children shut up in the house. Every day she would yell into the street: "Vittorio," and I would go up and answer her: "Kuza, what?" I already had a nickname then. They called me "Vittorio Kuza." I would leave early in the morning and go to Ramat Efal. Today it's a very expensive area with nice houses. In our time, it was Kibbutz Efal, a kibbutz that had fallen apart. And around it there was a fence with sabra fruits. You go to the sabras at five o'clock in the morning, the briars are still wet, in order to pick them. There was a wonderful well there and we would go straight to it and wash off the sabras. That was a wonderful experience. And we would sell the sabras where the rich people lived and, relatively, we would make a lot of money. I would go home with ten Israeli pounds. Do you know what that is? A construction worker made five and I made ten as a child. I would work selling ice. There weren't refrigerators then. I would deliver the ice from the store to the houses. I made a make-shift wagon, connected it to my body, and dragged it. It was a baby carriage. I put a crate on it and inside it a few blocks of ice. I would charge three pennies for a piece of ice, which was a third of the block. I made a lot of money from jobs like that. And that's how I learned how to manage and I also helped out at home a bit. Today I work near Efal. Where are the sabras and where is the well? You know what? I swear to you, if I could have that experience again, I would. But I can't, it's over.

Vittorio looks out the window, lost in nostalgia. We sit quietly for a few minutes and then I ask: "Can you tell me a little bit more about your immigration to Israel?"

I don't remember dates and periods because I was a little boy. We spent a short time in Italy and we needed to immigrate. We could have stayed there, but my brother immigrated before us and my mother was crazy about him. She wanted to see him and she pressured Father to leave. We got to a transit camp in Italy. They put us up and we needed to go on. But then they found that my father . . . they didn't let him immigrate like that. They needed to take care of him there. My mother wasn't prepared to wait for Father: "Stay here, we are going." The trip on the ship to Eilat, it was a miracle that we arrived in Israel. We thought we were going to drown during the whole trip. The entire boat filled up with water and all the people came out: "Ho, go out and pray, start fasting, put on your *tefillin*" [phylacteries worn while praying]. People actually prayed because the waves covered the boat. I guess the boat was old and not suitable for trips of that sort. We barely managed to arrive. That's the way we arrived in Haifa.

And then we went through that experience where they put everyone into a little shack of about three feet by three feet and they deloused us. They sprayed us with DDT. They took us from there in trucks to immigrant camps, to tents, the kind that you see in the army. And that same night we were in a tent like that, the burrs reached the bed. They didn't have tractors then to clean the area and you couldn't clear them away with your hands. And I remember that during that night there were winds and the tent flew away and I was a little boy. I won't forget that we had a sugar jar made of aluminum with a top that had a little knob on it and it flew away in the wind and I ran after it to catch it because it was still empty. That's what we brought with us.

"What did you know about Israel from abroad?"

Nothing. What did we have to do with Israel? My brother was influenced by the propaganda that they had when the State was established. That's why he left home and everything. He left school, he left everything with a lot of other young people. They put themselves in danger. I think that he was a legal immigrant, but there were a lot of illegal immigrants. They would board a ship and immigrate. I remember the riots in Libya, those I remember. It was Shevuot, I think, and my aunt was visiting us, and we lived in the center of town and, all of a sudden, we felt that there was a change. I didn't see anything, but my brother did, and he told us about it. He saw an older woman, a Jew. They caught her at the junction, they butchered her and . . . the riots began. They killed everybody that came along. But then the British came and they got involved. An hour after the rioting began, the British soldiers arrived and they fell into their ranks, I remember. As if they were making order. They always made sure to arrive after things were over because they were also afraid of the Arabs. I think that they were British that had been expelled from Israel to Libya. That's what they told us anyway. One day there was a big march and they arrived, they were expelled from Israel.

"What did you know about the Holocaust?"

I told you about how we complained that we didn't have electricity or water and conditions were hard. They had it good. They were happy. Because they had come straight from the concentration camps. And we had no idea what they had gone through. When we saw it later on in films, what they went through, so of course for anyone who went through the experiences of the concentration camps, it was paradise to move into a tent. But for people like us, who had lived well, it wasn't good for us to live even in a house like that without work and without anything. They also immediately had that arrangement of payments [restitution from Germany]. And then all of the Europeans, I don't want to say the Ash-kenazim, all of the Europeans that lived there, our neighbors, all got a lot of money from Germany, and they left to live in the center of Ramat Gan. In their place came the Yemenites. The neighborhood became a Yemenite neighborhood. We didn't get along so well with those new neighbors.

"Did you hear about what they went through in Europe?"

When we arrived in Israel, my brother joined the nationalist Herut [later Likud] party. He brought a picture of Zeev Jabotinsky, a sort of poster, and he put it up on the wall of the hut. One day a neighbor came in, an Ashkenazi. He was a big, bald man. He came in and saw the picture and that man went into shock. "What's gotten into you?" "Ahh," he said, "if we had listened to that man, then there wouldn't have been a Holocaust. He warned us, I will never forget that, I was a little boy. 'Leave Germany and go to Israel. There's nothing for you here. We need to build a State.' We sent him away, we took him off the stage. We spat at him and said: 'Get out of here, we don't want to hear you talk. You are speaking nonsense.' We were living there like kings and that man saw it coming. He saw the Holocaust coming, Jabotinsky. Nothing helped. If we had listened to that man, there wouldn't have been a Holocaust. Six million Jews would still be alive." I will never forget that scene.

We grew up with Beitar [the Herut youth movement]. To this day, Liat is still carrying it on. During the elections, we worked for Beitar a lot. We gave one of our rooms to Beitar. We had one room and we gave it to Beitar. Every Saturday we had a youth meeting of Beitar. We would have meetings there before the elections. We would get the glue ready. It's not synthetic glue like there is today, there were barrels of flour and water and we would heat it on the fire in our house. We did all of that as volunteers. Today there is only a certain board that you are allowed to paste notices on. Then, one covered up the other. We covered entire buildings. We would hide. Then, there wasn't the Labor party, there was Mapai. They would go out to put up their signs at two o'clock at night and we would ambush them. We would come with ladders and work on a two-story building, covering it completely.

What you saw in the Intifada, when they threw flags on the electrical wires—we did the same thing. But instead of the Palestinian flag, we would take the letter "H" with a white string and fly it above the electrical wires. The other parties did the same thing, that was the system. It's not like today, where each party has their own board, a specified place where you come and put up notices. That's the way we worked. We volunteered. Nobody got paid anything.

At home we talked angrily about their "pull," about how they managed everything. They came educated, they were people that studied. So it's natural that when someone of that type came they got help. It's possible that if I had been a clerk and someone from my ethnic group would have come, it's possible that I might have helped him more. Do you understand? But children in the streets, in the classroom, or in the neighborhood—we were friends. There was no difference between an Ashkenazi, a Yemenite, and a Moroccan. It depends on the person, that's all. You hear Moroccan and you are already afraid. Once you get to know the

Moroccan, you see that he's a person. Not all of the Moroccans and not all of the Tripolians are like that and not all of the Ashkenazim are like that. There are people like that in every ethnic group. So first people say that people from a certain group aren't good and then you get to know the person.

I am beginning to understand Vittorio's "social map": Beitar means Zeev Jabotinsky, who warned about the Holocaust. The Ashkenazim got reparations, they are educated, and they have special "pull" with their (Labor) party's help. On the other hand, we the children are not concerned with ethnicity, but with relating to people. I ask: "Where did you serve in the army?"

I served in the military police. I had the job of traveling with a convoy at night. It's not work that you do in the daytime where you travel quickly at forty-five or fifty miles per hour. A convoy travels at three miles per hour going uphill and barely gets to seven miles per hour going downhill. My job was to accompany convoys to the south. It was a very hard period. One night I needed to accompany some piece of equipment. We need to transfer all kinds of secret equipment at night, but there wasn't any way to do it. It's cold sitting on a motorcycle and we would ride and ride. After an hour and a half you reach Beer-Sheva. You get off there at the main southern base, you make dinner, me and the drivers. You go on until you reach, what's it called, Tel Yeruham. I can't drive anymore. I am finished.

I say: "Guys, I can't drive any more." "Okay, let's make coffee." Meanwhile, I go sit in their truck to nap a little. They make coffee on a little stove. They give me a cup of coffee and I can't open up my hand because it's so cold. They need to get the equipment to the base before dawn. It's forbidden that anybody see it during the day. They were very slow journeys. I said: "Guys, I can't, I can't go on with you. Go on by yourself or wait here." So they went on by themselves, and I started wandering around there. They said that there was a base somewhere nearby at Tel Yeruham. I got there at eleven o'clock at night but there was no one there. I arrived and asked the guard to let me in and sleep. "What are you doing here?" I said: "I got stuck." He called the officer and said: "There's a guy who has come to sleep here." He said: "Okay, let him in." They gave me a bed. It's a battle-cruiser and they get up at four o'clock in the morning to make their rounds. It was before Sinai, when the border was here in Nizzana, in Gaza. I got up with them, I want to get back to my base. I barely move for the first few miles. Such winds! Storms! It's impossible to ride. I go into first gear, second gear, third gear, I can't ride. The rain was going into my eyes. I stood that way on the road. Everyone who goes by thinks that I am waiting to give someone a report. And I stand there with my motorcycle waiting for someone to come by. But I got used to it. You're not sensitive to water anymore. You are completely wet anyway, it doesn't matter, it's all the same.

A truck comes by, I wave it off the road, I stop it. They probably think that I want to check it or something. "What's up?" "I'm stuck." I said: "My motorcycle is broken and I can't get it going." I was ashamed to tell them that I couldn't ride my motorcycle. "Okay." We put it onto the truck. You know those trucks that bring supplies for the morning? We got to Beer-Sheva and they went into the gas station to fill up with gas and I see another truck. "Where are you going?" "Castina." I said: "Please come here." I am a policeman, right? He turned around and we transferred the motorcycle from one truck to the other. Meanwhile, they hadn't heard from me at the base. I hadn't arrived at Ketziot at night with the convoy and I had disappeared. They had begun searching for me. There weren't incidents like there are today where soldiers are kidnapped, but they were worried anyway until I got back to the base the next morning.

Now, with his way of making do and "managing," Vittorio sounds completely Israeli.

There were other experiences. I worked with deserters, I caught them. One day I was in Natanya at an army resort. I met a military police corporal. He said: "Perhaps you know—I have a picture of a deserter—his name is Eli. Maybe you know him?" I said: "Yes." It's not enough that he is a deserter, he went to work in the house of the corporal from the military police *(laughs)*. And that is the deserter that I caught at night in Ashkelon. I went into his house: "Is Eli here?" "No, he's not home." But I saw on their faces that he was home. I was already an expert in such matters. I said: "Okay, I want to make a search." "Look." I look here and there and I see that in the kitchen there is a sort of curtain that is low. It's a sort of niche. I move back the curtain and I see his feet. I took him out, that bastard, I put handcuffs on him and brought him to the base.

The next day on Shabbat I went home. It was for a memorial service for my father. I told the officer on duty: "Take care of him." He said:

"Don't worry, he won't escape." They sent him in the middle of the day to do something in the kitchen and he never returned. I always walked around with his picture in my pocket. Where didn't I look for him? I looked everywhere. Once every two weeks I would go to the Dead Sea Works, it's easier there. I came with the pictures and with the names. They check their list of names. There weren't computers then. They call them on the loud speakers. Everyone who deserted would go to work there, at the Dead Sea Works, to far-off places. They would come to the office: "They are looking for you."

Paula returns from the kitchen with a tray of fruit and cold drinks, and the conversation continues among the three of us. Vittorio and Paula talk more about their families in Libya, about their family names, their holidays, and the relationships between them and their cousins in Israel. When I leave them at the entrance to their house, Vittorio waves to me until I reach the end of the street. His warm look continues to accompany me for many more hours.

[Dan Bar-On and Noga Gil'ad:] Like Laura, Vittorio begins his biographical reconstruction with the critical events in the framework of his family. He narrates his story without mentioning dates and external events. The first dates he gives are those of the 1945 and 1948 riots in Libya. He and Paula begin with stories about the secure atmosphere of their Libyan household and what it was like to be the children of a warm, well-to-do family insulated from the outside. At the beginning it seems that the family, as in Laura's story, will be the dominant theme upon which Vittorio's life story is based. Like his mother, Vittorio ends his studies and goes to work. He too is fatherless at a young age.

After the early death of his father, Laura's influence on the decisions Vittorio made was very strong: he chose to learn plumbing and construction trades; he married a student-neighbor, whom his mother saw as a replacement for the daughter who died at a young age; his second marriage was to a cousin. This may be typical of North African families, in which parents do influence such decisions. However, it is less typical of the generation that grew up in Israel, where the traditional authority structures came under severe strain. We sense in Vittorio a certain fear, translated into dependency on his mother, that is reminiscent of Tzipke's or Dina's feelings toward their mothers. It is quite unusual, however, for a man to express such dependency openly, especially a man from a North African family.

During his illness and hospital stay (about which we do not have exact information: Was it a mental illness? Was it a physical illness accompanied by a medication-induced depression?), the familial pattern is reinforced when his wife, mother, and mother-in-law rally around to support him. At the same time, and perhaps in spite of his somewhat idealized description of family life, during the three years of his illness, Vittorio and his wife have more and more quarrels. In addition to her husband's illness, Paula has a crisis over her miscarriage. Vittorio concludes with the honest statement: "I think that we didn't get a divorce [then] because she was my cousin. I don't know why, we were embarrassed . . . I had already been divorced once." Perhaps at this point, Vittorio started working through some of his fears, distancing himself from his mother's dominant influence and acting more independently.

At that time also, things began to take a more hopeful turn. Vittorio recovered from his illness, Liat was born, and a year afterward, David. Vittorio began working, made a good living, and undertook the difficult process of building himself a house—his life's dream (which basically meant that he was moving up the socioeconomic ladder). He describes how he persuaded Paula to agree to give up their apartment in Ramat Gan to move to Ashdod and then to their unfinished house in Savyon. Through this story we learn about Vittorio's ambitions and his willingness to take chances, even at the price of "manipulating" his wife. Clearly, he hoped to become integrated into Israeli society.

But his wish for status in Israeli society takes over, especially his desire to live like the "rich." It is not difficult to understand this ambition, especially in view of his parents' extreme hardship after their immigration from Libya. For his parents, it was an economic, cultural, and psychological crisis. Vittorio did not study as a child because of the family's move to Israel: "During that time we became street children." He also adds: "I was never an excellent student, I was always the one who bothered others." A direct expression of his feelings of inferiority comes out in his description of his meeting with his first wife: "To this day I believe that she deserved someone better than me. Somebody on her level, with her education." He learns a profession, but soon there is a recession in the building industry. Over the last few years he has become a meat salesman.

With this statement, he quickly ends his free narration. Is he expressing his success in disengaging himself from his mother's dreams and hopes? During the whole interview, Vittorio has never criticized her.

In relation to his fears about his lack of education and his professional problems, external events also shape his story: his immigration to Israel, the description of his father's exhausting work (as opposed to his wealthy status in Libya), the death of his sister, the period of austerity, and the hard living conditions in the transit camp, all of these are the antithesis of his descriptions of their life in Libya, where he felt protected, prosperous (in his grandmother's house), and happy (in his mother's house). His older brother left for Israel after the Arab riots and the apathetic response of the British, but Vittorio reacted differently: "What did we have to do with Israel?" Is this his way of suggesting that if his brother had not been exposed to the Zionist propaganda and if his mother had not longed to be near her older son, they would never have left Libya or continued on to Israel from Italy?

It is possible to imagine that Vittorio would blame all his failures on the dramatic economic "fall" caused by immigration to Israel. In his narrative, however, a different tendency can be observed, a tendency toward an active struggle for social recognition. Vittorio points to his fights at a younger age: "Here in Israel [in school], I made trouble like no one else had." He continues: "I came to Israel and fit in with all the Sabras." He describes himself leaving home early, freeing himself from his mother's worrying, picking sabras, selling them and making twice what a construction worker made. "If I could have that experience again, I would. But I can't, it's over," he says with sadness, without explaining what exactly was "over." Probably the wish to become an Israeli also helped Vittorio establish a more independent position in his family.

Vittorio also becomes involved in the political struggle in Israel, which for many of the North African Jews was a means of social recognition. "What you saw in the Intifada, when they threw flags on the electrical wires—we did the same thing." At home, in a symbolic manner, they prepared the glue that was used at night to paste up notices by members of Beitar in their confrontation with members of Mapai. It is a war over control, but it is also an ethnic clash: North African Sephardic Jews trying to overcome European Ashkenazi political hegemony. From the perspective of today, Vittorio's external struggles were successful. The struggle with Mapai ended with the election victory of the Likud party in 1977. This was his victory over the Ashkenazi, the "educated" Europeans who reaped government benefits, sprayed him and his family with DDT upon their arrival in Israel, humiliated his father with back-breaking work, and were probably connected in Vittorio's own mind with his sister's death (which Laura attributed to a lack of medical attention at the hospital).

The fact that some of the Ashkenazim were Holocaust survivors did not spare them from the basic rift between North African and European Jews. First, Vittorio relates to them with ironic scorn: for them, the transit camp conditions were "deluxe" after what they went through. Later, in the encounter around Jabotinsky's poster, Vittorio's hidden criticism of them is further revealed, although framed in the words of his neighbor: " 'If we had listened to that man, then there wouldn't have been a Holocaust . . . Six million Jews would still be alive.' I will never forget that scene." Perhaps unintentionally, Vittorio has adopted the judgmental Israeli view prevalent toward Holocaust survivors in the fifties and sixties, which was based on the accusation that they went "like lambs to the slaughter."

Unlike his mother, who at least tried to express—at a distance—her sorrow and identification, Vittorio shows no sympathy or emotion about the fate of Holocaust survivors. In his attitude it is possible to read a kind of double message: "If the subject is suffering, we also suffered and our pain is no less legitimate than theirs. If the subject is extermination, then we did not go through that because we came from a civilized country like Libya and because you did not heed people's warnings like those of Jabotinsky." However, in Vittorio's reconstruction there is no bitterness toward those who persecuted his family. He does not react to the "Europeans" with a zero-sum attitude—if you win, I lose. Is it due to his settling down in Savyon? To the Likud coming into power? To his easygoing nature? Whatever the case, he concludes: "it depends on the person," not his or her ethnic origin.

Vittorio has slowly but steadily constructed his narrative as a success story, starting when he freed himself from the control of his own fears and his mother's expectations, and when his material success helped him by introducing hope. Clearly, however, it was not always a success story. One can still sense the fear and helplessness that dominated several periods of his life (immigration, school, his divorce, and his illness). In that respect, both of his tales from the days of his military service as an MP express this combination: on the one hand, during the night convoy, his remark, "Guys, I can't drive any more" is a symbol of his anxieties about measuring up to his own as well as to society's demands. At the same time, the power he feels in becoming part of the establishment shows through when he catches the deserter: "I took him out, that bastard, I put handcuffs on him and brought him to the base."

Vittorio's reconstruction is reminiscent of Dina Anisevitch's: like her, he sanctifies "Israeliness" with symbols and nostalgia. His struggle has a personal character (freeing himself from his mother's expectations) as well as a political one (freeing himself from the way Europeans defined his people). In Dina's reconstruction we identified a hidden wish to be independent of her mother, to enjoy herself, and to liberate herself from the Israeli values imposed on the Holocaust (redemption versus survival). However, there are also differences between the two. Socially and politically, Dina is "in," since she is a member of the dominant group of European Jews. She does not even need to mention it in her narrative. But Vittorio has had to fight his way to social recognition. He chose to build a house in Savyon as a sign of his new social status. On the other hand, it is relatively easy for him to move back and forth between the past "there" and the present "here." He can relate to his personal and family life in Libya as his mother does, without risking the threatening presence of the Holocaust, a presence that seems to have paralyzed not only Dina's freedom of recollection, but also that of Tzipke, Hannah, Ya'acov, and Tamar.

Liat

"My motto was to prove myself"

When Liat leads me to her room, a thought goes through my head: it is like a dream—everything is pink. She sits down across from me, her dark hair falling around her shoulders. Her large eyes remind me of her grandmother. She is very reserved—perhaps embarrassed by the interview? Her hands rest on her thighs throughout our conversation. In the Guetta family, for the first time, I have to ask an opening question: "Can you tell me something about yourself? If you wish, you can start from childhood."

From the beginning, from age zero, ahh? I was born in 1972—the eldest child. The first place that I lived in was Ramat Gan. A year and two months later, my brother was born. At age five I moved to Ashdod. There my other brother was born. At age seven I moved to Savyon and, since then, I am still here. What do you mean by "tell about myself"? Just in general, about everything?

"About anything you want."

My life story? Good. At age five I went through a crisis when my grandfather died. I was very close to him. And when my grandfather died, I grew up a lot all at once. I remember the incident well. He died, it was before my birthday. He died suddenly and I didn't really understand what people were telling me, but I understood that something was missing. I remember those days as if it was yesterday. It was really one of the hardest periods that I went through. All of a sudden, I was grown-up. I think that since then, since then I have become more mature, because I, the way that I look at it, the way that others look at it, I am a few years older than children in my age group. The things that I am doing today I will talk about later. And the things that I always did, I was always different. It also has its negative side, but that doesn't matter. It really made me more mature. The feeling of . . . of loss, that since then, I haven't had that same feeling again. I hope that I won't feel it again, it was really, really hard.

The second time that I went through a very difficult thing was when I moved to Savyon. Until then, my childhood had been very nice. I really enjoyed living in Ashdod. I was the leader of my group of friends, and all of a sudden, I moved here and my self-esteem went way down, as they say. I became very introverted, very difficult, I didn't get along, I didn't find myself for a long time. I had a hard time in school. I had a hard time with the other children. It was very difficult for me. But I also found a few friends that . . . I got along with. It was okay. Later on, I was twelve when I went into junior high, it was really a wonderful period. A very nice period of . . . feeling "in" in the group, being one of the leaders. Again, the feeling of being important.

I didn't start off so well in school, but I had a teacher who gave me the right reinforcement in order to succeed. And so I progressed more and more quickly so that in the end, my achievements were good. But then, I was struck by a lack of trust from the teacher with whom I finished. When I went into high school, she recommended a very low level program for me. And I accepted it at the beginning, without . . . without fighting it. It's a very important matter, because it determines the future, I think. Just in order to emphasize the point, I finished the ninth grade with an 89 percent grade average and they recommended that I go into a non-academic program. About a month into summer vacation, I decided by myself to go to the high school counselor and to ask to be transferred to another program. They transferred me into the humanities program with the intention of transferring me into the biology program later, but I didn't want to go so far. Okay, high school, which is what I am finishing now, was three years of fun. It was a little hard, but with ambition and the right dreams, you can succeed. I really enjoyed the social aspect. No, I don't give a lot of importance to friendships in high school, because I never wanted a special relation with them. Maybe, due to the circumstances, I didn't want a special relation. I just preferred to have my friends from wherever they came from and I didn't actively pursue that part. Not like the kids who go to school in order to make friends.

I think that this year was significant for me. It's my last year. During this year, what happened to me is that I began working. By coincidence I found a job and I stayed there. I am working for the Likud party in the *Histadrut* [workers' union]. I began working during the elections and I remained because I wanted to stay and so I put all of my heart and soul into the work and it was really a lot of work. It's possible to work and go to school at the same time, but it's not simple. I didn't believe that I would finish out the year. But, I am extremely happy, I learned a lot there. The work makes me think about things and I was exposed to bigger issues. It widens one's horizons to an amazing extent. I discovered things that had been very distant from me, and today I think I can say that it is one of the important things that has happened to me. It also adds additional desires for the long run. I give up on going out in order to put all of myself into my work. I know that I need to do well in school, [it may be due to] social pressures or other things, but I need to do well. And I do the work because I love it. And when I love something, I am willing to work hard at it. I think that if I have central traits, they are stubbornness and principles. I stand up for my principles, I don't give in a lot or easily and . . . again, it's ambition. Whatever I want I will try to get, even if it costs me a lot. Even if it costs me a lot.

I am surprised at the clear opinions and self-awareness of an eighteen-

year-old girl. I notice that Liat speaks in the present tense in the same way her grandmother did.

Okay, so I had a pair of parents, parents who are cousins. In my opinion, that only adds because . . . it's one big family. It's amazing how good I feel at home. I just enjoy myself. Both of them are good company. That sounds very harmonious, but that's the way it is. At home, I get a lot of admiration . . . sometimes I think that they exaggerate a bit, but I really do get a lot of esteem. I am very much involved in what goes on here and . . . it gives me the feeling that I feel good about myself. It's great being involved. It's very good for me to be involved in everything. I like knowing everything about everyone. Maybe it's negative, but it's good for me. In our house, our way of life is like a nest. And I believe that everyone needs the same nest, the same family that will defend and take care of you. My feeling is that . . . that here, all of my needs are met.

No matter how many good friends I have, and no matter [if I am] in how many places, of all different types, I always feel that at some point I will be betrayed. But the family will always be here, I can always find refuge here. My parents, I openly admire both of them. There are other things that I agree with a little bit less and I love less about them. I have two brothers; with one I get along better, with the other less so. He is more of a rebel and he compromises less. I already said that I am stubborn and so it doesn't go so well together. With my younger brother, since he was born, I gave him a lot, I loved him a lot. So when he was born, I was six years old, he was my entire world. I put everything into the relationship, I did everything for him, so we became very close. I think that since then, we have become very close due to that. So I really live with him in harmony, because it is simply fun.

I suddenly recall Laura's story about how she raised her little brother after her father's death.

Now in my social life, I always had girlfriends. But, I trusted them too much and I always got hurt. Perhaps today I am wiser, because today I won't let situations like that repeat themselves, but there were times when I got hurt. Sometimes from those that I was sure were my good friends and they would do anything for me and it turned out that the exact opposite was the case. I think that those things made me not only critical but also distrustful. I still have my good friends that I trust, but ahh . . . it's not like it once was. I won't give everything into these friendships, I won't give my whole self. I will not trust any of them one hundred percent. Friends are not family, and friends are a function of how much they need me. That gave me a lot to think about.

I understand from Liat's tone of voice that she is hurt, but she gives me no clue to what exactly she is speaking about.

I am very possessive. I like it when people are mine and I will know that they are mine and only mine. I am also very loyal, that is, I remain loyal. I don't know how others will look at that, but when I belong to someone, I will really be all of myself and I will never think about other things. Perhaps I hurt others, I am sure that I hurt others, but it . . . it was never done with malice, perhaps naively. Today I am more, my thinking is sharper in the way that, I would say . . . I think how they will think about things in an improper way. Perhaps I learned that from my place of work, because it is a political organization. You take everything into account in these areas, so I will look at things differently. But I will still remain basically naive. It's a sort of childish naiveté. I look at the purity and perhaps I will be let down and hurt, but that is the force of fate and coming face to face with cruel fate will teach me more and more until, in the end, I will change.

I wonder whether Liat is referring to relationships between men and women but is not able to give it a name. She seems to read my thoughts.

My experience with loyalty and . . . love and all that, I have only experienced the bitter side of love. That is, with how terrible it was . . . things were small in proportion, but they had a big influence on me. I was very much affected, I always got hurt. I know that it sets me up for future failures and that it makes me wiser, but somewhere I say: "I don't want to be like that, I don't want to be wiser." They really were small instances, just a small number of boys, three or four. They all made me think twice about . . . about relationships with boys . . . in a different light. My girlfriend said that I was like those cats that fall and, even though they crush their legs, they stand up on them. That is true, because even if I am hurt, cut down and hurt at my deepest and most sensitive point, I will act as if nothing had happened, as if nobody hurt me, as if I am fine, and I will smile and laugh and have a good time. Only way down inside, I may be crushed and really feel the pain, but I will act as if nothing bothers me. Maybe it's good and maybe it's not. There is a category of people who know when I feel good and when I don't. These people know me and read me. They know when I am acting and when I am being genuine. But, I am basically an actress and I act as if the situation is different. There are people who find all kinds of traits in me that I don't agree with. There are those that say that I am a snob, conceited, perhaps because I don't smile at everyone on the street. I don't know why. I know that I, it's one of my most basic traits, I will give everything to my people. I will also not look for the negative side in people, rather focus on the positive points, and I really try to be all right in this aspect. I think that I also live in the shadow.

I always tried . . . my motto was to prove myself. I already mentioned that they told me in junior high school that they were sending me into the nonacademic program and I insisted on going into the humanities program. The fact is that I finished with high grades. And there was someone who tried . . . I don't know whether or not to stop me, I don't know whether it was intentional or not, but she looked at me differently, and I always needed to be strong and to prove myself. That was a matter of principle. If I look at that, during many stages of my life I needed to work, to work hard to show that I am capable and . . . it was at home that I got support and encouragement. There were times when I also needed to prove myself to them. Even during the move from junior high to high school. They also thought that I should go into an easier program, that I would work less hard and that my grades would be okay. I don't know how much they knew I was capable of doing. So I became ambitious and it pushed me forward. They say that you are born with it, it's a matter of character. So, maybe I wasn't born with it, but due to the circumstances, I became like that.

If there is something that I respect in myself, it is in this area. Even if I go against the stream—and even if I am at the edge of . . . the breaking point, I will do everything in order to succeed. I don't know whether it is to prove to others or to myself, but I need to prove myself. Really, when everyone said that I wouldn't succeed in the twelfth grade, you won't succeed . . . so okay, I got back at seven o'clock in the evening from work and I sat until one o'clock in the morning doing my homework. I did it, because I loved it and I wanted to show the others that I can do it. I am the kind of person who likes asking questions, the more that I get to deeper questions, the fewer answers I have. I am curious, yes, I am always very curious. I think I was blessed with perhaps too much of this trait. I think that I am also thorough, that whatever they give me to do I will try to do in the most thorough manner. The part about my negative traits, I am sensitive about that. No matter how I pretend to be, I am very sensitive and I may get hurt. I will get hurt only by those who are dear to me. But I care about many people . . . when I get hurt it really leaves a scar. Even though scars, in the end, make you tougher, until you become tougher, you only feel the pain more and more, and that really is negative. There are those who say that to be sensitive is a blessing, to a limited extent, that is. For me, however, it is not so limited.

"The more that I get to deeper questions, the fewer answers I have." A deep thought for a young person. However, Liat means that some of these questions are also very painful for her. "You mentioned your grandfather as being very significant for you. Do you remember him?"

A lot. I think that he is one of the best people that I had the honor of knowing. Indeed, he died when I was five, but I remember him very well. It was the fact that he went at least twice a week from Bat Yam or Ramat Gan to wherever I lived in order to come and be with me. At that time, I was a very significant part of his life. He was very loving, he was very giving. It was he who taught me to write my name, something that I will never forget. At some point he suffered from a disability, he lost a leg. However, he continued to be the same grandfather that gave a lot of himself. He didn't function as well, but he always gave of himself. Every day that he would come with his wafers and chocolate and he would sit with me twice or three times in the afternoons. I think that that period of childhood, the time when a child learns trust, so it is exactly then that I learned to trust him and I learned to trust other people, but with him it wasn't the same *(pause)*.

Maybe it was because of this aspect that his death affected me so much. He got sick before that and they tried to prepare me for it, as much as you can prepare a little girl, but all of a sudden, one day they came home and said that Grandfather, that Grandfather had died. Where did he go? My grandmother from my father's side explained that he went to heaven, so I asked to go up to heaven too and things like that. They really saw that I was having a crisis. Until I slowly understood what happened and that he would never come back. He . . . he was a wonderful man, a very good man. Until this day, when they talk about him, about me, they always bring up the part about how much he loved me, that he loved me more than anyone else *(crying)*.

When I got to the hospital I couldn't, I couldn't see him. It wasn't only embarrassment, it was . . . perhaps, it was mixed with a sort of fear. After all, I was a little girl. Perhaps I was four. I assume, I don't know, that when I went to the hospital, I didn't like it, perhaps I was even a little bit disgusted by him for a certain period of time afterwards. It is possible that all of a sudden a grandfather came to me who limps a little. A little girl, maybe I was a little bit embarrassed that I would see him like that. But that passed very quickly. That is, very quickly I learned to accept him the way he was, but I will never forget that visit to the hospital. I even remember the chocolate that he tried to give me to eat and I didn't want it. That's exactly the way that it was.

I remember how we sat and he taught me how to write my name one afternoon. I remember it really well, as if it was yesterday. And also after the surgery, I now remember more about the specific event. He would slide with me down the slide, he would do everything. That is, he returned to being completely active with me. I enjoyed him very much. It's just that that part comes back to me often, the part with him. Because maybe the fact that it happened so suddenly, I remember the day that the neighbor came and told me to wake up Mother and I said: "Mother said that she doesn't want to get up." Then she said: "Wake her up, something has happened." And my mother went down and her sister and boyfriend were downstairs and they said that he had died. He just got onto the bus and he died of a heart attack. Those are the things that I remember and I don't think that I will forget them. That's my grandfather's story.

"How was your relationship with your grandmother?"

Always good. To this day, if I thought that he was the best man in the world, then she is the best woman in the world for me. I really think that there aren't a lot of women who are better than my grandmother. It's simply that no matter what you do or whatever happens, she will look at it from the most positive perspective in the world. If somebody will steal something from her she will say: "The poor man, he must have needed it." She is simply a woman who does not know how to look at the world from a more egocentric angle. And her children and grandchildren are the most important things in her life. She will do everything for them. I mean everything. She also knows how important I was to Grandpa. She and him, they always had a wonderful relationship.

I love her very much, she is simply a woman who does not know how to do a little bit less than her best for everyone. I am not saying this because she is my grandmother. Everyone will say that about her. There is someone who says that I am like her. I think he is mistaken, I don't reach her level, even if I really try. With her, it is simply natural. That's the way she is, she is like that. She will simply look at everyone and have mercy for everyone. Perhaps she is naive, perhaps there is even a bit of silliness, but it is harmonious to live with someone like that, the most perfect of the perfect. I haven't met so many people that I can say something like that, but I still allow myself to say that there aren't many people like her, and it is not because she is my grandmother.

"Did you hear stories from your grandmother and grandfather about their childhood? About your mother's childhood?"

Yes. To this day I hear from my grandmother about the good life that they had abroad and about the hard time of immigration to Israel. They pretty much lost their status; to enjoy life there and to come here and learn about life the hard way. They immigrated via Italy, part of the family remained in Italy and they could have stayed there too, but they came here. My grandfather was simply broken. If it is because in the beginning his daughter fell in the transit camp and died when she was little or because he got sick and . . . died. Somebody said that if he continued the good life there, without having to fight over money, and suddenly come here and feel what it is like to live under austerity. All of a sudden, they take away all of the good things to which you are accustomed, then the suffering is really significant. It was a drastic change for both of the families because in many ways they felt good abroad. When the persecutions and pogroms began, my grandfather from my mother's side became very Zionistic and he fought for what he believed, even if he got into trouble over it. And he did get into trouble. But the main part that they tell me about is their immigration process and all of the stages. They had it very hard. People looked down on the group from North Africa. Those are the painful things, things that leave deep, deep scars.

But, in my opinion, both of them succeeded in the task of raising children, having families. They raised them in Jaffa in a neighborhood that wasn't so good. Still, fourteen and seventeen are ages at which you pick up things from the environment. If there is something that I remember, that Grandma would emphasize, it isn't really the part about how good they had it abroad, but rather how hard it was here in Israel. She needed to work three jobs just in order to make sure her children would get everything she thought she needed to give them. I think that the same story comes back to her each time she feels a little hurt about family matters. Then she really goes back to it and emphasizes it. She will remember to remind me about those same days when she suffered in order to provide for them.

I needed to do a family project and I came to her and said: "Go ahead and tell me." I remember that things I really didn't know that much about I discovered all of a sudden. Then I discovered just how much of a Zionist my grandfather really was. I didn't know that he was like that at all. Actually the stories about him really interested me. The stories about the trouble he got into with his Arab neighbors. I really admired that part about his being a patriot, to feel the values that are deep and real. There is even a specific story that he almost lost his right eye from an incident like that. I also remember the story about the market street. Then they took out some postcards, I don't remember so well, I did that project when I was twelve. I think that is already an age when one begins to know what questions to ask, but it was really a chance to get answers.

"Do you remember what made you decide to go to the counselor in order to change school programs?"

It is an amazing story. I went clothes shopping in the Indian Head store. And the saleswoman said, we just began talking, and she said: "You are finishing junior high school and going to high school. What high school are you going to? Three years of fun." She said that in those words. "You will have fun." I said yes, okay, good. Then she said: "What program? The nonacademic program? Can't you get into another program? What are your grades like?" I said: 89 percent, that was my exact average, with a very good grade in biology. "Are you going along with that? Don't you want them to admire you?!" That was really the slap in the face that woke me up. The next day I phoned the school. The counselor was out of the country, I got a hold of her. She told me that she would take out my file and that I should come. I arrived, she came out of her room and said: "It's okay, it's final, you are in the humanities program. If you want to, you can even go into the biology program."

To this day, I am thankful that I didn't go into the nonacademic program because I know what would have happened to me. I would have caught on very quickly that it is not for me. Not only would they not evaluate my potential, but I would have only used up a small percentage of it. Really, the level there is very low. The program is for learning how to be a nanny, and once a week they have practical work at a daycare center. There are stories about students who lost their potential because of mistakes like these. And I almost lost mine. And it was all due to the same teacher, who didn't really believe in me.

I remember, by coincidence, exactly one week ago, there was a graduation party last Thursday and I met her and she said to me: "So, Liat, did you finish?" She liked me very much but had no faith in me. I said: "Yes, Regina, I finished quite well." And it was like a type of sweet revenge to tell her. I felt very hurt. Later on, I found out that she told my girlfriends: "Liat will not manage to do well on her matriculation exams." It amazed me that she could reach such conclusions. Based on what? That is what proved to me that if someone is motivated, sometimes it is more important than their potential. Two weeks ago I went clothes shopping in another store and the same girl from Indian Head was working there and she didn't remember me, but I remember her well.

It was the saleswoman she met by chance rather than the teacher who "loved" her who helped her find her way. It is clear why she questions whom can she trust. "You mentioned your work in the Likud party. Can you tell a little more about it?"

Yes. I was always in the Likud youth. And I always volunteered when there were elections. I liked giving of myself because I believed in it and I wanted to. Last summer our director said that before the elections to the *Histadrut,* we are having primaries and we need to work for pay. We will film voters' stories and all kinds of things like that. So I went to work for them. It was really very nice. One day someone from the Likud party in the *Histadrut* came up. He was in charge, but we didn't have direct contact with him and he said: "We are missing a secretary today. Send me one of your girls." They sent me down. On the first day, I didn't know how to function. I answered phones and that's all I needed to do. On the second day as well as on the third that's what I did, and then one of the clerks decided that he needed me to be his secretary. That flattered me a lot and I immediately decided that I was going to work for him, and of course, I didn't hesitate for a moment. I got along with him very well, everyone was amazed at how I managed with him, because he was a difficult man, really something. First, I didn't understand what the big deal was. Very quickly I discovered that he was not as easy a man as I had thought. Within two days I was into things and it was really good; all the work of accounting, money, and personnel. At the beginning, perhaps I understood less what I was doing, but very quickly I got responsibilities and authority, much more than I had expected.

I remember that alongside me, they brought in another secretary to learn the job because I had begun twelfth grade, and it wasn't expected that I would manage to do both things. So they brought in another secretary and I . . . and I didn't try to mess her up, but I didn't help her succeed either in taking over my job quickly. Really, I didn't do anything bad. But I felt that I had achieved something and I wanted to keep it. In less than two days he called me into his room and said: "Liat, listen, I can't go on this way. The funds will wait until four o'clock in the afternoon when you arrive here from school." At that moment, I felt that I had earned my place in the world. And then I really worked hard, because before the elections we worked so hard you wouldn't believe it. I would arrive at work at four o'clock and go home at eight or nine at night after a lot of work. Organizing all of the funds before the elections is really, not just responsibility, it's really an effort. And we got to the point where the woman who worked with him kept for me . . . collected all of the work from the day and only helped me when I arrived. Then I really enjoyed myself, I really enjoyed myself.

All of a sudden I felt all of the positive rewards from my environment. "Look, a girl sixteen and a half, seventeen years old and look what she does and how she holds things together." And all of a sudden all my friends were over thirty-five and forty, people with families. I was little, but I managed very nicely with them. And I think that if something good happened to me lately it was just that. It also made the time go by very quickly. All of a sudden I stood up for myself, all of a sudden I was more stubborn, gave up less. I had what to learn and from whom to learn. And I think that I managed to inspire trust because people learned what I was really capable of doing. The person I work with says: "No university will teach you as well as work, because it is a different kind of university. It is, it is life." To learn from life about real situations—less theory and more real fieldwork. Sometimes I find myself saying: "After all, you are seventeen and a half, see yourself with your head on your shoulders, without big dreams." And then I say that without big dreams, it is impossible to succeed. I have a conflict with myself over that, but it doesn't matter. I also felt economic independence, because all of a sudden I was making money and not only from baby-sitting. I took driving lessons and paid for them, things like that, in order to show that I can manage by myself. Nobody reaches success on the straight path. There are always a few curves. There are those with more and those with less. I really worked hard on that part, I worked hard because that was my job and that is what I took upon myself and it didn't have a lot of complications. That is a very important thing that happened to me.

"No university will teach you as well as work, because it is a different kind of university. It is life." Liat and I talk a little bit more about holidays in her family and about Jewish tradition, but I feel that it is much less interesting to her than the dreams and possibilities opening up before her and making them come true.

[Dan Bar-On and Noga Gil'ad:] Like her father and grandmother, Liat reconstructs her biography within the framework of her family, starting with the death of her grandfather, which became such a critical event in her life (as the deaths of their fathers were to Laura and Vittorio?). However, Liat's narrative is dominated by her struggle for social recognition within the Israeli context. If we thought that Vittorio's decision to move to Savyon opened the way for his daughter to feel well established, we hear from Liat that it only marked the beginning of her struggle. Liat shows an extraordinary degree of self-awareness. As a young woman, she is faced with a social reality very different from the familiar one Laura or Vittorio's wife, Paula, encountered in Tripoli, and she has to find her own way by herself.

Liat's narrative begins, much like Dafna's and Idit's, with brief formal statements ("I was born in 1972") of a kind that are conspicuously absent from the beginning of the interviews with her father and grandmother, and she continues on a course of intense self-examination. In comparison to her grandmother, who comes to terms with her life and with herself, and to her father, who had his own difficulties with acceptance, Liat is much more focused on her efforts to gain external recognition. It is interesting that her first reaction to the request to tell her life story is to describe two crises, her grandfather's death and her move to Savyon. (Ganit Belinsky responded in a similar way.) These two events perhaps symbolize the tensions in Liat's life—between love and rejection, helplessness and control, and the family's prosperous past and difficult present.

The death of her grandfather when Liat was five marks the loss of a figure from "there" who loved her unconditionally. Later, it becomes clear that Liat was the grandchild he loved the most, as everyone is constantly reminding her. This is her first experience of such loss: "All of a sudden, I was grown-up." Does she consider this the end of her childhood (as it was for her grandmother when her father died)? Did her struggle begin then? The crisis of the move to Savyon is one of seeking a place in society: "I was the leader of my group of friends, and all of a sudden, I moved here and my self-esteem went way down." Indeed, Liat found her place in Savyon, but this achievement was the result of a struggle to feel "in," to be one of the leaders, to feel important. Later on, she outlines the new rules of the game: "I will smile and laugh ... Only way down inside, I may be crushed." In Ashdod, she had been a natural leader; in Savyon she is a leader only through enormous effort and self-control.

The tension between the image of the harmonious family that protects and is protected, and the external world in which she constantly has to struggle, is a second theme that recurs throughout Liat's interview. To begin with, there is her loving grandfather, who visits her and teaches her to write her name. After a brief crisis at the hospital, when she is afraid to confront his disability, she was able to return to enjoying him until the day he died. Her grandmother is "the most perfect of the perfect." People say that she is like her, but Liat adds, "I don't reach her level ... With her, it is simply natural." It is that way with her younger brother and with her parents as well. "It's amazing how good I feel at home. I just enjoy myself." And then, the contrast: "No matter how many good friends I have ... of all different types, I always feel that at some point I will be betrayed. But the family will always be here, I can always find refuge here." And again, "friends are not family, and friends are a function of how much they need me."

The home is a harmonious refuge. Out in the world there are betrayals and relationships based on utility. Liat's sensitivity causes her to be hurt again and again: she is naive, she trusts people, and even her best friends breach her trust. She is aware of the fact that perhaps she hurts others, but she adds immediately, "it was never done with malice." Hurt and disappointment also accompany her first experiences with boyfriends, but she only hints at these relationships and does not provide any details. At another point, Liat suggests that motivation is "more important than potential." Is she hinting here that she constantly has to make up for something missing in herself? Perhaps she is afraid she does not have enough ability, echoing her father's and her grandmother's feelings of intellectual inferiority.

This fear becomes obvious at the time of her move from junior high to high school. Her teacher, who "liked me very much but had no faith in me," referred her to a nonacademic program. Liat had almost come to terms with that decision, but after a coincidental conversation with a young saleswoman in a store, she decided to fight and asked to be transferred to an academic program. At that point, even her parents, who had always given her support, proved indecisive: "I don't know how much they knew I was capable of." Liat proves to herself and others what she is capable of. In the twelfth grade, in addition to her matriculation exams, she works for the Likud party in a responsible position. She earns her own living and she simultaneously achieves high grades. At the end of the year, she tells her teacher: "Yes, Regina, I finished quite well." It is a "sweet revenge," and Liat does not let her teacher know how much she has been hurt.

Through her work in the Likud party, she realizes what she can learn from her job. "Less theory and more real fieldwork." "It is, it is life." It is clear to her that she wants to progress; the question is how and in what way. In her struggles for love, power, and a place in society, we also see a continuation of Laura's and Vittorio's story in the third generation of immigrants from the North African countries. But Liat is the first one who speaks openly of the way they were treated in Israel: "They had it very hard. People looked down on the group from North Africa. Those are the painful things, things that leave deep, deep scars."

For Liat the wonderful past in Libya and the difficult beginning in Israel are much more black and white than they are for her father or grandmother. She tells wonderful stories of Libya along with those about the hard times that they had during the immigration process, Miriam's death in childhood, and the loss of social status that "broke" her grandfather.

While working on her roots project, she contributes new knowledge (which we did not hear from Vittorio or Laura) to the family story: "I discovered just how much of a Zionist my grandfather really was," how he fought against the Arabs, and how he almost lost his right eye. Beyond idealizing the past, does Liat's story also transform it into what is valued as heroism in her present-day context?

Past, Present, and Future

Like the other families whose voices we have heard in this book, the Guetta family lived through war and immigration. But unlike the others, they did not experience the Holocaust as a personal catastrophe that reached into the most private corners of their lives. In the first generation, Laura lived under a fascist regime in Libya that clearly identified with the Nazis. In order to understand the overwhelming differences between the two regimes, however, we would point out that the Italian fascist regime did not undertake a total and systematic annihilation of the Jews, as the Germans did in Europe. Laura went through her own personal suffering—the death of her father, her brother, her husband, and her daughter—but most of her family lived through the war quite safely (the Arab riots occurred later, during British rule). They too immigrated to Israel and put down roots, just as the families of Holocaust survivors did. How are these similarities and differences reflected in the life stories of Laura, Vittorio, and Liat?

We have noted that members of the Guetta family did not use calendar dates. Beyond the cultural practices that may account for this difference, it might also symbolize the minor role of external events in the inner life of a Libyan family. Organized dating of events in the Guetta family began during the riots in Libya and their immigration to Israel. Only Liat—in Israel—begins her life story with her date of birth. Along with the absence of dates, the stories from abroad focus on the private life of the family. External reality begins to influence family life only during the war, gathers momentum during the Arab riots of 1945 and 1948, and continues when the family faces the cultural shock of immigration to Israel.

In Laura's, Vittorio's, and Liat's stories the movement between different time perspectives (past, present, and future) is relatively easy. There are no traumatic periods that are either repressed or especially emphasized.

The stories begin with childhood and continue smoothly into the present. Indeed, all of them reveal an orientation of hope that is associated mainly with the present and the future. While reflecting on the past, the Guetta family can compare it to the present without reviving the piercing pain of Holocaust survivors' memories. Some aspects of the past are idealized in their narratives, while some are not. This is especially conspicuous in Laura's story. One would expect the past to become more and more idealized and to conform to Israeli reality, but we can find signs of this trend only when Liat talks about it. This is also true in relation to tradition. Religion is still a natural part of Laura's life. But Vittorio mocks religious practice when he recalls Yom Kippur (why say "we sinned" over and over when once is enough), and in Liat's story, there is no mention of religion or religious practice.

This does not mean that everything always went smoothly in the Guetta family: fear, personal suffering, distress, confrontation with sudden death, and similar events run through the family's history, and they have left scars that are revealed in their stories. Laura still has guilt feelings about "abandoning" her mother and sisters during the war, and Vittorio had difficulties over the "decline" that occurred when his father went from being a "king" in Libya to a simple laborer in Israel. He was also unnerved by his illness and his professional failures. Liat has her own fears and worries (how much is she worth?). There is a tension between the past and the present, between fear and hope, between remembering and living, but this tension has not been artificially reduced by retreating to one extreme. All three generations of Guettas have tried to deal in an open dialogue with both poles at the same time, a capacity much less evident among the survivors' families.

Their particular perspective allowed the Guetta family to relate to the Holocaust in a different way than the other four families. Laura, the closest to the survivors by age and experience, talked of what she had read and what she heard a few years ago from her cousin about her experience in a concentration camp. She expressed her sympathy and sorrow even though the experiences were remote from those she had gone through. For Vittorio, however, the Holocaust is part of the struggle for social recognition in Israel. This struggle has caused him to develop a superficial scale of suffering: the survivors' suffering was reimbursed by German reparations but his family's suffering went unrecognized. He talked about survivors he met during his childhood with a mixture of jealousy and ridicule and expressed his opinion about the Holocaust in his story about his neighbor and Jabotinsky's picture. In contrast, in Liat's story, the Holocaust has disappeared altogether. Liat does not mention it, probably because it is not a milestone on her personal map of socialization and maturation. The Holocaust may be part of her national-political consciousness (while working for the Likud party), and it is clearly part of the public discussion of her time, but it has no part in her personal or family life story.

The Guettas provide a kind of "control group" for the portrait of Holocaust survivors' families we have tried to portray. In our opinion, the stories of these families are more vulnerable to the influence of the external world. Indeed, the external world invaded their stories in unexpected and extremely brutal ways. The Holocaust was a man-made calamity, which not only sowed massive destruction but inhibited free recollection and reflection in later years. The survivors and many of their children find it impossible to move back and forth between the past and the future, between remembering and forgetting, between life and death. The continuity—and thus the protective framework—of the institution of the family was disrupted in these biographical reconstructions, which also report the painful losses of individual family members. Even though the impact of this rupture may have diminished over time, the residue of fear can still be felt in most of the third generation's life stories.

Epilogue

We have presented these biographical reconstructions of three generations in each of five Israeli families in order to gain a fresh perspective on a complex and difficult question: What are the aftereffects of the Holocaust on the descendants of survivors? We wondered how we could distinguish them from those related to the often parallel process of immigration, to a particular family structure, or to individual differences. We hoped to identify what aspects of this experience had been transmitted from one generation to another and what had been worked through. As we began, we tried to free ourselves from traditional concepts like "identity" and "personality," since we felt that they could easily become constricting labels, unwarranted by our subjects. We wished instead to develop "softer" concepts based on each storyteller's reconstructed life story rather than on the researcher's or interviewer's interpretation.

The task we tried to accomplish was ambitious, perhaps impossible: to follow the biographical reconstructions of survivors and their family members and see what they could teach us. We assumed that biographical reconstruction is not a random process. The choices people make in telling their life story reflect the choices they make, consciously or unconsciously, in their lives. Specifically, we wanted to learn which aspects of the Holocaust experience, as expressed in the biographical reconstructions of the first generation, were transmitted to the second and the third generations, and which were worked through and underwent change. The obstacles were immense, both in essence and in method; we will thus divide our

discussion into two sections: in this final chapter we will discuss our findings, and in the methodological appendix, the ways in which we tried to
analyze our data.

Ganit, Yoav, Orit, Dafna, Idit, and Liat live in an Israeli society very
different from the European and North African societies of their grandparents. For them, the Holocaust is more myth or legend than ongoing
reality. There are very few moments in their own lives (one being, for
example, the Persian Gulf War [January–February 1991], when the threat
of Iraqi missiles was a real one) to which they can point and say: "Here
it comes again." Still, their own family history has affected their reconstruction of reality. It has intensified the ongoing dialogue between their
fear and their hope—a dialogue more intense than the usual one between
existential fear of the unknown and hope for a better future, which is
probably true for most of us. As the youngster we quoted at the beginning
said: "We are like the support graft of the family."

The aftereffects of the Holocaust, with which Genia, Ze'ev, Olga, and
Anya have had to cope over many years, have not simply vanished. Either
expressed in suspicion (as in Genia's and Anya's cases) or hidden in pain,
anger, or fear (as in Ze'ev's and Olga's cases), they have been transmitted
to the next generation. Compared to Laura (and to some extent also to
Olga), the continuity of the family framework was disrupted for Genia,
Ze'ev, and Anya in both their memory and their reconstruction of events
as a direct consequence of the massive and painful losses they experienced.
These produced a feeling of disjunction—beyond the usual uprootedness
of immigration (Aroian, 1990)—which was passed on, in different inten-
sities, to their children and grandchildren. We found that this sense of
disjunction was still quite severe for Dafna and Idit, and perhaps a bit less
so for Ganit, Yoav, and Orit. This dialogue—between fear and hope, between being uprooted and becoming a "support graft" for the grandparents—we interpret according to various degrees of intergenerational
working through of the past.

Even Liat, who is not from a Holocaust survivor's family in the usual
sense, was not free of this ongoing dialogue. One could, of course, argue
that everyone carries the burdens of past generations, who have in turn
suffered from one form of man-made violence or another: sexual and
physical abuse in the family, at work, among friends and partners; social
domination and delegitimation; hatred between enemies; war or terror-

ism. We now know that many abusive parents were themselves abused in childhood (Herman, 1992). And during a recent stay in the United States I met a number of clinicians who work with Vietnam veterans with post-traumatic stress disorder (PTSD). These patients came from families with a history of PTSD: the father had come back with similar effects from World War II, the grandfather from World War I, even the great-grandfather from the Crimean War. At the time, these post-traumatic aftereffects had no name; they were considered "part of life." Only recently have we recognized them as the result of psychological intergenerational burdens.

As the first generation to learn about the extent of these traumatic aftereffects, we may actually be in a unique situation. Yet this very awareness can be frightening: we have few means and too little knowledge to be able to cure or prevent these intergenerational reverberations. It takes so much clinical intervention to help even a few people, and in the meantime, every day, further manmade violence takes place, setting off further aftershocks. One can read in the current Bosnian crisis, for example, the aftereffects of past relationships of violence stemming from World Wars I and II. Our goal in this study, therefore, was to try to identify and evaluate the *spontaneous* processes of transmission and working through within families in which the first generation had suffered from a severe, well-identified trauma like the Holocaust.

In this sense, the Anisevitch family, and to some extent also the Belinsky and Lerman families, were a source of hope: without formal knowledge or conscious intent, they have managed to devise an intergenerational healing process in which constraints or repressed conflicts from the past can be openly questioned by a younger generation. While Tzipke consciously tried to reflect on and involve herself in the education of her children, Hannah did so unwittingly and paid the heavy price of her own delayed independence. And it was Orit who started to reexamine the untold legends in her family through her trip to Warsaw with her grandmother. In all three families, these actions, feelings, and thoughts limited the uncontrolled effects of fear, anger, guilt, and pain. Yet, although we might hope that this would diminish the transmission of these effects to the following generations, there is, of course, no guarantee. And new traumas, new violence, could revive these old patterns and undermine that fragile hope.

To Remember, to Forget—the Living, the Dead?

In trying to follow the transmission of the trauma of the Holocaust and its working through in life stories, we have made certain assumptions. First, it is clear that there are many ways of reconstructing a life story. Telling any story is an ongoing choice-making process: one decides what to talk about in detail and where to be brief; what to narrate and what to leave out or gloss over; what to describe and what to argue about. When is silence about background and biographical facts of great import and when is it trivial? We must also recognize that these choices become extremely difficult when the narrator is trying to connect in one coherent story such radically different life sequences as the years before, during, and after the Holocaust (Rosenthal, 1993).

The example of Dvora (in the Prologue) represents some of the myriad possible explanations one can ascribe to a dream, each one relative to what is going on now and to what happened in the past. But most people seldom have an opportunity to consider all these possibilities. Therefore, we examined the particular patterns the interviewees chose, as well as their tendency to adhere to certain patterns over time. Identifying these chosen patterns was our first mission. This task—this "soft" conceptualization—seemed much more interesting than "strong" identity name-tags, because we saw the tellers as active participants in this drama. They constructed and reconstructed their stories from conflicting needs and new life experiences, which they tried to integrate into the narrative so it would sound coherent to them—and to us. Instead of labeling, and thereby revictimizing our interviewees, we preferred to approach their active reconstruction as a dynamic process.

While adhering to a consistent pattern in reconstructing their life stories, interviewees moved between two conflicting poles: the need to refashion the story in light of events that took place in their life, which they had learned to see differently over time; and the desire to preserve the story, to appear consistent over time and coherent in different situations.

The tension between these two poles becomes even greater when one's past encompasses an event as extreme as the Holocaust. On the one hand, one desires to go on—to live, to free oneself from the horror, to put it out of one's mind. On the other, one needs to preserve family continuity, to crystallize exactly, and thereby remember, what happened. Given the extreme and random acts of violence during the Holocaust, there was almost no way to keep both of these vectors together within one person, within one life story. Usually one became dominant (Danieli, 1980), while the other was repressed. As a result, some stories express more hope, while others express more fear. Only a few seem able to express the ongoing dialogue between them.

The tendency to want to live, to move forward, to forget what happened, was naturally more functional, especially for those who immigrated to Israel, a young, temperamental nation struggling for its own existence. However, even among those survivor-pioneers we identified an underlying wish or need: the opposing tendency to preserve everything that had been lost, which one did not want to "give up" by going through the psychological process of separation and mourning (Bar-On, 1986). With the passing of years, did it eventually become possible to mourn and openly integrate the need to remember with the need to move forward? As we saw, Olga demonstrated this capacity, but less through her story-telling than through her trip to Warsaw with her granddaughter Orit. When we discussed the intergenerational transmission of life stories, we suggested that children of survivors did not take advantage of some of the possible life-story reconstructions theoretically available to them (such was the case with Tamar) because of what they had absorbed from their parents as children. This showed us the extent of the intensity of the "then versus now" tension.

We next asked ourselves: What exactly was it that was transmitted in families of Holocaust survivors: the need to preserve the past or the need to forget it? When we talked about "working through," we wondered if the possibility of reconstructing one's biography was ever reopened for the survivors, their children, and their grandchildren, especially in view of their ability to move back and forth between what happened there and then and what is happening here and now? How did they make peace with the memory of death, which was such a profound and horrifying experience?

Intergenerational transmission can take place in several different ways: in the story itself through the telling of what happened (in this way, one generation's story can influence and shape the stories of the next generations); as one generation acts in a particular way and the younger generation attempts to imitate or rebel against these actions; or through feelings that have not been expressed in words, the "untold" story we have pointed out in previous chapters.

It was precisely this gap—between what was transmitted verbally and what was transmitted nonverbally—that most strongly influenced the next generation. Why? Perhaps because it bypassed the *possibility* of choice, a necessary step in the reconstruction process that determines which parts of my predecessor's story I "take with me." Working through, on the other hand, requires the ability to uncover the prior loss of choice, to conceptualize in a new way the link between now and then. We will look at each of these in turn.

THE FIRST GENERATION:
THE TENSION BETWEEN PRESERVATION AND RENEWAL

In this book we have presented life stories from five Israeli families. We have characterized each family according to the personal history of the survivors, the first generation: Genia was in the extermination camps of Majdanek and Auschwitz; Ze'ev was with the partisans; Olga spent the war in the Warsaw ghetto and in hiding at her gentile father's home in Aryan territory; Anya escaped to Russia shortly after the Nazi occupation; and Laura lived under a fascist Italian regime in Libya. All of them had large extended families before the war; with the exception of Laura, they lost most of these family members in the Holocaust. After the war, the five members of the first generation immigrated to Israel and married there, made their home there, and had children who, for the most part, also settled there.

We have tried to view the biographical reconstructions of the interviewees against the background of their very different life experiences. As we have noted, we undertook a difficult task, because the experience of the Holocaust is interwoven with other personal and familial events, such as the immigration to Israel. It was difficult to isolate any one component and talk about its ultimate effect. In addition, so many years have passed since the Holocaust, it was unclear whether it is even possible to identify in the biographies any dominant pattern of choices (those made years ago? those made today?).

Our question now is to what extent the biographical reconstructions of the survivor-interviewees reflect the tension between the desire to go forward and the need to preserve the past? Were the differences in the five sets of stories the result of a tension between these two poles, one that drew them backward into what happened there and then, and another that pushed them forward into the reality of here and now? Could they successfully integrate this tension into their lives?

For us, the stories of Anya Segal and Genia Belinsky represent, in different ways, the dominance of the first pole, the pull of the past. Olga Anisevitch's story, in contrast, represents the dominance of the second pole, the need to move forward at any price. In Ze'ev Lerman's story the movement forward, based on his active involvement in the partisan fighting, coexists with a latent pull toward fear and weakness, which remains unresolved. Only Laura Guetta represents the free movement between the memory of the past and present daily life, and their successful integration.

Genia lives painfully and consciously in the past ("our hearts were burned in the camps"), and it continues to affect her ability to function as a mother ("We were like animals. The children were the victims"). There is a marked discrepancy between her ability to act in extreme situations and her negative view of those actions now. The "circle of suffering" dominates her story. Is it unprocessed mourning and guilt about her mother or other family members or is it the ongoing awareness of death she encountered before, during, and after her time in the camps? We do not really know the answer. Anya, in contrast, states that "there is no need to talk about things that no longer exist." Yet her life story embodies just the opposite message: an inability to let go of certain aspects of the past. Her suffering and mourning reappear constantly between the lines of her narrative. Her daughter, Tamar, defines it in her own hard words: "She has a monopoly on the Holocaust . . . on death."

Olga moves forward to "rebuild life," although new events pull her back again and again. This attitude had practical expression in her pioneering days in Israel and her comment that what is important is the future. Later events, however, such as her brother's visit to Israel, and the deaths of her husband and her father, bring her back to the past she broke away from but has not actually parted from. And all of this is highlighted by her recent visit to Warsaw, about which she does not tell us. Her stepfather, whom she loved but now has no contact with, symbolizes for us the pain she has not successfully integrated into her narrative.

The drive to be active, to move forward, is also conspicuous in Ze'ev's life story—along with fragments of the past that still make him uncomfortable: his conscious thoughts (his revenge against the gentiles in his town) and his unconscious ones (his helplessness in saving members of his family). Unlike Anya, his heroic partisan experience has helped him in his struggle for existence in Israel. Still, when he speaks of his beloved grandson's recruitment into the army, a residue of fear surfaces, one that was not evident earlier.

Laura suffered the loss not only of her father (at an early age), but also of her brother, her daughter, and her husband. She experienced the violent riots against Jews in Libya after the war. Even though she lived under the fascist Italian regime, we cannot, strictly speaking, define her as a Holocaust "survivor," since she did not experience the loss of most of her family in that man-made calamity. Perhaps this has allowed her to move freely, as she tells her story, between the past and the present, just as she has in other areas of her life (the religious, the secular, the Christian, the Arab, and the Israeli). Indeed, there is some idealization of the past in her words (her childhood was "paradise"), as well as some blame toward the family that "abandoned" her. However, there is not the powerful pull toward the past that we found in Genia's story or in Anya's arguments, nor is there the strong movement forward we found in Olga's or Ze'ev's.

What we have, then, are "snapshots" of the life stories of our first-generation interviewees made relatively late in their lives. Have their stories undergone changes over the years? We have no clear answer. We might infer from the second generation's stories that such changes did occur, the most conspicuous example being the appearance of Olga's brother, which forced her to reveal the existence of her father and her mixed origin to her children for the first time. However, even then, Olga managed to keep to herself those facts she was uncomfortable with—the existence of her stepfather in London and the fact that she has no contact with him.

One could hypothesize that Genia's painful awareness is a result of events of the last few years: her daughter's divorce and her geographic distance from her son. And we have already noted Ze'ev's fear in response to his grandson's recruitment into the army. In these three instances, we would point out a "softening" of the original reconstruction, one that signals an emotional reaction repressed earlier in the interview (as in life?). In contrast, we do not find any change in Anya's story beyond the inclusion or exclusion of particular details; her reconstructions remain as they were. Unfortunately, Genia's and Ze'ev's children may not perceive this emotional softening. They have built their own "wall" against their parents' original patterns, and they are not open to testing the reduced need for such a defense as they grow older.

We have found many examples of the tension between holding on to the past and moving forward in the survivors' stories. What is more difficult to determine is whether this tension originated in the Holocaust. We know that the shaping of a life story is not based on some objective index of suffering. There is no way to compare the suffering of Genia and Anya, or Ze'ev and Olga. We could, however, propose that Laura's ability to move more freely between the past and the present is related to the fact that her experience of the Holocaust was not as immediate as it was for the others.

Keilson (1992) asserts that all Holocaust survivors went through a cumulative process of three traumatizations: their separation from parents before the Holocaust, their experiences during the Holocaust, and their encounter with the external world after the Holocaust. In his opinion, it is the third phase that was decisive. According to this view, Anya's difficulty in moving forward perhaps began with her earlier decision to run away from home with her boyfriend, which was reinforced by the loss of her baby and her husband during the war, and finally crystallized in her alienating encounter with her family in Israel after the war and her "not for love" marriage. On the other hand, Olga may have developed the ability to move forward during her childhood, a tendency reinforced by the fact that part of her (gentile) family survived and helped her survive, although she views them negatively in her biographical narrative. This tendency only became stronger with each "slap in the face" she received during and after the war. We might surmise from both of these examples that the shape one's life story will take emerges long before the life story is under way. It is possible, however, that later development might help it change and, as we saw with Genia and Ze'ev, reintegrate "lost" parts.

The survivors' reconstructions, each in its own way, reflect the tension between the past and the future, and a dominant regression toward one or the other. But with the passing of time, these individuals might discover the ability to integrate and live with this tension, to entertain a dialogue between these two opposing realities. We did not, therefore, simply equate hope with the push forward and fear with the pull backward. We found fear in both patterns (even if one was more functional or practical than the other). The deeper quest for hope would open a dialogue between preserving and reformulating both legitimate needs in relation to the trauma of the past.

The question now becomes: Which part of the working-through process was transmitted to the survivors' children and grandchildren? How were these tendencies passed on and how did they influence the biographical reconstructions of the succeeding generations?

THE SECOND GENERATION:
TRANSMISSION AND WORKING THROUGH

Beyond the difficulties we have already noted in identifying the patterns in the survivors' stories and their connection to the Holocaust, we confronted an additional problem: how to compare the life stories of people in different stages of their lives. We interviewed the survivors in an optimal stage of life for their biographies. But the seven members of the second generation—Tzipke, Hannah, Dina and her brother Benny, Tamar and her husband, Ya'acov, and Vittorio—were in their forties, squarely between their aging parents and their growing children, a period customarily characterized as the "mid-life crisis." We want to consider how the patterns in the parents' reconstructions were transmitted to their children. In doing so, we should remember that this transmission usually crystallized a few years after the Holocaust, when, we would suggest, the tension between past and future was at its peak. Parents did not always resolve the tension in the same way. Did this confuse their children when they constructed their own stories or did it make it easier to choose a pattern that was better suited to them?

In contrast to the common view that most of the survivors did not speak to their children about what they had experienced, it is important to note that in our sample, the second-generation interviewees mention stories they heard from their parents. Of course, this may be a bias in our sample: we deliberately chose families that were willing to tell us their life stories. However, the more important issues are what was told and how it was told. In general, the survivors we did not interview for our study spoke less about the Holocaust than the interviewees did. Dina's father said less than Olga, and this was also true of Tamar's father, Tzipke's father, and Hannah's mother. The problem of legitimacy also arose. Genia tells us that Ben-Gurion said there was "no need to speak with the children," but they did so anyway; their children were able to talk in school about their parents' experiences in the Holocaust. At the same time, the children raised questions that required answers: Why was there a number tattooed on Grandma's arm? Why don't I have grandparents?

Beyond the initial readiness to speak, however, we found evidence of filtering in the stories: *conscious, directed filtering,* the result of a decision, such as Ze'ev's, when he refrained from describing what happened during the Holocaust (and his revenge) in detail; and *subconscious filtering,* which is evident in Olga's story (if her children did not ask about something, she did not speak about it). Her son Benny says they concluded only that things were "not good" between Olga and her father.

We also found active filtering in the second generation: Tamar holds back Anya's stories because she is inundated by them: "they change according to my mother's needs." Dina is angry with her grandfather, who rejected her mother when she needed his support. This active filtering confirms the analogy of the "double wall" we spoke of in the Introduction: each side preserves both itself and the other. Ze'ev's reticence, probably based on good intentions, silenced Hannah. She absorbed his stories of heroism and belittled herself in relation to them, not hearing the helplessness and fear he omitted, intentionally and unintentionally. When children or parents tried to make an opening in their own wall, they usually encountered the other side's wall. Rarely did one "emotional window" align with the other as it did during the unusual conversation between Olga and her son Benny.

Transmission can take several shapes—paralysis, for example, or admiration. Tzipke admires Genia's ability to withstand suffering and searches out forms of suffering (diets, her friend's cancer) in order to experience something of what her mother had to confront in the camps. Tamar criticizes Anya while admiring the way her mother worried about her, in contrast to her father's indifference. Compared to Ze'ev, her father, Hannah feels that she has no story of any interest to tell. Dina attempts to continue her parents' pioneering spirit, but she begins with the statement that "the pioneering spirit of the eighties is not like that of the fifties." In all of these instances, the parents' stories have had the effect of dwarfing the personal stories of the second generation.

Transmission also takes place through the parents' actions, but here their effect on the second generation is varied. Dina is enchanted by her parents' pioneering, their ability to offer hospitality to others, their modesty. But Tzipke rebelled against the demands of her parents and became a difficult and obstinate child. Tamar also describes her adolescent self as someone "who made my mother's life miserable." However, we know that rebellion is not like working through. Tzipke attempts to raise her children to be free, the antithesis of the invalidating "child raising methods" related to food, clothing, and school used by her parents. Only when her son reaches adulthood does she discover that her methods have produced a similar rebelliousness. She begins a project, working through her parents' pattern to liberate herself and her son from its ongoing effects. Similarly, she looks for a way to accommodate her need to be close to her children with their need for independence.

Tamar is unsuccessful in freeing herself from the need to respond to her mother, to argue with her, and thus she perpetuates her mother's argumentative pattern. She responds to the story Anya tells, but she does not uncover the power of the "untold" story—Anya's weakness, her desperate urge for warmth, support, and intimacy. Hannah likewise absorbs her parents' stories but is unable to acknowledge the source of her own feelings of mourning. This may be a reaction to the "untold" segment of their story. Dina is not clear about the existence of borders between her mother and herself until her uncle's story is uncovered. The myth of her "closeness" to her mother falls apart when Dina finds out that Olga has hidden part of her life story from her. Similarly, Benny describes the identity crisis he went through when his father died: although his father had been ill, he conveyed a feeling of undefeatable power. It is only when his father dies that Benny perceives his weakness for the first time.

Did both parents transmit conflicting messages through their stories, their actions, and their "untold" stories? On the manifest level, Dina tries to have the festive Shabbat night dinner her father wished for but finds herself failing and gives up, following Olga's way of "no religion." On the latent level, Tamar moves between open feelings of anger toward Anya's control of her and admiration for her mother's concern. Did her father, as distant as he seems to have been, demonstrate a different kind of loving relationship to her? Toward the end of the interview Tamar asks, "Where are the images, the fantasies?" as if she felt the missed opportunity in the interview and perhaps not only there. The key difference between the two levels, the manifest and the latent, is that the former allows new ways of integration, like Dina's and Tzipke's attempts, while the latter reinforces the persistent duality, as in Tamar's and Hannah's reconstructions.

Do we discover changes in the second-generation's reconstruction of their biographies? Hannah finds it difficult to tell her story, but owing to the persistence of the interviewer, it becomes evident that she has developed a version of her life story. She has found her own way of doing things: working with immigrants and with literary groups. During the interview she cried a lot, still feeling the burden of the past, but she is optimistic about the future. We have already mentioned the changes in Tzipke's reactions, especially when her son's difficulties demanded her attention. It was the aging of her parents that brought back the "symbiotic" process of worrying too much, of mutual dependence. In this sense, Tzipke still lives between the old and new patterns of behavior, still working through her dependence-counterdependence with her parents.

The main lesson we learn from the interviews relates to the second generation. If until now they have been presented in the literature of the Holocaust as reacting to or resisting their parents, the survivors, in our study we have met several who are actively searching for a path between their children and their parents. Instead of being "memorial candles" (Vardi, 1990) who respond only to the survivors' stories, actions, and "untold stories," they present a significantly different picture. Tzipke, Hannah, and to some extent also Dina, Benny, Vittorio, and Ya'acov, have maneuvered their way between the generations, each of them with his or her own needs and perspective. Several have succeeded in developing delicate strategies of caring for their parents and their children, and mutually linking them together, while also developing a career of their own. Clearly, they were motivated by their wish to "start a life of their own," independent of their parents and the Holocaust.

It is only after they were well ahead in their "project" (using Tzipke's terminology) that they had the time to worry about their own professional careers and to construct their own life story. Tamar also tried to find her way, professionally speaking, but she was less successful emotionally in constructing a life story independent of her mother's and in giving emotional support to her daughters. Ya'acov began a professional career, but when his daughters matured and needed emotional help, he made time for them and sought psychological help to work through the influence of his parents' past on him and on Tamar. Benny began asking himself questions about the effect of the past after his father's death and the appearance of his mother's brother. From Vittorio's story it is unclear whether he began to examine his mother's expectations of success in marriage and work in light of his own failure to withstand her demands.

Viewing the second generation only through the framework of their parents and the Holocaust has distorted the picture and created serious misunderstandings—even unjust judgments—of how well they coped with their parents' painful heritage. The interviews allow us to get to know them for themselves, through their own narratives, as innovators who have managed to navigate between their children's needs and the conflicting demands of their parents. This has enriched our understanding and added an important dimension to our work.

THE THIRD GENERATION: THE NATIVE AMERICAN AND THE ESKIMO MYTHS

We did not have great expectations of our interviews with the grandchildren. In theory and in practice, they have just begun to construct a life story. Ganit, Yoav, and Dafna were interviewed just before or during their army service, Idit and Liat at the end of high school, and Orit when she was in the tenth grade. It is natural that these young adults are preoccupied with the present and the future and are less interested in examining the problems of the past (Erikson, 1968). Compared to their parents, the third generation grew up in a much more protected atmosphere economically, socially, and psychologically speaking, a generation and a half away from the terror.

The possibility of identifying intergenerational transmission and working through in the third generation's stories was small to begin with. We did, however, examine one question: What was the actual relationship between the survivors and their grandchildren?

We knew of two opposing myths: the Native American myth in which young adults respect their elders because of their great experience, and the Eskimo myth in which the young send the elders out to die in the snow because they are no longer relevant or useful in the struggle to survive.

All six young adults tell us about their everyday experience, which is colored by their varying backgrounds. Yoav has by far the most vibrant life story to tell, full of events and struggles and accompanied by sensitive reflections on himself and others. His reconstruction radiates love and happiness, and stands out in relief against the pain and sadness in his mother's story. His statement "Life isn't the time that you are alive, but rather what you do with it" could have been taken from his grandfather's story. In another comment, "Friends leave, family remains," he expresses the sense of security he feels in his family. For Yoav, Ze'ev, the partisan, is an object of pride, even competition. He defines his grandmother as "indirectly obsessive," thereby mixing criticism with affection. Even though Hannah does not mention her part in Yoav's life history and story, we have no doubt that so much love and caring came from somewhere.

Orit's story is brief in comparison to Yoav's, but she radiates a similar positive outlook in the way she relates to herself (and we should not forget that she is two years younger than Yoav). Her descriptions are full of humor and sensitive observations of family members. She can let her reality happen, unlike her mother, who is still busy controlling it. Like Yoav, Orit speaks warmly and lovingly of her grandmother. Their joint trip to Warsaw added a great deal to the deepening relationship between them, and to Orit's reflections on the past, which are beyond what one would expect from a girl her age and even beyond what we found in interviews with the other young adults in our sample.

Ganit describes her present reality in the army in grayer tones, and when she speaks of the past, she exhibits a controlled irony that reminds us of her grandmother, Genia. Her positive assertions concern only the future: the creation of a "big" family, how she will celebrate the holidays, her plans to study psychology and work with people. Yet in the present she is able to enjoy privacy and distance herself from others without feeling guilty. She is also emotionally expressive, particularly in terms of her grandmother. Genia's suffering (on Holocaust Day) is painful to Ganit, but she feels unable "to really help her, to compensate her for what she lost." Ganit exhibits a rare maturity that combines emotional closeness with a necessary distancing. Even though, like Yoav and Orit, she does not mention (or is not aware of) her mother's contribution, it is difficult to understand how a relationship of this nature could occur without the thoughtful and respectful example of her parents.

Liat struggles for recognition in school and in society. Compared to members of her parents' generation, she is still struggling toward her own achievements. It is hard for her to describe, and perhaps also to enjoy, her experiences. When she talks about her present work in the Likud party and her studies, her main concern is about how much others esteem her and her actions. Her difficulty in building stable relationships and her fear of failure belong to the same picture: a constant jockeying for her social place, with ethnic origin and economic status as background factors. It is possible to connect her struggle over the place of women in her social context with the similar struggle of her grandmother in Libya and later, in Israel. From her father Liat learned to love her grandmother, but she is also searching for a way to move away from the traditional North African society in which Laura grew up.

Idit is also concerned with the struggle for a place in society, and Dafna too expressed a feeling of being on the periphery. Their lack of self-confidence, however, can be accounted for by issues other than those that characterized Liat's story. A sense of alienation runs through Tamar's story, which has its origins in Anya and her husband and was never worked through. In comparison to "real" survivors, War of Independence fighters, and her ultra-orthodox religious relatives, Tamar feels herself to be on the periphery. Given this background, the girls' relationships with Anya are interesting. Idit sees her grandmother as a symbol of what she is afraid of: a bent back, old age, loneliness, a diaspora-orientation, the "Eskimo myth." Dafna relates to her in a warmer manner. She recognizes Anya's ability to love and empathizes with her pain and her difficulties. Dafna views her father's mother as Idit does Anya—she is a symbol of what Dafna is afraid of becoming: "she is absorbed in herself and she destroys everything around her ... she doesn't try to do anything with herself."

When members of the second generation were unsuccessful in making their way between their parents and their children, their difficulty was reflected in the way the younger family members talked about themselves and their grandparents in their narratives. Their concern about finding a place in society, their feeling of being an outsider, their difficulty in experiencing reality as it is—these are the conspicuous expressions of their parents' failure that emerge in Liat's and Idit's life stories. It also affected how Idit and Dafna relate to the Holocaust. Idit describes her fear as "a black, ghostlike void" and feels helpless in dealing with this part of her family's past. She feels that she missed a lot during her trip to Poland: she could not deal emotionally with what she saw there. Dafna tells of a recurring dream about Nazis chasing her; she does not know how to run away and protect her sisters.

It is interesting to compare the details of Idit's and Orit's trips to Poland. Idit's was based on normative social pressure, while Orit's was based on her own personal curiosity (even though it began as competition between Orit and her brother). Idit's journey was organized "from above," while Orit's was a family trip that emerged "from below." Instead of encouraging Idit's working-through process, the trip magnified her fears just as closer exposure to such a painful subject can result in an oversimplified view of the relevance of the past to the present (Assa and Degani, 1989). This does not mean that no one should study the Holocaust or go to Poland on organized educational tours. What we are cautioning is that one should be careful to process the experience at a pace suited to each individual's maturing processes.

Not in vain does Ganit tell us about how beautiful Genia's mother was in her youth, how she went to the opera, almost in contradiction to what we heard from Genia herself ("I didn't have a chance to know what the word *mother* is"). Because she loves Ganit in a new way, Genia could recall for her happy childhood memories, which did not come to mind when she was talking to us or to Tzipke. Orit tells us about her trip to Warsaw and describes how at home Olga felt there and her love for her father—things Olga was unable to express even to her daughter. Dafna is sensitive to Anya's weakness, her need for intimacy, in a way that her sister, her mother, and even Anya herself are not.

The ways in which the young adults related to their grandparents (affection, intimacy, distancing, or rejection) helped us reexamine the concepts of intergenerational transmission and working through. We were impressed by the commonality: all the young people in our sample were well integrated into their extended families, and family members remain very important in their biographical reconstructions. Liat and Yoav used almost the same words in expressing their feeling that "friends change, you cannot always trust them, but family is safe and steady." This renewed confidence in the family framework might be seen as their response to the disruption of their family's continuity in the Holocaust and to the disjointed and fragmented life stories of their grandparents.

To Live with Memory

The Holocaust charged survivors with two basic responsibilities: the first, explicitly expressed as an obligatory act, to remember, preserve, and transmit this terrible experience from one generation to the next; the second, to overcome what happened and serve as living evidence that the Nazi attempt at annihilation had ultimately failed. These were usually carried out through actions: returning to "normal" life, marrying, having children, actively building a continuation of a prewar life.

The survivors saw themselves as the sole representatives of an entire population that had not managed to stay alive. They felt that it was their duty to pass these two responsibilities on, just as their forefathers had passed on religious traditions. There were disagreements over the content of these responsibilities and the best way to implement them, yet there was also a kind of consensus (to the extent that one can expect to find one in a large and varied Jewish population) about the task itself.

Some survivors, for example, have talked about their personal experiences during the Holocaust, while others have not. Yet in principle, all agree on the need to transmit this message to their children as well as to the children of those with no direct connection to the Holocaust and even to other nations, confronting revisionists who assert that the Holocaust never happened.

What has never been resolved is the contradiction, the almost unavoidable tension, between these two responsibilities—to remember and to live, to fear and to hope. Within the first, it is between the memory of life as it was before the Holocaust and the memory of death, the horror and the evil, the cold-blooded destruction of children, women, men, and elders that was planned and carried out by human beings. It is almost impossible to think of one without thinking of the other, because both are interwoven with the past, and it is this past that must be transmitted to the following generations.

The second, to live, assumes a lesser emphasis on the past and a movement forward into the future. But this also requires an act of forgetting—of repressing memory, especially the inhumane memory that was internalized so that it would not influence the present—while also pursuing the second. The actions that are proof of life are intermingled with tense anticipation of an unknown future and thoughts of an uncontrolled past, which appear unexpectedly like ominous shadows.

The relationship between the threatening past and the threatening future (Rosenthal, 1989) engaged the interviewees' "thoughts of the heart," consciously or unconsciously, when verbal expression was not possible. It included a question, one full of awe and anxiety: Did I come through it "normal"? Or is there something invisible in me, absorbed against my will through my exposure to such inhumanity, that might appear as a terrible flaw, heaven forbid, in a generation or two? After all, I was exposed to hatred, violence, degradation, helplessness, starvation, and illness for years, and I often behaved like an animal. What from all this has stayed with me?

Can this unspoken tension be brought forward into open dialogue? Psychologists assume, sometimes naively, that one can work such tension through by talking about it, and thus reduce its effect. If during the years immediately after the Holocaust it was important to move forward at the cost of not remembering, in the ensuing years new situations have arisen, mainly concerned with raising children, that have urged a reexploration of long-repressed feelings. For many, bearing children and grandchildren offered an opportunity to mourn their losses while getting on with their lives. The working-through process means the chance to create a dialogue, to achieve a kind of balance, between memories of life and death, between remembering the past and creating a life in the present. Its aim is not to abolish memory but to weaken its control, enabling the experience of pleasure in the present. The way to reduce fear and resume hope is to accept both of them as legitimate feelings.

Psychologists usually discuss planned working through within therapeutic frameworks, although they agree that it can also occur spontaneously (Danieli, 1983). A changing reality may encourage this process. Positive experiences in societal, professional, and familial spheres, for example, may reduce fear of the future and, by doing so, enable an individual to get in touch with threatening memories from the past. The biological process of transition from generation to generation entails similar possibilities: the threatening power of the past may weaken from one generation to another as new occasions for examining the relationship between past and present realities arise. However, these processes may also bring about the opposite result: a reality saturated with hardship and loss can aggravate unresolved tensions. Biological and psychosocial processes may pass on unresolved conflicts from earlier generations.

In this book, we have tried to evaluate the potential of a changing reality and of biological forces and psychosocial processes to reconstruct personal and family biographies. We have discovered that the old solutions, based on the tension between fear and hope, can be transformed through open dialogue. We have found that new opportunities for living with memory bring up new choices in the reconstruction of life stories in each generation. Still, we should not forget the ruins that the Holocaust left in the souls and memories of the survivors (Langer, 1991). One of our survivor-interviewees reflects on how hard this process was for her: "Who will I remember? the living? the dead? Who will I forget? the dead? the living? What else is there for me to do but to remember and forget, to live and die, to fear and hope?"

Appendix ✦ *Notes* ✦ *References* ✦ *Index*

APPENDIX

Life Stories as Scientific Inquiry

We have described how we analyzed the interviews in this study. Here we address three of the major questions in the professional literature on the scientific value of biography reconstruction:

1. The relationship between the ways of thinking and the discourse of the interviewer, the storyteller, and the analyst.

2. The relationship between reality and the life story: What is a fact?

3. The question of generalization or representation.

Method: Biographical, Linguistic, and Content Analysis

The method we used in this book was developed in a seminar given by Gabriele Rosenthal during the academic year 1988–89. In addition to the mode of interviewing and transcribing, the method included three consecutive levels of analysis: biographical, linguistic, and content analysis.

BIOGRAPHICAL ANALYSIS

As a first step, we abstracted all the dates (and the events that characterize stages in the interviewee's life) from the interview text. What happened, according to the storyteller, on a given date? We noted these details in chronological order and presented the main features in the brief family chronology in each chapter. We also tried to find out which historical and political events occurred on those dates and in those places. For example, when Laura describes 1940 as the year in which the war in Tripoli caused her to move to Garian, it was important to research what happened during the war in Tripoli at that time. How were the Jews treated? To what extent were Libyan Jews able to move freely and to places such as Garian?

By using biographical and historical details, it was possible to come up with some initial hypotheses before we even began reviewing the interview text itself. Some of these hypotheses appear in the introduction to each chapter. For example, in comparing the details of Genia's and Ze'ev's biographies, we noted a partial similarity, along with several basic differences, in their experiences during the Holocaust (death camps versus partisans). This brought up a question: To what extent does this difference color their life stories when viewed against the background of their similar biographies?

At this stage of the analysis we noted contradictions in dates in the stories of family members. Laura asserts that her daughter Miriam died in an immigration camp in Israel when she was a year old. Vittorio says his sister died when she was four or five. According to the child's date of birth as reported by Laura, it is logical to assume that Vittorio's date is the correct one. Contradictions such as these may occur by chance; sometimes, however, they are significant in the construction of the life story. Why did Laura distort the date of her daughter's death? Is it somehow related to the death of her younger brother, whom she took care of after her father died, when he was less than a year old? We will not always be able to find answers to these questions in the text, but it is important that we raise them.

Next, we estimated how the interview would continue, based on each of these preliminary hypotheses. For example, if the difference in their experiences during the Holocaust colored Genia's and Ze'ev's entire life stories, we would expect to find in Genia's a residue of helplessness and fear from the time she spent in the death camps, while Ze'ev's would include stories of the heroism of a partisan fighter. If Laura provides no dates at all in her narrative until 1940, does this mean that external events had no significance for her until then or that after that date, historical and political events had begun to penetrate her private life?

LINGUISTIC ANALYSIS

At the next stage, we divided each interview into sections according to subject matter. We tried to give each section a name in order to help us clarify for ourselves what the interviewee was telling us. Sometimes the division was simple and straightforward, because the storytellers organized their own stories. But sometimes it was complicated and demanded further discussion. Then we defined the linguistic mode of each section: When does the interviewee narrate a story that has a beginning, a middle, and an end (told in a temporal and spatial sequence) and when does the interviewee report, describe, or argue (speech acts without spatial and temporal sequences)?

Now it became possible to raise questions of a different nature: When and about what did the interviewee narrate, describe, report, or use arguments and why? This type of analysis assumes that in the act of narrating, the storyteller becomes emotionally involved and loses some control of the nature of the discourse. Descriptions and reports, which are external to the story itself, are more neutral, and may suggest control and/or difficulty in expressing emotions about the content or the process of the interview. In addition, arguments, as a rule, often have an invisible partner; the argument may be aimed at the interviewer, yet the interviewee may actually be arguing with himself or with someone else.

In the interviews with Laura and Vittorio, for example, the narrative mode was the dominant linguistic form, in contrast to the argument mode in Liat's interview. Similarly, it was suggested that Anya was argumentative in order to justify (to her lost family members?) her escape from Poland (and thus her failure to help them survive). It was also suggested that Ze'ev had difficulty telling about moments of weakness during his escape: he reported them or described them briefly. The rest of his story, telling about his meeting with his future wife's family in the forest (the story of the bucket) and about his nighttime excursions, expressed a sense of control and heroism.

CONTENT ANALYSIS

The major part of the analysis begins here, in content. We have read the interview according to the sections we previously prepared. We now try to discover to what extent there is support for any of the hypotheses we raised in the first stages of the analysis (the biographical or the linguistic), or for those that have emerged out of the initial sections. The opening sentences of each interview were central. When Hannah began and ended her interview with the words "I am not"/"I don't," it was very important in understanding her way of thinking about herself. We then asked: To what else was this related? From what did it derive?

Genia's first sentence was "To tell you that I didn't have a chance to know what the word *mother* is." What drove her to begin in such a way, a way that was not even factually true? Was the word *mother* too difficult for her (perhaps due to her own problems with mothering)? Were the memories of her mother too painful to her because her mother died before the Holocaust? We searched for support for each of these possibilities. The interview spread out like a maze, with myriad entrances and exits, and we looked for a thread to follow into its heart.

We often chose an especially problematic section that seemed to us to be central for understanding the interview. We examined it closely, as if with a magnifying glass: What was the meaning of each word, each phrase? Why were things said in one way and not another? Where were the silences, and what nonverbal expressions accompanied statements and silent moments? Our detailed analysis of the first five sentences of Dina's interview helped us generate hypotheses that were confirmed in the later sections.

For the neophyte, this type of work can seem tedious, even endless. After all, it is always possible to come up with new hypotheses and reject old ones, while never uncovering all the possible meanings. Yet even though this may happen, as a rule, many of the initial hypotheses converge into a small cluster that recurs in the different sections of the interview. In the final stage of our analysis we try to decide which strategy the interviewee used in constructing his or her life story. This we termed the person's "choice pattern." We still needed to discover what purpose this pattern served, at what stage of life it was created, and whether it changed over time, especially when external demands changed.

We carried out the content analysis in pairs and sometimes within the framework of the entire seminar. The discussion and the uncertainty, how to understand a certain expression, how to define a specific hypothesis were clarified within the group frame-work by repeatedly returning to the text. Sometimes as a result of our rereading of the interview, or our reading of an interview with another family member, questions that had been in the background or had not been previously raised became central. In Orit's interview, for example, when she tells about her visit to Warsaw with her grandmother, the question arises: Why did neither Dina nor Olga tell us about this trip? This sent us back to their interviews to look for an answer to a question that had not occurred to us earlier.

One could ask about the internal reliability of each analyst and the external relia-bility between different analysts. For a given interview, will each of us come up with the same hypotheses and confirm them in a similar way? A positive answer to this question would provide firm scientific validity for the method according to the criteria of quantitative analysis. But the answer is not so simple. It is not in fact always possible even to expect that this will happen. This question leads us to a further aspect of our method.

Thinking and Discourse:
The Interviewer, the Storyteller, and the Analyst

The interview and its analytic process form a complex combination. Even though it first appears that we are analyzing the linguistic expressions of another person (the interviewee), in actuality, his or her verbal statements are the reciprocal activity of three thought-language structures: those of the interviewee, those of the interviewer, and those of the analyst.

Let us assume that the interviewer begins with the question "Please tell me what happened to you during the Holocaust." At this first moment, knowingly or unknow-ingly, the interviewer has set the framework for the interviewee's verbal response. The storyteller now knows what the interviewer wants to hear. He or she may answer (trying to be a good interviewee) or may choose not to answer (wittingly or unwit-tingly). In such cases, the thought structure of the interviewer frames the verbal answers of the storyteller in a way that also places obligations on the analyst. The analyst cannot know whether the interviewee spoke mainly about her experiences during the Holocaust because the interviewer directed her to, or because that is the focus of the interviewee's life story.

Interview subjects have the freedom to choose what to talk about and how to talk about it, a freedom that would be taken away completely if the interviewer gave the subject a structured questionnaire of multiple-choice items to list in order of pref-erence or to answer yes or no to. We purposely tried to minimize as much as possible the influence of the interviewer's leading question on the storyteller. We simply asked all interviewees to "tell us their life stories." In this way, we minimized the possibility that the storyteller would know a priori what the interviewer was looking for. Yet this was not always so simple for either the interviewer or the interviewee. Hannah, for example, asked—almost demanded—that Bosmat frame the interview by asking her questions. Perhaps it was difficult for her to admit, even to herself, that she had a life story of her own. When Bosmat insisted, Hannah began her story, but it is quite possible that this would not have happened had Bosmat given up and asked questions as Hannah demanded.

We were aware that the interviewer also had nonverbal ways of framing the structure of the interviewee's story. Facial expressions, attentiveness, oversensitivity or insensitivity, all of these greatly influence what the storyteller chooses to talk about and in what way. All are unpredictable to a great extent, since we have little or no control over them. This is what we mean when we talk about the "chemistry" between interviewee and interviewer. Tova did not intend to cry during her interview with Genia, but after what Genia told her and the associations it elicited in her own life, she was unable to control her emotions. However, her crying was authentic and did not interfere with the interview.

In this respect, the interviews with Holocaust survivors are especially difficult. Even after so many years, language is inadequate to describe the emotions and the experiences it must represent (Kripke, 1982). Indeed, if it was difficult then to make sense of what had happened, it is still difficult. Perhaps this explains why, during the years immediately afterwards, survivors could not find words to express what they had experienced, nor could they sort out their inner confusion.

The fragility of language was also an aspect of the formation of the "double wall" between parents and children: when the children were beginning to formulate their own emotional expression, their parents could offer no guidance. Where else could they learn to do this? At the same time, psychologists who have tried to provide their own discourse often create the opposite problem: their meaning structure dominates and disrupts the fragile structure of their survivor-patients (Keilson, 1992).

As an interview progressed, the maze that at first appeared endless became a kind of tunnel whose end could be anticipated. The words chosen so far, the stories told—even those not told—created a structure that omitted some options and left others open for continuation. These options gave the false impression that the story was finished. At this stage, the hardest task for the interviewers was to continue to see the interviewee's story as an unfinished structure, one whose forthcoming parts could offer new surprises. Anya, for example, avoids speaking about her first husband and her baby, who died in Russia, even when Bosmat tries to encourage her to talk about it. It would seem that this structure is closed. However, toward the end of the interview, Anya suddenly talks about them, and this story could actually evolve into a new interview.

The same process occurred with Tamar when, in her final sentences, she begins to talk about "the fantasies, the other things" that she missed in the interview (in life?). By doing so, she is actually asking to begin a new cycle of questions. Similarly, it would be interesting to follow up on the way the grandchildren reopened the possibilities that did not exist in the survivors' stories to their children or to us. In this way, Ganit heard things about her grandmother from Genia that she did not tell either Tzipke or us.

Up to this point we have focused on the reciprocal relations that exist between the structures of the interviewer and the storyteller. How do these relate to the thought-language structure of the analyst? There are situations in which these structures are identical: for example, in a therapeutic setting, the interviewer is the therapist who listens and simultaneously analyzes the interviewee's words. The analyst's structure sets the framework for the therapeutic interview as well as for the meaning of words and silences. This is also true of police investigations and legal proceedings. However, as opposed to therapy, in these situations it is possible that the analysis and the judgment will be rejected by the defending lawyer, the jurors, or the judge. On the other hand, in quantitative studies, the analyst decides a priori what the framework will be for analyzing the subject's answers. Thus, the thought-language structures of the interviewee are dismissed as unimportant.

We emphasized the thought-language structure of the storytellers as an integral part of their biographical reconstruction. It is possible to understand interviewees' life stories in many different ways, depending on the context that interests the researcher. We might have tried to assess psychological pathologies, psychic processes analyzed according to Freud, or intra-family processes according to Minuchin. The analyst's structure in each such analysis would have effected a certain reductionism on the structure brought forth by the interviewer. In hindsight, some reductionism of this kind occurs in every interview and analysis.

This reductionism is especially problematic when both the interviewer and the analyst are too emotionally involved (or not emotionally involved enough) in the interviewee's story. It is known that many therapists were unable to relate to the difficulties of patients who went through the Holocaust (survivors as well as perpetrators) because they were themselves unable to deal with their own emotional turmoil in relation to the Holocaust: their own fear, guilt, rejection, and anger (Danieli, 1980). In the psychological literature dealing with the Holocaust, one can find clear signs of a linguistic-conceptual barrier between the survivors and the researchers. If the analysts are afraid of (or feel guilt or anger toward) the significance of these feelings for themselves, there is a problem in analyzing these stories.

Even when the issue of emotional involvement is resolved, the question To what extent does the analyst's structure fit the structure of the interviewee? may still be unresolved. Do the two structures produce reciprocity? For us, the method of raising hypotheses and looking for support in the text itself created a sense of such a fit. However, it is not our place to state whether we were successful in achieving this fit. We assume that this is not a final process; it is comparable to the evolution of a biblical text: each generation has added numerous new analyses based on the language-thought structure of that period. It must be remembered that our analysis of transmission and working through between one generation and another was done from within our own perspective as members of the second and third generations: it probably determined our expectations and the linguistic tools available to us at the time of the analysis.

To a certain extent, the process of writing *Fear and Hope* created additional problems, independent of the previous ones. Here we had to decide how much to impose on readers. Did we want them to listen to the stories of the survivors and their children, did we want them to listen to our stories as researchers, or did we perhaps want both? How much should be presented from the interviews and how much from the analysis? We needed to put all the complex elements mentioned earlier into a final sequence of words with a beginning and an end, a story that would be accessible, and this influenced our choices. In addition, we felt the need to leave the puzzle open to some extent, to enable readers to come to a conclusion according to their own language and thought structures.

Reality versus the Life Story: What Is a Fact?

There are many who, from the outset, are skeptical of the scientific value of biographical reconstructions. People tend to tell what comes to mind, they say, to tell different stories each time, to fit their story to the situation (who is the interviewer, what is the interview style?). If this is true, why should we assign value to what is being said and the way it is being said? In principle, these assertions have some truth, but is there an alternative? Would it be possible to know something about people that does *not* include ambiguity or some amount of randomness as part of the structure of the scientific study? We are not only dealing with factual validation of what we already know, we are dealing with the relationship between the known and the unknown.

Spence (1980) asked: What is the goal of psychological therapy? Is it the disclosure of a "historical truth" similar to the attempt to put together an ancient vase whose pieces have been found in an archeological dig? When such a truth is not feasible, is it not more like a participatory examination of "narrative truths"? According to Spence, Freud tried to reestablish the historical truth with the help of free association and slips of the tongue; to try to clarify what had actually happened, then been perceived as traumatic, and been repressed.

By gradually and carefully bringing the repressed into consciousness, Freud initiated a working-through process intended to free the patient from the unconscious control of these events. According to Spence, there is actually no possibility of reconstructing one truth. There are already a multitude of attribution possibilities in the patient's mind, to which new ones are added from the patient's ongoing life experience. To these are added the complex encounter between the different discourse and emotional structures of the patient and the therapist-analyst.

However, Spence did not try to clarify what became a fact under these conditions (Bar-On, in preparation). What is the connection between what has actually taken place and what has been thought or told? If only "narrative truth" exists, are the actual facts unimportant? If what happened is important, how does it interact with the narrative truth? Is it possible to assert that the life stories of Ze'ev, Genia, Olga, and Anya did not deal with their life history, that is, with what they experienced during the Holocaust? Did not their biographical reconstructions reflect an emotional complexity originating in cruel and sudden loss? Did they not come out of the vacuum of trying to make sense of what had happened, and give it significance?

We accepted Spence's theory where the children and grandchildren of survivors were concerned. In their case, the significant traumatic experiences were not their own and had actually been transmitted to them as "narrative truths." However, when we analyzed the survivors' life stories, we were especially interested in the relationship between hard fact and what had happened in the years since. In this sense we looked at the discourse as a reflection of internal facts and feelings, which tried to signify the experienced facts. That one cannot "see" these internal facts does not detract from their effect and value in discussing life stories.

Indeed, the problem of biographical reconstruction in the light of the Holocaust might be just the opposite. It is difficult to present external and internalized horrors in a uniform verbal sequence that seems logical to both storyteller and listener. There is no discourse that can simultaneously express the emotional whirlwind of pain, of memory, and of desire about what happened. On the other hand, the normalization of the discourse (Rosenthal, 1989) helped maneuver the chaotic into a logically coherent sequence. The world did not stop to develop a new language for communicating the horror, and to become insane (and try to do justice to the experience in daily discourse) would in the mind of the victims only serve the purpose of the aggressor, so the only way was to use ordinary discourse.

It was similarly impossible to expect that Olga, for example, would talk five times about her escape from the ghetto, each time from a new perspective: as a child, as an adult in Israel today, and from her mother's, brother's, and father's viewpoints. Such possibilities exist only for the analyst, to the observer in the film *Rashomon,* or in mystery stories like those of Edgar Allan Poe (Lacan, 1966). Dvora is an exception. She was able to relate to her dream in three different ways, to give it a different meaning each time, and finally to assert that "it was not that way at all," and thereby begin the process all over again. We could expect children, especially grandchildren, to come up with new versions of old stories and, by doing so, to uncover possible explanations that were not clarified by the survivors themselves. Orit was able to relate verbally to Olga's problems in loving her father and her feeling of being "at home" in Warsaw: this did not emerge in Olga's and Dina's discourse.

One may assume that words clarify ambiguities between external and internal facts, and between past and present events. Yet they can also create ambiguity. Therefore, our wish to find out through the life stories what had happened, to understand the story told and the story left untold, became a time-consuming investigative back-and-forth process, which we followed until we were satisfied with the outcome and came close to understanding what we had tried to figure out. In our opinion, there is no one way to get at this meaning in a manner that would be acceptable in the positivistic research tradition.

In order to clarify what the facts are in a life story, we needed to ask ourselves a number of questions simultaneously: What was "the truth"? What should have been the truth, and according to whom? Which stories actually "worked" (that is, provided a narrative that one could live with and created options for problem-solving in the present)? What untold stories, whose presence affected the told ones, were missing?

We have not emphasized one possibility, that one can create a *new* reality through one's discourse. Dina created a different reality than Tamar had, not because she was more Israeli, but rather because she saw herself as a "pioneer of the eighties" and constructed her reality and her story accordingly, within limits that were constantly changing. Unlike both Dina and Tamar, Hannah claimed that she did not have a life story, although she was well along in constructing one in her consciousness and in reality. Committing herself to its existence through her own discourse was still too threatening for her. While she was speaking to Bosmat, she had no language with which to talk about being a mother, although we have no doubt, after listening to Yoav's story, that her motherhood was her creation: she was very important in her children's lives and her children were probably very important in hers.

The Question of Generalization or, What Is Representative?

It is possible to say, okay, these are stories of five families. We even accept your way of analyzing them. But what do they signify for the thousands of other families that had similar life histories and life stories? In what ways do the five "represent" the many, if at all? Is it possible to make generalizations based on five families? This is a serious assertion. It is actually impossible to claim generalization and representation in the way these concepts are usually used in the social sciences. But first we should ask ourselves what was presented, about whom, and what does it represent? Is it possible to suggest that the five families included in this book represent the phenomenal range of those connected to transmission and working through between the generations in Holocaust survivors' families?

There are two basic approaches in relation to representation. One sees the average as the most representative value of the sample or population, normally distributed (Hays, 1981). In such cases, the variance is considered a deviation from the mean, which can be standardized and estimated. Without doubt the combinations of the mean and its standard deviation are final values and easy to use. Every time we can employ them, it is preferable that we do so. In order to employ these values, however, we need a large, randomly selected sample in order to assert that it represents the population and that its mean represents the population's mean.

Yet there are circumstances in which one simply cannot make claims of this sort. When I was researching the influence of their fathers' actions on the children of Holocaust perpetrators in Germany (Bar-On, 1989), I attempted to build a varied sample from a social, economic, religious, and geographic perspective. But I could not claim representativeness, since there are no available data about the population of perpetrators. When we discuss Holocaust survivors, we do have information, but the number of variables that influence the diversity of this population is enormous: Where was the person during the Holocaust, during which period, at what age? Did the survivor arrive in the camps alone or with his or her family? Did the survivor escape by him- or herself, or was he or she assisted by someone? What happened before the Holocaust in the family and in his or her life, and what happened as a result of it? How did the survivor make sense of what happened to him or her or to others at each stage? As we stated in the Introduction, it is impossible to pinpoint exactly what the effect of the Holocaust is, since it is compounded by other factors, such as immigration, absorption, and family and personal dynamics.

Any attempt to sample randomly in a case like this will be extremely problematic. One has to give up the strong assertion of representation. One has to accept the not-at-random procedure of sampling, even if one tries to present the variance of the principal variables that influence the issue under discussion. In our case, this led us to choose families that presented different life histories from the period of the Holocaust. We had no illusion that this procedure made these families representative of even that limited aspect, not to mention all the others. We do not claim that the Belinsky family represents all families that went through the death camps or that the Lerman family represents all partisan families. Even if they were different from one another, they did not preclude other possible life histories. We were interested, for the purposes of our discussion, in the difference between them and within them. The question of the relationship between these differences and a representative sample is a subject for discussion and is not assumed a priori.

Problems of generalization and representation exist above and beyond the question of sampling. We wanted to analyze qualitatively the life stories of three generations and to estimate the amount of transmission that took place between them. This was a new subject about which no systematic or valid information existed. We chose to begin with a small number in order to identify the phenomenon and thus initiate discussion. In examining life stories we had to give up values like mean, median, or even mode. On the one hand, we were searching for uniqueness; on the other, even when dealing with uniqueness we were still interested in its relationship to the entire whole. The role of conceptualization in this kind of analysis is to bring up topics that will enable us, at a later stage, to test the question of generalization.

We asserted that, for the Anisevitch family, for example, the move from physical safety to a psychological feeling of security was a central issue. If we proved the internal validity of this assertion (was it a problem in this family?), we might then attempt to look at its external validity as well: Is it *only* a problem of the Anisevitch family, or is it a problem that exists in many other Israeli families, with or without a Holocaust background? The same is true of the other issues we tried to identify in our sample—the issue of weakness and strength (in the Lerman family), loss and a feeling of belonging (the Segal family), remembering and forgetting (the Belinsky family), or the penetration of collective events into personal life stories (the Guetta family).

According to our evaluation, the issues we identified in our small sample may represent typical problems of intergenerational transference and working through in Israeli society, with or without any relationship to the Holocaust. We make no claim that we have shown that they are representative. This could be the subject of future quantitative research. We saw our role, at this early stage, as that of presenting the topic in a manner both coherent and valid. If we have accomplished this task in a clear and reliable way, it will be helpful to the future examination of issues like generalization and representativeness.

◆ ——— ◆

Notes

Prologue

1. The Palmach was a special unit of kibbutzim armed forces, inspired by the legendary figures of Ord Wingate and Itzhak Sadeh, who combined agricultural work with military training. They were actually the backbone of Jewish military forces during the 1948 war but were dismantled in a controversial act by Ben-Gurion shortly after the war ended.

Introduction

1. In the meantime, we have evidence that it had more to do with the difficulties of the German research team. Recently, Professor Rosenthal has been interviewing German families, three generations in a family, in the former East and West Germany as part of a comparative study with a similar Israeli sample.
2. The use of strong, or hard, and soft conceptualization relates to the assumptions underlying the research methods (Schon, 1983). Under strong assumptions one can expect to find answers concerning ultimate truth. Under softer assumptions one will tend to rely heavily on the meaning making of the subjects themselves, since no single ultimate truth can be defined (Bar-On, Facthood of Facts, in preparation).
3. Akira Kurosawa's recent movie *Rhapsody in August* gives a vivid example of the family of a survivor of the atom bomb dropped on Nagasaki. The grandchildren are the first to become curious about what their grandparents went through during those horrible hours. Their parents are completely absorbed in existential issues and perceive only their parent-survivors' ongoing grief and mourning. Their own children's interest pulls them into reflecting on the past for the first time.
4. I differentiate here between identity and biography reconstruction. *Identity* is a construct developed from the outside (for example, Holocaust survivor), which

thereby assumes a kind of objective meaning, although of course individuals participate in their identity formation (Erikson, 1968); *biography reconstruction,* in contrast, is a process that works from within, though clearly also affected by external events and normative pressures. Here there is no underlying assumption about an objective truth.

5. Discourse analysis involves several more complicated aspects—for example, how can we distinguish genuine from as-if discourse? How are undiscussable facts kept out of the discourse?—which we will not be able to address here. Those interested can find them in Bar-On (in preparation).

6. The criterion for inclusion or omission was generally how much we could prevail on the reader to follow repetitious or trivial sections of the life story. However, this assertion needs double-checking so that we are not perceived as trying to get rid of something that does not fit our theory. The original tapes and texts are extant (in Hebrew) for the curious.

1. The Belinskys

1. "Canada" was the name of a unit of Auschwitz inmates who sorted the belongings of those who had been gassed. They were called "Canada" because they had everything. However, they also knew too much and were therefore under daily danger of extermination.

2. The right-wing youth movement established in Poland in the twenties by Zeev Jabotinsky.

2. The Lermans

1. In that sense the interview with Hannah was unusual, because it required many more questions than the others to keep it moving forward.

3. The Anisevitches

1. The border beyond which no field crops can grow without being irrigated.

2. A poor development town in the desert, inhabited mainly by Asian Jews.

3. During the early fifties, before the Sinai campaign in 1956, there was no organized Palestinian army or liberation movement, but there were many individual saboteurs who terrorized the new Jewish settlements along the borders, which were not yet closely guarded.

4. The Jewish Agency was the authority that provided the basic investment for new agricultural settlements. It was sponsored by world Jewry.

4. The Segals

1. Shiva: an act of mourning performed by orthodox Jews when a son leaves religious practice.

2. Righteous Gentiles: gentiles who helped rescue Jews during the Nazi occupation are granted a special recognition by the Israeli government, and a tree is planted in their name in the forest of Righteous Gentiles at Yad Vashem.

References

Abelson, R. P. 1976. Script processing in attitude formation and decision making. In J. S. Carrol and J. W. Payne, eds. *Cognition and Social Behavior*. Hillsdale, N.J.: Erlbaum.

Aroian, K. J. 1990. A model of psychological adaptation to migration and resettlement. *Nursing Research*, 39: 1.

Assa, T., and E. Degani. 1989. Voluntary visits to Poland: Refusal and collaboration. In D. Bar-On and O. Selah, eds. *Psychosocial After-effects of the Holocaust on Second and Third Generations: Readings*, pp. 131–177. Ben-Gurion University, Beer-Sheva. In Hebrew.

Bar-On, D. 1986. *The Pantomime's Stick*. Tel Aviv: Meirav. In Hebrew.

—— 1989. *Legacy of Silence: Encounters with Children of the Third Reich*. Cambridge: Harvard University Press.

—— 1990. Children of perpetrators of the Holocaust: Working through one's own "moral self." *Psychiatry*, 53: 229–245.

Bar-On, D., and I. Charny. 1992. The logic of moral argumentation of children of the Nazi era in Germany. *International Journal of Group Tensions*, 22: 3–20.

Bar-On, D., and O. Selah. 1991. The "vicious circle" between current social and political attitudes and attitudes towards the Holocaust among Israeli youngsters. *Psychologia*, 2: 126–138. In Hebrew.

Bar-On, D., and P. Hare, M. Brusten, and F. Beiner. 1993. "Working through" the Holocaust? Comparing questionnaire results of German and Israeli students. *Holocaust and Genocide Studies*, 7: 230–246.

Bar-Semech, M. 1990. Partnership and complementarity in the Kibbutz family. *Igeret Lachinuch*, 88: 47–51. In Hebrew.

Bastiaans, J. 1988. Vom Menschen im KZ und vom KZ im Menschen. In D. Bar-On, R. Beiner, and M. Brusten, eds. *Der Holocaust*. Wuppertal: University of Wuppertal.

Bergmann, M. S., and M. E. Jacuvy. 1982. *Generations of the Holocaust*. New York: Basic Books.

Berlazki, I. 1991. Aspects of interviews with Holocaust survivors. In K. Brendler and G. Rexilius, eds. *Drei Generationen im Schatten der NS-Vergangenheit.* Wuppertal: University of Wuppertal, no. 4, pp. 15–24.

Browning, C. R. 1992. *Ordinary Men.* New York: HarperCollins.

Carter, B., and M. McGoldrick. 1988. *Changing Family Life-Cycle: Framework for Family Therapy.* New York: Gardner Press.

Chang, J. 1991. *Wild Swans: Three Daughters of China.* New York: Simon and Schuster.

Cohler, B. J., and H. U. Grunnebaum. 1981. *Mothers, Grandmothers and Daughters: Personality and Child Care in Three-Generation Families.* New York: Wiley-Interscience.

Danieli, Y. 1980. Countertransference in the treatment and study of Nazi Holocaust survivors and their children. *Victimology,* 5: 3–4.

—— 1983. Families of survivors of the Nazi Holocaust: Some long- and short-term effects. In N. Milgram, ed. *Psychological Stress and Adjustment in Time of War and Peace.* Washington: Hemisphere Publication Corporation.

Davidson, S. 1980. The clinical effect of massive psychic trauma in families of Holocaust survivors. *Journal of Marital and Family Therapy,* 1: 11–21.

Dvir-Malka, B., and N. Gil'ad. 1989. The characteristics of European immigration to Palestine between 1933–39 of those who lost their family in the Holocaust. In D. Bar-On and O. Selah, eds. *Psychosocial After-effects of the Holocaust on Second and Third Generations: Readings,* pp. 61–95. Ben-Gurion University, Beer-Sheva. In Hebrew.

Erikson, E. H. 1968. *Identity: Youth and Crisis.* New York: Norton.

Felman, S., and D. Laub. 1992. *Testimony.* New Haven: Yale University Press.

Fischer-Rosenthal, W. From identity to biography: On the social construction of biography and the question of social order in modern times. In preparation.

Freud, S. 1914. Remembering, Repeating, and Working-Through (Further Recommendations on the Technique of Psycho-Analysis, II). *Standard Edition of the Complete Psychological Works,* vol. 12: 147–156. London: Hogarth.

Friedlander, Sh. 1980. *When Memory Comes Back.* Jerusalem: Adam. In Hebrew.

Grossman, D. 1986. *See under: "Love."* Jerusalem: Keter. In Hebrew.

Gutman, L. 1990. *The Encyclopedia of the Holocaust.* Tel Aviv: Yediot Achronot. In Hebrew.

Habermas, J. 1971. *Knowledge and Human Interests.* Cambridge: Harvard University Press.

Hays, W. L. 1981. *Statistics.* New York: Holt, Reinhart and Winston.

Herman, J. 1992. *Trauma and Recovery.* New York: Basic Books.

Janoff-Bulman, R. 1992. *Shattered Assumptions.* New York: Free Press.

Keilson, H. 1992. *Sequential Traumatization among Jewish Orphans.* Jerusalem: Magnes.

Kestenberg, J. S. 1972. Psychoanalytic contributions to the problem of children of survivors from Nazi persecution. *Israeli Annals of Psychiatry and Related Sciences,* 10: 311–325.

Kripke, S. A. 1982. *Wittgenstein: On Rules and Private Language.* Cambridge: Harvard University Press.

Krystal, H., ed. 1968. *Massive Psychic Trauma.* New York: International Universities Press.

Lacan, J. 1966. *Ecrits.* Paris: Editions du Seuil.

Langer, L. 1991. *Holocaust Testimonies: Ruins of Memory.* New Haven: Yale University Press.

Lehman, D. R., C. B. Wortman, and A. F. Williams. 1987. Long- term effects of losing a spouse or child in a motor vehicle crash. *Journal of Personality and Social Psychology,* 52: 218–231.

Levi, P. 1988. *The Drowned and the Saved.* New York: Simon and Schuster.

Mandela, I., and M. Frankel. 1990. Testimonies of surrvivors of the Kastner train and their children. Ben-Gurion University, Beer-Sheva.

McGuire, W. J. 1973. The yin and yang of progress in social psychology: Seven koah. *Journal of Personality and Social Psychology,* 26: 446–456.

Monk, R. 1990. *Wittgenstein: The Duty of Genius.* London: Penguin.

Novey, S. 1962. The principle of "working through" in psychoanalysis. *Journal of the American Psychoanalytic Association,* 10: 658–676.

Porath, D. 1986. *Entrapped Leadership.* Tel Aviv: Am Oved. In Hebrew.

Reick, M., and L. Eitinger. 1983. Controlled psychodiagnostic studies of survivors of the Holocaust and their children. *Israeli Journal of Psychiatry,* 20: 312–324.

Rosenthal, G. 1987. *"Wenn alles in Scherben fallt...": Von Leben und Sinnwelt der Kriegsgeneration.* Opladen: Leske and Budrich.

———— 1989. Leben mit der NS-Vergangenheit heute: Zur Reparatur einer fragwürdigen Vergangenheit im bundesrepublikanischen Alltag. In *Vorgange: Zeitschrift für Bürgerrechte und Gesellschaftspolitik,* 3: 87–101.

———— 1993. Reconstruction of life stories: Principles of selection in generating stories for narrative biographical interviews. *The Narrative Study of Lives,* 1: 59–91.

Rosenthal, G., and Dan Bar-On. 1992. A biographical case study of a victimizer's daughter repair strategy: The identification with the victim of the Holocaust. *Journal of Narrative Life and History,* 2: 105–127.

Rothstein, A. 1986. *The Reconstruction of Trauma: Its Significance in Clinical Work.* New York: International Universities Press.

Schmidt, C., and B. Heimannsberg. 1994. *The Collective Silence.* San Francisco: Jossey-Bass.

Schon, D. 1983. *The Reflective Practitioner.* New York: Basic Books.

Segev, T. 1991. *The Seventh Million.* Jerusalem: Keter. In Hebrew.

Solomon, Z. 1989. A three-year prospective study of post-traumatic stress disorder in Israeli combat veterans. *Journal of Traumatic Stress,* 2: 59–74.

Spence, D. P. 1980. *Historical Truth and Narrative Truth.* New York: Basic Books.

Vardi, D. 1990. *The Memorial Candles: Dialogues with Children of Holocaust Survivors.* Jerusalem: Keter. In Hebrew.

Wax, S., and R. Belah. 1989. Emotional responses to the Holocaust among youngsters in Israel. In D. Bar-On and O. Selah, eds. *Psychosocial After-effects of the Holocaust* on *Second and Third Generations: Readings,* pp. 90–130. Ben-Gurion University, Beer-Sheva. In Hebrew.

Wittgenstein, L. 1953. *Philosophical Investigations.* New York: Macmillan.

Yablonka, Ch. 1990. The problem of absorption of Holocaust survivors in the emerging Israeli society. Ph.D. diss., Hebrew University, Jerusalem.

Zuckerman, I. 1990. *Those Seven Years.* Tel Aviv: Hakibbutz Hameuchad. In Hebrew.

Index